The epigram in England, 1590–1640

Manchester University Press

The epigram in England, 1590–1640

James Doelman

Manchester University Press

Published by Manchester University Press
Altrincham Street, Manchester M1 7JA

www.manchesteruniversitypress.co.uk

British Library Cataloguing-in-Publication Data
A catalogue record for this book is available from the British Library

Library of Congress Cataloging-in-Publication Data applied for

ISBN   978 0 7190 9644 0 hardback

First published 2016

The publisher has no responsibility for the persistence or accuracy of URLs for any external or third-party internet websites referred to in this book, and does not guarantee that any content on such websites is, or will remain, accurate or appropriate.

Typeset by
Servis Filmsetting, Stockport, Cheshire
Printed in Great Britain by
TJ International Ltd, Padstow

This book is dedicated to the memory of my father and mother, Jacob (1919–85) and Marytte (1923–2009) Doelman, who inspired a love of learning in me.

Ego autem coacervavi omne quod inveni.

Nennius, *Historia Brittonum*

Contents

Acknowledgements

Much of the work for this book was made possible by a multi-year grant from the Social Sciences and Humanities Research Council of Canada; this was also supported by ongoing funding from Brescia University College of the University of Western Ontario. While I am indebted to many libraries and archives, I wish particularly to thank the staff of Beryl Ivey Library at Brescia for their years of patient assistance, and the Interlibrary Loan Department of D. B. Weldon Library, who tracked down many books and microfilms on my behalf.

Colleagues at Brescia, faculty, staff and administration, have been supportive and encouraging of the project from its beginning, and I particularly thank my fellow faculty members Brian Diemert, Dominick Grace, Monika Lee, Sister Mary Lou McKenzie, Sister Mary Frances Dorschell and Sara Morrison.

I am also deeply grateful to the student research assistants I worked with over the years: September Teeple, Beth Reid, Helen Button, Stephen Carter and Christina Wiendels.

Some sections of this book appeared earlier in the following articles, and I thank those journals for permission to offer them here in revised form: 'Epigrams and Political Satire in Early Stuart England', in *Huntington Library Quarterly* (2006); 'The Religious Epigram in Early Stuart England', in *Christianity and Literature* (2005); 'Circulation of the Late Elizabethan and Early Stuart Epigram', in *Renaissance and Reformation* (2005); '"A Libell, for an Epitaph": The Parodic Epitaph in the Early Stuart Period', in *Appositions* (2008); and 'Charles Fitz-Geffry and the 'Wars of the Theatres'', in *Early Theatre* (2008).

I thank Matthew Frost, editor at Manchester University Press, for his guidance through the publishing process, John Banks for his careful copy-editing work and the anonymous readers for Manchester University Press for their helpful responses and suggestions.

Finally, as with all my work, this could not have been accomplished without the unfailing love, support and encouragement of my family: Nancy, Sarah, Esther, Elizabeth and Elliot.

Abbreviations

BL	British Library, London
Bodl.	Bodleian Library, Oxford
Camb.	Cambridge University Library
CSPD	*Calendar of State Papers, Domestic*
Crum	*First-line index of English Poetry, 1500–1800*
DNB	*Oxford Dictionary of National Biography*
Early Stuart Libels	*Early Stuart Libels*, ed. Bellany and McRae / www.earlystuartlibels.net/htdocs/index.html
EETS	Early English Texts Society
Folger	Folger Shakespeare Library, Washington, DC
HLQ	*Huntington Library Quarterly*
HMC	*Historical Manuscripts Commission*
Huntington	Huntington Library, San Marino, CA
OED	*Oxford English Dictionary*
PRO	Public Record Office, London
SEL	*Studies in English Literature, 1500–1900*
SR	*A Transcript of the Stationers Register*, ed. Arber
STC	Pollard and Redgrave, *Short-Title Catalogue of Books Printed in England, Scotland & Ireland and of English books Printed Abroad, 1475–1640*
Sutton	Sutton, Dana F. *The Philological Museum.* www.philological.bham.ac.uk/
Tilley	*Proverbs in England*
TLS	*The Times Literary Supplement*

A note on the texts

To facilitate finding poems across a range of editions, epigrams have generally been identified by number, or book and poem number (rather than page or leaf number), in the following format: Ep. 3 or Ep. 2:55.

All quotations from Ben Jonson are from *The Cambridge Edition of the Works of Ben Jonson*, eds David Bevington, Martin Butler and Ian Donaldson, 7 vols (Cambridge; New York: Cambridge University Press, 2012). Poems cited 'Ep. 15', etc. are from his *Epigrammes* in the 1616 *Workes*; his uncollected epigrams are cited as '*Underwood* no. 4', etc.

The epigrams of Sir John Harington raise difficult numbering problems. The first print publications (1615, 1618) were divided into books and numbered. N. E. McClure's *The Letters and Epigrams of Sir John Harington* (Philadelphia: University of Pennsylvania Press, 1930) served as the standard edition through the twentieth century; it presented the epigrams numbered, but undivided into books. For this study I have chosen to quote the recent edition by Gerard Kilroy, *The Epigrams of Sir John Harington* (Farnham: Ashgate, 2009), which takes its text (and numbering) from the gift manuscripts prepared by Harington himself. In Harington's case, the manuscript sources are more authoritative than the posthumous printed ones. A cross-index to the seventeenth-century printed texts and McClure is found in Kilroy at pp. 311–21.

Unless otherwise identified, classical texts and translation are quoted from the Loeb Classical Library.

Original spelling and punctuation have been maintained with all quotations from manuscript and printed sources from the sixteenth and seventeenth centuries; however, i/j and u/v have been regularized except in titles. Contracted spellings and abbreviations have been expanded in italics.

Unless otherwise indicated, all translations from Neo-Latin texts are the author's.

Introduction

What is an epigram in the Renaissance sense of the term? While a more nuanced exploration of this question will follow in the first two chapters, a working definition and description is in order here: an epigram is a polished, witty, tightly focused brief poem, often of as little as two lines. Its hallmarks are witty sharpness and brevity (*argutia* and *brevitas*), and individual human behaviour is its prime subject. Some, usually directed toward named figures, offer an epitome of praiseworthy virtues; more often, however, epigrams are obscured by a fictional name and deride an individual's faults. Although epigrams are theoretically vehicles of both praise and blame, the latter dominates, both in terms of the number of poems and in their popularity in manuscript circulation. Social behaviour and interaction, the superficial, physical and tawdry qualities of individuals, are at the heart of the genre; an epigram book of the period is rather a gallery of rogues, populated by greedy churchmen, jealous husbands, frivolous wives, cowardly soldiers, dishonest merchants and prostitutes. The fleshly shortcomings of greed, lechery and gluttony are frequent topics. Ironic wit and wordplay are the usual means and the required brevity encourages focus and restraint. While there is some variation, the pentameter couplet is the typical metrical form of the English epigram; this structure fosters a quotable character, even in epigrams that exceed two lines. In spirit, epigrams are typically urbane and worldly-wise, and more often marked by a sense of resignation than satiric outrage. Such a tone implies that, when it praises, the epigram also does that from a position of objective judgement.

This attitude of objectivity is central to the genre: an epigram seems not to emerge from the mind or heart of its author, but merely responds to the actions, persons or even texts of others. In identifying such 'responsiveness', as I call it, as a hallmark of the genre, I build upon theoretical discussions reaching back to Gotthold Lessing, for whom the prompt to composition took the place of the original monument or statue upon which the earliest epigrams were inscribed. Peter Hess continues in this tradition by arguing that the epigram is defined partly by its property of having a 'specific "Objektbezug," by which he means that the poem refers to a certain material object, either realistically or metaphorically'. On the basis of this idea, Hess believes that 'epigrams are never about their authors, but always about things'.[1] Karl A. E. Enenkel qualifies this assertion by arguing that the '"Objektbezug" is more a poetic point of departure than an essential characteristic of the poem' and, furthermore, that the author is concerned with defining himself or herself in relation to that object.[2] My contention is that the essential brevity of the epigram renders it substantially dependent upon something outside itself, whether that something is a thing, person or text. The epigram works by responding to this commonly known element, often by exploiting the implicit irony in a specific object, occasion or character's name.

One of the most famous epigrams of the period may serve here as an example: Sir John Harington's 'Of Treason':

> Treason doth never prosper? What's the Reason?
> for if it prosper none dare call it treason.[3]

The poem's popularity stems from its clever undermining of the openly proverbial and moralistic first clause: 'Treason doth never prosper' sounds like conventional wisdom, but this statement is then challenged by the shifting semantics suggested in the ensuing line of the poem. The failure of treason is not from any higher justice in the cosmos, but the relativism of the political sphere, where success validates any assumption of power and may order words to its pleasing. As is typical of the genre, the second and final line neatly offers the sharp 'sting in the tail', and the epanalepsis (repetition of a word or phrase at the beginning and end of a passage) that rounds the poem by returning to 'treason' further contributes to its memorable quality.[4] It has the argutia most central to the genre, and its resigned tone, partly achieved through brevity, holds out little hope that this grim reality will ever be overturned. This epigram also reflects the pattern that Lessing long ago identified as the hallmark of the genre, where the opening sets up an expectation ('Erwartung'), which is then quickly followed by an explanatory twist ('Aufschluss').[5]

Heavily influenced by the Latin poet Martial (ca. AD 40–103/4) and to a lesser degree by the compendium of Greek epigrams preserved as

The Greek Anthology, the epigram in England burgeoned as a genre in the later 1590s and early 1600s, when a self-conscious generation of epigrammatists emerged. Their epigrams were distinct from medieval and early sixteenth-century manifestations of the genre, such as the didactic epigrams ascribed to Cato that were popular in the Middle Ages, and the more proverbial and folk-based iterations of the genre that are reflected in the mid-sixteenth-century poems of John Heywood. While the present study is not organized by author, it is appropriate to sketch the works of the most notable practitioners, all of whom developed collections of epigrams numbering in the hundreds. Through the 1590s and early 1600s Harington reworked his sizeable collection of epigrams, offering gift manuscripts to a range of important figures; only after his death in 1612 did a print collection reach the public. However, at least some of his epigrams were known in manuscript circulation and he was generally recognized by his fellow epigrammatists as a leading figure. The poems of Sir John Davies (whom one contemporary referred to as 'the English Martial') were likely the first of this generation of epigrammatists to reach print: his were surreptitiously published in a volume with Christopher Marlowe's versions of Ovid's elegies in the mid-1590s. Thomas Bastard's *Chrestoleros* (1598) was the first volume solely dedicated to English epigrams to appear in print and as such helped Bastard to attain an epigrammatic reputation similar to that of Harington and Davies. However, his renown was also built upon a well-established reputation for poetic libel achieved as a student at Oxford. John Owen achieved in Latin what Harington and Bastard had in English: beginning in 1606, he presented ever-growing collections of epigrams, which, as was typical of the Neo-Latin tradition, engaged in a more evenly balanced distribution of poems of praise and blame. Finally, Ben Jonson largely preserved his epigrams for publication as part of his much grander literary collection in his folio *Workes* of 1616. For him, epigrams were a significant part of his very deliberate public poetic career.

However, such a description of the most notable epigrammatists should not obscure the breadth of epigram composition in the period, and the chapters that follow draw upon a wide range of authors. *Time's Whistle*, written about 1616 by an unidentified 'R.C.', points to both the sheer number and the social range of epigrams in the early seventeenth century: 'Scribimus indocti doctique epigrammata passim' [Both the learned and the unlearned, we all write epigrams].[6] The dominance of the genre in the period has been confirmed by numerous scholars: Leicester Bradner suggests that interest in epigrams was 'one of the characteristic elements of Jacobean literature'.[7] Alastair Fowler also points to the primacy of the epigram in the seventeenth century, noting its predominant influence upon a range of other kinds and its role in establishing the dominance of the pentameter couplet.[8] May and Ringler's first-line index of Elizabethan poetry lists approximately 2500 epigrams in their cross-index of 'Poetic Kinds', far more than in any other category, and approximately 110 for the sub-genre of the epitaph.[9] If a similar index were compiled for the early Stuart period, there would be many more – probably far too many on the repeated subjects of taverns, tobacco, wine, dice, cuckolds and drabs[10] – but also intriguing ones on politics, religion, places and the human vagaries of behaviour, both good and ill. In addition to published and manuscripts collections of epigrams, they also appeared embedded in plays and prose works, and as commendatory or dedicatory verses. Epigrams were written to mark occasions and to comment on public affairs, to praise the worthy and satirize the ridiculous. They were practised as educational exercises and used in both festive and vitriolic exchanges.

With the English blossoming of the epigram as a genre in the 1590s, there was a high degree of self-consciousness about the form: more so than with other genres, practitioners refer to other contemporary epigrammatists in their poems. In other words, there was a strong sense of competition and of a building tradition. While many of these references are direct, some are hidden behind the fictional names typical of the genre.

Scholarly attention to date

Given that the epigram was among the most frequently composed and influential of early modern literary genres, it has received remarkably little scholarly notice. The most inclusive English study is T. K. Whipple's *Martial and the English Epigram from Sir Thomas Wyatt to Ben Jonson* (1925),[11] but as the title suggests its principal concern is the influence of Martial. While Whipple referred to the rest of the field as an 'untracked jungle',[12] few have attempted to map that jungle. Neither of the planned volumes on the epigram in Renaissance England by mid-twentieth-century scholars were completed. Hoyt Hopewell Hudson's work remained unfinished at his death, with the completed section (which ended in the late sixteenth century) published as *The Epigram in the English Renaissance* in 1947. James Hutton wrote his *The Greek Anthology in Italy* (1935) and *The Greek Anthology in France and in the Latin Writers of the Netherlands to the Year 1800* (1946) as preparation for a volume on the influence of the *Greek Anthology* on the English epigram as mediated through those continental literatures. However, he never completed that culminating study. Continental literary criticism, especially German, has gone further than British in considering the genre in both its vernacular and Neo-Latin forms. Ironically, some of the most substantial scholarship on Owen and the influence of his Neo-Latin epigrams has been in German. Lessing's 'Essay on Epigram' is a perpetual touchstone for later scholars such as Peter Hess, who offers a book-length overview of the genre, which he sees as defined by its tendency to challenge received ideas.[13]

The sub-genre of the epitaph has received more substantial treatment of late in Joshua Scodel's *The English Poetic Epitaph: Commemoration and Conflict from Jonson to Wordsworth*[14] and Scott Newstok's *Quoting Death in Early Modern England: The Poetics of Epitaphs Beyond the Tomb*.[15] Their work allows my chapter on the epitaph to focus on a subset: the mocking or 'feigned' epitaph.

The epigrams of some major authors have also been better served than the genre in general: Harington's complex social and religio-political use of epigrams has been explored by Jason Scott-Warren's *Sir John Harington and the Book as Gift* and Gerard Kilroy's *Edmund Campion* (2005) and his edition, based upon the gift manuscripts, *The Epigrams of Sir John Harington* (2009). Jonson's epigrams figure prominently in many of the general studies of his works, and they have been the sole subject of many articles. Nevertheless, still wanting is a thorough book-length study of his use of the genre.

Considerable scholarly attention towards libels (some of which are epigrams) has recently been directed by such scholars as Thomas Cogswell, Alastair Bellany, Andrew McRae, Pauline Croft, C. E. McGee and Andrew Gordon.[16] Lacking from some of these, however, is any distinguishing between literary kinds: ballads, epigrams, prose satire etc.; the present study's contention is that these generic differences are important, that with them came both expectations and a sense of audience.

Why has the epigram been relatively ignored despite its acknowledged prominence in the period? One of its two hallmarks, 'brevitas', renders individual examples too flimsy for rigorous discussion, and, as published in massive collections, they lack significant development or organization, again forestalling critics who might desire to provide an overview or find meaning in the structure of the whole. Certainly, the slenderness of the genre is part of the problem; however, this has not prevented massive attention to that other short form of the period – the sonnet. The other broadly accepted feature of the genre, its 'argutia', would seem to appeal to New Criticism's appreciation of wit, irony and paradox. Unfortunately, however, the reality that the epigram so frequently manifests its argutia in obvious wordplay has discouraged critical discussion. Lawrence Manley helpfully demonstrates how epigrams 'relied primarily not on tropes but on clever schemes of repetition, balance, and antithesis, and on witty concluding turns like *epiphonema* and *acclamatio*'.[17] Even many scholars of Renaissance literature will have to turn to a literary handbook to recall those last two schemes, and that illustrates something of the problem. The epigram has suffered because of twentieth-century unfamiliarity or discomfort with the rhetorical tradition. Unlike proverbs, whose metaphors can be unpacked, and hence with which the 'interpretation game' can be played, the epigram calls only for bemused admiration of its rhetorical turns. By being schematic rather than figurative they have frustrated the techniques and interests of many critics.[18]

The ancients saw the epigram as the least worthy of the literary genres,[19] and that sense carries over as an apologetic or dismissive attitude on the part of many Renaissance epigrammatists, and subsequently to today's scholars who consider them. Gideon Nisbet, in writing of the skoptic (that is, mocking) epigram of classical Greek, notes that it 'seems almost to have embarrassed the Academy; at any rate, it has been consistently side-lined'.[20] I acknowledge in myself a similar scholarly awkwardness about my interest in a genre that is so ephemeral and seemingly trivial. In the course of this project there are times when I have been troubled by qualms because of the subject's triviality, fearful that Christ's words in *Paradise Regained* might apply: that I have been

> collecting toys,
> And trifles for choice matters, worth a sponge;
> As Children gathering pebbles on the shore.[21]

Such are the thoughts of darker moments, and perhaps stemming from reading too many epigrams at one sitting; as will be explored in Chapter 6, epigrammatists sometimes described their public offerings as sweet or salty treats that ought to be consumed sparingly, a few at a time to fill empty moments. I must also note that amongst the thousands of epigrams from the period I have been delighted and prompted to thought by the wit, invention and polish of many.

Approach

Broader developments in the field over the past few decades render this book's approach significantly different from that of Hudson or Hutton.

While, like theirs, my study begins with a fairly traditional overview of the genre's history and general features, it moves beyond this to approach the genre in historicist terms, fully locating both epigram books and single epigrams in their social, political and religious contexts. One of my guiding assumptions is that a genre-based approach is compatible with a historicist approach, and I affirm Heather Dubrow's assertion in *The Challenges of Orpheus: Lyric Poetry and Early Modern England*: 'The renewed interest in form in many reaches of literary and cultural studies is one of the most promising developments of the first decade of the twenty-first century.'[22] Many of the epigrams treated in the following chapters have been used by scholars engaged in historicist readings of them in their political context; my conviction is that such readings can be enhanced by an awareness of genres and the conventions and expectations that they bring with them. It makes a difference when a poem is thought of as an epigram or epitaph, rather than a libel, satire, beast fable or elegy.

My focus is on the genre from about 1590 through the early 1640s: such captures both the flurry of epigram books published in the late 1590s and the consolidation of the genre in the early decades of the century. It stops short of attempting to pursue its development and particularly its use in the very different literary and political culture brought about by the Civil Wars. Many epigrams are firmly rooted in very particular social or political moments, and are thus ripe for historicist readings; however, these have been limited in scholarship. In this way, it is like its sister form, satire, which as McRae points out, while heavily contextual and frequently political, has received less attention from new historicists than other less likely genres.[23] McRae is also exceptional in having considered aesthetic aspects of this material while engaging in a necessarily political reading. Throughout this study, I am concerned with context, and recognize that each epigram potentially goes through a series of contexts: from original responsive composition (to a current event), to quotation and manuscript circulation, and finally, in some cases to a more fixed situation in a printed book of epigrams.[24]

Authors

This study deliberately avoids an author-focused approach, as the culture of epigrams – more so than that of any other poetic form of the period – is very subject-focused. In some epigram collections the use of the first-person singular is rare, and the processes of circulation led to situations in which these poems were frequently detached from their author. With this approach poets who have been largely ignored in recent scholarship but who were significant in their own day (for example, Bastard, Henry Parrot, Charles Fitzgeffry) receive as substantial attention as more canonical writers (such as Jonson and Harington). This also allows for a more integrated consideration of those epigrams that were anonymous or whose authorship was doubtful. My concentration on the means of circulation, along with the sub-genres of the epigram, leads to certain authors – and even a few individual poems – being discussed in more than one place.

A genre-based approach can correct the tendency in some studies of better-known writers of epigrams (like Jonson) to ascribe to the individual poet what is in fact typical of the genre. Conversely, it can highlight where an author pushes against or beyond generic norms. Such an approach also brings to notice the 'minor' but fascinating figures often overlooked in literary studies, where the canon-questioning assumptions of the past few decades have not significantly affected which writers are highlighted in published studies. In particular, it remains imperative, it seems, to include 'Shakespeare' in a monograph title: I regret that Shakespeare wrote no epigrams (beyond those embedded in his plays) and hence to call this book 'Epigrams in the age of Shakespeare' would be an intolerable fudge.

Likewise, while epigrams written in English are my main focus, I also consider at times the rich store of Neo-Latin epigrams from the period, as the two cultures largely overlapped. As will be explored in Chapter 3, most writers of English epigrams had the early experience of writing Latin ones as school exercises. A few, most notably John Hoskins, composed in both languages. Sir John Stradling and Fitzgeffry, writing in Latin, celebrate Harington (who wrote in English) as their fellow, just as English-language epigrammatists were very aware of the work of the noted Neo-Latin ones like Owen. Many manuscripts preserve, mingled together, the best-known epigrams in both languages. Better familiarity with the wealth of Neo-Latin epigrams in the period can guide our assessment of what epigrammatists were doing in English; for example, Jonson seems less of an outlier when his epigrams are read in the context of those by Fitzgeffry, Stradling and Owen, rather than those of Harington and Sir John Davies.

Manuscript and print

This study also very intentionally devotes full attention to epigrams in both manuscript and print formats, and as far as possible the fragmentary evidence of them in oral circulation. Such is a reflection of the renewed

attention over the last few decades to manuscript verse. Pioneering studies by Arthur Marotti on the manuscript circulation and collection of
lyric verse, Harold Love on the varieties of manuscript 'publication' in
the period and the wealth of information in Peter Beal's *Catalogue of
English Literary Manuscripts 1450–1700*,[25] have forced both critics and
textual editors to reconsider the bases of their work. Thus, the field of
epigrams looks quite different now than it did for Hudson or Hutton. No
longer is attention so narrowly fixed on the first publication of a poem,
and the resulting literary history has become much more nuanced. These
changes have made possible the studies of Harington's manuscripts by
Scott-Warren and Kilroy, as noted above, along with the genre-based
approach of Joshua Eckhardt's *Manuscript Verse Collectors and the Politics
of Anti-Courtly Love Poetry*.[26] My work has been much informed by that
of these earlier scholars. This study examines both those epigrams (like
Harington's and Bastard's) that circulated in manuscript before print
publication and some that never entered the print market. Overall, I hope
that the approach achieves a fuller picture of the rich variety of the genre
in the period.

Overview of chapters

As this book attempts neither a straightforward chronological history of
the genre nor an author-based organization, it might best be understood
as presenting 'Dimensions of the epigram'. That is, it attempts to understand the tradition of the genre and its relationship to other literary kinds,
its means of transmission (oral, manuscript and printed book) and how
it functioned in relation to the social, political and religious contexts in
which it was written and read. It also recognizes that 'epigram' is a broad
category and hence pays due attention to a number of sub-genres.

The opening chapter outlines the tradition of the epigram in the classical, medieval and Renaissance periods: this chapter is most similar to the
sort of genre histories written in the past. I am particularly concerned with
exploring how literary and rhetorical handbooks defined an epigram, and,
moreover, with how the term seems to have resonated for actual poets and
readers. Many epigrammatists of the period struggled with the genre's
reputation as licentious and cynical.

Chapter 2 attempts to achieve a better understanding of the epigram
in the period by considering it in relation to a range of proximate and
competing genres, including satire, the jest, the libel and the sonnet, and
the distinction between the epitaph (a sub-genre of the epigram) and the

elegy. It also examines the range of terminology that was at times applied to the epigram.

The third chapter concerns the contexts, both educational and convivial, in which many epigrams were composed and initially circulated. The genre's central place in the educational practices of the period was particularly significant; I argue that it established an 'epigram habit' that poets took with them into later life, one that solidified the genre's place in the literary landscape of the period. In contrast to some recent scholars, I argue that this earlier context of school and university was more important than the Inns of Court in the flowering of the genre in the 1590s and early 1600s.

The next three chapters (4, 5 and 6) explore the means of transmission for epigrams in the period. Chapter 4 considers the topical, ephemeral origins of individual epigrams, and how at least some came to circulate, both by word of mouth and as posted poems. Here, I aim to show how recent attention to manuscript culture is insufficient in that it frequently ignores a preliminary oral stage of transmission. Over time, at least some of these ephemeral poems achieved a more permanent place in a variety of manuscript miscellanies; Chapter 5 examines the nature of different types of surviving manuscripts – authors' working copies, collectors' miscellanies and gift manuscripts in which epigrams appear. Chapter 6 considers epigrams as presented in printed books: their physical form, their place in the print marketplace, the rationale for print publication, and the concerns of epigrammatists in appearing in this more public medium.

Chapters 7 and 8 are complementary in considering questions of authorship and readership respectively. In the culture of epigrams there was a continuing tension between anonymity and acknowledged or even emphatic authorship. The free-floating transmission of poems meant that they might be either disavowed by their author and left as 'bastards' or taken by another and worn as 'stolen feathers'. A special case was 'illustrious authorship', where epigrams came to be 'fathered upon' notable public figures as a way of enhancing interest in them. Chapter 7 presents a variety of readers of the printed epigram book: the general reader against whom the epigrammatist extended habitual scorn, the ideal reader that a few imagined and the expected (or dreamed of) role of patrons of epigram books. The chapter ends with rare evidence of an actual reader, one who left his or her marginalia in a copy of Harington's *Epigrams*.

Chapter 9 is concerned with two central elements of the genre: naming and responsiveness. As the majority of epigrams are ultimately concerned with the summary identification of vice, folly and virtue in individuals, the identifying of those through either fictional or literal naming is of great importance. The 'lemma' or title most often provides the link between the epigram and its human subject. In their brevity epigrams are dependent on and responsive to things and people beyond themselves. They are not self-generating, but take their bearings from an often well-known event, person or even other epigram.

The final chapters (10, 11 and 12) focus on three major sub-genres: the political epigram, the mock or feigned epitaph and the religious epigram. Chapter 10, on political epigrams, examines the limits of political comment in printed epigram books, with a special focus on Bastard's *Chrestoleros*. A number of case studies follow, including an extended survey of epigrams on the life and career of the prominent legal and political figure Sir Edward Coke. Many of these were savagely partisan, but the final part of the chapter turns to epigrams by Robert Ayton, Richard Corbett and George Herbert that were nuanced and stoic in their political explorations.

Chapter 11 explores how the main conventions of the epitaph were adapted in 'feigned' or satiric epitaphs. Here, widely circulating hostile epitaphs on Sir Christopher Hatton, Robert Cecil, Earl of Salisbury, and the Duke of Buckingham maintained the partisan use of libellous epigrams beyond the grave (although some were countered by epitaphs and epigrams supporting the dead). The chapter concludes with the curious case of Owen's tomb in St Paul's Cathedral, which came to function as a site for mocking epitaphs in response to the ornateness of the tomb and the commendatory epitaph by Archbishop John Williams.

The Martialian epigram does not seem a likely candidate for Christian use; however, a strikingly large number of poets turned the genre to a religious purpose, sometimes of devotion or meditation, and at other times for the purpose of religious satire or polemic. The final chapter (12) considers how such a conversion of the genre was made difficult by its scurrilous reputation and conventionally cynical tone. These qualities would seem to be more promising for epigrams of religious satire, but many of the polemical epigrams composed lost the genre's characteristic sharpness and brevity.

A number of the chapters move toward one or more case studies in order to explore a dimension of the epigrams of the period. Such an approach raises some methodological issues: no epigrammatist is completely 'typical', and I hope that I have not flattened out their particularities in working in this fashion. As with any literary genre, epigrams are marked by variety and experimentation.

Finally, there are dimensions of the epigram that have not received sufficient attention here: epigrams of praise were a significant part of the more ambitious and literary volumes of epigrams, but less significant in other modes of circulation. Their relative neglect in this study is, I hope, somewhat made up for by a number of excellent studies that have focused on Jonson's epigrams of praise.[27] Similarly, my relative neglect of Herrick stems from both the date of *Hesperides* (1648), lying just beyond the range of my focus, and the fact that his volume has been admirably treated as an epigram book by Ann Baynes Coiro.[28] Other worthwhile epigrammatists – Thomas Campion in Latin, John Davies of Hereford and Thomas Bancroft in English – have not been given the attention they deserve, and I hope that they will attract such in the future. If the present book opens up some of the richness of the epigram culture of the period, explores the contexts of its composition and transmission, and highlights possibilities for further study, it will have fulfilled its aim.

Notes

1 Karl A. E. Enenkel, 'Introduction: The Neo-Latin Epigram: Humanist Self-Definition in a Learned and Witty Discourse', in Susanna De Beer, Karl A. E. Enenkel and David Rijser (eds), *The Neo-Latin Epigram: A Learned and Witty Genre* (Leuven: Leuven University Press, 2009), p. 10. This discussion (pp. 1–24) offers a worthwhile introduction to the theoretical issues surrounding the genre, which have been much more rigorously pursued by continental critics on the Neo-Latin epigram than those writing on the Renaissance English epigram.

2 Enenkel, 'Introduction: The Neo-Latin Epigram', p. 11.

3 Harington, Ep. 3:44 (Kilroy ed.).

4 See Rick Bowers, 'Sir John Harington and the Earl of Essex: The Joker as Spy', *Cahiers Elisabéthains*, 69 (2006), pp. 13–21, on Harington's playful and ironic approach to politics in more particular contexts.

5 Gotthold Lessing, 'Essay on Epigram', in *Fables and Epigrams*, trans. J. and H. L. Hunt (1825), pp. 165–208.

6 *Time's Whistle: or, A new daunce of seven satires, and other poems: compiled by R. C., gent.*, ed. J. M. Cowper (London: EETS, 1871), p. 132. The sentence is a slight adaptation of Horace, Epistle 2.1.117: 'scribimus indocti doctique poemata passim'.

7 Leicester Bradner, *Musae Anglicanae; A History of Anglo-Latin Poetry, 1500–1925* (London: Oxford University Press, 1940), p. 78.

8 Alistair Fowler, *Kinds of Literature: An Introduction to the Theory of*

Genres and Modes (Cambridge, MA: Harvard University Press, 1982), p. 196.

9 Steven W. May and William A. Ringler, Jr (eds), *Elizabethan Poetry: A Bibliography and First-line Index of English Verse, 1559–1603*, 3 vols (London and New York: Thoemmes Continuum, 2004), vol. 3, pp. 2096–9.

10 This list, with some additions, is from Henry Parrot, *The Mous-trap* (1606), no. 92.

11 T. K. Whipple, *Martial and the English Epigram from Sir Thomas Wyatt to Ben Jonson* (Rpt New York: Phaeton Press, 1970).

12 Whipple, *Martial and the English Epigram*, p. 280.

13 Peter Hess, *Epigramm* (Stuttgart: Metzler, 1989).

14 Joshua Scodel, *The English Poetic Epitaph: Commemoration and Conflict from Jonson to Wordsworth* (Ithaca, NY: Cornell University Press, 1991).

15 Scott Newstok, *Quoting Death in Early Modern England: The Poetics of Epitaphs Beyond the Tomb* (London: Palgrave Macmillan, 2009).

16 Andrew Gordon, 'The Act of Libel: Conscripting Civic Space in Early Modern England', *Journal of Medieval and Early Modern Studies*, 32 (2002), pp. 375–97. For an overview and historiography of the study of verse libels in the early Stuart period see Alastair Bellany, 'Railing Rhymes Revisited: Libels, Scandals, and Early Stuart Politics', *History Compass*, 5 (2007), pp. 1136–79.

17 Lawrence Manley, 'Proverbs, Epigrams, and Urbanity in Renaissance London', *English Literary Renaissance*, 15 (1985), pp. 247–76, p. 251.

18 For an insightful commentary on scholarly embarrassment over Renaissance rhetoric and style, see David Scott Wilson-Okamura, *Spenser's International Style* (Cambridge: Cambridge University Press, 2013), pp. 14–17.

19 William Fitzgerald, *Martial: The World of the Epigram* (Chicago: University of Chicago Press, 2007), p. 25.

20 *Greek Epigram in the Roman Empire: Martial's Forgotten Rivals* (Oxford: Oxford University Press, 2004), p. xvii.

21 John Milton, *Paradise Lost*, 4:328–30.

22 Heather Dubrow, *The Challenges of Orpheus: Lyric Poetry and Early Modern England* (Baltimore, MD: Johns Hopkins University Press, 2008), p. 13. Her earlier *Genre* (London and New York: Methuen, 1982) remains a commendable brief introduction to the topic of genre, particularly as she recognizes the limitations of adopting an excessively restrictive definition of what constitutes a 'genre'. Such flexibility is helpful with a category like the epigram, which is often, but not always, prosodically fixed, and often, but again, not always, concerned with a certain type of utterance.

23 Andrew McRae, *Literature, Satire, and the Early Stuart State* (Cambridge: University Press, 2004), p. 4.

24 I am indebted to Kathryn J. Gutzwiller, *Poetic Garlands: Hellenistic Epigrams in Context* (Berkeley, CA: University of California Press, 1998), which has provided something of a model of this approach.

25 Arthur F. Marotti, *Manuscript, Print, and the English Renaissance Lyric* (Ithaca, NY: Cornell University Press, 1995); Harold Love, *Scribal Publication in Seventeenth-Century England* (Oxford: Oxford University Press, 1993).

26 Joshua Eckhardt, *Manuscript Verse Collectors and the Politics of Anti-Courtly Love Poetry* (Oxford: Oxford University Press, 2009).

27 See, for example, Eric Partridge, 'Jonson's *Epigrammes*: The Named and the Nameless', *Studies in the Literary Imagination*, 6 (1973), pp. 153–98; Richard Helgerson, *Self-Crowned Laureates: Spenser, Jonson, Milton and the Literary System* (Berkeley, CA: University of California Press, 1983), pp. 168–72; Jennifer Brady, '"Beware the Poet": Authority and Judgment in Jonson's *Epigrammes*', *SEL*, 23 (1983), pp. 95–112; Jonathan Z. Kamholtz, 'Ben Jonson's *Epigrammes* and Poetic Occasions', *SEL*, 23 (1983), pp. 77–94; A. D. Cousins, 'Feigning the Commonwealth: Jonson's *Epigrams*', in A. D. Cousins (ed.), *Ben Jonson and the Politics of Genre* (Cambridge: Cambridge University Press, 2009), pp. 14–42.

28 Ann Baynes Coiro, *Robert Herrick's Hesperides and the Epigram Book Tradition* (Baltimore, MD: Johns Hopkins University Press, 1988).

1

The classical, medieval and Renaissance inheritance

In a prefatory poem to his collection of epigrams printed in the 1616 folio, Ben Jonson addressed the stigma associated with the genre:

> It will be looked for, book, when some but see
> Thy title, 'Epigrams', and named of me,
> Thou shouldst be bold, licentious, full of gall,
> Wormwood, and sulphur; sharp and toothed withal;
> Become a petulant thing, hurl ink and wit
> As madmen stones, not caring whom they hit.[1]

This quotation captures well the complex set of expectations surrounding this problematic genre: it was frequently used for scandalous material of a sexual nature, for libellous attacks on individuals, both minor and well-known, and with a troubling lack of moral concern and responsibility. As Jonson puts it in his dedication of the epigrams to the Earl of Pembroke, the name 'carr[ies] danger in the sound'. Not mentioned here, but frequently noted in other prefatory poems, is that, even at its most innocuous, the epigram manifested a trivial concern with the mere surfaces of human life. At the same time, it was a genre with a strong classical pedigree, well-developed descriptions by Renaissance theorists and longstanding and widespread use as a pedagogical tool. This chapter maps the reputation of the epigram in the period, tracing the paramount influence of Martial, the more limited role of the *Greek Anthology* (a large compilation of epigrams spanning more than a millennium of the classical age), and the continuing role of a native tradition of distichs, reaching back into the Middle Ages.

'That pleasant and conceited Poet Martiall' or 'the Prince of all writers in this kind'[2]

Henry Peacham, himself a composer of epigrams, encourages the use of Martial's epigrams in the education of an early Stuart gentleman:

> In *Martial* you shall see a divine wit, with a flowing puritie of the Latine tongue, a true Epigrammatist: his verse is cleare, full, and absolute good, some few too wanton and licentious, being winked at.[3]

Peacham identifies the elements for which Martial was admired and widely imitated: wit and precision of diction. However, like nearly all early modern descriptions of Martial, this statement also concedes that his epigrams were marred by licentiousness. Furthermore, his subject matter, even in the purest of his poems, was admitted to be at best trivial. His work, thus, was a prime store upon which the proverbial activity of 'sucking honey from the weed' might be practised. However, despite Martial's trivial, and often licentious, subject matter, most epigrammatists adopted the concise and pointed style of their Roman forebear, and the tone and organization of his epigram books were imitated by self-consciously literary writers like Jonson and John Owen. Jonson challenged his 'mere English censurer', who might fault his epigrams for being unlike those of Sir John Davies or John Weever: he claims his 'is the old way and the true', that is, the way of Martial.[4] These literary epigrammatists were often to invoke the 'ghost of Martial' to defend their work, and strive to become English Martials themselves.

Unlike some classical Latin poets, Martial remained prominent and influential throughout the Middle Ages; he was imitated by some early Christian poets, and was known during the Carolingian revival and by at least some figures in the succeeding centuries.[5] However, with the Renaissance cultivation of classical models for verse style, and with the advent of the printed book, he rose into overwhelming prominence: J. P. Sullivan notes over 110 fifteenth-century manuscripts of his epigrams, and he figures among the earliest printed books.[6]

The influence of Martial continued to be widespread in sixteenth-century Europe; among many others, he was imitated by such notable figures as Clement Marot in France, and Giovanni Battista Marino of Naples (1569–1625), who in turn heavily influenced the English and Latin epigrams of Crashaw. Sullivan argues that the early seventeenth century was the high-water mark for the popularity of Martial and 'agudeza' [pointedness] across Europe,[7] and that this ultimately led to a valuing of pointedness across the poetic landscape.[8] While Martial's influence was widespread, it should *not* be assumed that all who wrote epigrams were directly modeling themselves on him. Frequently, his influence was mediated through the widespread humanist practice of epigram composition, Renaissance theorists and home-grown English epigrammatists.

Editions and translations

The late sixteenth and early seventeenth centuries saw a spate of significant scholarly editions of Martial, in which Jesuit scholars were particularly active. Among the more influential was the expurgated edition by Matthaeus Raderus (mocked by John Donne as 'gelded Martial'[9] and by Jonson as 'ille Jesuitaru*m* castratus, eviratus, et prorsus sine Martiali Martialis' [that castrated, effeminate one of the Jesuits, utterly Martial without Martial]),[10] which first appeared in 1599, with many subsequent printings.[11] A host of major scholar produced significant editions: Jan Gruter's of 1602,[12] and that by Peter Schrijver (Scriverius) in 1618/19;[13] in England the widely respected schoolmaster and scholar Thomas Farnaby produced an edition (1615) with extensive marginal commentary. While described as 'rather inferior' by Sullivan, it was very influential in early seventeenth-century England. Farnaby is a great neglected literary and scholarly figure of the period: he was widely renowned as a schoolmaster and his editions of classical texts were much depended on across Europe. Jonson, a deep reader of Martial, extolled his edition as that which should be 'Toto notus in orbe' [known in the whole world], borrowing the words of Martial himself.[14] The epigrammatist Thomas Bancroft praises not only Farnaby's work on Martial but also that on *The Greek Anthology* and other classical literature.[15]

Translating Martial is a particularly difficult literary task, as so often the point of the epigram depends upon wordplay. In addition, the brief scope of an epigram leaves the translator little room to rearrange materials to fit an English meter and rhyme scheme. Thus, translations and imitations of carefully *selected* epigrams of Martial were much more common than translations of his *complete* works; for some, this practice was also encouraged by the variety of subject matter and the desire to avoid the licentious or crude specimens. Ironically, Martial 10:47, an epigram more typical in spirit of Horace than Martial, was the one most often quoted and translated (beginning with Surrey 'On a happy life'). Relatively thorough translations were attempted by Thomas May (*Selected Epigrams of Martial* (1629)) and John Heath.[16] The latter focused on *Liber Spectaculorum*,

Martial's collected epigrams on the buildings and public celebrations of Rome; this was a popular section for translation, probably since they were more consistently decorous than his other books.

All this editorial and translation work established Martial as one of the best-known of classical writers in late Elizabethan and early Stuart England: few of the educated would not have read at least some of his epigrams. The hallmarks of his style, brevity and pointedness, rendered him very apt for commonplacing and quotation. He is echoed in plays, sermons and treatises, and found on the title pages of a wide range of works. John Webster's preface 'To the Reader' in *The White Devil* cites Martial's epigrams four times, and he offers a quotation from Martial in place of an epilogue. A surprising number of sermons use quotations from Martial (while sometimes denouncing his immorality in the same breath). The well-known preacher Thomas Adams seems to have been particularly fond of him. John Withal's oft-reprinted *Shorte dictionarie for yonge begynners* (1602) regularly includes examples of Martial to illustrate the definitions and usage of Latin words. This educational use of Martial is more fully explored in Chapter 3.

Norms inherited from Martial
Mocking, satirical epigrams are frequently called 'skoptic' (or 'scoptic') epigrams in the classical studies tradition (from σκώπτειν (*skoptein*), 'to mock'). While skoptic epigrams were found in the *Greek Anthology* (principally in Book 11), it was Martial who established the primacy of this type among the various epigrammatic tones.[17] Even as this was the dominant note in Martial inherited by his Renaissance imitators, that he also wrote inscriptions, sententious epigrams and panegyric epigrams – most notably in the *Spectaculorum* – did not escape them, and his example helped establish the tendency for English epigram collections (in both print and manuscript) to be mixed bags of tones and subjects.

Martial offered English followers a strong sense of the physical and social reality of first-century Rome in verse that was vivid, urbane and somewhat jaded. Martial wrote, 'hominem pagina nostra sapit' ['tis of man my page smacks] (10:4), rejecting mythological subject matter and celebrating ordinary life in Rome. This found its equivalent in the everyday life of London in particular,[18] a city which also had its panders, whores, cuckolds, braggarts and fools, its jockeying for political position, conspicuous consumption and striving for poetic fame, all of which English epigrammatists might observe and wryly comment upon. As with Martial, the cumulative effect of all these mini-portraits is to suggest a crowded urban scene.[19]

Martial also established the idea that the epigrammatist ought to aspire to whole *books* of epigrams, in spite of the unrelated, disparate nature of the individual items. He shrugs off the accomplishment of Sabellus in composing a few good epigrams, ending with this dictum: 'facile est epigrammata belle / scribere, sed librum scribere difficile est' (7:85) [it is easy to write a beautiful epigram, but difficult to write a book of them]. He seemed to admire the sheer bulk of epigrams rather than individual poems, even where some poems might be inferior.[20] Such books invited readers to browse, select and approach the work in a leisurely way. The majority of published English epigrammatists followed Martial in organizing their poems into books, most often of approximately a hundred poems each, called 'centuries' by some.[21] Finally, the fact that Martial 'published' (in the sense of that word for imperial Rome) his epigrams offered a precedent for English Renaissance poets: despite the trivial, ephemeral nature of the individual items, collectively they were worth a broader audience, both in space and time. Individual epigrams might be effective, but were more likely to perish, or at least to lose connection with their author. Thus, Martial clearly took pleasure in the broader public they reached when published: 'Laudat, amat, cantat nostros mea Roma libellos' (6:60) [My Rome praises, loves, sings my little books].[22]

'A good wit ill imployed': Martial's bawdiness
While Martial was highly venerated as a stylist, his frequent obscenity was a significant difficulty for both Renaissance readers and those poets who wished to rehabilitate the form for Christian use. Although some epigrammatists, like Everard Guilpin, might hold themselves excused because 'wanton words' are simply 'the language of an Epigrame',[23] more common was some sterner defence or rehabilitation of the form. A range of writers attempted adaptations and censored editions to render Martial suitable for a Christian readership. Jesuit scholars in particular developed these expurgated texts,[24] which culminated in the widely used edition by Raderus discussed above. Taking a different approach was the Lutheran Johann Burmeister, who in 1612 published a faithful edition of Martial that combined the original epigrams with more edifying paraphrases or parodies on the facing page.[25] Burmeister's endeavours may seem extreme, but are the logical culmination of a longstanding desire to make Martial's supreme style serve a Christian purpose. All this was akin to late medieval and Renaissance allegorizing and moralizing of Ovid.

Some who aspired to a Martialian career as epigrammatists bemoaned

the facile identification of bawdiness with wit; thus, Abraham Holland
addresses his epigrammatic Muse:

> But tell me when thou into'th world art come,
> How wilt thou please the multitude, when some
> Unlesse thou canst outbaudy *Martial*,
> Or loose-pen'd *Arbiter*, will stiffly call
> Thee slight and witlesse.[26]

Holland is not rejecting the influence of Martial wholesale, but calling for
a restrained Martialian style that at least does not go *beyond* him in bawdiness. Some, however, did reject him completely, and for them his name
was a byword for obscenity. Gabriel Harvey wrote, 'better the dogges-
meate of Agrippa, or Cattes-meate of Poggius, then the swines-meate
of Martial, or goates-meate of Arretine'.[27] In this hierarchy of disrepute
Martial finds himself, with the notorious Aretino, ranked beyond the frequently vitriolic occultist Cornelius Agrippa and the sometimes licentious
fables of the Italian humanist Poggio Bracciolini.[28]

A most extended attack on Martial comes in *Ulysses upon Ajax* (1596),
a response to John Harington's *Metamorphosis of Ajax* (1596), where
'Misodiaboles' notes how Martial has been invoked by Harington as 'the
foremost to fighte the battaile for him'.[29] He then turns his attack upon the
classical epigrammatist:

> But what is this Martial? Faith a good wit ill imployed like himselfe. This is
> hee, (I speake it in his commendations) that writ epigrams of *Aethons* fart-
> ing in the capitol, of his boyes kisse; This is the incourager of letcherie, in
> victor, *Misacmos* neede not feare to alledge him about *Cacacanit* [he sings of
> excrement], that gloried to fill Emperours eares with flatterie, bauderie and
> Sodomie. *vaugh spurciciem, nugas* [bah, filthiness, trifles]. It is pittie that as in
> Catalogina, there is a lawe, that everie Cuckold shoulde paie a fine or tribute;
> So among us there is not a statute that such as teach such filthinesse, should
> be publiquely punished. I will not examine the *Epigrams*, for they are too
> obscene to be lookt uppon; and who so rubbeth stincking weedes, shall have
> filthy fingers.[30]

Clearly, this is not simply motivated by hatred of Martial but is primarily
a disparagement of Harington achieved through castigating the classical
writer whose standard he has adopted. However, it shows the explicit
elements of Martial that were most often attacked by those concerned

with the classical writer's moral influence. He was, as Misodiaboles so memorably puts it, 'a good wit ill imployed'.

A Martialian tradition

Such attacks are also testimony to the significance of Martial for English poets of the 1590s. Repeatedly, aspiring epigrammatists were hailed as the 'new Martial' or the 'English Martial'. In 'The Excellencie of the English Tongue', Richard Carew identifies contemporary English authors to match classical counterparts: for Martial, he cites 'Sir John Davies and others',[31] and Davies, whose epigrams were published in the same volume as Marlowe's versions of Ovid's elegies in the mid-1590s, was referred to by a number of other writers in the late 1590s as the 'English Martial'.[32] Thomas Freeman celebrated John Heywood and Davies as ones in whom 'successively descended Martialls soule'.[33] Similarly, for his Neo-Latin epigrams Owen became known across Europe as the 'British Martial' or 'Martial redivivus'.[34]

Jonson's copy of Scriverius's 1619 edition of Martial survives,[35] replete with his markings and marginalia (some of which are quotations and emendations from Farnaby's 1615 edition). They show that he read Martial thoroughly and closely, and also fully annotated the prefatory material which reproduced the comments of humanists on Martial. At times he points to other epigrams in the collection, thus finding a sense of unity in what seem to be these disparate compilations. This immersion in Martial formed a basis for his own epigrams. Sullivan summarizes Jonson's approach to Martial: he 'shed direct translations, Latinate names for standard characters and Latin titles; he revived the eulogistic epigrams Martial had sent his patrons, and adopted the thematic cycles of interconnected epigrams which were a feature of Martial's books'.[36] While other scholars have most often cited the significance of more stoic and moral classical influences, Bruce Boehrer suggests that 'Jonson's debt to Martial is heavier than to any other Latin poet with the possible exception of Horace'.[37]

Jonson's reworking of Martial's model in English was matched by the achievement of Owen in Latin. His epigrams, published first in 1606, and then in ever-expanding volumes, show Owen as the most Martialian of England's Neo-Latin poets, especially in style and structure; his poems are ultimately less indecent and more impersonal in their attacks.[38] His wide readership, not just in England but across the continent, helped to reinforce the Martialian style as the paradigm for epigrams. Hence, by the 1630s, Thomas Bancroft is able to place himself within a epigram tradition that extends from Martial through Owen and Jonson:

Reader, till *Martiall* thou hast well survey'd,
Or *Owen's* Wit with *Jonsons* Learning weigh'd
Forebeare with thankelesse censure to accuse
My Writ of errour, or condemne my Muse.[39]

Thus, by the 1630s, there was not only the undisputed sovereignty of
Martial in the field of epigrams but a Martialian tradition among British
poets writing in both English and Latin. For those of literary aspirations,
to write epigrams was to follow Martial, and to share with him a sense that
such poems were in themselves 'trifles' ('nugae'), yet worthy of authorly
care and deliberate publication or circulation in collected 'books' that
mingled poems of praise and ridicule, covering the full breadth of human
subject matter.

Catullus

While Martial served as the chief model for English epigrammatists of
the late Elizabethan and early Stuart periods, a rival tradition based upon
Catullus and the *Greek Anthology* was recognized.[40] Although we most
often think of Catullus as a lyric poet of sensual love poetry, in the first
couple of centuries after the rediscovery of Catullus in the late thirteenth
century he was most frequently discussed as an epigrammatist.[41] Julia
Gaisser argues that because Catullus was *discovered after* Martial readers saw him within a Martialian framework,[42] and Bruce Swann finds
that Renaissance commentators across Europe tended to group Catullus
with Martial and the *Greek Anthology* rather than with Propertius and
Tibullus as later scholars did. At the same time, his very different style
from Martial was well noted. In his widely known *Poetices*, Scaliger distinguishes between the sweet and soft type of epigram, typical of Catullus,
and those of Martial, which are 'vivida, vegeta, acria' [vivid, lively,
sharp].[43] This distinction was commonplace in the period, with atten-
dant debates on the relative merits of the two types of epigrams. Overall,
and despite some shifts during the sixteenth and seventeenth centuries,
continental commentators were more likely than their British counterparts to value Catullus. In early sixteenth-century Italy Catullus was preferred over Martial (although both were seen as inferior to the *Greek
Anthology*),[44] and the French humanist Marc-Antoine Muret (1526–85)
saw Martial as having corrupted the earlier elegance of Catullus. The
seventeenth-century French commentators Guillaume Colletet, Pierre
Nicole and Francois Vavasseur continued the debate over the relative

merits of Catullus and Martial.[45] According to Thomas Campion, Catullus 'Cantabat Veneres meras' [used to sing mere love songs],[46] in contrast to the breadth of subjects in Martial, and 'the former [Catullus] is great in the eyes of the multitudes, while the latter [Martial] is well-liked by those of cultivated taste'.[47] That Campion comes to favour Martial as the more rarified taste is typical of the English tradition, where the influence of Catullus (and the *Greek Anthology*) was not to become widespread again in epigrams until the 1630s. The general shape of influence is that the Martialian pointed epigram dominated the late Middle Ages; the 'sweeter' epigram in the style of Catullus and the *Greek Anthology* supplanted it for the first half of the sixteenth century, particularly on the continent, only to give way gradually to the Martialian epigram again in the late sixteenth and seventeenth centuries.

Other Latin epigrammatists

Other classical Latin epigrammatists were relatively little known in Renaissance England. A few epigrams ascribed to Virgil often appeared in Renaissance collections of his works, under the title 'Catalepton'. John Penkethman, who offered English translations of the epigrams of both Virgil and Cato for the edification and instruction of readers, presented those of Virgil in this way:

> (notwithstanding they were for the most part, the fruits of *Virgils* minority, being by him composed at his age of 15 yeeres, as I note in his life written by *Donatus*) [they] doe containe such variety of good doctrine, and exquisite inventions, that to me they seeme rather to have beene brought forth in his Majority, or else the greatest number of them to have issued (as *Scaliger* and other Commentators conceive) from the learned heads of more ancient Poets.[48]

Although overshadowed by his *Satyricon*, Petronius's epigrams were included in the 1579 edition of his work by Claude Binet.[49] A broader gathering of Latin epigrams by disparate authors appeared in Pierre Pithou's *Epigrammata et poematia vetera* (1590), including material that is now frequently described as the 'Anthologia Latina'.[50]

The epigrams in Latin and Greek of the late classical author Magnus Ausonius (ca. 310–95) were known and exerted some influence, especially his custom of writing epigram sequences or catalogues on people and places, which was picked up by the humanist Neo-Latin tradition.[51] Many continental editions of him (some with commentaries) appeared in the sixteenth century, but he was probably best known through the inclusion of some of his epigrams in the oft-printed primer *Disticha Catonis* (which will be more fully discussed in Chapter 3).[52] Samuel Shepherd's 1651 epigrams depict Martial and Ausonius in parallel fashion on the frontispiece: Martial is 'the life and soule of SENCE', Ausonius 'in ARTS SCHOLE most great'.[53] Like Martial, the epigrams of Ausonius and the 'Priapeia' (a collection of about eighty anonymous epigrams supposedly to be placed on garden statues of the fertility god Priapus) were marked by a bawdiness that contributed to the scandalous reputation of the form in the period.[54] However, in comparison to Martial the influence of these epigrams on the English-language tradition was negligible.

The *Greek Anthology*

The other major classical influence on the Renaissance epigram was the *Greek Anthology*, itself an 'anthology of anthologies' that preserves a wide range of Greek epigrams by disparate authors from the seventh century BC to the tenth century AD.[55] The best-known epigrams in this collection were not satiric and biting like Martial's but sweet and playful variations on a vast range of topics – love, friendship, morality and architecture figure prominently. It became widely known in Western Europe from the late fifteenth century, especially through the first printed edition by Janus Lascaris in 1494.[56] Its contents were translated and imitated, first by Italian humanists, and then their counterparts in France and the Low Countries.[57] Collections of Neo-Latin verse of the sixteenth century are scattered with translations '*e Graeco,* which generally means the Anthology'.[58] James Hutton describes it as among the most frequently reprinted classical works of the sixteenth century, widely known in selections and schoolbooks.[59]

One section of the *Greek Anthology*, known as 'Meleager's Garland' (ca. 100 BC), is organized into four categories: erotic, epitaphic, anathematic and epideictic, all of which became standard in Martial and Renaissance epigram collections.[60] This work was also wide-ranging in the subject matter covered: a dedicatory poem (4:3) remarks on the variety of types of epigrams that are in the collection of new epigrams that Meleager is presenting to Theodorus: poems in praise of the old gods, inscriptional epigrams on buildings or statues and works of art (ecphrastic),[61] epitaphs, poems on the 'devious paths of life and the deceitful balance of inconstant Fortune', 'scurrilous rhyme', poems on 'sweet love' and Bacchic verse.[62] In a pair of scholarly studies, Hutton explores the significance of the *Anthology* for Renaissance Italian and French poets. He shows how it peaked in its influence upon French writers of the sixteenth century, but was eventually displaced by the more pointed Martialian epigram in the seventeenth century.[63] Unfortunately, Hutton's work stopped short of an account of its influence in England. However, a stream of influence, especially in educational circles, can be traced there as well. Thomas More's Latin epigrams were more heavily indebted to the *Greek Anthology* than to either Catullus or Martial,[64] and later in the century the influence of the *Anthology* in England was largely through More rather than direct. This reflects what Hutton suggests about the *Anthology* in Italy as well: that it was more broadly known through translations and adaptations by humanist poets into Latin than in its original Greek form.[65]

The widely known educational volume by John Stockwood, *Progymnasma Scholasticum* (1597), offered selections from the *Greek Anthology*, followed by various Latin translations of these epigrams. In each case he begins with a literal version in prose, and then offers Latin verse renderings by such famed humanists as Henry Stephanus and Paul Melissus, always concluding with one of his own. However, the clearest manifestation of the *Greek Anthology*'s significance in early seventeenth-century England is Thomas Farnaby's *HE TES ANTHOLOGIAS ANTHOLOGIA Florilegium epigrammatum Graecorum* (1629), which offers selections of the original Greek epigrams with Latin translations by a range of important humanists including More, Scaliger, Stephanus, Janus Secundus, Theodore Beza and Farnaby himself. Translations of *Anthology* poems into English were much less common. Surviving in manuscript is a small selection translated by the antiquary and scholar Richard James, many of which are politically charged and provide James with an indirect way of commenting on what he perceived to be the King's high-handedness.[66]

From the 1620s, anacreontic elements in the *Anthology* were increasingly imitated. John Leech's *Epigrammatum libri quatuor* (1623) is among the earliest to show this influence, and it was to find its finest English language expression in the poetry of Robert Herrick, much of which was written in the 1620s, but not published until 1648. William Drummond of Hawthornden was another poet whose epigrams savour more of the *Anthology* than Martial, with most involving classical, mythological references. Finally, beyond the 'sweeter' sort of epigrams for which it was most famous, the *Greek Anthology* included some examples of late classical Christian epigrams, which, as will be explored in Chapter 12, offered justification for adapting the form to sacred material.

In the Renaissance, the *Greek Anthology* was perceived as generally more chaste and gentle than Martial, but what of the undeniably bawdy and savagely mocking epigrams within it? Marc D. Lauxtermann argues that poets of the sixteenth century simply tended to translate and imitate the milder ones within the collection,[67] and, as the *Anthology* for the common reader was most often known through the redactions described above, its image as somewhat purer than Martial was secure.

Thus, by 1628 Robert Hayman was able to extol both the sweeter Greek epigram and the 'sour' Martialian one as models: 'Short Epigrams relish both sweet and sowre, / Like Fritters of sowre Apples, and sweet flowre.'[68]

Epigrams in the English Middle Ages

While Martial came to be widely known in the later Middle Ages, the most significant collection of epigrams throughout the period was the *Disticha Catonis*, moral verses commonly ascribed to Marcus Cato ('Cato the Censor', 234–149 BC).[69] Despite the wider body of classical epigrams known in the sixteenth century, the *Disticha* continued as one of the most commonly required texts for beginning students at grammar schools, and thus were known to virtually all of the reading public.[70] English translations were also common, as in John Penkethman's *A handful of honesty. Or, Cato in English verse* (1623) and Richard Baker's *Cato variegatus or Catoes morall distichs: translated and paraphras'd, with varations of expressing, in English verse* (1636). While the *Disticha* shared the brevity of the Martialian epigram, the homely wisdom of these maxims and the austere reputation of their author set them far apart. Ultimately, they came to influence the more native medieval English tradition of the proverbial epigram. This line continued through the sixteenth and seventeenth centuries, most notably in the work of John Heywood (1497?–1580?), whose epigrams continued to be read and cited through the seventeenth century.[71] Cato represented a sternly chaste counterpart to Martial; thus, Jonson, however indebted to Martial, could claim in the prefatory dedication to his epigrams that they formed a 'theatre, where Cato, if he lived, might enter without scandal'.[72]

Lawrence Manley has explored the overlapping boundaries of proverbs and epigrams, and notes that in the educational process both were valued for their summarizing of established wisdom. At the same time, they differed in their origins: the proverb ostensibly emerged from the oral folk tradition, and the epigram from a chirographic literary one.[73] However,

Manley helpfully illustrates how epigrams at times borrowed from and responded to the oral proverb tradition, adapting its rhetorical techniques and making explicit and specific its metaphoric generalities.[74] Sullivan as well notes this 'native Anglo-Saxon tradition of brief poems incorporating satire, realism and humour, which tended to rely on subliterary farce, proverbs and folk anecdote', and argues that the 'classical formalism of Martial pared down this expansiveness'.[75] John Heywood's epigrams, first published in 1550, show such a coming together of the proverb and epigram traditions. While the sharper Martialian epigram was to come to dominate in England by the 1590s, the continuing tradition of Heywood's proverbial approach is evident, at times even sporadically within books that lay claim to the more satiric tradition. However, some more classically minded epigrammatists, like Jonson, were to resist this tendency to include aspects of the non-Martialian tradition, or at least to deny these elements in their own work.

Renaissance practitioners and theorizing

A theoretical understanding of the epigram in the Renaissance may be derived from both the poetic treatises of the period – such works as Julius Caesar Scaliger's *Poetices Libri Septem*, Jacobus Pontanus's *Poeticae Institutiones*, and Puttenham's *Arte of English Poesie* – and from the prefatory material to published epigram collections.[76] Treatises were fairly uniform in their description of the genre, but Scaliger was the most frequently cited by later writers.[77] His work is decidedly Aristotelian in approach, breaking down poetry into a set of related categories and subcategories. Thus, the epigram is discussed in relationship to lyric poetry and the elegy, and after the epigram he discusses the inscription, which is actually its source. Like most theorists of the time, Scaliger emphasized the range of epigram subjects and its unifying stylistic features of brevity and sharpness, which he recognizes as the body and soul, respectively, of the epigram.[78] This summation was widely known, and the quotation of it on the title page of the 1634 edition of Owen's epigrams indicates its centrality for the foremost British Neo-Latin epigrammatist.[79] Because Martial never varied from these attributes, Scaliger values him over Catullus: 'hac Catullus non semper est assecutus: Martialis nusquam amisit' [Catullus does not always achieve this: Martial never slips].[80] Scaliger's approach is clearly normative rather than descriptive, and he highly values originality of argutia as well.[81]

Another influential work, Pontanus's *Poeticae Institutiones*, first

published in 1594 and appended to Johannes Buchler's *Sacrarum profanarumque phrasium poeticarum thesaurus*, was used in schools across
Europe.[82] As such, Pontanus's influence was likely even greater than
Scaliger's. Like Scaliger he identified brevitas and argutia as the central
features of the epigram,[83] but, while Scaliger notes that there are as many
types of epigrams as subjects,[84] Pontanus classified epigrams into three
main categories:

> Unam eorum, quibus ad rerum inscriptiones utimur, unde nomen ipsum est
> natum, quaeque prima origo Epigrammatis fuit. Alteram quibus laudes ali-
> cuius, aut vitia explicamus, sive, quibus laudamus aut vituperamus. Tertiam,
> quibus fortuitum quippiam, vel novum, vel admirabile, quod acciderit, argute
> exponimus, vel ipsi aliquid excogitamus, & comminiscimur.[85]

> [We use one of these for inscriptions on things, whence comes its name, which
> would be the initial origin of the Epigram. We use the other for any whose
> praises or faults we are setting forth; with these either we praise or criticize. We
> use the third for any chance occurrence, whether new or admirable, as it hap-
> pens; these we present with a point, whether we contrive and invent anything.]

Pontanus also offers another threefold division of epigrams, corresponding to the three great Aristotelian literary categories: tragedy, comedy
and epic. From the first are derived poems on the death of individuals (epitaphs), in epigrams derived from comedy 'auctores aliena pec-
cata patefaciunt, insectantur, atque rident' [authors bring to light others'
sins, reproach, and mock] and from epic 'sumit Epigramma laudationes
imprimis excellentium virorum, urbium, fluviorum, portuum, locorum,
fontium, monumentorum, etc.' [the epigram takes the praise of excellent
men, cities, rivers, harbours, places, springs, monuments, etc.].[86] While
both Scaliger and Pontanus suggest a breadth of subject matter, in practice the genre was best known for taking ordinary human behaviour, in all
its tawdriness, as its focus.

The primary feature of the genre, brevity, was recognized by all
Renaissance commentators, with some urging a strict line limit of two,
four or ten lines.[87] This radical brevity emerged from the genre's inscriptional origins,[88] and a frequent concern among commentators was that
the genre might become too loose and thus extended into what are prop-
erly elegies or long songs.[89] This emphasis on brevity in turn brought
about certain rhetorical approaches. Owen argues that the epigrammatist,
because of the need for brevity, must be a 'steganographon', not a 'poly-

graphon'; that is, one who proceeds through secret or hidden writing, who leaves things unsaid or merely glanced at.[90] Such an approach meant that some epigrams were condensed to the point of being cryptic. Thomas Fuller refers to 'the enigmatical epitaph set up at Bononia: "Aelia Laelia Crispis, &c." Which many think merely made by a conceited brain, on design to puzzle intellects, to create sense by their ingenuity and industry, which was never intended therein.'[91] This brevity might also result in a dense texture: as Francis Osborne writes of a political epigram, it does 'contain as many Stories as Lines'.[92]

The second term, 'argutia', was particularly prized in the final line of an epigram, where it might serve as the 'sting in the tail'. According to Pontanus, 'iure optimo anima, vita, & tanquam spiritus eius, nervi, succur, sanguis vocari potest' [it can be called by best opinion, the spirit, the life, and such is its soul, nerves and vigour, its blood].[93] Desired was a certain urbane and polished wit leading to a sharp point. Argutia was not limited to the witty 'turn' typical of the Martialian epigram, as those more dependent on the *Greek Anthology* or Catullan tradition also offer a sharp focus on a single figure or situation, which came to a head in the final line. Thus, the 'point' might be a turn of thought or wordplay, but generally involved the unexpected. The 'brevitas' and 'argutia' of epigrams were not merely separate ideals, but were intimately related: epigrams were brief because they presented a sharp observation on a single subject. Such a definition did not fix the epigram to a certain number of lines, and in one poem Martial responds to the complaint that his epigrams are too long; his defence is that his tight focus and lack of superfluous material render a longer epigram acceptable: 'non sunt longa quibus nihil est quod demere possis' [Things are not long from which you can subtract nothing].[94] In Renaissance practice this meant that, while typically epigrams were anywhere from two to about twenty lines, occasional examples of up to a hundred lines can be found. The licence allowed by Martial's example and Renaissance handbooks was open to abuse: there are numerous examples of printed and manuscript Renaissance poems that are titled 'Epigram' but which are neither brief nor sharp.

As a way of providing the required 'argutia', punning (especially on names) was a widespread technique in both Latin and English epigrams. In Pontanus's formulation this 'Echo' is identified as a worthwhile technique:

periucundum, argutum, & lepidum est Epigramma, attentumque retinet lectorem, cum in Fine, aut medio versus eiusmodi, vocula ponitur, quae vel tot verbo praecedenti, vel eius similis caudae, aut eandem sententiam illustrat, aut diversum aliquid, & nonnunquam contrarium, aut prorsus inexpectatum, aut par, aut maius, aut minus deinque complectitur. Haec Echo dicitur.[95]

[Very pleasing, pointed and elegant is the Epigram, and it retains the attentive reader, when in the end, or in the middle of the verse, a little word is placed, which whether such a word has a similar beginning or ending, or depicts the same sense, or another; and sometimes the contrary, or entirely unexpected sense, whether the same, or more or less, then it is completed. This is called 'Echo'.]

Such wordplay, not always to twenty-first-century tastes, was widespread in Renaissance epigrams, and was here given a classical justification. Scaliger also discusses the use of 'Echo', but is less enthusiastic about the technique, as it must involve the unexpected to be successful.[96]

According to Scaliger, argutia was not of one flavour, as he distinguished four varieties of the pointed epigram by metaphor: they could be of salt, vinegar, gall, or a substance he forbore to identify.[97] He also notes that many epigrams combine elements of all four: 'Beyond this is that form, which we are accustomed to call urgent, stuffed, intense, manifold'.[98] English epigrammatists make frequent reference to these four metaphoric categories, and defend their own poems by distinguishing them from other varieties.

While brevitas and argutia were widely accepted as the two hallmarks of the epigram, scholars debated whether sweetness might be an acceptable ornament for the genre as well. Pontanus affirms this quality, drawing examples not only from the expected Catullus and the *Greek Anthology* but also from Martial.[99] Martial himself, however, had mocked epigrams that were sweet rather than salty (7:25). In some discussions, these 'sweeter' epigrams were referred to as 'naive', and Scaliger extended his metaphoric framework to describe them as 'honey-like'. Composing epigrams in the 1620s, Robert Hayman drew on this framework and extended it: in a programme poem he suggests that epigrams are like oxymel (a medicinal mixture of honey and vinegar):

> *Hony*, and sweet in their invention,
> *Vineger* in their reprehension.
> As sowre, sweet *Oxymell*, doth purge though fleagme:
> These are to purge *Vice*, take them as they meane.[100]

Here, the qualities of epigrams go beyond flavouring to medicinal corrective – the language of Scaliger's metaphoric categories has been given an
ethical dimension.

This language of physical taste was to play a significant role in framing
the epigrams of the period. Both the titles and prefatory materials of collections refer to collections as 'banquets' or 'feasts', wherein the individual
epigrams are the delicacies of a variety of flavours.[101] Such language may
also suggest that the epigram was a 'consumable' article in both senses[102]
(rather than a 'still unravished bride of quietness'). Among the types
identified by Scaliger, 'saltiness' seems to have been particularly valued:
epigrams are often referred to simply as 'sales' [salty things]. Thomas
Porter (ca. 1614) writes of his that they are 'sine felle, sales' [salty verses,
without bitterness].[103] Pontanus suggests that Greek Old Comedy was
the source of epigrammatic saltiness.[104] While this saltiness was central
to Renaissance understandings of the genre, not all agreed on what constituted it. Jonson describes one 'Playwright' who laments, 'I want the
tongue of epigrams; / I have no salt'. However, Jonson then asserts that
'Playwright' has mistaken 'salt' for 'bawdry': in a sense, he has confused
the categories laid out by Scaliger.[105]

Finally, Renaissance theorists also considered the rhetorical function
or purpose of epigrams. O. B. Hardison, Jr, has shown how theorists,
from Aristotle to the Renaissance, argued that poetry ultimately addressed
human behaviour through either praise or blame, with epic on the praise
side balanced by satire on the blame side; tragedy by comedy, etc.[106]
Unlike most genres, however, the epigram is not limited to one function,
but might either praise or condemn, and this was central to its defence.
It can participate in the humanist venture of improving conduct, the epigrammatist 'illos passis gloriae velis evectos clarat et aeternat; hos convitii
velut fulmine afflatos traducit' [makes shine and live for ever those carried
away by the spread out sails of glory, even as he publicly mocks by a light-
ning bolt those who are puffed up].[107]

This section has largely been concerned with the humanist understanding of the epigram articulated in Neo-Latin treatises. What of native
English descriptions of the epigram? The most extensive definition is
found in the *Arte of English Poesie* by George Puttenham, who was well
read in both classical and continental poetry, and heavily reliant on Scaliger
in much of Book 1 of the work.[108] He shares with Scaliger and Pontanus
an emphasis upon the brevity of the form, but strikingly he places it in
more mundane social and domestic contexts. Rather than being a monumental inscription or a literary text, the epigram is 'but an inscription or

writing made as it were upon a table, or in a window, or upon the wall or mantel of a chimney in some place of common resort'.[109] These oral and social aspects of the epigram tradition in England are more fully explored in Chapter 4. While Puttenham mentions Martial, more than half of his chapter on epigrams is devoted to a witty epigrammatic episode involving Virgil, the emperor and a rival poet. For Puttenham, the genre is rooted in social exchanges, whereas the continental theorists present it as a fixed, literary category.

The humanist epigram

This widespread theorizing on the epigram was reflected in the strong tradition of Neo-Latin epigram composition within Renaissance humanism. Burckhardt refers to Rome as the 'capital city of epigrams and inscriptions', and suggests that 'under Leo X [1513–21], Latin epigrams were the daily bread',[110] and a recent study suggests that 'From the end of the fifteenth century, we find hardly any humanist who did not write epigrams'.[111] However, few scholars have pursued the implications of this reality for the development of the epigram, in both its English and Latin forms, in Britain. The Neo-Latin epigram was a pan-European phenomenon, practised by a range of figures who shared a strong sense of culture despite national differences. The learned reputations of many of these epigrammatists could also be invoked by later poets to overcome the sullied reputation of the form. The list of prominent scholars and churchmen across Europe who wrote and published epigrams is striking: More, Theodore Beza, Buchanan, Dousa, Paul Melissus, Hugo Grotius and many more. Clearly, these epigrams cut across confessional lines – and they were frequently used to battle across those same lines. As is explored more fully in Chapter 3, these epigrams often flourished in academic settings and were part of the currency of friendship [*amicitia*] among the elite. This dynamic seems to have been more common than epigrams being written to would-be patrons, as was customary in the classical tradition.

Among those of English humanists, Thomas More's Latin epigrams (a mixture of satirical, admonitory and panegyric ones)[112] were the most influential in the century after his death.[113] While More is popularly perceived as predominantly a scholarly humanist, his epigrams display something of the jest tradition of England, involving what Bradner calls a 'robust, healthy medievalism'.[114] They were first published with the third edition of his *Utopia* (1518), and, while not printed in England that century, were included in many continental collections of More's work.[115] Helping More's epigrams reach a wide sixteenth-century audience was Timothy Kendall's *Flowers of epigrammes, out of sundrie the most singular authours* (1577), which in addition to those of More also offered translations of Greek and Latin epigrams (especially those of Martial). Appended to this large compilation were Kendall's own compositions in the form. The epigrammatists of 1590 to 1640 recognized Kendall, along with More, as a forebear in their tradition.[116] English versions of More's epigrams continued to appear in seventeenth-century collections of popular verse, such as *Wits Recreations* (1641).

More was similarly invoked as a precedent by John Parkhurst, Bishop of Norwich, in his Neo-Latin collection, *Ludicra, sive, Epigrammata juvenilia* (1573).[117] Parkhurst's example went beyond More's in that he willingly published them during his own lifetime, and in his preface he asserts the acceptability of so doing on the basis of the reputation of More:

> Nam de Thoma Moro summo aliquando Angliae Cancellario, viro pro illis temporib*us* Latine Grece*que* doctissimo, nihil dico. Is enim quamvis huiusmodi ludicra, & lasciva, aliquando etiam parum pudica carmina quaedam scripserit, tamen postea inter Divos Indigetes relatus est, et nunc a suis divino honore colitur. No*n* equidem illi invideo hanc apotheosin. Sed quod in illo ferri, & probari potuit, nolim damnari in aliis. Scripserunt etiam in hoc genere multi nostrorum temporum Poetae, eximii illi quidem, & praestantes viri.[118]

> [For I say nothing of the most worthy Thomas More, sometime Chancellor of England, a man for those times most learned in Latin and Greek. Truly although he sometimes wrote ludicrous and lascivious songs of this type, even a little shameful ones, afterwards he was said to be among the native gods, and now is revered with divine honour. Certainly, it is not that I envy his apotheosis, but that I would refuse to have condemned in others, which in him can be borne and approved. Even many poets of our times have written in this genre; indeed they are distinguished and eminent men.][119]

In the next century, Thomas Fuller would still recognize Parkhurst's achievement in the genre, and defend his publication of the epigrams because of their wit and modesty:

> It grieved him most of all that he lost the fair copy of his Epigrams, though afterwards with much ado he recovered them from his foul papers. These at last he put in print, *et juvenilem foetum senex edidit* [and the old man brought

forth the young brood], without any trespass on his gravity; such his poems being so witty that a young man, so harmless that an old man, need not be of them ashamed.[120]

Parkhurst, like More, was an important figure linking the continental humanist tradition with the native English one that followed in the late sixteenth century.[121] That it is hard to imagine an English bishop of the early seventeenth century print publishing as an epigrammatist in the manner of Parkhurst suggests something of how the genre declined in reputation in that later period. As with More, Kendall's *Flowers* provided a large selection (87) of Parkhurst's epigrams translated into English.[122]

In these same decades the multi-talented Scottish humanist Buchanan composed and published a significant body of epigrams, both satiric and epideictic. These have historically been 'overshadowed' by his other works of poetry and his writings on history and political theory.[123] Like those of many humanist writers, Buchanan's epigrams engage in the virulent religious strife of the period, featuring 'flings at the Roman church and especially at members of monastic orders'.[124] Some of Buchanan's epigrams were published in his lifetime and a full collection was printed in 1584, two years after his death. The continuing influence of Buchanan is suggested by the numerous editions that appeared through the seventeenth century, and occasional translations of his epigrams into English.[125] Paul Melissus (or Schede) was another widely respected epigrammatist of the second half of the sixteenth century. He had contact with the French poets of the Pléiade, visited England in the 1580s, and as a firmly Protestant humanist he was particularly attractive to English poets.

Through the first four decades of the seventeenth century British writers published a striking number of large collections of such Latin epigrams that derived from this humanist tradition. In addition to Buchanan and the well-known Owen, the following, now almost completely unread, were printed:

Bruch, Richard. *Epigrammatum Hecatontades Duae* (1627)
Craig, George. *Specimen epigrammatum* (1624)
Dunbar, John. *Epigrammaton Ioannis Dunbari* (1616)
Fitzgeffry, Charles. *Affaniae* (Oxford, 1601)
Johnson, Jacob. *Epigrammatum libellus: sive, schediasmata poetica* (1615)[126]
Johnston, Arthur. *Epigrammata* (Aberdeen, 1632)
Leech, John. *Epigrammatum libri quatuor* (1623)

Leech, John. *Joannis Leochaei Scoti, musae priores, sive poematum pars prior* (1620)

Ogilvie, W. *Epigrammaton therapeutikon centuriae duae* (Paris, 1624)

Plumptre, Huntingdon. *Epigrammaton Opusculum Duobus Libellis Distinctum* (1629)

Reynolds, John. *Disticha Classis Epigrammatum* (ca. 1609)

Reynolds, John. *Epigrammata, Auctore Ioanne Reinoldo in LL* (1611)

Stradling, John. *Ioannis Stradlingi Epigrammatum libri quatuor* (1607)

Scholars of early modern English literature are still coming to terms with the significance of these late manifestations of the Latin humanist tradition. Did they deeply inform the culture of English epigrams of the period? Did Harington or Jonson see themselves as doing in English what these figures were doing in Latin? Overall, the answer is, yes, the habits of mind and rhetorical techniques central to Latin epigrams were absorbed by English epigrammatists. As I argue more fully in Chapter 3, the role of Latin epigram composition (based upon imitation of others) in education was essential to this process of cultural translation. The chief composers of epigrams in the period, 1590 to 1640, drew upon both these Latin precedents and a more common English tradition that included oral distichs, jests and proverbial wisdom.

Pre-1590s English epigrammatists

John Heywood and Robert Crowley were the most significant English epigrammatists of the mid-sixteenth century. Of the two, Heywood was the more prolific; his folksy and proverbial epigrams were first published in 1549, and continued to grow through subsequent editions. He based each epigram on a common English proverb, which was then responded to or developed in the epigram.[127] While they emerge from the vernacular proverb tradition, these poems are still epigrammatic in their pointedness. Lawrence Manley, exploring the relationship between proverbs and epigrams, suggests that in Heywood 'a proverb of potentially indefinite extension is limited by a more pointed comment', and that frequently the epigram makes explicit that which was hidden by metaphor in the traditional proverb.[128] At least as often, however, the epigrams of Heywood subvert or deny the wisdom embodied in the proverb. They question or reinterpret – from a far more cynical (and thus epigrammatic) perspective – what the proverb passed along as conventional wisdom. Crowley's *One and Thyrtye Epigrammes* (1550) are more in the vein of social satire, and, like Heywood's, they exhibit a definite medieval flavour.[129] However, there is little reference to him as an epigrammatist in subsequent decades, and his influence is limited. Thus, along with More, Heywood was the most often cited British predecessor by epigrammatists of the period 1590–1640. For example, in his 'Epigrams upon English Proverbes' John Davies of Hereford addresses his predecessor:

> Ile gather some Proverbes thou gatherdst before,
> To descant upon them as thou didst of yore:
> But yet not as thou didst for now that were sin,
> But as my Muse prompteth,[130]

The reference to that which is now 'sin' is likely a glancing at Heywood's Catholicism, which led to his exile on the continent during Elizabeth's reign. Davies was himself suspected of adherence to the old faith, and is taking pains to avoid the fate of his predecessor.

Showing more of the Neo-Latin humanist tradition of the epigram were the scattered English epigrams by Nicholas Grimald in *Tottel's Miscellany*, and George Turberville's epigrams, published in 1567 in *Epitaphes, Epigrams, Songs, and Sonets*. The work of both poets shows the strong influence of the *Greek Anthology*, probably derived from Latin sources.[131]

General reputation of epigrams, 1590–1640

The prefaces to epigram collections of the period are striking for the frequency with which the *insignificance* of their work is noted. However, the authorial tone adopted in the light of this varies between two poles: at one extreme are those epigrammatists who apologize for the triviality and idleness of their work, noting with apprehension the wasting of the poet's and the readers' time with such 'trifles'; others, while making no higher claim for their epigrams, brazenly and nonchalantly put them forth, acting unconcerned with any readerly response, and importing the jaded attitude of the epigrams into the words that introduce them.

Typical of this self-dismissive attitude toward epigrams is Charles Fitzgeffry's reference to his three-hundred-some Latin epigrams as 'a scurvy cargo of trifles, blitherings, and nonsense'.[132] Thomas Wroth entitled his century of epigrams 'The Abortive of an Idle Houre', and dismissed them in this way:

If any aske me now, whose booke I am,
I cannot answere without signes of shame;
For he that owns mee, very often saith,
I am the worst of all the bookes he hath,
And which more grieves me, calls me triviall rymes,
Th'untimely issue of his idle times.[133]

An anonymous collection from 1620 presents another typical apology:

These Epigrams I made seven yeeres agoe,
Before I rime or reason scarce did know.[134]

Henry Fitzgeffrey excuses his from criticism by acknowledging their basis in idleness:

These *Idle Verses* (which I *Idle* made)
None but the *Idle* I request to read.[135]

As a counterpart to the spirit of composition in idleness, Fitzgeffrey is suggesting that readers might turn to them in times of idleness, or, as *Tyros Roring Megge* puts it, 'when thou art lazie'.[136] The trifling nature might be excusable because of their brevity; as Richard Turner writes, 'if bad, the time you lost was brief'.[137] Such examples could be easily multiplied. While the slightness and ribaldry of epigrams stood as a serious barrier to their acceptance, the many illustrious practitioners of the genre described earlier in this chapter could be invoked in their defence.

Notes

1 Ben Jonson, 'To my Book', Ep. 2.
2 The first quotation is from William Camden, *Remaines concerning Britaine* (1637), p. 452; the second from Richard Niccols, *The Furies. With Vertues Encomium. Or, The Immage of Honour. In two Bookes of Epigrammes, Satyricall and Encomiasticke* (1614), sig. A3r.
3 Henry Peacham, *Compleat Gentleman* (1622), pp. 89–90.
4 Jonson, Ep. 18.
5 J. P. Sullivan, *Martial: The Unexpected Classic: A Literary and Historical Study* (Cambridge: Cambridge University Press, 1991), pp. 258–61.
6 Sullivan, *Martial*, p. 264
7 Sullivan, *Martial*, pp. 278–9.

8　Sullivan, *Martial*, pp. 271–3.

9　Paul J. Stapleton, 'A Priest and a "Queen": Donne's Epigram "Martial"', *John Donne Journal: Studies in the Age of Donne*, 28 (2009), pp. 93–118, offers the fullest account in English of Raderus's edition, including an appendix that lists all epigrams omitted (over three hundred) or changed by Raderus.

10　C. H. Herford and Percy Simpson (eds), *Ben Jonson*, 10 vols (Oxford: Clarendon Press, 1925–52), vol. 1, p. 216 [my trans.].

11　A popular similar work is Andre Frusius's *Martialis expurgatus* (1558); Frusius was secretary to St Ignatius.

12　Sullivan, *Martial*, p. 292.

13　Frank-Rutger Hausmann, 'Martialis, Marcus Valerius', in Paul Oskar Kristeller (ed.), *Catalogus translationum et commentariorum: Mediaeval and Renaissance Latin Translations and Commentaries*, 6 vols (Washington, DC: Catholic University of America Press, 1960), vol. 4, pp. 256–8. The first printed edition of Schrijver's edition came out in 1618/19; however, in his preface to his 1615 edition of Martial, Farnaby alludes to the role Jonson played in procuring him a manuscript copy of the Dutch scholar's work.

14　Letter to Richard Briggs, Herford and Simpson, *Ben Jonson*, vol. 1, p. 216.

15　Thomas Bancroft, *Two bookes of epigrammes* (1639), Ep. 1:45.

16　Unpublished; BL Add. MS 27343, BL Egerton MS 2982.

17　Gideon Nisbet, *Greek Epigram in the Roman Empire: Martial's Forgotten Rivals* (Oxford: Oxford University Press, 2004), puts forward the argument for a stronger Greek tradition of the skoptic epigram upon which Martial was dependent.

18　Sullivan, *Martial*, p. 287.

19　See Fitzgerald, *Martial*, p. 5, on the dynamics of such close proximity in Martial.

20　See Martial, Eps 1:45, 7:81, 7:90.

21　This organization of published epigrams will be explored more fully in Chapter 5 below.

22　My trans.

23　Everard Guilpin, 'To the Reader', *Skialetheia: or, A shadow of truth, in certaine epigrams and satyres* (1598), ed. D. Allen Carroll (Chapel Hill, NC: University of North Carolina Press, 1974), Ep. 47.

24　Bruce W. Swann, *Martial's Catullus: The Reception of an Epigrammatic Rival* (Hildesheim: Georg Olms Verlag, 1994), p. 90.

25　*Martialis Renati. Parodiarum Sacrarum partes tres Quibus obposita M. Val. Martialis Epigrammata*. See Sullivan, *Martial*, p. 281. The most thorough discussion of Burmeister is found in Fitzgerald, *Martial*, pp. 190–6.

26 Abraham Holland, *Naumachia* (1622), sig. ¶¶v. 'Arbiter' is another name for Gaius Petronius, author of the *Satyricon*.

27 Gabriel Harvey, *Pierces supererogation* (1593), sig. E4r [*sic*] for sig. F4r.

28 It was rumoured that a demonic black dog was released at Cornelius Agrippa's death. The *Facetiae* of Poggio Bracciolini (1380–1459) were frequently published in England in the sixteenth and seventeenth centuries, both in the original Latin and in English.

29 Harington, sig. C6v.

30 Harington, sig. C7r. A marginal note points to Eps 2:78 and 11:11.

31 William Camden, *Remaines concerning Britaine* (1637), p. 44.

32 Guilpin, *Skialetheia*, Ep. 20; cf. Richard Carew, *The Excellency of English*, in *Elizabethan Critical Essays*, ed. G. Gregory Smith, 2 vols (Oxford: Clarendon Press, 1904), 2:293; *The Second Part of the Return from Parnassus* in *The Three Parnassus Plays (1598–1601)*, ed. J. B. Leishman (London: Nicholson & Watson, 1949), 1.2.257–8.

33 Thomas Freeman, BL Sloane MS 1889, fol. 28v.

34 On Owen's continental reputation, see P. N. Wilson, 'A Best-Seller Abroad: The Continental Editions of John Owen', in Ton Croiset van Uchelen et al. (eds), *Theatrum Orbis Librorum: Liber Amicorum Presented to Nico Israel on the Occasion of His Seventieth Birthday* (Utrecht: HES, 1989), pp. 242–9.

35 Petrus Scriverius, *M. Val. Martialis nova editio* (1619), in the Folger Shakespeare Library.

36 Sullivan, *Martial*, p. 288.

37 Bruce Boehrer, 'Martial', *Ben Jonson Journal*, 14 (2007), pp. 259–62, p. 259. This brief article offers a helpful summary of Martial's significance for Jonson and an overview of scholarly work on the topic. Jonson also owned a copy of the heavily expurgated edition of Martial, *Chorus Poetarum Classicorum Duplex*, for which he took the time to 'suppl[y] all the omitted lines and passages in the margin' (Herford and Simpson (eds), *Ben Jonson*, vol. 1, p. 216n).

38 Bradner, *Musae Anglicanae*, pp. 86–8.

39 Bancroft, *Two bookes of epigrammes* (1639), Ep.1:2.

40 Swann, *Martial's Catullus*, p. 87. See, for example, Thomas Campion, *Tho. Campiani Epigrammatum Libri II* (1619) (1613?), Ep. 2:27, 'De Catullo et Martiale'.

41 Swann, *Martial's Catullus*, pp. 95–7.

42 Julia Gaisser, *Catullus and His Renaissance Readers* (Oxford: Oxford University Press, 1993), ch. 5.

43 Julius Caesar Scaliger, *Poetices* (Stuttgart: Frommann-Holzboog, 1987), Book 3, Caput CXXVI, p. 170.

44 Swann, *Martial's Catullus*, p. 108.

45 Swann, *Martial's Catullus*, pp. 132–5.

46 Campion, *Two bookes*, Ep. 2:27 [trans. Sutton].

47 Campion, *Two bookes* [trans. Sutton].

48 John Penkethman, *The epigrams of P. Virgilius Maro* (London, 1624), sig.
    A8v. Gaius Suetonius Tranquillus also identifies the epigrams as the work of
    Virgil's youth. *Suetonius*, trans. J. C. Rolfe, vol. 2, p. 469.

49 N. M. Kay, *Epigrams from the Anthologia Latina: Text, Translation and
    Commentary* (London: Duckworth, 2006), p. 20.

50 Kay, *Epigrams*, p. 20.

51 See, for example, Arthur Johnston's 'Encomia Urbium', recently repub-
    lished in Robert Crawford (ed. and trans.), *Apollos of the North: Selected
    Poems of George Buchanan and Arthur Johnston* (Edinburgh: Polygon, 2006).
    Roger Green notes the influence of Magnus Ausonius on the Scottish
    humanist poets George Buchanan and John Johnstone.

52 See Kay, *Epigrams*, pp. 37–8.

53 Samuel Shepherd, *Epigrams Theological, Philosophical, and Romantick*
    (London, 1651).

54 See N. M. Kay (ed.), *Ausonius: Epigrams* (London: Duckworth, 2001), pp.
    19–20, on the relative obscenity of Martial and Ausonius. See Anne Reynolds
    (ed. and trans.), *Renaissance Humanism at the Court of Clement VII: Francesco
    Berni's Dialogue against Poets in Context* (New York and London: Garland,
    1997), p. 290, on Renaissance Italian familiarity with the 'Priapeia'.

55 *The Greek Anthology* survives in two forms: the Planudean, which was that
    collection known throughout the Middle Ages and early Renaissance, and
    the Palatine Anthology, a tenth-century collection that came to light again
    only in 1607. At that point its contents circulated in more scholarly circles
    and prompted renewed attention to the collection, but it was not published
    in the century. As James Hutton points out, the Planudean was thus *the*
    Greek Anthology for sixteenth- and seventeenth-century writers (*The Greek
    Anthology in Italy* (Ithaca, NY: Cornell University Press, 1935), p. 1).

56 Hutton, *The Greek Anthology in Italy*, p. 36. For a more thorough treatment,
    see Marc D. Lauxtermann, 'Janus Lascaris and the Greek Anthology' in
    Susanna De Beer, Karl A. E. Enenkel and David Rijser (eds), *The Neo–Latin
    Epigram: A Learned and Witty Genre* (Leuven: Leuven University Press,
    2009), pp. 41–66.

57 See Hutton, *The Greek Anthology in Italy*, pp. 37ff.

58 Hutton, *The Greek Anthology in Italy*, p. 37.

59 Hutton, *The Greek Anthology in Italy*, p. 38.

60 Fitzgerald, *Martial*, p. 26.

61 This ecphrastic tradition had much less influence on English Renaissance epigrams, but there are some on household objects among Campion's Latin ones (see, for example, in *Two bookes*, his 'De Horologio portabili' [About the Portable Clock] (Ep. 1:131), and 'On a Penknife' (Ep. 2:13).

62 *The Greek Anthology*, vol. 1, pp. 123–5.

63 James Hutton, *The Greek Anthology in France and in the Latin Writers* (New York: Johnson Reprint, 1967), p. 57.

64 Swann, *Martial's Catullus*, p. 142.

65 Hutton, *The Greek Anthology in Italy*, p. 49.

66 Bodl. James MS 35, pp. 16–19.

67 Lauxtermann, 'Janus Lascaris and the Greek Anthology', pp. 58–9.

68 Robert Hayman, 'Of Epigrams', *Quodlibets* (1628), 4:16.

69 In *Poetices*, the Renaissance scholar Scaliger reassigned them to the fourth century AD, and suggested that a 'Dionysius Cato' was the author instead.

70 J. Howard Brown, *Elizabethan Schooldays: An Account of the English Grammar Schools in the Second Half of the Sixteenth Century* (Oxford: Blackwell, 1933), p. 75.

71 Sir Thomas Urquhart, *Epigrams, divine and moral* (1641) stands as a late example of this tradition.

72 Jonson, dedicatory epistle to the Earl of Pembroke, *Epigrams*, in *Workes* (1616) in *The Cambridge Edition*, vol. 5, p. 112.

73 Manley, 'Proverbs, Epigrams, and Urbanity', p. 250.

74 Manley, 'Proverbs, Epigrams, and Urbanity', pp. 256–65.

75 Sullivan, *Martial*, p. 287.

76 Francesco Robortello also included a section ('de epigrammate') as an appendix to his *In librum Aristotelis de arte poetica explicationes* (Florence, 1548); see the discussion of Robortello in Swann, *Martial's Catullus*, pp. 114–16. Enenkel, 'Introduction: The Neo-Latin Epigram', p. 4, also identifies a number of treatises devoted to the epigram: Tommaso Correa, *De epigrammate* (Venice, 1569); Matthaeus Rader, *De epigrammate* (Ingolstadt, 1602); and Joannes Cottunius, *De conficiendo epigrammate* (Bologna, 1632). None of these, however, would have had the influence of the widely known Scaliger and Jacobus Pontanus.

77 Enenkel, 'Introduction: The Neo-Latin Epigram', p. 21. Among epigrammatists, see John Owen, *Ioannia Audoeni Epigrammatum*, ed. John R. C. Martyn, 2 vols (Leiden: Brill, 1976), where Ep.1:16 makes reference to Scaliger.

78 Scaliger, *Poetices*, p. 170. Hutton notes how in early sixteenth-century treatises, *lepor* [charm] rather than *argutia* [sharpness] was understood as the second distinguishing feature (*The Greek Anthology in Italy*, p. 60).

79 *Epigrammatum Ioannis Owen.*
80 Scaliger, *Poetices*, p. 170.
81 Enenkel, 'Introduction: The Neo-Latin Epigram', p. 18.
82 Ann Moss, 'Theories of Poetry: Latin Writers', in Glyn Norton (ed.), *The Renaissance*, vol. 4 of *Cambridge History of Literary Criticism* (Cambridge: Cambridge University Press, 1999), p. 105.
83 Jacobus Pontanus, *Poeticum institutionem*, in Johann Buchler, *Sacrarum profanarumque phrasium poeticarum thesaurus* (1632), p. 485.
84 'Epigrammatum tot sunt genera, quot causarum' [There are as many kinds of epigram as there are subjects] (Scaliger, *Poetices*, p. 170).
85 Pontanus, *Poeticum institutionem*, p. 474.
86 Ponatnus, *Poeticum institutionem*, p. 475.
87 Enenkel, 'Introduction: The Neo-Latin Epigram', p. 19.
88 See Thomas Farnaby, *HE TES ANTHOLOGIAS ANTHOLOGIA: Florilegium epigrammatum Graecorum, eorumque Latino versu à variis reddito-rum* (1629), sig. A2r.
89 Pontanus, *Poeticum institutionem*, p. 490.
90 Owen, *Ioannia Audoeni Epigrammatum*, Ep. 4:274.
91 Thomas Fuller, *The history of the worthies of England* (1662), vol. 2, p. 21. He notes that Richard White wrote a long commentary on it.
92 Francis Osborne, *The works of Francis Osborne* (1673), p. 504.
93 Pontanus, *Poeticum institutionem*, p. 488.
94 Martial, Ep. 2:77, trans. Walter C. A. Ker.
95 Pontanus, *Poeticum institutionem*, p. 485. Martial himself seems to ridicule the use of echo in Ep. 2:86.
96 Scaliger, *Poetices*, p. 170.
97 Scaliger, *Poetices*, p. 170.
98 Scaliger, *Poetices*, p. 171.
99 Pontanus, *Poeticum institutionem*, pp. 490–1. This was most famously trans-lated into English by the Earl of Surrey as 'Martial, the things for to attain'.
100 Hayman, *Quodlibets*, Ep. 2:2. 'Fleagme' = phlegm.
101 Henry Peacham, *Thalia's Banquet* (1620); *The Philosopher's Banquet* (1614, 1633, 1636); *A banquet of jeasts* (1630).
102 Fitzgerald, *Martial*, p. 3.
103 Thomas Porter, 'Ad Lectorem', Bodl. Holkham MS 436, Ep. 2:34.
104 Pontanus, *Poeticum institutionem*, p. 476.
105 Jonson, 'To Playwright', Ep. 49.
106 O. B. Hardison, Jr, *The Enduring Monument: A Study of the Idea of Praise in Renaissance Literary Theory and Practice* (Chapel Hill, NC: University of North Carolina Press, 1962), pp. 26–9.

107 Farnaby, *HE TES ANTHOLOGIAS ANTHOLOGIA*, sig. A2v.

108 George Puttenham, *The Art of English Poesy: A Critical Edition*, ed. Frank Whigham and Wayne A. Rebhorn (Ithaca, NY: Cornell University Press, 2007), pp. 26–30, 38–40.

109 Puttenham, *The Art of English Poesy*, p. 142.

110 Jacob Burckhardt, *The Civilization of the Renaissance in Italy*, trans. S. G. C. Middlemore, rev. and ed. Irene Gordon (New York: Mentor, 1960), p. 201.

111 Enenkel, 'Introduction: The Neo-Latin Epigram', p. 1. See also H. C. Schnur, 'The Humanist Epigram and Its Influence on the German Epigram', in J. IJsewijn and E. Kessler (eds), *Acta Conventus Neo-latini Lovaniensis, Louvain 23–28 August 1971* (Munich: Fink, 1973), pp. 557–76.

112 Hoyt Hopewell Hudson, *The Epigram in the English Renaissance* (New York: Octagon, 1966), p. 45.

113 Thomas More was only the best known of the notable English scholars and clerics writing competitive Neo-Latin epigrams in the early sixteenth century: significant ones were also produced by William Lily, Robert Whittington and John Leland. These were not forgotten by the poets from the late sixteenth century who will be at the centre of this study. Leland's epigrams, for example, were finally printed in 1589.

114 Bradner, *Musae Anglicanae*, p. 16.

115 Hudson, *The Epigram in the English Renaissance*, pp. 36–7.

116 See Francis Meres, *Palladis Tamia* (1598).

117 Bradner, *Musae Anglicanae*, p. 21. The preface is dated 1558 from Zurich, and many of the poems date from the 1530s and 1540s

118 John Parkhurst, *Ludicra sive Epigrammata iuvenilia* (1573), sig. Aiiii.

119 My trans.; another is offered in Hudson, *The Epigram in the English Renaissance*, p. 142.

120 Fuller, *The history of the worthies*, vol. 3, p. 209.

121 See Hudson, *The Epigram in the English Renaissance*, pp. 90–100, on the relative neglect of Parkhurst's epigrams.

122 Hudson, *The Epigram in the English Renaissance*, p. 102, suggests that it was largely through Timothy Kendall (see *Flowers of epigrammes, out of sundrie the most singular authours*, 1577) that later English epigrammatists knew Parkhurst's epigrams.

123 Hudson, *The Epigram in the English Renaissance*, p. 108.

124 Hudson, *The Epigram in the English Renaissance*, pp. 116–17.

125 Hudson, *The Epigram in the English Renaissance*, pp. 119–20. Writing in 1638, Simond D'Ewes remarks that 'those verses which that learned poetical Scot, Mr. George Buchanan, made, touching a Pope of his time', are so

'vulgarly known', that he does not need to quote them (*Autobiography*, ed. James Orchard Halliwell, 2 vols (London, 1845), vol. 1, p. 390).

126 Another edition appeared in the same year with the title flipped: 'Schediasmata poetica: sive, epigrammatum libellus'.

127 See Burton A. Milligan, 'Humor and Satire in Heywood's Epigrams', in Don Cameron Allen (ed.), *Studies in Honor of Thomas Whitfield Baldwin* (Urbana, IL: University of Illinois Press, 1958), pp. 16–33.

128 Manley, 'Proverbs, Epigrams, and Urbanity', p. 260.

129 Whipple, *Martial and the English Epigram*, pp. 303–6.

130 John Davies of Hereford, *The Scourge of Folly* (1611), Ep. 293.

131 Whipple, *Martial and the English Epigram*, pp. 313–14.

132 Charles Fitzgeffry, *Affaniae* (1601), Ep. 3:142 [trans. Sutton]. The full text of the original Latin passage reads, 'reversi / Ut merces nimium malas feramus, / Nugas, affanias, ineptiasque'.

133 Thomas Wroth, *The Destruction of Troy* (1620), p. 23.

134 Anonymous, *A Description of Love with Certain Epigrams* (1620), sig. B7r.

135 Henry Fitzgeffrey, *Satyres: and satyricall epigrams* (1617), sig. B1r.

136 T. Tyro, *Tyros Roring Megge Planted against the walles of Melancholy. One Booke cut into two Decads* (1598), sig. A2v.

137 Richard Turner, *Nosce Te* (1607), sig. F4r.

2

'A Curter kind of Satyre'?[1] The epigram, proximate genres and terminology

> It is the mark of a trained mind never to expect more precision in the treatment of a subject than the nature of that subject permits.[2]

While all might agree that 'Epigrammatis duae virtutes peculiares: brevitas & argutia'[3] [Epigrams have two particular attributes: brevity and sharpness], the actual epigram culture of the period 1590 to 1640 was far more complex. The relationship between the epigram and proximate genres – especially satire – was a vexed question. While the literary theorists described in the previous chapter might precisely define what an epigram entailed, in both the practice of poets and in references by readers, letter-writers and even the courts there was clearly a great deal of slippage between terms, and overlapping of concepts. As a genre it shared some of the spirit of satire, but used very different methods. It was often connected with the jest, a term deriving from more popular vocabulary and culture, and 'libels', a term or concept based in the legal world. Its brevity linked it with other short forms of the period, such as the sonnet, aphorism, prose character and proverb, but its pointedness generally set it apart from these. Finally, a variety of competing terminology (especially in Latin) used to describe the epigram itself contributed to the murkiness of its generic boundaries and identity.

Alastair Fowler's theory of generic modulation is helpful in considering the relationship between the epigram and these neighbouring poetic kinds. He suggests that the conventions and elements of one genre can have a modal effect on surrounding ones, and he uses the epigram in the late sixteenth and seventeenth centuries as an example, arguing that the period saw a 'great epigrammatic transformation' as the genre's emphasis on pointed wit and concision was absorbed by a range of other literary kinds.[4] However, the effect was in two directions: '[the epigram] could assimilate features of other kinds, or it could contribute its own to them'.[5] Fowler sketches how the epigram influenced a range of other genres, but my concern here is more with how other genres, especially satire, modulated the epigram. Those poets who self-consciously committed themselves to the epigram struggled to maintain its distinctiveness from the proximate genres of satire, proverb and libel. It is more with that *struggle* than the straightforward influence of the epigram upon other kinds or the culture in general that this chapter is chiefly concerned. The affinities discussed in this chapter have a twofold dimension: influence and reader's perceptions. However, these are not completely separate: epigrammatists might be led to deny influence to challenge readers' perceptions that they were engaged in a proximate genre. Thus, poets' distinguishing of epigrams from these other genres was an important element in the defining of the genre and the maintenance of their status as epigrammatists.

Fowler's idea that literary genres are more like families than distinct botanical classes, where there is resemblance but not necessarily an always-appearing feature, is also pertinent here.[6] It allows us to see epigrams as a distinct family, while acknowledging limited and varying degrees of kinship with related genres. Hence epigrams share qualities of both subject and style with satires, jests, libels and characters; their brevity, and, in those influenced by the *Greek Anthology*, their sweetness, links them with sonnets,[7] but they share almost nothing with epics.

Genres in the climate of the 1590s

Single-author books of epigrams emerged in the 1590s, a very self-conscious and vibrant period of generic development. Epigram books thus jostled for position in the literary marketplace with other forms newly in vogue: Ovidian verse, sonnet sequences, verse epistles and satires. What did the epigram offer in competition with these? In *Skialetheia* Guilpin sets epigrams and satires apart from the other fashionable genres of the time:

> The Satyre onely and Epigramatist,
> (Concisde [*sic*] Epigrame, and sharpe Satyrist)
> Keepe diet from this surfet of excesse,
> Tempring themselves from such licenciousnes.
> The bitter censures of their Critticke spleenes,
> Are Antidotes to pestilentiall sinnes,
> They heale with lashing, seare luxuriousnes,

They are Philosophicke true *Cantharides*
To vanities dead flesh.[8]

They are antidotes to the excess and licentiousness of other unnamed genres (Guilpin may have in mind Ovidian verse in particular), constituting what Claudio Guillen has called a 'countergenre'.[9] Their sharp, dry wit stands in contrast to the sweet, florid quality of the love sonnet and Ovidian verse that dominated the first half of the 1590s, and they stand apart from other poetic work through their philosophical temperance, detachment and judgement.

The epigram and other short forms

Sixteenth-century Italian and French humanists often presented the sonnet as the 'equivalent' vernacular form to the classical epigram.[10] However, in English practice these forms, alike in brevity, came frequently to be perceived as contrasting. This had less to do with formal qualities than the way in which the two forms had become identified with particular tones and subject matter. While the model of the *Greek Anthology* provided a wide range of subject matter for epigrams, and a sweeter, more flowery style, by the 1590s the form in England was associated with urbane, Martial-like wit, which set it apart from the sonnet. Harington's 'Comparisons of the Sonnet and the Epigram' sums up the difference in tone: 'Well though I graunt sugar may please the taste / Yet let my verse have salt to make yt last.'[11] He thus sees 'sugared sonnets' as a passing fashion, where the salty epigram has a classical past and a future. Likewise, in spite of Sir John Davies's 'gulling sonnets', that genre was dominated by the suffering of the poet-lover not the detached judgement and ridicule of the epigram. An anonymous epigram, addressed to one 'Madame Fowler', reflects this distinction; it begins

Good Madam Fowler doe not trouble mee
To write a sonnett in the praise of thee
I dare not crosse wise nature for to frame
A sonnet where shee ment an Epigram,[12]

The woman's expectation of a sonnet will never be fulfilled: each of her 'members' and the children she will bear will require an epigram, presumably of derision. This is more than a distinction in subject matter: the poet resists the humbling position of sonneteer for the more independent and cynical role of epigrammatist. The poet in this role will be true to nature, not to the wishes of his subject.

Again, the aphorism and proverb shared the epigram's brevity and at times influenced the genre. However, the proverb represented common folk wisdom, while the epigram was generally set apart by its urbane individual wit. While both epigrams of praise and ridicule might convey (indirectly) an ethical point, they stood apart from the maxim and aphorism in their specificity.

Epigrams and the jest tradition

The native jest tradition, as exemplified in such popular printed works as *A Hundred Mery Talys* (1526?) and *A banquet of jeasts* (1630), drew on popular comic anecdotes that circulated by word of mouth in variant forms, and whose humour was often broadly physical or situational. Adam Fox has shown how the jest tradition mingled oral and written modes: what began as anecdotal conversation came to be written down for future use by individuals, and offered as collections by printers. Further oral use sometimes came from both these written forms.[13] Something of the early seventeenth-century reputation of jests can be garnered from a passage in Overbury's *Characters*. 'The True Character of a Dunce' (possibly by Donne) describes a dunce as one whose 'jests are either old flayed proverbs or lean-starved hackney apothegms, or poor verbal quips outworn by servingmen, tapsters, and milkmaids, and even laid aside by balladeers'.[14] Here the disparagement of worn-out 'folk' genres is tightly bound up with the idea of social descent, from serving-men to balladeers.

The fear of social contagion from the jest tradition is found frequently in the prefatory material to epigram books, as the poets try to show their form's respectable literary pedigree. Like the jest, the epigram frequently enjoyed a pattern of mixed and freewheeling circulation, one which in its intensity aroused concerns about social and literary distinctions. The more Martialian tradition of the epigram might look askance at such relatively unsophisticated works and their wide circulation, but in reality some major (and respected) epigrammatists of the period such as Sir Thomas More and John Harington are clearly indebted to it.[15]

Ben Jonson said of both Harington's and Owen's epigrams that they were mere 'narrations', by which he seems to have meant that, rather than being brief witty reflections on an individual or situation, they were jest-like in their relating of a short tale leading to a humorous conclusion. Similarly, the epigrammatist Henry Fitzgeffrey, who never quite decided

whether his epigrams were Martialian or common, complains of those
who compose verses by such borrowing of jests:

> Such as they at Table sit
> Each Jest you speake, will to a Metre fit.
> And thus your Witt's sell for their private gaine
> And bee accounted Poets for their paine.[16]

Most epigrammatists of the period 1590 to 1630 would be open to the
charge of *at times* composing in this way, offering mere narrations, deeply
indebted to a common store of anecdotes and jests. Those epigrammatists like Harington who recognized this dimension of their work tend
to defend themselves by arguing that execution not originality was the
defining feature, and that they offered a more polished version of the jest,
one worthy of being fixed in written form.

Harington seemed unconcerned that many of his epigrams are ultimately polished jests, as he quite openly admits their popular sources.
One of his epigrams begins, 'I heard among some other pleasant tales':[17]
he acknowledges that his 'matter' is borrowed, but takes pride in what he
does with it. In this way he counters accusations of literary theft:

> When *Sextus* heard my ryme of Raynsford reeding
> with lafter lowd he cryes, and voyce exceeding,
>> That Epigram was mine, who ever made it,
>> I told him that conceyt: from me he had yt;
> Ah barbarisme, the blynder still the bolder,
> will *Sextus* near grow wiser, growing older.
>> When *Phidias* framed had in marble pure
>> Joves goodly picture, would a man indure,
> A Pioner to challenge half the prayse
> that from the Quarr, the ragged stone did rayse
>> Or should a Carman boast of his desart,
>> bycause he did unlode it from his Cart
> I thinke that Sextus selfe would never say 't
> So in like manner, *Sextus*: that conceyt
>> Was like a ragged stone dig'd from thy foollish head
>> now tis a statue carv'd by us, and pullished.[18]

The source of the jest is merely the 'pioner' (that is, 'pioneer', in the
sense of sense of quarrier or miner), whereas Harington presents himself

as the carver and finisher, the one who achieves with the raw material the urbane polish and sharpness that makes it an epigram rather than a mere jest. He is the Phidias-like artist, the others mere labourers. (In terms of the traditional stages of rhetoric, his is the elocution rather than the invention.) Harington's prose work *A Supplie or Addicion to Bishop Godwin's Catalogue of Bishops* provides similar evidence of his method: he collected jests by and about churchmen, some of which became the source of epigrams. Thus, he recounts some jests of Bishop Bonner that he had probably received orally: he 'having twice lost his bishoprick, walking with his tippet in the strete, one begg'd it of him in scoffe, to lyne a coate; "No, (sayth he) but thou shalt have a fooles head, to lyne thy cap." And to another, that bad him "good morrow bishop *quondam*;" he straight replyed, "Farewell, knave *semper*".'[19] These jests of Bonner are reformulated as epigrams by Harington:

> Fat Bonner late that Bishop was of London,
> was bid by one good morrow bishop quondam,
> > he with the scoff no whitt put out of temper,
> > replyde incontinent, Adew knave semper.
> One other in such kynde of scoffing speeches,
> Would beg his tippet needes, to lyne his breeches,
> > Not so quoth he, but it may bee thy hap,
> > to have a foollish head to lyne thy cap.[20]

Henry Parrot's similar polishing of a widely known political jest may demonstrate how the epigram's formal qualities shaped material. Early in his English reign James's prolific knightings prompted a widely circulated quip that it was now more illustrious to be a gentleman than a knight: 'two walking espyed one a farr of, the one demanded what he sholde be, the other answered he seamed to be a gentleman, no I warrant you, sayes the other I thinke he is but a knight'.[21] A few years later this idea was reproduced in this more developed poetic form by Parrot:

> *Battus* beleeved for a simple truth,
> That yonder gilt-spur spruce and velvet youth
> Was some great personage or worthy wight,
> Untill one told him he was but a knight,
> A knight (quoth *Battus*) vaith I chud a zworne,
> He had at least been zum gud gen-man borne.[22]

Unlike the original quip or jest, this epigram points in more than one direction, mocking not only the proliferation of knighthoods but also the excessive clothing of the new young knight, and the west country dialect of Battus, the observer of the situation. He is not the voice of the poet but one whose provincial naivety is used by the more urbane author to point a truth.[23]

Even a volume using the word 'jests' in its title might recognize the worn and unfashionable reputation of the form, and hence use the vocabulary associated with satire and epigram to identify itself. Thus, the 1634 edition of *A Banquet of Jests* promises 'in the stead of Dainties, you shall finde *Dicteria*: for Junkets, *joci*: and for curious Sallets; *Sales*'.[24] Here typical terms from the titles of jest books and poetry collections of the 1500s ('dainties', 'junkets', 'sallets') are replaced with the vocabulary of the Latin epigram tradition ('dicteria', 'joci', 'sales').[25] Among the collections that had 'dainty' or 'dainties' in the title were *The banquett of dainties* (1566), but the reference is likely to the oft reprinted *The Paradyse of Daynty Devises* (1576 and many subsequent editions up until 1606). The sense that 'sales' (a term frequently used in reference to Neo-Latin epigrams) were *urbane* witticisms is supported by one of the definitions of the term in Thomas Cooper's *Thesaurus Linguae* (1565): 'Civile & courteise jestes, or pleasant sayinges without rusticitie': they are 'Nati sales intra pomoeria'[26] [salty things born within the city walls]. This shows a distinction between epigram and jest based upon polish and urbanity. The printer's preface in the same volume rejects a number of popular jest books by name:

> Pasquels conceits are poore, and Scoggins dry,
> Skeltons meere rime, once read, but now laid by.
> Peeles Jests are old, and Tarletons are growne stale,
> These neither bark nor bit, nor scratch, nor raile.[27]

The worn jests are being replaced by ones associated with the harsher violence of modern satire, with their emphasis on barking, biting, scratching and railing. Sidney Godolphin picked up on this distinction as well, after Jonson's death prophesying that later readers will marvel how 'in Jest, what urbanity hee uses'.[28]

Epigrams and satire

While early Stuart poets and readers might identify the epigram as 'A Curter kind of Satyre',[29] its reputation and formal qualities significantly

set it apart from other ventures in the broad category of 'satire'. The predominant brevity of the epigram gave it a focus lacking in satire, which
often tended in the direction of an expansive catalogue. It also tended
toward an urbane cynicism distinct from the overwhelming splenetic rage
found in the formal satires of the 1590s and early 1600s. The classical epigram, particularly as practised by Martial, was noted for its detachment,
and hence it was unlikely to be a *railing* rhyme, in the style of formal
verse satire. William Fitzgerald has noted how Martial differs from the
Juvenalian satirist; while he does point out human vice and folly, his
role is also at times to praise and seek patronage.[30] Similarly, Jonson's
reliance on epigrams rather than satire has been read by Jack D. Winner
as a deliberate response to the excessive voices of 1590s formal satire.[31]
Where the satirist of the 1590s was a figure driven by indignation to a
savage roughness in his treatment of vice, the epigrammatist maintained
a cool, discerning judgement reflected in the polish of his production. As
described by Alvin B. Kernan, the verse satirist was a figure who himself
was distorted, driven by his humour of melancholy to lash out at both
the deserving and undeserving.[32] No such instability of mind was associated with the epigrammatist, who offers instead a detached and balanced
judgement. This is also reflected in style; where formal verse satire was
often notoriously crabbed and difficult, epigrams of the period are largely
clear and direct. There are wordplay and double meanings, but seldom
tortured syntax.

Renaissance commentators like Scaliger made similar remarks, but in
practice, and even in the self-conscious reflections of poets active in the
field, such generic boundaries were far from clear or fixed, and epigrams
were frequently modulated by satire in the late sixteenth and early seventeenth centuries. Even such a self-conscious epigrammatist as John
Owen collapses any distinction other than length between epigrams and
satires:

> Nil aliud satyrae quam sunt epigrammata longa.
> Est, praeter satyram nil, epigramma, brevem.
> Nil satyrae si non sapiant epigrammata pungunt,
> Nil satyram sapiat, nil epigramma iuvat.

> [Satyres are but long Epigrams; And these
> Are but short Satyres, to displease, or please:
> Satyres avail not, if they be not tart;
> Nor Epigrams, unless like Satyres, smart.][33]

Similarly, John Stradling's two poems 'On Lolianus' complain that Lolianus is not satisfied with his epigrams, at one point saying they are more like satires, at another accusing them of being too short, all of which suggests of course that the prime difference is length.[34] (While Stradling is clearly frustrated with Lolianus's carping, he does not quarrel with his critic's assumption that length is the primary marker of the epigram). An epigram by Hayman also assumes length to be the primary distinction between the genres:

> Thou art not worthy of a Satyres quill:
> An Epigram's too short to shew thine ill.[35]

That a number of authors (Guilpin, Henry Fitzgeffrey) published both genres within the covers of one book also encouraged such conflation. In his 'Satyre Preludium' Guilpin aligns satire and epigram, and suggests that as a pair they are distinct from such decadent forms as the sonnet, elegy and comedy.[36] However, his description of the epigram that follows seems to ignore what others had seen as its distinctiveness. He describes it:

> An Epigrame
> Is popish displing, rebell flesh to tame:
> A plaine dealing lad, that is not afraid
> To speake the truth, but calls a jade, a jade.[37]

The first clause compares the epigram to an irritant that mortifies the flesh, thus giving it a stern social purpose, similar to satire itself. The second enforces this similarity between the two genres by replacing the more traditional urbane epigrammatist with the plain-spoken satirist of the English tradition, most famously found in the figure of Piers Plowman.[38] This shows that even a practitioner of the genre could be uncertain of (or unconcerned with) its primary classical associations. However, Guilpin does recognize the epigram as a more limited genre, both in scope and in severity. The satire is a 'strappado' and 'rack', but 'the Epigram's Bridewell, / Some whipping cheere: but this [satire] is follies hell'.[39] A slightly different distinction is offered by John Davies of Hereford: epigrams might have the same corrective role as satire, but aim at less distinguished figures:

> *Aretine*, whom *Fame*
> Stil'd *Scourge of Princes* (such I leave to such)

> Kept them in awe: So may an *Epigram*
> With other soft-brow'd Sinners, doe as much,[40]

It is this blurring of the distinctions between the genres that Winner argues compelled Jonson so carefully to maintain that his epigrams were not satire-like.[41]

A sharply defined single focus is central to the epigram; where the satire catalogues a seemingly endless array of human vice and folly, the individual epigram is selective and limited. Thus, even those epigrams that through length and the development of a short narrative move in the direction of satire still maintain a sharp unifying feature. This is the case in Guilpin's 'As Caius walks the street ...' (no. 68): like many satirists Caius roams the streets encountering a range of human spectacles, but the whole is focused on Caius himself, and unified by Caius's single repeated response: 'oh rare!' is all he can say. Ultimately, he, not the city life encountered, is the satirized subject of the epigram.

A few published volumes describe themselves as epigrams (perhaps because of fashion), but are satires in all but name. The preface to the reader in *Tyros Roring Megge* (1598) calls the poems 'epigrams', but it also identifies them as having emerged from the poet's melancholy, the humour typically associated with satire. Overall the poems' frequently crabbed and cryptic syntax feels much more like satire. The first, for example, relates the encounters of the fictional persona Tyro with a series of ridicule-worthy figures, and then a series of poems mocking Tyro himself. The effect is much more diffuse than in Guilpin's poem on Caius. Thus, like Guilpin's of the same year, the volume points to the overlapping of satire and epigram, and the fashion (and perhaps marketability) of the term 'epigram'. Working the other way, William Goddard entitles the short epigram-like poems of *A Mastiff Whelp* 'satires', even though they are just like the epigrams of his volume *A Neaste of Waspes*. 'R.C.', the author of the manuscript collection of satires entitled 'Times' Whistle' (ca. 1614–16) opens his collection with a twenty-line poem he entitles 'Epigrammisatiron',[42] and J.H.'s *The house of correction* (1619) is subtitled 'Certayne satyricall epigrams'.

Despite such overlapping, there were many poets who maintained a distinction in tone between the two genres: Stradling, for example, writes: 'Dente licet mordent epigrammata, felle carebunt / Spurcities absit, sint sale sparsa levi' [though epigrams bite with a tooth, they will lack spleen. Let filth be absent, let them be lightly sprinkled with salt].[43] Thus, in the place of the splenetic tone of satire, his epigrams will have the saltiness encouraged by Scaliger and other humanist commentators. *The Whipping of the Satyre* (1601) distinguishes among the satirist, epigrammatist and humorist thus:

> One should outrayle him by invective vaine,
> One all to flout him like a countrey clowne;
> And one in action, on a stage out-face,
> And play upon him to his great disgrace. (831–4)

Here the epigrammatist is distinct by his 'flouting' (that is, mockery) rather than the railing invective of satire; however, it is noteworthy here that the epigrammatist is figured as rural rather than urbane. (The humorist in this account is a figure of the stage.) Similarly, John Taylor distinguishes among 'temporizing Humorists, sharpe Satyrists, or Aenigmaticall Epigrammatists'.[44] Taylor's description of satire as 'sharpe' is consistent with the long tradition of seeing it as a genre that 'bites' those whom it attacks (which Stradling had presented as a quality of epigrams as well); however, his description of the epigrammatist as 'aenigmaticall' is itself, well, rather enigmatic: possibly he is pointing toward the epigram's tendency at the time to indirectly identify the follies of a particular individual, leaving the reader to puzzle out the identity. Likewise, at the end of *Strappado for the Divell* (1615), Richard Brathwaite (who throughout his volumes uses 'epigram' to describe longer satire-like works) explains his terminology:

> My answer's this to him that saies I wrong
> Our Art to make my Epigrams so long;
> I dare not bite, therefore to change my nature,
> I call't an Epigram which is a Satire.[45]

Brathwaite in a preceding poem threatens to advance to more biting material if this is not well received.

The epigram's limited length also affects tone and approach, and helps distinguish the epigram from formal verse satire: while both may comment from an ethical basis on topical concerns, epigrams are restrained by their length: two or four lines are little room to 'rail', but quite sufficient to launch a 'squib'. The mounting criticism of satire, the sense of disdain and vituperation accomplished through a cataloguing of errors (the sort that bursts into Wyatt's 'I cannot, I. No, no, it will not be' in 'Myne owne John Poynz'),[46] is impossible in the epigram. Vehemence would seem nonsensical in such a context, and hence the detached ironic tone of mere observation. The voice is most often quiet or neutral, or even wryly accepting. Freeman suggests that, in spite of their appearance of invective, his epigrams are not satires, because they laugh at that which they dislike and 'in th'end [do] smile'.[47] At the same time, the smile of epigrammatists was a wry, uncommitted one.

The libel: 'a damnable storie ... in goodlie verse'[48]

Both satires and epigrams also frequently overlapped with the law-based category of 'libel'. As M. Lindsay Kaplan suggests,

> Doggerel rhyme, ballads and satire became such popular expressions of detrac-
> tion that defamation is increasingly associated with poetry. This connection
> is so strong by the beginning of the seventeenth century that Chief Justice
> Edward Coke can define a libel as 'an epigram, rhyme, or other writings'.[49]

Not all libels were epigrams, and certainly not all epigrams were libels, but in the period 1590 to 1640 there was considerable overlapping of the two terms, and many contemporary references suggest that a libel was expected to be in epigram form. Alastair Bellany convincingly argues that the early Stuart verse libel represented a coming together of a home-grown tradition of political satire with the 1590s fashion of classically inspired satire and epigrams.[50]

The authorless nature of many epigrams in oral and manuscript circu-lation also connects them with common conceptions of libel, as it is clear from many references that anonymity was conceived as a determining element of 'libels', and hence an illegitimate form of political discourse. Harington, for example, advises that 'a booke without name may be called a libel'.[51] An exchange in Webster's *The Duchess of Malfi* confirms this: when Antonio charges 'You libel well, sir', Bosola responds 'No, sir. Copy it out, / And I will set my hand to't'.[52] Finally, Donne notes in a letter from 1612 that writings of the Lucifer, Bishop of Cagliari, against the Emperor Constantius 'did a little escape the nature of libels, by being subscribed and avowed: which excuse would not have served in the Star-chamber, where sealed Letters have been judged Libels'.[53] Here we see the strong suggestion that, while traditionally libels were anonymous, in the early seventeenth century there was a perceived legal broadening of the definition to include those acknowledged by an author.

For the broader category of satire the more usual defence against the charge of libel was that the poem chastised the general vice rather than the individual. While epigrams acknowledged a firmer basis in individuals, they would claim that identity was sufficiently obscured that those who complained were only indicting themselves. As a legal defence, however, this seems to have fallen short if the identity could be easily discerned by readers. A manuscript in the Huntington Library preserves the records of court cases in Gloucestershire where individuals were charged with libel because of short mocking poems. The judgement notes:

> Althoughe the names of the complainants & others meant by the libell were not plainely named, yett by ynference and Circumstance so pointed at that the inhabitantes easely understoode the parties therein meante. etc.[54]

Some literary epigrams are also quite obvious: one by Harington leaves little doubt that a woman named 'Penn' is the subject:

> Her name I must not name in playne recyting,
> But thus the chiefest instrument in wryting.[55]

Such easy identification seems to have at least partly motivated the 1599 'Bishops' Ban' on satire and epigram.[56]

At a number of points Jonson counters accusations that his epigrams are libels:

> Chev'rel cries out my verses libels are,
> And threatens the Star Chamber and the Bar.
> What are thy petulant pleadings, Chev'rel, then,
> That quit'st the cause so oft, and rail'st at men?[57]

However, the 'tu quoque' argument that libel is practised by others besides poets hardly discredits the allegation. His *Poetaster*, a play deeply concerned with poetic libel, offers a quite different defence of satiric epigrams at the end of Act 3, scene 5 in the 1601 Quarto. Trebatius warns Horace (the Jonson figure) to be careful: 'There's justice, and great action may be sued / 'Gainst such as wrong men's fames with verses lewd' (128–9). Horace responds with this distinction between the poet and the mere libelist:

> To be sure, in case of ill verses. But what if a man compose good verses, and Caesar's judgement approve? If he has barked at someone who deserves abuse,

himself all blameless? The case will be dismissed with a laugh. You will get off scot-free.

Here is then another – and far more subjective – way of distinguishing between libels and epigrams: poetic craft and a deserving subject elevate the work beyond legal action. Laughter will triumph over law, the monarch's poetic just favour is supreme, and the 'blameless' character of the poet preserves him.[58]

Characters

Finally, there is some affinity between the epigram and the Theophrastian character, which became popular in England about a decade after the late 1590s flurry of epigram books. While both genres are concerned with succinctly capturing the essence of a recognizable figure. the epigram differs in usually assigning a specific fictional identity to that which the prose character leaves generalized. With a few sure strokes, the character depicts the essence of a type, say, the courtier, while the epigram depicts Paulus, a courtier, and often with simply one representative feature. However, the affinity between the two is reflected in that the fictional lemmas of some epigrams are simply taking the quality and turning it into a Latin name. For example, a number of epigrams with the lemma 'In Superbum' would be rendered 'On the proud man' if they were characters, but with the epigram that pride becomes the name itself, and generally epigram is felt to depict an individual rather than a type.[59]

Epitaphs and elegies

The epitaph as a sub-genre of the epigram is distinct from a range of other poetic genres associated with death, in Renaissance theory and in both classical and Renaissance practice. Most of these distinctions were based upon the voice and moment of utterance. The classical form of the epicedium was understood to be uttered over the body as part of the funerary process; in Renaissance England this type of poem slowly came to be called an 'elegy' or 'funeral elegy' instead. The emphasis is upon personal grief and the search for consolation. Brathwaite explains the distinction in this way: 'the difference is betweene an *Epicede* and *Epitaph*, as *Servius* teacheth, that the *Epicede* is before the corps be interred, an *Epitaph* or inscription upon the Tombe'. The epitaph offers less momentary grief and commemoration, and a more detached, longstanding reflection upon the dead individual. As Scott Newstok puts it, the epitaph is distinguished by its 'here-ness', that is, whether or not it uses the formulaic opening 'here lies', the epitaph 'always retains a connection to its place of enunciation [the grave], even if only a fictive origin'.[60] He argues that epitaphs were a way of offering closure to the ongoing grieving process represented by the elegy.[61] From this emerges the frequent scenario of an elegy concluding with epitaph, as most famously in Carew's elegy on Donne. However, in spite of these widely acknowledged distinctions, there was still a considerable slippage of terminology, with the same poem being titled an epitaph in one manuscript and an elegy in another.

Terminology

As outlined above, the epigram culture of Renaissance England was rich and multi-faceted, with significant modulation and mingling of genres; it was rendered more complicated yet by a range of competing and overlapping terminology, particularly in Latin. Certain words echo through literary handbooks of the period and prefatory material to books of epigrams: Latin terms used to identify what were more generally called 'epigrams' include 'lusus' [amusements],'lepores' [pleasantries] 'parerga' [secondary things, appendices], 'pauculae' [little, trifling things], 'affaniae' [trivial matters], 'ludicra' [playthings], 'ioci' or 'nugae' [trifles], all of which suggest the inconsequential nature of the form.[62] Some of these competing terms went back to Roman times. While Martial helped fix the term 'epigram', he also frequently labels his epigrams 'nugae', and Swann argues that 'nugae' was 'the programmatic word of Catullus' as well.[63]

Pliny the Younger also recognizes a wide range of possible terms: 'Proinde, sive epigrammata sive idyllia sive eclogas sive, ut multi, poematia, seu quod aliud vocare malveris, licebit voces, ego tantum hendecasyllabos praesto' [Call them, if you think proper, Epigrams, Idylls, Eclogues (as many others have), Little Poems; in a word, give them what name you please, I offer them only as *Hendecasyllabics*].[64] Pliny thus settles upon the metrical term hendecasyllables, which after the elegaic couplet was the most common form used by Martial. In the Renaissance, poems in this metre (also referred to as Phaleuci) came to be associated with milder, but still salty, epigrams. Two volumes of Latin hendecasyllables had been written by Giovanni Pontano in late fifteenth-century Italy, and these proved to be of great influence on the humanist poets who followed. Melmoth, in a footnote to his edition of Pliny, suggests that the term 'became a synonym for erotic poetry'; while this may be true of the Italian

use of the term, in England its use seems to have been wider. [65] Charles
Fitzgeffry repeatedly refers to his own epigrams in *Affaniae* as 'Phaleuci'.
Their distinction from other forms is made clear in one addressed to
Degory Wheare:

> Si nil blanditiis, papyri, si nil
> Blanda profueris precatione,
> Iras adsere mox, minaciasque,
> Et post molliculos leves phaleucos,
> Expectet tetricos truces iambos,
> Sed plures, sed amarulentiores,
> Sed quales socero ferox Lycambri
> Spartani rabies dedit poeta.

[If you achieve nothing with pleasant and friendly entreaties, my papers, then
soon introduce wrath and threats, and after your light, soft little Phaleucians,
let him expect harsh savage iambics, more numerous and more bitter than those
the fierce poet gave to his father-in-law, Lycambrus the Spartan.][66]

John Stradling similarly contrasts the milder hendecasyllabics with
'raging' iambics.[67] 'Phaeleuci' were also associated with a somewhat
leisurely, if not languid, approach to life.

Competing terminology was multiplied by a tendency (on the part
of authors or readers) to dismiss the significance of the form. A Latin
epigram by Fitzgeffry to Edward Michelborne discusses the competing
terms he and his addressee use:

> Quae tu carmina, quos sales iocosque
> Leporesque vocas facetiasque,
> Quas nos affanias ineptiasque
> Burras, quisquilias vocamus, atque
> Sordes candidulae nigras papyri,
> Haec tibi damus.

[These poems, which you call sallies, jokes, witticisms and pleasantries, but
which I call *affaniae*, *burrae*, rubbish and black smudges on white paper, I give
to you.][68]

Evidently, the terminology brings with it value judgements: Fitzgeffry
dismisses his own works with deprecatory epithets, while making it clear

that his friend and mentor would generously grant them somewhat more positive names.[69] Such struggles with conflicting labels could also work the other way; in his 1627 collection, Richard Bruch responds to one who has attacked his poems by calling them 'nugae' rather than 'epigrams':

Nuga nostra vocas, (sic sunt Epigrammata,) nugis
Postpono tamen his grandia (Macre) tua.

[You call ours (which are epigrams) 'trifling jests'; however, Macrus, I esteem your great things less than these.][70]

Bruch does not reject the term 'nugae' outright, but simply places his ambitious poetic rival even lower on the generic scale.

In common English usage there was a similar cluster of competing terms, but the overlapping terminology reflects more on the social role of the poetry rather than its relative significance: the terms 'epigram', 'libel', 'distich', 'squib' and 'Pasquil' show major overlapping and slippage. A libel could take a number of forms, and one of these was that of a distich, a fairly neutral technical term, simply identifying the poem as a single couplet. Many epigrams were distichs.[71] Such a poetic attack might be called a 'squib', which was literally a short-lived type of firework that ended with a sharp explosion. This term was most often used to denote a relatively inconsequential mocking attack, frequently in a dismissive sense, to suggest that writers were firing *mere squibs*. Likewise, epigrams of personal attack were sometimes called 'nips',[72] which may be a reflection of the satiric tradition of 'biting' one's objects of ridicule. As discussed more fully in Chapter 4, the term 'Pasquil' (or 'Pasquin'), which highlights the public posting of a short libel in a particular spot rather than mere circulation, might in form and spirit be an epigram. However, increasingly in the period the term came to be used to describe any short libel in verse or prose, and regardless of whether it was publicly posted or circulated in some other fashion.

Some poets extended the terminology, creating nonce words by playing on the roots of 'epigram' and 'epitaph'. Samuel Rowlands dismisses those who 'lay about with lowsie *Nitigrams*':[73] like a number of other references from the period, this term points in the directions of irritating insects. In a satire seemingly written in 1626, although not published until 1642, John Taylor, the Water-Poet, expresses the desire to erect 'some pretty *Epi-knave* upon [Ambrogio Spinola's] death'.[74]

Finally, some of the substitute terminology applied to the genre may have resulted from a desire to evade the prohibition on epigrams in the Bishops' Ban of 1599, discussed in Chapter 6. Thus, Robert Joyner in *Itis, or three severall boxes of sporting familiars* (1598), sends his 'Itys' out into the world protected by 120 'familiars'; that is, the short poems of the volume that are epigrams in all but name. Ironically, his preface to Itys acknowledges fully what he has done:

> To speake troth, thy Familiars are nipping grams.
> Yet doe thou conceale, that they be Epigrams.
> *Agrippa* (who knewe Arte Magike forbidden,
> Saide, he wrote but of Phylosophie hidden.
> When a trade is bad, give it a new name,
> And with credit, then one may use the same.
> Epigrams as obscaene [*sic*] vearse each one hates,
> Say then thy vearses are familiar mates.[75]

These various terms then presented a range of emphases and connotations; discussion in the chapters that follow, however, for the most part relies on the broader term 'epigram'.

Notes

1 Bancroft, *Two bookes of epigrammes*, Ep. 1:3.
2 Aristotle, *Nicomachean Ethics*, 1094B23.
3 Scaliger, *Poetices*, p. 170. Cf. also Pontanus, *Poeticum institutionem*, cap. 472.
4 Fowler, *Kinds of Literature*, pp. 191–212.
5 Fowler, *Kinds of Literature*, p. 197.
6 Fowler, *Kinds of Literature*, pp. 40–1.
7 See Rosalie L. Colie, *The Resources of Kind: Genre-Theory in the Renaissance*, ed. Barbara K. Lewalski (Berkeley, CA: University of California Press, 1973), pp. 67–9, and Fowler, *Kinds of Literature*, pp. 183–5, on hybrids of the epigram and sonnet.
8 Guilpin, 'Satyre Preludium', in *Skialetheia*, p. 61.
9 Claudio Guillen, *Literature as System: Essays toward the Theory of Literary History* (Princeton, NJ: Princeton University Press, 1971), pp. 146–7.
10 Hutton, *The Greek Anthology in Italy*, p. 56. Paul F. Grendler, *Critics of the Italian World (1530–1650); Anton Francesco Doni, Nicolo Franco & Ortensio Lando* (Madison, WI: University of Wisconsin Press, 1969), p. 43, recounts Nicolo Franco's use of satiric sonnets.
11 Harington, Ep. 1:68 (Kilroy ed.).

12 Rosenbach MS 187 edited as David C. Redding, 'Robert Bishop's Commonplace Book: An Edition of a Seventeenth-Century Miscellany', PhD, University of Pennsylvania, 1960, p. 275.

13 Adam Fox, *Oral and Literate Culture in England, 1500–1700* (Oxford: Clarendon Press, 2000), pp. 39–40.

14 Sir Thomas Overbury (And Others), *Characters, together with Poems, news, Edicts, and Paradoxes based on the eleventh edition of 'A Wife Now the Widow of Sir Thomas Overbury'*, ed. Donald Beecher (Ottawa: Dovehouse, 2003), p. 220.

15 Hudson, *The Epigram in the English Renaissance*, p. 59

16 Fitzgeffrey, *Certain Elegies*, sig. A5v.

17 Harington, Ep. 2:15 (Kilroy ed.).

18 Harington, 'How Sextus layd clayme to an Epigram', Ep. 2:86 (Kilroy ed.).

19 Harington, *Nugae Antiquae*, 2 vols (1804; Rpt New York: AMS, 1966), vol. 2, p. 33.

20 Harington, 'Two Answers of Bonner Bishop of London', Ep. 1:57 (Kilroy ed.).

21 See Philip Gawdy, *The Letters of Philip Gawdy, 1579–1616*, ed. I. H. Jeayes (London: J. B. Nichols and Sons, 1906), p. 138 (early August 1603).

22 Henry Parrot, *Epigrams by H.P.* (1608), sig. B2v.

23 In Parrot's later volume, *Cures for the Itch* (1626), Battus is mocked for his habit of breaking jests that are already broken (sig. C2r).

24 Archie Armstrong, 'To the Reader', *A banquet of jests. Or Change of cheare Being a collection of moderne jests. Witty jeeres. Pleasant taunts. Merry tales* (1634), sig. A3v.

25 See below on 'sales'.

26 Thomas Cooper, *Thesaurus Linguae* (1565), sig. SSSss3r. This echoes Juvenal, Satire 9:11.

27 Archie Armstrong, 'The Printer to the Reader', *A banquet of jests* (facing title page); for Pasquil, see Chapter 5 below; John Scoggin was a possibly legendary jester of the fifteenth century, well known through the printed volume *The jestes of Skogyn* (first printed ca. 1570, with many later editions). Douglas Gray in the *Oxford DNB* notes that Scoggin was frequently grouped with John Skelton in the seventeenth century. While George Peele is best known to later readers for his drama, Reid Barbour in the *Oxford DNB* refers to his 'strange afterlife as a jest-book hero', which seems to have begun with *The Merry Conceited Jests of George Peele* (1607).

28 Jonson, 'Elegy XIV', Herford and Simpson (eds), *Ben Jonson*, vol. 11, p. 450.

29 Bancroft, *Two Bookes of Epigrammes*, sig. A3r.

30 Fitzgerald, *Martial*, pp. 8–10.

31 Jack D. Winner, 'Ben Jonson's *Epigrammes* and the Conventions of Formal Verse Satire', *SEL*, 23 (1983), pp. 61–76.

32 Alvin B. Kernan, *The Cankered Muse: Satire of the English Renaissance* (New Haven, CT: Yale University Press, 1962).

33 John Owen, Ep. 2:181, trans. Thomas Harvey, *John Owen's Latine epigrams* (1677).

34 John Stradling, *Epigrammatum libri quatuor* (1607), Ep. 1:42; Ep. 3:177.

35 Hayman, 'Worse then naught', *Quodlibets*, Ep. 1:18.

36 Guilpin, 'Satyre Preludium', in *Skialetheia*, line 65.

37 Guilpin, 'Satyre Preludium', in *Skialetheia*, lines 75–6.

38 See Kernan, *The Cankered Muse*, pp. 49–50.

39 Guilpin, 'Satyre Preludium', in *Skialetheia*, lines 82–3.

40 John Davies of Hereford, *Wits Bedlam* (1617), sig. A4v. 'Soft-browed' does not appear in the *OED*; from the context it would seem to mean those who are amenable to correction.

41 Winner, 'Ben Jonson's *Epigrammes*', p. 69.

42 Richard Corbet, *The Times' Whistle: or, A new daunce of seven satires, and other poems*, ed. J. M. Cowper (London: N. Trübner, 1871), p. 2.

43 Stradling, *Epigrammatum*, Ep. 2:38 [trans. Sutton].

44 John Taylor, *Water-workes: or the scullers travels, from Tiber to Thames* (1614), sig. A2r.

45 Richard Brathwaite, 'To the Captious Reader', in *Strappado for the Divell* (1615), sig. ¶2r.

46 Sir Thomas Wyatt, 'Myne owne John Poynz', in *Collected Poems*, ed. Kenneth Muir (London: Routledge and Kegan Paul, 1949), p. 185, line 76.

47 Thomas Freeman, *Rubbe, and a great cast: Epigrams* (1614), Ep. 2:34.

48 Sir John Harington, qtd in Catherine Drinker Bowen, *The Lion and the Throne: The Life and Times of Sir Edward Coke, 1552–1634* (London: Hamish Hamilton, 1957), p. 59.

49 M. Lindsay Kaplan, *The Culture of Slander in Early Modern England* (Cambridge: Cambridge University Press, 1997), p. 30.

50 Alastair Bellany, 'Railing Rhymes Revisited: Libels, Scandals, and Early Stuart Politics', *History Compass*, 5 (2007), pp. 1136–79, p. 1143. See also Andrew McRae, 'The Literary Culture of Early Stuart Libeling', *Modern Philology*, 97 (2000), pp. 364–92.

51 Sir John Harington, *A New Discourse of a Stale Subject, Called The Metamorphosis of Ajax*, ed. Elizabeth Story Donno (New York: Columbia University Press, 1962), p. 204. Cf. also the first Martin Marprelate tract, *The Epistle*, in *The Martin Marprelate Tracts: A Modernized and Annotated Edition*, ed. Joseph L. Black (Cambridge: Cambridge University Press,

2008), p. 35, where he denies its status as libel by 'setting my name to my book'.

52 John Webster, 2.3.41–3, in *The Duchess of Malfi*. Cf. Jonson, *Poetaster*, 5.3.51–2.

53 John Donne, *Letters to Severall Persons of Honour*, ed. John Donne, Jr (1651), p. 79.

54 Huntington, Ellesmere MS 2727 (5. Jas. I), fol. 2r.

55 Harington, 'Of casting out Spirits', Ep. 2:3 (Kilroy ed.).

56 See Chapter 6.

57 Jonson, Ep. 54.

58 This passage is toned down considerably in Jonson's 1616 Folio:

> 'Ay, with lewd verses, such as libels be,
> And aimed at persons of good quality.
> I reverence and adore that just decree;
> But if they shall be sharp yet modest rhymes,
> That spare men's persons and but tax their crimes,
> Such shall in open court find current pass,
> Were Caesar judge, and with the maker's grace' (130–6).

Here poetic worth is replaced by modesty, and the defence is the more conventional one that the verse is attacking the crime not the person.

59 Donald Beecher recognizes the strong affinity between character and epigram in Guilpin's *Skialetheia* and James Hutton's *Follies Anatomy* (Overbury (And Others), *Characters*, p. 43).

60 Scott Newstok, *Quoting Death in Early Modern England: The Poetics of Epitaphs Beyond the Tomb* (Basingstoke: Palgrave Macmillan, 2009), p. 54.

61 Newstok, *Quoting Death*, p. 31.

62 Fitzgerald, *Martial*, p. 25. He includes a helpful extended discussion of the Latin terminology for short poems in the classical period. See also M. Puelma, '*Epigramma*-epigramma: Aspekte einer Wortgeschichte', *Museum Helveticum*, 53 (1996), p. 137.

63 Swann, *Martial's Catullus*, p. 120, referring to Catullus 1.4.

64 Pliny the Younger, *Letters*, 4:14, trans. William Melmoth.

65 William Melmoth, in Pliny, *Letters*, p. 319.

66 Fitzgreffy, *Affaniae*, Ep. 2:5 [trans. Sutton]. The 'fierce poet' referred to is Archilochus, who famously brought about the death of Lycambes and Neobule through his biting iambics.

67 Stradling, *Epigrammatum*, Ep. 2:96.

68 Fitzgeffry, *Affaniae*, Ep. 2:2 [trans. Sutton]. Thomas Porter, in his manuscript collection of Latin epigrams dedicated to Sir John Heveningham

in 1614, refers to them as 'affaniae' as well (Bodl. Holkham MS 436, Ep. 4:99).

69 The trio of terms 'burras, quisquilias and ineptiae' is drawn from the late classical author Decimus Magnus Ausonius (*Decimi Magni Ausonii opera: recognovit brevique annotatione critica instruxit*, ed. R. P. H. Green (Oxford: Oxford University Press, 1999), p. 5).

70 Richard Bruch, 'In Macrum', in *Epigrammatum Hecatontades Duae* (1627), Ep. 1:15.

71 In a listing of poetic types, Harington lists 'Disticks' and 'Epigrams' separately, suggesting that they are two distinct genres ('Of Lynus poetry', Ep. 1:16).

72 Guilpin refers to Sir John Davies's epigrams as 'his close nips' ('To Candidus', in *Skialetheia*, Ep. 20).

73 Samuel Rowlands, *A Fooles Bolt is Soon Shot* (1614) in *The Complete Works of Samuel Rowlands, 1598–1628* (Hunterian Club, 1880: Rpt. New York: Johnson Reprint, 1966), sig. C2v.

74 John Taylor, *I Marry Sir, heere is newes indeed* (1642), p. 4.

75 Robert Joyner, *Itis, or three severall boxes of sporting familiars* (1598), sig. A4v.

The contexts of epigram composition

While Chapter 1 explored the broad classical, medieval and Renaissance roots of the epigram, and Chapter 2 its relationship to other genres, this chapter turns to consider more precisely the contexts in which late Elizabethan and early Stuart epigrams were written. While a range of geographical locations and social situations provided these contexts, educational experience seems to have been the common element that led individuals to write epigrams in later periods of life. The first half of this chapter shows how grammar-school emphasis on Latin epigram composition and the intense social milieus of the English universities were the most important factors in the flourishing of the epigram genre in the period. The latter half examines a circle of Oxford poets centred on Degory Wheare and Charles Fitzgeffry in the latter years of the 1590s as a case study of epigram composition in an academic setting.

The late Elizabethan and early Stuart Inns of Court have often been identified as thriving centres of poetic activity. In his study of John Marston, F. J. Finkelpearl presents them as 'the literary center' of England for the period, and associates them particularly with the witty, ironic and anti-Petrarchan verse (such as epigrams) that came to the fore in the 1590s.[1] He also identifies Inns of Court men as significant readers and patrons of such verse.[2] Similarly, Lawrence Manley has noted that 'Nearly all of the first generation of epigrammatists – Davies, Guilpin, Bastard, Thynne, and Weever – were associated with the Inns of Court', and sees their epigrams as emerging from their uncertain social situation there.[3] However, upon closer examination, this sweeping claim becomes doubtful. It is not clear what evidence Manley has for either Weever or Bastard being at the Inns of Court. Weever went to London around 1600, and, while moving in the literary circles that included Inns of Court men, he was not formally entered in any of them. The *Oxford DNB* also makes no mention of Bastard attending the Inns of Court, and the particular references in *Chrestoleros* (1598) suggest that Oxford and Dorset, where Bastard was a parish priest, were the main settings of his epigrams.[4] Finkelpearl also lists Bastard among 'some important figures at the Inns of Court', but does not specify an Inn or dates.[5] Similarly, Manley's is also a rather selective list: notably absent are the most accomplished epigrammatists of the period, Owen, Jonson and Harington (who had briefly been at Lincoln's Inn in the early 1580s, well before his main period of epigram composition in the 1590s). Thus, from Manley's list, Thynne, Davies and Guilpin are the sole figures whose epigram composition was firmly based upon their life at the Inns of Court.[6] This is not to deny the Inns as a social setting for epigram composition, but to assert that we must consider other contexts as well, primarily the grammar schools and universities attended by the epigrammatists of the period 1590 to 1640.

While the Inns of Court offered a cultural context that valued wit and repartee, and their close proximity to both City and court offered further material and stimulation for epigrammatists, I will argue that the beginnings of such work lie much earlier in the lives of most, in their grammar school and university educations, and that these institutions provided direct explicit encouragement of the composition of epigram and other varieties of short verse. Such writing began with the educational practices themselves, not just the social context offered by the school or college. My thesis here is that cohorts emerged from these schools and universities for whom writing epigrams was habitual, and, while this habit found its roots in the educational experience, they took it with them to further stages in their lives: to their roles as priests, courtiers, tutors or country gentlemen, or to further study at the Inns of Court. While their educational compositions would have been in Latin, the emerging poets ultimately came to write in both English and Latin as adults. (The Appenix shows the educational experiences of the major epigrammatists of the sixteenth and early seventeenth centuries.)

In addition to emphasizing the Inns of Court, scholars such as Manley have tended to see epigram culture as closely associated with the City of London.[7] Certainly, it is true that many English epigrams in the late Elizabethan and early Stuart period emerged from London, and reflect the life of the large city. Their urbanity is a reapplication of Martial's Rome-focused epigrams, and as with Martial the corruptions of city life offer rich material for poetic treatment. While writers of pastoral or poetry of Horatian retreat simply reject urban life in favour of ideal rural escape, epigrammatists stoically or even cynically accept it as the way of the world

– or at least the way of the city. Richard Niccols, in the introduction to his collection, *The Furies: with Vertues Encomium* (1614), describes how he went from Oxford, 'the Eden of my soules desire', to his native seat of London, where in seeing the vice there his Muse 'the Furies she doth raise / With snakie whips to scourge such idle Apes'.[8] Manley quotes an epigram of Bastard that wonders if the genre can 'flourish outside of 'London, England's Fayrest eye'.[9] However, the epigram itself, 'Ad Henricum Wottonum' (2:4), while acknowledging that Wotton enjoys London as the 'foode and life of poetry', ultimately argues that poetry written *outside* London might also have a role, as it concludes:

> And yet the country or the towne may swaye,
> Or beare a part, as clownes doe in a play.[10]

The implication is that Bastard himself is writing from outside London (as he did most of his life), and is defending a broader basis for poetic composition. Thus, while Martialian epigrams are often thought of as a supremely urban phenomenon, a significant part of the English culture of the epigram emerged from the universities and the provinces. As least as much as the Inns of Court, the universities were 'hothouse' social environments that bred the close examination of others' faults and foibles as any larger city would. Likewise, the friends, family and patrons in the counties from which students had come and to which they often returned also served as the subject matter of epigrams.

Epigram composition in the schools

Composition of various literary forms was central to the educational process in late Renaissance Europe, including Tudor and early Stuart England,[11] and, in some cases, school statutes required such exercises.[12] In his unfinished book on the Renaissance epigram Hoyt Hudson traced the pervasiveness of epigram composition (over other sorts of poetry) in sixteenth-century schools.[13] The humanist reforms in education led by William Lily at St Paul's School in the early sixteenth century placed verse composition at the centre of education.[14] While initially prominent in a few such advanced schools, as the century went on it became a wide-spread practice. John Brinsley's *Ludus Literarius*, a popular and frequently reprinted educational manual, emphasized verse composition as a central part of Latin education, with a number of features that are significant for this study. The first was the goal of contracting in the process of versifying;[15] the second, a desire to write in a way indistinguishable from the Latin masters, that a reader 'shall hardly discerne in many verses, whether the verse be Virgils verse, or the schollars'.[16] Finally, academic verse composition encouraged responsiveness: poems took their bearings from a specific event or work outside the poet's self. As the epigram fulfilled all three features, it was widely adopted in schools and colleges; in particular, as a brief form it was well suited to daily exercises. Ultimately, this use of the epigram in education led to what I call an 'epigram habit'; that is, a tendency to turn to the form in a variety of situations in later life.

The ability to 'contract' a wealth of material into a short verse was a standard objective in both the theory and practice of education at the time.[17] In Brinsley's model, students were to learn to compose nearly *ex tempore* upon their assigned themes for the day, 'to bring the sum of their Theams written under their Theams, comprized in a disticke, or two or moe'.[18] Proverbs and public occasions such as royal birthdays also served as subject matter for epigrams, as did biblical readings: for example, students at Westminster were required to versify in brief the Sunday sermon, gospel or epistle.[19]

A close connection to classical forebears was maintained, by encouraging either stylistic imitation or the adaptation of classical epigrams to present situations. Such a process is described in Richard Willes's *Poematum Liber*: among the many types of exercises modelled is 'Ex Epigram. antiquo novum', where an ancient epigram, in this case by Virgil, is rewritten and applied to a contemporary situation. The text explains:

> Secundum genus imitationis est, quum certo versuum genere conscriptum poema alio nos genere, simili tamen eventu, reteximus.[20]

> [The second genre is one of imitation, when we rewrite a poem written in a certain genre in another genre, but on a similar event.]

The original that Willes uses is

> Nocte pluit tota, redeunt spectaeula mane,
> Divisum imperium cum Jove Caesar habet.

> [It rains all night, early the shows return:
> God and Caesar do reign and rule by turn.][21]

and his rewritten version is

Moguntiae 1565
Tota pluebat nocte, reversus dedit
    Sol denuo spectacula:
Divisa plane regna cum summo Jove
    Elector hic Princeps habet.[22]

[**Mainz 1565**
All night it rained; the returning sun brought the shows again;
Clearly, this Prince Elector shares the kingdoms with highest Jove.][23]

Willes explains this particular adaptation in this way:

> ipsum illud quoniam ludis Autumnalibus aliquando in Germania contigerat
> Reverendissimo Archiepiscopo, eodemque illustrissimo principe Electore
> Moguntino biduum spectatore, ex epigrammate Virgiliano feci novum.[24]

> [It is the same thing; occasionally at the Autumn games in Germany he touched
> upon the most reverend Archbishop, and at those the illustrious prince Elector
> Moguntino was for two days a spectator; from the Virgilian epigram I have
> made a new one.][25]

Such rewriting and reapplication of epigrams thus began in grammar
schools and continued as a feature in adult epigram composition, as
attested to by the numerous imitations of Martial and the *Greek Anthology*
found in the published epigram collections of the period.

While Martial and the poets of the *Greek Anthology* were the primary
models for students engaged in epigram composition, over time native
English poets came to serve the same purpose. More's epigrams were
widely known and imitated, and Charles Hoole in 1660 recommended
that students translate Owen's epigrams, or 'those collected by Mr.
Farnaby, that is, his *Anthologias anthologia*, a 1629 anthology of Neo-
Latin epigrams.[26]

Education in the period also encouraged *responsae*; that is, verses that
responded to other poems or writings in a dialectic fashion.[27] Hutton has
suggested that this educational practice 'must probably be associated with
a revival in the Renaissance schools of the *controversiae* of ancient rhetoric'.[28] Frequently, academic epigrams responded to a proverb or theme,
which then supplied the title (or lemma) of the poem.[29] (Such responsiveness, I would argue, became central to the genre: epigrams take their
bearings immediately from their subject, often an event, or even from

another written work, such as someone else's epigram.) This maintains the brevity for which the epigram is prized: that is, the subject is taken as a given, understood by the readership, and the poem merely responds to it. For example, an epigram upon the Gospel story of the Wedding at Cana would assume that readers had the whole story in mind, and the task of the epigram would simply be to reflect wittily upon it.

The surviving schoolbooks of Simond D'Ewes (BL Harl. MS 118–21) show such educational composition in practice. As a child, D'Ewes had enjoyed a fairly intensive Latin education under private tutors (including Henry Reynolds, father of the polyglot poet and scholar Bathsua Reynolds), before going to study under John Dickinson at the Bury grammar school.[30] While D'Ewes was later to speak disparagingly of Reynolds, he acknowledged his master's role in teaching him to compose Latin verse at a young age:

> I lost not my time altogether at this school, but amended much my Latin tongue in respect of prose, being able to make reasonable large themes and epistles, with verses to them, in which I had no knowledge at all before my coming hither, but grew so ready at the hexameter and pentameter before my departure thence, as I could ordinarily make a distich or tetrastich extempore, or on the sudden, upon a theme given, and so repeat them without any long study or delay.[31]

One of the manuscripts includes a section of these poetic compositions dating from 1617–18, the time when D'Ewes (aged fifteen) was at Bury. It shows that on a typical day he might write an anagram, an ode and an epigram, all on the same topic. For example, the pages for 14 April 1618 have the heading 'In regis nobiliss. et maxime Christian &c.' , and the first exercise is an anagram/epigram on the name of Prince Charles. D'Ewes's autobiography also expresses his satisfaction in the verses he made while at Bury and records that he had an exercise book (presumably that which survives as BL Harl. MS 11821) containing some 2850 verses, Latin and Greek.[32] From this, we get some sense of the intensity of the typical training in verse composition at the pre-university level.

Many English schools of the period enlivened these routine poetic exercises by making them competitive,[33] a practice that seems to have had medieval roots. John Stow recounts how in the schools established in the reigns of King Stephen and Henry II,

> the boyes of diverse Schooles did cap or pot verses, and contended of the principles of Grammar: there were some which on the other side with Epigrams and

rymes, nipping & quipping their fellowes, and the faults of others, though sup-
pressing their names, moved thereby much laughter among their Auditors:[34]

A later volume on education, Charles Hoole's *A New Discovery of the old
Art of Teaching Schoole* (1661) encouraged this same competitive aspect:
'They [students] should also vie wits amongst themselves, and strive who
can make the best Anagrams, Epigrams, Epitaphs, Epithalamia, Eclogues,
Acrosticks, and golden verses, English, Latine, Greek, and Hebrew.'[35]
Such competitive versifying seems likely to have carried over into later
poetic composition, and many clusters of epigrams and epitaphs on a
range of figures, both serious and sportive, are a reflection of this tendency
to competition on an occasional subject. For example, Mary Hobbs suggests that the many surviving poems on the death of the relatively inconsequential 'Hobson the carrier' of Cambridge (who transported goods
– and news – between London and Cambridge) reflect a poetic competition on a set topic.[36]

In the example drawn from D'Ewes, the student was composing a
variety of verse forms on a single topic. However, also popular was the
exercise of writing a series of epigrams on a set topic, or variations of the
same epigram.[37] Brinsley encourages this approach, and points to John
Stockwood's influential volume of translations from *The Greek Anthology*
as a model:

> For turning of Verses divers waies, M. Stockwood his *Progymnasma scholasti-
> cum* is *instar omnium*, to direct and to incourage young schollars. In which booke
> towards the end of it, you shall have one Disticke or couple of Verses varied
> 450 wayes.[38]

Stockwood's example may offer an explanation for the radical variation,
especially of word order, found in some famous Neo-Latin epigrams.
Whether such variation stems from this authorial playfulness in composition or later recasting of the poem as it circulated orally is not always easy
to discern.[39]

While such versifying was widespread in English grammar schools
of the period, Westminster and Winchester became especially noted
for fostering poets.[40] Among the epigrammatists who emerged from
Westminster in the late sixteenth and early seventeenth centuries were
Richard Edes, Henry Fitzgeffrey and Jonson. Even more significant for
the composition of epigrams, Winchester produced John Hoskins, John
Owen, John Reynolds, John Heath, Sir John Davies and Bastard. Willes's

Poematum Liber (1573) was dedicated to 'the masters and scholars of the Winchester School', and some of its poems may have been written while Willes himself was a student there in the early 1560s.[41] Similarly, Heath credits Winchester with any wit his epigrams might have:

Ad Collegium Wintoniense

If in this booke dulnesse doe chance to lurke,
I'le Father it, t'is mine owne handy-worke.
If in this booke there be one witty line,
I utterly disclaim't, t'is wholly thine.[42]

The epigrams of Hoskins most fully reflect this Winchester origin: his epigram on a Winchester servant was among the most widely circulating verses of the time.[43]

Richard Crashaw's career shows the connection of early education with poetry composition later in life. He seems to have begun writing his Latin (and a few surviving Greek) epigrams while a student at Charterhouse in the late 1620s and early 1630s;[44] he credits his schoolmaster Robert Brook with the encouragement of this practise, and as a Foundation scholar he was required to write and post both Greek and Latin epigrams upon one of the biblical readings for the day.[45] The school statutes required that 'they of the highest Form shall every Sunday set up in the Great Hall four Greek and four Latine verses apiece, upon any part of the Second Lesson appointed for that day, for the Master of the Hospital, or any stranger, to view and examine'.[46] The first schoolmaster of Charterhouse, Nicholas Grey, had come from Westminster School and Christ Church, Oxford,[47] and it may be that he brought this emphasis on publicly displayed verse composition with him from those earlier experiences. Unlike most educational exercises of this sort, Crashaw's had a wide and significant influence, as they became part of his poetic lifework and reached publication. They also reflect a process of development: while most began as four-line academic essays, some were later expanded into longer epigrams, and many were translated into English by Crashaw himself.[48]

In turn, they came to influence others. Already in 1637 Richard Holdsworth, Master of Emmanuel College, Cambridge, was recommending that his students read Crashaw's epigrams,[49] and William Sancroft, later to become Archbishop of Canterbury, was among the students who responded to this, translating some of Crashaw's Latin epigrams into English.[50] Later in the century they continued to be recommended as models by Cambridge tutors.[51] Thus, rather than directly imitating

Martial, students might now work from the more edifying Martialian epigrams of Crashaw.

Crashaw was not alone in reworking his school-based poetical exercises.[52] James Duport, a significant churchman and classicist, published religious epigrams in 1662 that stemmed from schoolboy exercises at Westminster School in the 1610s,[53] and those of John Suckling on the days of the Christmas season likely arose from this same tradition.[54] The poems that emerged from these academic exercises frequently went by the Latin term 'Progymnasmata',[55] and that word recurs in titles of collections of sixteenth-century humanists, who set apart this schoolboy work from their later writings. However, that they included it at all suggests the recognition of its value in their development.

Epigrams at the universities

Most poets primed for epigram composition at their grammar schools went on to the universities, and this later educational influence on their poetic cultivation has also been underestimated by scholars. Owen describes his book of epigrams as having been 'peppered' at Winchester and 'salted' at Oxford;[56] he may be suggesting that different stylistic elements were fostered in the two environments, or that the two institutions were balanced in their seasoning of his verse. Crashaw went on from Charterhouse to Pembroke College, Cambridge, where he had a similar obligation to fulfil the requirements of the Watts scholarship, which called for the composition of an epigram on one of the lectionary readings each Sunday.[57] This Watts scholarship was held by other notable figures as well, including Lancelot Andrewes, Matthew Wren and Roger Williams; presumably they composed and posted individual sacred epigrams also, which may very well survive somewhere in manuscript.[58] Austin Warren points out that the Watts scholarship requirements were not unique: a similar requirement was in place for a fellowship at Peterhouse,[59] which was attended by the epigrammatist Thomas Campion.

While the grammar schools established rudimentary skills in epigram composition and initiated the careers of a number of epigrammatists, the colleges at Oxford and Cambridge to which most students went on provided a more sophisticated context for such poetry. Verse composition was less often a required educational exercise and more often an art that flourished among circles of friends at particular colleges. Many of these poems were relatively private or coterie-based, praising (and mocking) friends, maligning ridiculous and vicious fellow students and professors, and at times reflecting on the non-academic town life of Cambridge and Oxford. The same poetic culture was responsible for the more public Neo-Latin university anthologies published on such occasions as births, deaths and anniversaries of royal – and, at times, non-royal – figures.

Such verse-writing tended to be common at those colleges that were the usual next steps following from the more significant public schools. Winchester boys most often went to New College, Oxford,[60] and the most significant body of English epigrammatists of the period 1580–1620 followed this route: Bastard, Heath, Reinolds, Hoskins, and Owen; Sir John Davies attended Winchester and then Queen's College, Oxford. A similar, if smaller, cohort of poets followed a well-beaten path from Westminster to Christ Church, the main centre of poetic activity at Oxford in the late Elizabethan and early Stuart periods.[61] In the 1580s the college served as the context for a flourishing Neo-Latin literary culture, centred on such figures as Richard Edes, William Gager, George Peele, Richard Latewar and Matthew Gwynne.[62] As Bradner notes, most of these 'had received their earlier training at Westminster'.[63] Its continuing literary significance is reflected in the large body of manuscript miscellanies of poetry from the 1620s and 1630s that emerged from the Christ Church.

Less noted has been the literary activities at Broadgates Hall and Gloucester Hall, Oxford, in the last two decades of the sixteenth century. Of particular significance for the epigram tradition in England were three shadowy, but important, figures who were at Gloucester Hall, Oxford, at least intermittently, from the 1580s on: the brothers Edward, Laurence and Thomas Michelborne. As adherents of the old faith, the Michelbornes were likely to have remained at Oxford in an unofficial capacity, and Gloucester Hall, under the leadership of Thomas Allen, offered a comfortable situation for Roman Catholics.[64] While very little of their own poetry survives, they are repeatedly referred to by contemporaries as masters of the Latin epigram, and Bradner suggests that the Michelbornes played a significant role in fostering the form at Oxford in the 1580s.[65] From a later perspective, Anthony à Wood refers to Edward Michelborne as 'the most noted Latine Poet of his time in the University, as divers copies of his composition printed in several books, shew; which if put together, would make a Manual'.[66]

Repeated references are made by other poets to the Michelbornes' Latin epigrams, but, apart from commendatory poems to others' volumes and contributions to occasional University collections, none of their work is known. Hence they met the fate of which Charles Fitzgeffrey warned Edward Michelborne: 'Eternal death will obscure your work'.[67] An epigram in Campion's *Poemata* 1619 makes clear that Edward had circulated a *book* of his epigrams in manuscript, one that included both *ioca* and *seria tecta* [jokes and serious matters],[68] and, like Fitzgeffry, Campion chastises Michelborne for refusing to publish. This poem is among those by Campion from the late 1610s, which would suggest that Edward Michelborne was an abiding influence, and still refusing to publish at that late date. Likewise, when Campion published his enlarged collection in 1619 he still directs it to 'my two dear Mychelburnes'.[69] The poetic atmosphere established by Gloucester Hall is noted by Campion in his epigrams on Edward Michelborne (1:192) and in that to William Percy (2:40).[70] In the latter he recreates an anacreontic atmosphere where such poetry is closely associated with wine and leisure. The Michelbornes also included Percy and Thomas Bastard, both of whom composed significant collections of epigrams, among their wide circle of poetic acquaintances.[71] In his 'Oxford Libel' Bastard referred to his 'father' who had commissioned him to his work, a reference which Percy glossed as 'Myne Author Larence Mychelborne, He was his patron, Els Hoskins his freind'.[72] (Hoskins was an exact contemporary of Bastard at both Winchester and New College, expelled from the latter for his scandalous libelling.) Bradner speculates that two later Oxford epigrammatists, John Stradling and Owen, must have also known the Michelbornes.[73]

Case study: Degory Wheare and the Broadgates Hall circle

Connected with the Michelbornes is a slightly younger circle of poets at Broadgates Hall from the 1590s, whose activities can be more closely examined because of the survival of two related volumes: Charles Fitzgeffry's Latin epigram collection *Affaniae* (1601) and Wheare's manuscript letterbook. These volumes provide a more complete picture than usual of the university culture in which epigrams were written and circulated. As Bradner notes, the *Affaniae* includes an 'extraordinary number of poems addressed to contemporary writers and to personal friends'.[74] Further connections can be traced through commendatory and dedicatory poems to *Affaniae* and other works. Ultimately, a loose network of friends and poets surrounding Wheare, and particularly associated with Broadgates Hall, Gloucester Hall and Exeter College, can be constructed from the surviving evidence. *Affaniae* 3:141 acknowledges the basis of the poems at Broadgates in particular, as Fitzgeffry hopes to be remembered as alumnus of that hall. In an epigram on his own birthday (3:44), he laments that he is far from the Muses and Wheare, suggesting that for him poetic composition is rooted in the Oxford social setting. Furthermore, the circle worked together in bringing *Affaniae* to print: Francis Rous and George Spry (part of the same cohort at Broadgates) saw *Affaniae* before its publication with an eye to correction, and Wheare's letters show his involvement in shepherding it through the printing process when Fitzgeffry himself had left Oxford for the south-west.[75] The sense of Wheare as the centre of this group is not just an accident of the survival of his letters, as Fitzgeffry in *Affaniae* 3:131 identifies him as their leader.

Fitzgeffry and Wheare were part of a group of students from Cornwall and Devon at Oxford in the 1590s who wrote Latin and English poetry, particularly epigrams, and very self-consciously saw themselves as part of a literary circle. They were students at Broadgates Hall and Exeter College, both of which were heavily populated by men from Cornwall and Devon.[76] This sense of a regionally derived community is frequently reflected in Wheare's letters: he refers to himself and his friends as 'Danmonii' [Danmonians],[77] after the ancient tribe of the south-west. Their poetry manifests this commitment to their counties: Fitzgeffry's first published work was on Sir Francis Drake, and, beyond his university associates, Cornish figures are frequent subjects of his epigrams of praise.[78]

Like some of the poets noted above, the Fitzgeffry/Wheare circle looked to the Michelborne brothers as models and guides. Fitzgeffry's *Affaniae* is dedicated to Laurence, Edward and Thomas Michelborne, 'ille Triumvirum nostratium poetarum' [our Triumvirate of native poets].[79] While expressions of poetic indebtedness are conventional in such dedications, this case is supported by frequent references to the Michelbornes in the letters of Wheare. Wheare and Fitzgeffry clearly had seen the Michelbornes' poetry and aspired to more work of the same type: Wheare praises Thomas's 'jocos sales et facetias'.[80] A preliminary poem to *Affaniae* by Wheare asks Edward Michelborne to reread Fitzgeffry's epigrams, suggesting that he saw them previously in manuscript. Michelborne responds in a commendatory poem: 'Vera quibus censura favet, Ralaeaque parcit / Virgula, quid vates punctula nostra petit?' [Why does he seek my critical notes for work which Vere's censure approves, and Raleigh's rod spares?].[81]

The association of these figures (and possibly their poetic interaction) predates their arrival in Oxford. It would seem that Wheare, Fitzgeffry and the brothers Francis, Richard and Robert Rous were educated together in Cornwall under the tutelage of Henry Wallis, a priest of St Dominic's, Cornwall, and, later, just across the Tamar in Plymouth.[82]

Repeatedly in Wheare's letters Wallis is referred to as 'nostro Vallesis' and at one point as 'mecenate meo' [our Maecenas], that is, patron or encourager,[83] and he was obviously an early literary as well as religious influence. Wheare describes their youth under the tutoring of Wallis as a 'consortio studiorum'.[84] Thus, the time at Oxford continued and fostered local associations, while exposing the young men to a broader society as well.[85] They often played the role of disseminating family and political news to a range of associates scattered across the country. They would also frequently circulate books, especially more scholarly ones, among a wide range of acquaintances.[86]

These young men all went up to Oxford in the early 1590s, with Fitzgeffry matriculating at Broadgates Hall in 1590, and Wheare and the Rous brothers at the same hall in July of 1593. As an adjunct to Christ Church, Broadgates seems to have been a further centre of poetic activity. Fitzgeffry refers to it as 'this house of the nine goddesses, always a residence for Phoebus and his bards',[87] and the late sixteenth and early seventeenth centuries saw 'a brilliant list of scholar-poets and statesmen, men of action and of letters' educated at Broadgates.[88] It attracted a larger percentage of gentleman commoners than many colleges, men who were not necessarily going on to a clerical career.[89] The last decades of the sixteenth century saw a mingling of different types of students at Oxford colleges and halls: the more traditional student, studying for the ministry, was still a large part of the student body, but gentlemen with the very different aim of a life of administration at home or court, or legal studies at the Inns of Court, increasingly took their places.[90] The Fitzgeffry/Wheare circle included about equal numbers of these two types, and both sorts engaged in poetic composition, particularly of epigrams. While the poets of this circle began their Oxford education at Broadgates, a number moved on to Exeter College, which also drew its students largely from the south-west. Looking back years later, John Prideaux (rector of Exeter and then Bishop of Worcester) was to remark on the cohort of scholars who emerged from Exeter College in the 1590s and early 1600s.[91] In a memorial volume of 1613, *Threni Exoniensium in obitum illustrissimi viri D. Iohannis Petrei*, Nathaniel Carpenter has a long poem which acknowledges the patronage of poetry in Devon and at Exeter College.

The association of *Affaniae* with Fitzgeffry's roots in the south-west is especially evident in *The Cenotaphia*, a collection of epitaphs that ends the volume. While Fitzgeffry honours a range of continental and English figures, at least a third of them are from Cornwall and Devon, and even such a nationally important man as John Jewel is identified in the title of the poem as 'Ioanni Iuello Danmonio, Sarisburensi Episcopo' [John Jewel, Danmonian, Bishop of Salisbury].[92] Fitzgeffry also praises many famous alumni of Broadgates, most of whom were of the south-west.[93] In a number of places it is also clear that Cornishmen are the subject of Fitzgeffry's satiric epigrams, as in a poem 'To Aldus' who was 'born atop St. Michael's Mount'.[94]

For Fitzgeffry and Wheare the regional association seems to have been stronger than that of the College in general or that which may have been inspired by a shared religious sensibility; there are few letters by Wheare to Broadgates or Exeter men who were *not* of the West Country. While the group as a whole (like Broadgates itself) had a tendency to advanced Protestantism, Fitzgeffry's epigrams reflect a breadth of association: he praises both Whitgift and the Puritan Reinolds in Book 3 of *Affaniae*. Of the circle, Francis Rous was to become the most notably 'Puritan', and he published a large body of religious writings from the 1620s to the 1650s. He also figured prominently in the parliaments of the 1640s and 1650s, including as the Speaker of the 'Barebones' Parliament. The late 1590s circle can be best described as consisting of young men (late teens to twenties) from the West Country who were typical conforming Calvinists, but the regional identity predominated. Warren Boutcher argues that scholars have stressed the universalizing aspects of education in the period and the ways in which education integrated individuals from the outlying areas into the central power structures of government, but that in doing so they have neglected a more complex dynamic at work: that local influences and identities were maintained at the universities, and that increasingly its education prepared students for a return to their provincial locales and work there. Students frequently were connected to tutors at the universities who had themselves come from the same counties. Boutcher writes, 'it is still legitimate to stress the weight of "local" cultural baggage which scholars continued to carry with them as a direct result of their university experience and the ongoing likelihood that they might return to points of local origin to participate in regional society'.[95] He is particularly concerned with the 'second-tier' areas such as the North and the Marches, examining these counties' patterns of sending of boys to particular colleges.[96] Boutcher does not discuss Cornwall in particular, but certainly all he writes applies to it and to this circle of writers as well. While their time at Broadgates introduced these students to a wider range of literary associates, they maintained a strong connections with their county roots, returning there as priests, tutors and gentlemen.

This 1590s cohort at Broadgates and Exeter differed from that of

Christ Church in the previous decade (as typified by Gager, Edes and
Richard Latewar) in that it cultivated a poetic culture of both Latin and
English. Major works completed by this circle in the 1590s and early
1600s were the English poem *Thule, or, Virtue's History* (1598) by Francis
Rous, and Thomas Storer's *Wolsey* (1599), which commemorates the
career of the Cardinal who first established Christ Church.[97] Prior to
Affaniae, Fitzgeffry had published an English poem *Sir Francis Drake
His Honorable Lifes Commendation, and his Tragicall Deathes Lamentation*
(1596). Stylistically, these poets seem very open to the influences of the
continental humanist poetic tradition in their Latin verse, and have a tendency to imitate Edmund Spenser in their English.

Affaniae was printed by Joseph Barnes, the Oxford printer, and seems to
have been intended for a largely Oxford readership.[98] Near the opening of
Book 1, Fitzgeffry writes, 'I am not so bold as to dwell in St. Paul's book-
stalls', and 'I am not a product of Bishop's press'.[99] The London printer
George Bishop had recently issued the *Workes* of Geoffrey Chaucer, the
impressive *Britannia* by William Camden (1600) and Frances Godwin's
Catalogue of Bishops (1601).[100] Fitzgeffry's newfound reticence signals
something of a retreat from his earlier poem on Drake, which, while
printed by Barnes, was 'to bee solde [by J. Broome, London] in Paules
Church-yard at the signe of the Bible'. This change in expected bookseller
may largely reflect the very different subject matter of this work. They
are, after all, 'Affaniae' – that is, 'trifles' – rather than a work commemo-
rating a figure of national (if unjustly ignored) significance.[101] The Latin
composition of the work also committed them to the more learned readers
of Oxford, as would the satirizing of individuals (whether of town or
gown) who might be recognized by this readership.

What becomes clear from Wheare's letters is how widespread the practice of composing and circulating Latin verse was within this circle, and
how Fitzgeffry's volume stands out only because it reached print. Wheare
himself wrote a substantial number of Latin poems, largely laudatory
epigrams that he shared with his friends; some of these poems are gathered at the end of his letterbook in Bodl. Selden Supra MS 81. The
majority are from the late 1590s, his student years at Broadgates, and
the period in which Fitzgeffry wrote those of *Affaniae*. Wheare mentions
receiving thirty hendecasyllabic poems from Richard Birkbeck (a priest
of Henstridge, Somerset) and promises to send a similar number of the
same to that older poet.[102] Like Fitzgeffry, he also presented a collection
of poems to Edward Michelborne.[103]

The above discussion might give the impression of an insular circle of

poets, concerned only with their roots in the South-West and the con-
viviality of Oxford. However, the stylistic features of Fitzgeffry's volume
point to the humanist collections of Neo-Latin epigrams that were a pan-
European phenomenon, and individual poems (and the letters of Wheare)
show a keen interest in current developments in Neo-Latin poetry of the
Low Countries. Near the end of the third book of his *Affaniae*, Fitzgeffry
presents about fifteen poems celebrating such continental Neo-Latin writers as Melissus, Scaliger and Jan Dousa the younger. Richard and Francis
Rous cultivated these connections by spending time in the late 1590s at
the University of Leiden, a hotbed both of advanced Protestantism and of
Neo-Latin culture.[104] Wheare and Fitzgeffry anticipate the return of the
Rous brothers, eager to hear of the humanist poets for which that university is famous.[105]

The late 1590s and early 1600s saw the physical proximity of this circle
being broken up as its members moved beyond Oxford. After their time
at Leiden, Francis and Richard Rous entered the Middle Temple, the
favoured Inn of Court for men of Cornwall.[106] Fitzgeffry, among others,
took holy orders and accepted livings in rural parishes, and George Spry
returned to his family's lands in Roseland, Cornwall. Wheare went at
first to serve as tutor to the children of the Audley family in Stalbridge,
Dorset; the notoriety of this family lay in the future: Eleanor (Davies, then
Douglas) became famous as a prophetess in the 1620s, and Mervin, later
Earl of Castlehaven, was executed in 1631 for his role in the sexual attacks
on his wife. After less than a year, however, Wheare returned to Oxford
to pursue higher studies, which ultimately led to his becoming Professor
of History. His letters from the years 1600–1 manifest a strong sense of
a community or brotherhood of scholar-poets that is slowly dissolving,
but which he wishes to hang on to as long as possible.[107] While serving as
a tutor to the Audleys he complains to one friend of how 'iactamur nunc
huc, nunc illuc, nec certam sedem habemus usquam; in motu semper
sumus' [we are thrown now here, now there, never with a fixed place].[108]
Verses that had formerly been exchanged through direct personal contact
at Broadgates were now circulated by post, but the most intense period of
epigram composition seemed to have ended.

As the years went on, the poetry writing of this circle seemed to decline
to far more occasional productions. Wheare apologizes to John Pym (step-
brother of the Rouses) in 1604 for not sending Pym's new bride verses
to celebrate the marriage: 'my Muses neglected me and they do not even
look at me any more',[109] and the verse in his letterbook that clearly dates
from subsequent decades is quite limited. Fitzgeffry published no further

poetry after his ordination (although a number of his sermons did appear in print). Francis Rous's most notable poetic work of later years was his part in the versification of the Psalms that was accepted by Parliament in 1643 as the official version for public worship.[110]

Epigram composition in other university circles

Because of Wheare's letterbook we have a more thorough picture than usual of the circumstances in which Fitzgeffry, Wheare and their friends wrote. However, less complete evidence related to other poets supports the conclusions drawn: that the university colleges fostered epigram composition in convivial circles that often predated arrival at Oxford or Cambridge. John Stradling's *Epigrammatum libri quatuor* (1607) shows many of the same contextual features as *Affaniae*: it too reflects the social circles of the university and strong and persistent regional roots.[111] Stradling also enjoyed the poetic society of the influential Michelbornes, and, while his epigrams reflect his Oxford experience, they are clearly written from the country, and affirm his affiliation with southern Wales.[112] Similar examples can be found in the next generation. John Russell's manuscript collection of epigrams in BL Add. MS 73542 stands as a marker of his university years at Cambridge in the mid-1620s. Although born in London,[113] Russell seems to have studied at the school of Matthew Stoneham in Norwich,[114] and other epigrams show Norwich connections. He arrived at Magdalene College, Cambridge, in the spring of 1625,[115] and most of the datable poems seem to come from the years 1625–26.[116] Poignantly, Russell's manuscript collection ends with two poems on the plague outbreak in Cambridge, probably either that of 1625, or the more severe one of 1630.[117] In a final epigram Russell reflects on the volume as a whole:

De meipso, quare epigrammata tam tristi tempestate in lucem
  edidisse cogitaram
Cur ego, cum mater tam tristia fata subiuit,
Pro lachrimis, ioculos carmine fundo leues.
Ingratum me me ne dicito candide lector
Hoc penetrat pectus terve quaterve meum.
Ante ego iam binos amios haec carmina chartis
Mandaram, quonam tempore laetus eram.
Tempora laeta iocos, poscunt elegeia maesta:
Qui vero nequeat carmine flere, tacet.

[Of myself, why I thought to have brought forth epigrams into the
   light in so sad a season.
Why do I, when my mother undergoes such a sad fate,
Pour forth light jokes in song, instead of tears.
Gentle reader, do not think me ungrateful:
This situation pierces my heart, three or four times.
Hitherto I committed the songs in these pages to two friends; then I was
      happy. Happy times produce jests, sad times elegies:
He who truly is unable to weep in song is silent.][118]

In this way the volume becomes a marker of happier undergraduate days,
to which the poet can never return. Like *Affaniae*, this manuscript marks
the end of a period of epigram composition at the university.

   While Neo-Latin epigrams like those of Fitzgeffry and Russell might
be expected to flourish in an academic setting, the epigrams of Bastard,
Weever and Gamage show that there were English-language counterparts. Bastard established a name for himself as a witty Oxford writer of
both Latin and English verse in the late 1580s and early 1590s; however,
his work edged towards libel, and as a result in 1591 he lost his fellowship
at New College. Anthony à Wood firmly places Bastard's writings within a
more widespread Oxford culture, writing that they are 'In my collection of
Libels or Lampoons, made by divers *Oxford* Students in the Reign of Q.
Elizabeth'.[119] The later 1590s saw Bastard, while a priest in Dorset, putting forth his Oxford-based epigrams in print in the volume *Chrestoleros*.
He continued to polish them in this period of country life in the mid-
1590s (see 2:37, 4:39 and 7:40), and in Books 4 to 7 there are epigrams to
Dorset figures that would seem to originate from these years. However,
ultimately the book reflects more of Oxford, and, like Fitzgeffry, Bastard
expects his epigrams will particularly appeal to this readership:

   My booke, some handes in *Oxford* wil thee take,
   And beare thee home, and lovingly respect thee
   And entertaine thee for thy masters sake:
   And for thy masters sake some will reject thee.[120]

Chapter 5 explores more fully the Oxford provenance of many of Bastard's
epigrams.

   Most of Weever's poems published in *Epigrams in the Oldest Cut and
Newest Fashion* (1599) seem to have been written while he was an undergraduate at Queens' College, Cambridge, where he had matriculated in

1594, and from which he graduated in 1598. As the collection was published in 1599, Weever apologizes in a prefatory epistle that they are a year out of date. They serve then as a record of the associates he observed during those college years, and E. A. J. Honigmann has argued that Weever used Latinate names to thinly veil the identity of the Cambridge individuals he was attacking.[121] While Honigmann may be somewhat overconfident in his identifications, his general claim that Weever's Cambridge readers would have recognized the depicted figures stands up well. Thus, like those of Fitzgeffry, Stradling and Bastard, Weever's epigrams are very much a reflection of the university culture that fostered them. Furthermore, like Fitzgeffry's and Stradling's Neo-Latin volumes, this one also reflects its poet's regional roots, as Weever addresses laudatory epigrams to a range of named figures from his native Lancashire.

Gamage's *Linsi-woolsie or two centuries of epigrammes* (1613) likewise balances regional roots (like Stradling, in south Wales) and a university context for composition. Glyn Pursglove describes his subjects as 'two overlapping circles – one formed by the gentry families of Glamorgan, the other by Oxford-educated clerics in south Wales'.[122] His publication of the volume the year before he left the university to take holy orders is like the parting gesture to a stage of life seen in Fitzgeffry.

In conclusion, the flourishing epigram culture of the 1590s and early 1600s was not merely a phenomenon of the Inns of Court and the London literary scene. Rather, the educational experiences of youth, whether with tutors or in small schools or in the more famous public schools of Winchester and Westminster, developed those skills and habits in epigram composition which students then took with them to the universities. Cambridge and Oxford provided a milieu in which freer and more extended epigram composition took place; epigrams of praise solidified circles of friendship, while satiric ones defined the limits of these by castigating the follies and vices of others. From the schools and universities emerged cohorts for whom writing epigrams was habitual, if not always intensive, and, while the practice found its roots in the educational experience, they took it with them – to life in the Church, the court, the country, or at the Inns of Court.

Notes

1 F. J. Finkelpearl, *John Marston of the Middle Temple* (Cambridge, MA: Harvard University Press, 1969), p. 24. See also Jessica Winston, 'Lyric Poetry at the Early Elizabethan Inns of Court: Forming a Professional

Community', in Jayne Elisabeth Archer, Elizabeth Goldring and Sarah Knight (eds), *The Intellectual and Cultural World of the Early Modern Inns of Court* (Manchester: Manchester University Press, 2011), pp. 223–41, which focuses on the earlier generation of Barnabe Googe, George Gascoigne and George Turberville. Susanna Hop, '"What Fame Is This?": John Davies's *Epigrammes* in Late Elizabethan London', *Renaissance Journal*, 2 (2005), pp. 29–42, likewise emphasizes the Middle Temple context of Davies's epigrams.

2 Finkelpearl, *John Marston*, pp. 26–7.

3 Manley, 'Proverbs, Epigrams, and Urbanity', p. 273.

4 Thomas Bastard, *Chrestoleros: Seven Bookes of Epigrams* (1598) addresses one epigram to William Sutton, vicar of Sturminster Marshall, the Dorset parish next to Bastard's own (Bere Regis); in it he vows to make an epigram a day, but lacks invention. The couplet, 'Sutton this losse thou well mayst recompense, / Taking out wordes and putting in some sense', suggests that Sutton was responding to or editing Bastard's epigrams as he composed them. Owen also wrote an epigram acknowledging Sutton's influence (Ep. 3:121).

5 Finkelpearl, *John Marston*, p. 261. Similarly, Finkelpearl's identification of Owen as of the Inner Temple is questionable; the *Oxford DNB* describes him as moving on from Oxford to a life as schoolmaster in a variety of places.

6 Francis Thynne's situation is distinct from that of Davies and Guilpin. He entered Lincoln's Inn in 1561, some three decades before the time of Davies and Guilpin, and the *Oxford DNB* suggests that 'there is no evidence of his staying there very long'.

7 Finkelpearl, *John Marston*, pp. 256–7; William Kerwin, 'Epigrammatic Commotions', in Katharine A. Craik and Tanya Pollard (eds), *Shakespearean Sensations: Experiencing Literature in Early Modern England* (Cambridge: Cambridge University Press, 2013), pp. 157–72.

8 Niccols, 'To the Right Worshipfull … Sir Timothie Thornhil Knight', in *The Furies*, sig. A2r.

9 Manley, 'Proverbs, Epigrams, and Urbanity', p. 257n.

10 Bastard, *Chrestoleros*, Ep. 2:4.

11 See Foster Watson, *The English Grammar Schools to 1660: Their Curriculum and Practice* (Cambridge: Cambridge University Press, 1908), pp. 468–86. This seems to be in contrast to Renaissance Italian education, in which, according to Paul F. Grendler, Latin verse composition was a not a general part of the curriculum; *Schooling in Renaissance Italy* (Baltimore, MD: Johns Hopkins University Press, 1989), p. 245.

12 Watson, *The English Grammar Schools*, p. 473.

13 *The Epigram in the English Renaissance*, pp. 145–68.

14 Hudson, *The Epigram in the English Renaissance*, p. 145. For the similar emphasis on educational epigram composition in the Low Countries in the same period, see Juliette A. Groenland, 'Epigrams Teaching Humanist Lessons: The Pointed Poems and Poetics of the Latin School Teacher Joannes Murmellius (C. 1480–1517)', in De Beer, Enenkel and Rijser, *The Neo-Latin Epigram*, pp. 255–73.

15 John Brinsley, *Ludus literarius: or, the grammar schoole* (1612), p. 194.

16 Brinsley, *Ludus literarius*, p. 194.

17 For an extensive discussion, see Harris Francis Fletcher, *The Intellectual Development of John Milton*, 2 vols (Urbana, IL: University of Illinois Press, 1956), vol. 1, pp. 228–40.

18 Brinsley, *Ludus literarius*, p. 195.

19 John Jay Parry (ed.), *The Poems and Amyntas of Thomas Randolph* (New York: Yale University Press, 1917), pp. 8–9.

20 Richard Willes, *In Suorum Poemat. Librum Ricardii Willeii Scholia* (London, 1573), sig. C7r. This *Scholia* was published with Willes's *Poematum Liber* (1573), but has separate signature numbers and no pagination. Like so many epigrammatists, Willes was a product of Winchester and New College (Hudson, *The Epigram in the English Renaissance*, p. 160).

21 This translation is by Puttenham, *The Art of English Poesy*, p. 143, who includes this epigram and its context in his chapter on the form. Both Willes and Puttenham would have found the poem in Aelius Donatus, *Vita Vergilii*.

22 Willes, *Scholia*, p. 13.

23 My trans.

24 Willes, *Scholia*, sig. C7r.

25 Willes had joined the Jesuits and lived in Mainz in the mid- to late 1560s.

26 Watson, *The English Grammar Schools*, pp. 481–2.

27 Hutton, *The Greek Anthology in France*, p. 30.

28 Hutton, *The Greek Anthology in France*, p. 30.

29 Hudson, *The Epigram in the English Renaissance*, p. 149.

30 J. M. Blatchly, 'Sir Simonds D'Ewes', *DNB*.

31 D'Ewes, *Autobiography*, vol. 1, p. 95.

32 D'Ewes, *Autobiography*, vol. 1, p. 103.

33 Brown, *Elizabethan Schooldays*, p. 145, cites a similar competitive rendering of verses in Latin and Greek, which was requited with a monetary reward.

34 John Stow, *A Survey of London: Reprinted from the Text of 1603*, ed. Charles Lethbridge Kingsford, 2 vols (Oxford: Clarendon Press, 1908), vol. 1, p. 72. Stow is quoting William Fitzstephen's *Description of London*, which was prefixed by Fitzstephen to his *Life of Thomas a Becket*.

35 Charles Hoole, *A New Discovery of the old Art of Teaching Schoole* (1661), p. 201.

36 Mary Hobbs, *Early Seventeenth-Century Verse Miscellany Manuscripts* (Aldershot: Scholar Press, 1992), pp. 30–1.

37 See Hudson, *The Epigram in the English Renaissance*, pp. 152–5, for further examples of elaborate variation exercises.

38 Brinsley, *Ludus Literarius*, p. 197.

39 Variation within oral and manuscript circulation is considered in Chapter 4.

40 On surviving Winchester schoolboy verses presented to Queen Elizabeth, see A. F. Leach, *History of Winchester College* (1899), pp. 291.

41 Bradner, *Musae Anglicanae*, p. 34.

42 Heath, *Two Centuries of Epigrammes* (1610), 1:50.

43 See Hudson, *The Epigram in the English Renaissance*, pp. 167–8, on some surviving Winchester collections.

44 Austin Warren, 'Crashaw's *Epigrammata Sacra*', *Journal of English and Germanic Philology*, 33 (1934), pp. 233–9, pp. 233–4.

45 Thomas F. Healy, 'Richard Crashaw', *DNB*.

46 Samuel Herne, *Domus carthusiana, or, An account of the most noble foundation of the Charter-House near Smithfield in London* (1677), p. 137.

47 Robert Smythe, *Historical Account of the Charter-house* (1808), p. 241.

48 While, in most cases, the sacred epigram takes its bearing from an incident or object in the Bible, there are occasional exceptions. In 'In Beatae Virginis', for instance, Crashaw seems to be responding more precisely to the iconographic tradition.

49 Lorraine M. Roberts and John R. Roberts, 'Crashavian Criticism: A Brief Interpretive History', in John R. Roberts (ed.), *New Perspectives on the Life and Art of Richard Crashaw* (Columbia, MO: University of Missouri Press, 1990), pp. 2–3.

50 Bodl. Sancroft MS 48, fol. 12r–v. Sancroft referred to Richard Holdsworth as 'his "card and compass"' (Patrick Collinson, 'Richard Holdsworth', *DNB*). The Tanner manuscript of Crashaw's epigrams, which belonged to Archbishop Sancroft later in the century, is entitled 'Mr. Crashaw's poems transcribed from his own Copie, before they were printed; among which are some not printed'; L. C. Martin (ed.), *Poems [of Richard Crashaw]: English, Latin, and Greek* (Oxford: Clarendon Press, 1957), p. lviii.

51 Thomas F. Healy, 'Crashaw and the Sense of History', in John R. Roberts (ed.), *New Perspectives on the Life and Art of Richard Crashaw* (Columbia, MO: University of Missouri Press, 1990), pp. 49–65, p. 58.

52 In an earlier article (James Doelman, 'The Contexts of George Herbert's *Musae Responsoriae*', *George Herbert Journal*, 2 (1992), pp. 42–54), I fol-

lowed most scholars in doubting Walton's accuracy in describing the Latin epigrams *Musae Responsoriae* as having been written by the young George Herbert at Westminster school. The picture of an eleven-year-old responding to the venerable Andrew Melville's attack on the English Church seemed unlikely. Now, having seen how widespread Latin epigram composition was in the elementary curriculum, I believe it is possible that *Musae Responsoriae* at least began in that context.

53 James Duport introduced the collection in this way: 'Adjunxi praeterea Circulum annuum Epigrammatum Sacrorum, seu Carminum, quae in anniversariis Ecclesiae festis & solennitatibus [*sic*] puer itidem pro more in Collegio nostro jam olim composui' [I have attached moreover a year's circuit of sacred epigrams, or songs, which I composed as a boy on the feast days and solemn days of the church, as part of a custom in our College] (*Ecclesiastes Solomonis*, (1662), sig. ¶6r).

54 These poems are grouped as 'Juvenile Religious and Christmas-Seasonal Poems' in *Works*, ed. Thomas Clayton (Oxford: Clarendon Press, 1971).

55 Hudson, *The Epigram in the English Renaissance*, p. 38. On the rhetorical discipline of a structured course of Progymnasmata, especially as found in Aphthonius of Antioch, see Francis R. Johnson's introduction to Richard Rainolde's widely used *The Foundacion of Rhetorike* (New York: Scholars Facs., 1945), pp. iv–xxiv. Rainolde's book was based upon Aphthonius.

56 Owen, Ep. 7:64.

57 Warren, 'Crashaw's *Epigrammata Sacra*', pp. 233–4. See also Aubrey Attwater, *Pembroke College Cambridge: A Short History* (Cambridge: Cambridge University Press, 1936), pp. 49–50. This scholarship was not new, having been established in 1571. It required both Latin and Greek epigrams; included in Crashaw's *Epigrammata Sacra* are a few of the latter.

58 Attwater, *Pembroke College*, p. 50.

59 Warren, 'Crashaw's *Epigrammata Sacra*', p. 233.

60 Hobbs, *Early Seventeenth-Century Verse Miscellany Manuscripts*, p. 89.

61 See Hobbs, *Early Seventeenth-Century Verse Miscellany Manuscripts*, pp. 116–29, for a study of a group of Christ Church manuscripts.

62 Dana F. Sutton, Introduction to *Phineas Fletcher's Sylva Poetica (1633): A Hypertext Critical Edition* (1 May 1999); www.philological.bham.ac.uk/sylva/intro.html.

63 Bradner, *Musae Anglicanae*, p. 36.

64 *DNB*. See Michael Foster, 'Thomas Allen (1540–1632), Gloucester Hall and the Survival of Catholicism in Post-Reformation Oxford', *Oxoniensia*, 46 (1982), pp. 99–128.

65 Bradner, *Musae Anglicanae*, pp. 79–81.

66 Anthony à Wood, *Athenae Oxoniensis* (1691), vol. 1, p. 854. Wood's statement about the number of Edward Michelborne poems printed in various volumes is difficult to comprehend. Either he exaggerated the number of commendatory verses penned by Michelborne or he knew of that poet's authorship of anonymous printed poems.

67 Fitzgeffry, *Affaniae*, Ep. 2:16.

68 Thomas Campion, 'Ad Ed. Mychelburnum', in *Poemata* (1619), Ep. 1:192.

69 Campion, *Poemata*, Ep. 2:3 [Sutton's trans.].

70 William Percy produced a large body of rather unpolished epigrams that survive in manuscript: Huntington MS 4 and Alnwick Castle MS F392 509. These are discussed in Chapter 5. Percy had as his tutor Dr John Case, who seems to have been intimate with the William Gager / Richard Edes / Gwynne circle noted above. Suspicion of Roman Catholic sympathies persisted throughout his life and at his death (Edward A. Malone, 'John Case', *DNB*).

71 Thomas Bastard's *Serenissimo potentissimoque monarchae Iacobo* (1605) includes a commendatory poem by Michelborne.

72 Mark Nicholls, 'The Authorship of "Thomas Bastard's Oxford Libel"', *Notes and Queries*, 52 (2005), p. 187.

73 Bradner, *Musae Anglicanae*, p. 81.

74 Bradner, *Musae Anglicanae*, p. 84.

75 Degory Wheare, Letter to Francis Rous and Geo. Spry, 22 Apr. 1601, Bodl. Selden Supra MS 81, fol. 15v.

76 On the relationship between particular colleges and counties, see Victor Morgan, 'Cambridge University and "The Country" 1560–1640', in Lawrence Stone (ed.), *The University in Society*, 2 vols (Princeton, NJ: Princeton University Press), vol. 1, pp. 183–245, which, while focused on Cambridge, notes that the pattern of close connections was found at Oxford as well. This essay reappears in a slightly revised form in Christopher Brooke, *History of the University of Cambridge*, vol. 2 (Cambridge: Cambridge University Press, 1988–2004), pp. 181–240. See also J. K. McConica, 'The Social Relations of Tudor Oxford', in *Transactions of the Royal Historical Society*, fifth series, 27 (1977), pp. 115–34.

77 Wheare, Letter to Francis Rous London, Oxford, 4 Non. Mai. 1601 [3 May], Bodl. Selden Supra MS 81, fol. 18r.

78 Fitzgeffry was connected with Sir Francis Drake through the Rous brothers, whose father, Sir Anthony, was a friend of Drake and the executor of his will (J. Sears McGee, 'A "carkass" of "mere dead paper": The Polemical Career of Francis Rous, Puritan MP', *HLQ*, 72 (2009), pp. 347–71, p. 351).

79 Wheare, Letter to Charles Fitzgeffry, Prid. Cal. Maia [30 Apr. 1601], Bodl. Selden Supra MS 81, fol. 17r.

80 Wheare, Letter to Thomas Michelborne, 5 Feb. 1600/1, Bodl. Selden Supra MS 81, fol. 14v.

81 Edward Michelborne, 'Hilario Vero Suo' [trans. Sutton]. The Raleigh mentioned here is not Sir Walter, but William Raleigh, also addressed by Fitzgeffry in a preliminary poem. He was of Buckinghamshire, and matriculated at St Mary Hall in 1581 (Wood, *Alumni Oxoniensis*).

82 The central figures of the circle were also all connected with Sir Anthony Rous, father of Francis, Richard and Robert, and patron of Wheare and Fitzgeffry. Fitzgeffry, *Affaniae*, Ep. 1:23, mentions that he lived for some time with the Rouses.

83 BL Selden Supra MS 81, 9 Sept. 1595, fol. 4v. Fitzgeffry mentions in *Affaniae*, Ep. 1:23, that Wheare and he were joined 'from our earliest years in an auspicious bond' [trans. Sutton].

84 Wheare, Letter to Gamon, 3 Kal. Jan. 1626 [29 Dec. 1625], *Degorei Wheari Prael. Hist. Camdeniani. Pietas erga benefactores* (1628), p. 90.

85 Warren Boutcher, 'Pilgrimage to Parnassus: Local Intellectual Traditions, Humanist Education and the Cultural Geography of Sixteenth-century England', in Niall Livingstone and Yun Lee Too (eds), *Pedagogy and Power: Rhetorics of Classical Learning* (Cambridge: Cambridge University Press, 1998), pp. 110–47, p. 124.

86 Victor Morgan, 'Cambridge University and "The Country" 1560–1640', in Lawrence Stone (ed.), *The University in Society*, 2 vols (Princeton, NJ: Princeton University Press), vol. 1, pp. 183–245, pp. 231–2.

87 Fitzgeffry, *Affaniae*, Ep. 3:141 [trans. Sutton].

88 Douglas Macleane, *History of Pembroke College, Oxford, Anciently Broadgates Hall* (Oxford: Clarendon Press, 1897), p. 96.

89 James McConica, 'The Rise of the Undergraduate College', in James McConica (ed.), *The History of the University of Oxford, Volume III: The Collegiate University* (Oxford: Clarendon Press, 1986), vol. 3, p. 40; Macleane, *History of Pembroke College*, p. 95. Broadgates published its own volume of Latin verse on the death of Prince Henry in 1612, *Eidyllia in obitum fulgentissimi Henrici Walliae Principis duodecimi, Romaeque ruentis terroris maxim.* The ascription of this to Broadgates scholars is based upon Bradner, *Musae Anglicanae*, p. 352. Broadgates became Pembroke College in 1624.

90 C. M. Dent, *Protestant Reformers in Elizabethan Oxford* (Oxford: Oxford University Press, 1983), p. 196.

91 John Prideaux, *A sermon preached on the fifth of October 1624: at the consecration of St Iames Chappel in Exeter Colledge* (1625), sig. ¶3r.

92 Fitzgeffry, *Affaniae*, Ep. 12.
93 Fitzgeffry, *Affaniae*, Ep. 3:141 [trans. Sutton].
94 Fitzgeffry, *Affaniae*, Ep. 3:105 [trans. Sutton].
95 Boutcher, 'Pilgrimage to Parnassus', p. 123.
96 Boutcher, 'Pilgrimage to Parnassus', pp. 110–47.
97 While Thomas Storer was neither of the South-West nor of Exeter College or Broadgate Hall, *Wolsey* (1599) does include a commendatory poem from Fitzgeffry as well as ones by the Michelbornes. Beyond the purely poetic works this circle also produced Peter Morlet's French grammar *Ianitrix sive institutio ad perfectam linguae Gallicae*, which is dated from Broadgates Hall, 1596.
98 Beyond those whom I identify as part of the 'Wheare circle', also attending Broadgates in these years were Richard Martin (famous as a leader of the wits at the Middle Temple in the late 1590s) and the poets Richard Corbett, Sir Thomas Wroth, and Francis and John Beaumont.
99 Fitzgeffry, 'The Book Speaks', in *Affaniae*, Ep. 1:7 [trans. Sutton].
100 In 1607, George Bishop was to print Stradling's *Epigrammatum libri quatuor*.
101 Fitzgeffry had previously published a poem that could claim a national significance, *Sir Francis Drake* (1596); it had commendatory verses from the same circle of friends.
102 Wheare, Bodl. Selden Supra MS 81, fol. 101r. Further poems exchanged by Wheare and Richard Birkbeck are found in fols 89v–90r, 100v–2r, 108r.
103 Wheare, Bodl. Selden Supra MS 81, fol. 94r.
104 Wheare's letters are addressed to them there in the late 1590s. Melissus was the Latin name adopted by Paul Schede; while of German rather than Dutch origin, he was well known to those in the Leiden circle; J. A. van Dorsten, *Poets, Patrons, and Professors: Sir Philip Sidney, Daniel Rogers, and the Leiden Humanists* (Leiden: University of Leiden, 1962), p. 30.
105 Fitzgeffry, *Affaniae*, Ep. 3:38; Wheare, Wheare to Francis Rous, Leiden, 12 June 1598, Bodl. Selden Supra MS 81, fol. 7r.
106 John Chynoweth, *Tudor Cornwall* (Stroud: Tempus, 2002), p. 64.
107 Wheare, Letter to Charles Fitzgeffry, 28 Oct. 1601, Bodl. Selden Supra MS 81, fols 27v–8r.
108 Wheare, Letter to Robert Bonithon, 12 Oct. 1601, Bodl. Selden Supra MS 81, fol. 27r.
109 Wheare [trans. Bergquist], 1 Nov. 1604.
110 Rous, of course, had a significant political role in the parliaments of the 1640s and 1650s, but his writings before this have been neglected; McGee, 'A "carkass" of "mere dead paper"', pp. 347–71, goes some way toward correcting this.

111 The general affinities between the volumes are traced by Dana Sutton in his introduction to Stradling's *Epigrammatum libri quatuor*; www.philological. bham.ac.uk/stradling/intro.html.

112 Later in 1624 Stradling was returned to Parliament for the seat of St Germans, a position he owed to William Herbert, Earl of Pembroke; Anne Duffin, *Faction and Faith: Politics and Religion of the Cornish Gentry before the Civil War* (Exeter: University of Exeter Press, 1996), p. 76.

113 John Russell, BL Add. Ms. 73542, Ep. 6:51.

114 Russell, BL Add. Ms. 73542, fol. 2.

115 Magdalene College still enjoyed close connections with the Howards of Audley End, by whom it had been founded in 1542 (Morgan, *History of the University of Cambridge*, vol. 2, p. 348). The hereditary visitor when Russell arrived at Magdalene was Thomas Howard, first Earl of Suffolk. Peter Cunich et al., *A History of Magdalene College, Cambridge, 1428–1988* (Cambridge: Magdalene College, 1994), p. 303.

116 *Alumni Cantabrigienses* supplies 'B.A. 1628; M.A. 1632. Ord. priest (Ely) Dec. 21, 1634. R. of Chingford, Essex, 1634–87'. STC attributes an elegy on Gustavus Adolphus (1633?), and a number of later works to this John Russell. While one, *The spy discovering the danger of Arminian heresie and Spanish trecherie: written by I.R.* (1628) is from this period, its style and political allegiance do not seem quite in keeping with the Russell of the epigrams. See McRae, *Literature, Satire, and the Early Stuart State*, pp. 104–5.

117 On the effect of the 1630 plague on Cambridge, see John Rous, *Diary of John Rous*, ed. M. A. Green (London, 1856), p. 55.

118 Russell, BL Add. Ms. 73542, Ep. 6:118 [my trans.].

119 Wood, *Athenae Oxonienses*, p. 368.

120 Bastard, *Chrestoleros*, Ep. 4:3.

121 E. A. J. Honigmann, *John Weever: A Biography of a Literary Associate of Shakespeare and Jonson, Together with a Photographic Facsimile of Weever's Epigrammes (1599)* (Manchester: Manchester University Press, 1987), p. 13.

122 Glyn Pursglove, 'Introduction' in William Gamage, *Linsi-woolsie or two centuries of epigrammes* (1613), The Philological Museum, www.philological. bham.ac.uk/gamage/intro.html. The fullest discussion of Gamage's volume is found here.

4

Buzzed, scrawled and printed: composition and circulation of topical epigrams

The epigram as a genre defies the most frequent pattern of literary forms: that is, a historical movement from oral to written modes. Instead, the epigram developed from the chirographic form of the classical epitaph, which consisted of short verses literally inscribed upon a tombstone. Throughout its history the epitaph offered the possibility of enduring remembrance of the deceased, as the engraved poetic lines promised to be as long-lasting and unchanging as the stone itself.[1] The written mode also dominated as the more literary non-funerary epigram developed, as can be seen in the *Greek Anthology* and the Latin poet Martial.[2] Thus, the classical legacy of the epigram offered a fixed, written form as the norm, one that the more ambitious epigrammatists of the Renaissance attempted to follow. However, in practice, the Martialian epigram existed in tension both with more oral-based forms, such as the anonymous political distich, and with what might be called the 'popular epigram',[3] which derived from the tradition of vernacular distichs and jests. The frequent slippage of the epigram between oral and written circulation was similar to a general pattern in the English Renaissance that Adam Fox has demonstrated in a wide range of literary forms.[4] This was partially reflective of a continuing tension between the ephemeral and the long-lasting elements inherent to the genre: was the epigram enduring or disposable?[5] William Fitzgerald refers to this dynamic as the 'tense coexistence of (occasional) ephemerality and lapidary permanence in the character of the genre itself'.[6] Political circumstances, the competing tradition of the popular epigram and the distinctive brevity of the genre all contributed to create overlapping oral, manuscript and print cultures of the epigram. This chapter explores the circulation of individual topical epigrams within the first period of their oral and manuscript transmission. Outlined first are the general dynamics of such circulation, and then a number of case studies are used to illustrate these at work with specific well-travelled epigrams. The final section considers how these individual epigrams were then embedded in more permanent written contexts.

Simple binaries of manuscript versus print, or oral versus written, are insufficient to describe the epigram in this period: the varieties of media within these categories need to be considered. As H. R. Woudhuysen has shown, there was a wide range of manuscript types in the period: authors' manuscripts, presentation or gift manuscripts and miscellanies, among others.[7] Charcoal upon a wall (the 'fools paper' as some called it)[8] or hastily penned lines pinned up in a tavern carry very different cultural weight than a gift manuscript of epigrams penned by a writing master with calligraphic skills. In the same way, Jonson's carefully and impressively produced epigrams in the 1616 Folio stand in striking contrast to the casual haphazard printings of the volumes of Henry Fitzgeffrey or John Cooke.[9] And in the oral realm much depended upon the circles within which the verses were uttered. All these distinctions reflect different social and aesthetic realities as well. Striking with the Renaissance epigram is the way in which it spilled over social and intellectual boundaries, managing to be both a highly self-conscious form in imitation of the classics and a vernacular, popular form that circulated among the widest publics. This ongoing tension between the various traditions of the epigram was never fully resolved, and throughout the period it was bound up with the question of modes of circulation.

The popular topical epigram made wide use of all three modes (oral, manuscript, printed), frequently shifting between them, and thus reaching wide audiences. This freewheeling circulation is reflected in Puttenham's description of the form in *The Arte of English Poesie*:

> this Epigram is but an inscription or writing made as it were upon a table, or in a window, or upon the wall or mantel of a chimney in some place of common resort, where it was allowed every man might come, or be sitting to chat and prate, as now in our taverns and common tabling houses, where many merry heads meet and scribble with ink, with chalk, or with a coal such matters as they would every man should know and descant upon. Afterward, the same came to be put in paper and in books and used as ordinary missives, some of friendship, some of defiance, or as other messages of mirth.[10]

This definition would fit not only the anonymous manuscript distich but also the epigrams of Heywood, whose poems were frequently 'printed separately on flyleaves or broadsides',[11] that is, as separate sheets suitable for public posting. Even the Protestant humanist and distinguished academic Beza had one of his French epigrams published on a broadside in England in 1588; Hudson notes that 'This was not the only instance of printing epigrams on broadsides for sale in the street, but it affords an interesting specimen of the occasional liaison effected between scholars and the popular audience'.[12] Like lines scrawled on a wall, or ones 'on everyman's lips', these printed epigrams were offered to all who might read – or be read to.

Juliet Fleming has argued that the wall-writing and window-writing mentioned by Puttenham were common, socially acceptable and non-transgressive in the Elizabethan and Jacobean periods, and hence 'sanctioned there in ways that are foreign to ourselves, and troubling to the categories within which we recognize graffiti'.[13] Thus, there was not necessarily a significant gap between epigrams scratched on a surface and ones that found their way into print. She also argues that such writings and their placement reflect premodern conceptions of subjectivity where authorship is 'collective, aphoristic and inscriptive, rather than individualist, lyric and voice-centred'.[14] As I explore more fully in Chapter 7 on 'Authorship', such epigrams belonged then to everyone and no one.

An epigram might begin as a very local and elite phenomenon, limited to a college, a courtly circle or the Inns of Court, but frequently the lines eventually spread much further. In Jonson's *Poetaster*, a play heavily involved in the question of defamation by libel, Captain Tucca complains of how a libellous epigram

> lives eternally to upbraid him [the defamed] in the mouth of every slave
> tankard-bearer or water-man; not a bawd or a boy that comes from the bake-
> house but shall point at him.[15]

This quotation illustrates what Fox has suggested about libels generally: once composed and let loose into the public domain, in oral form they could reach a very wide audience, repeated by courtiers, merchants, servants, apprentices and watermen.[16] While most often the author was an educated gentleman,[17] the readership was far broader.

In regards to a libellous epigram on the murder of John Lambe, physician to Buckingham, Mead notes, 'It seems there were some more copies scattered: for this fair time one Mr. Wright's man was fetched up for taking up one of them, and showing it to a saddler in London, as he was coming to the fair.'[18] Two months later, after the death of Buckingham, the same verses were the subject of another inquiry, which once again shows the social orders through which such libellous epigrams passed. A scrivener named George Willoughby, who had associations with the assassin John Felton, was examined by Lord Chief Justice Richardson for his possession of the verses. He claimed that

> He had the same from Daniel Watkins, the pantler at Hampstead, who had them from the baker's boy that brings in the bread there. On Monday or Tuesday last he sent them to one Mr. Moody, counsellor-at-law, by Mr. Moody's son, and Mr. Moody wrote the verses on the petition.[19]

While such circulation might occur with other poetic forms, the brevity of the epigram extended and complicated the situation by making oral circulation more likely.

Topical, and especially libellous, epigrams were circulated at the prime newsgathering points in London, such as St Paul's, the Royal Exchange and the Temple Cloisters,[20] and Alastair Bellany is right to present them as part of the emerging news culture of the early Stuart period.[21] Some were dropped surreptitiously at or near the royal court,[22] or even 'nailed upon the pulpit in the king's chapel'.[23] Many found their way into newsletters sent to the provinces or abroad, diaries, and eventually miscellanies of verse kept by individuals. Our evidence of course is now in manuscript – most often embedded (or attached) epigrams in newsletters – but these repeatedly point toward at least partially oral circulation. In his letters John Chamberlain frequently notes that a certain poem is 'being whispered' or refers to the 'buzz' of scandalous lines: both descriptions suggest oral transmission. The case studies below provide clear evidence of this type of circulation. It was not only anonymous popular epigrams that were heard rather than read; a number of both Jonson's and Harington's epigrams allude to a listening audience. Jonson's 'To Person Guilty' (no. 38) and 'To Groom Idiot' (no. 58) and describe situations of laughter as his epigrams are orally performed. This suggests another way in which epigrams might enter into circulation, but in forms not tightly based on the original.

This oral circulation might easily lead to further written copies, frequently with significant variations – as the gist or basic structure of the epigram, rather than its exact word order, is remembered. (Woudhuysen has identified the extent to which surviving manuscript miscellanies may preserve corruption due to 'the compiler's difficulties in remembering what he read or heard, whether it was sung or spoken'.)[24] In English epigrams the central conceit and the rhyme words are usually preserved, but there is often a great deal of variation beyond this. Thus, recurring versions of the same epigram cannot always be identified in first-line indexes. In topical Latin epigrams, the flexibility of word order allowed for even wider variation. This is especially clear in the case of Andrew Melville's famous Latin epigram on Sir William Seymour's imprisonment in the Tower for his secret marriage to Arabella Stuart in 1610. Melville himself had been imprisoned earlier for his mocking of the ornaments upon the altar at the Royal Chapel. The epigram runs thus:

> Communis tecum mihi causa est carceris, Ara-
>   bella tibi causa est; Araque sacra mihi.[25]

> [The cause of your imprisonment and mine is the same: a beautiful 'Ara' (Arabella) is the cause of yours, a sacred 'Ara' (altar) the cause of mine.]

Melville sent these lines to Seymour, and they also circulated widely at court in a variety of forms, all with the same basic sense, but different word order. For example, one manuscript has 'Causa mihi tecum communis carceris, Ara / Regia, bella tibi, Regia sacra, mihi',[26] a word order that simply cannot be attributed to scribal error, but must reflect oral transmission.[27] The popularity of such Latin epigrams, as reflected by their frequency in miscellanies and newsletters, supports Bellany's argument for a relatively cultivated and educated body of verse libellers, whose poems reached a socially broad readership – these were not coterie verses.[28]

The widely circulating epigrams of Harington also reflect these variations based on oral remembering. For example, one epigram begins 'Men say that England late is bankrout grown' in Harington's *Tract on the Succession*,[29] but in many manuscripts as 'England of late menne saie is bankrupte growne'.[30] Most such variations can be ascribed to circulation beyond control of the author, but in rare cases an author might even misremember his own composition, maintaining its basic point but rewording it in the present. Thus, the printed edition of Harington's epigrams include one entitled 'Against Momus' and beginning 'Lewd Momus loves mens lines and lives to skan'; however, when Harington recalled it in his *A Supplie or Addicion to Bishop Godwin's Catalogue of Bishops* in 1607, he began the poem 'Though Momus love mens lynes and lives to skanne'. There he introduces it as a poem he 'wrate ten years since to Dr. [Richard] Eedes'. This suggests an initial social context and individual reader for a *written* poem, which was then recalled from memory by Harington, reworded in the process and given a new context in his work on bishops.

A supreme example of the complexity of mingled written and oral epigram circulation in the period is found in a letter of Joseph Mead from the winter of 1622. He describes an entertainment at Cambridge where 'Dr. Richardson [probably John Richardson, Master of Trinity College] brought before the king a paper of verses, in manner of an epigram, which Bishop Neil read, and others. A friend of mine, over the bishop's shoulder, got two of them by heart.'[31] Once again, a mixed transmission is manifest: the lines – which may have been orally circulating before their presentation in written form to the King – have now entered into something once again closer to an unstable oral form. This example illustrates how easily the details of an epigram might have become bungled or changed as they were indirectly obtained, and how a longer epigram might be reduced to a fragment. The episode also has an illicit air to it: that which was circulating among the most elite group now has been surreptitiously obtained and will likely spread among a broader, more popular audience. Lines circulating in this fashion are subject to 'a scholar's fickle memory', as Mead puts it in one of his letters, as he passes along a distich he knows is metrically deficient.[32]

Because of this high degree of textual instability, surviving copies manifest frequent rewordings, inversions, badly fractured rhythms, lost or changed lemmas and even at times gibberish or incomplete works. In the public turmoil of the summer of 1613 Chamberlain reports on 'two lame hexameter verses, without head or foot to my understanding, for I know not what construction to make of them, and they go thus as I could carie them away at one hearing. Curans, Lord Compton, Whitlocke, Overberie, Mansfeld: Nevill, Starchamber, Sutton, Scot, Baylie, divorcement.'[33] Many of these can be identified as connected with the public scandal of the Howard–Essex divorce, but, with no syntax beyond this list of nouns, no title to identify what might bring these figures together, and with the added caveat that Chamberlain may have misheard or lost significant parts of the epigram, the lines remain a mystery.

These are all cases where the epigram seems to have been heard and remembered, however partially. It seems logical, then, to conclude that some variation in manuscripts may arise from the copy being dictated and occasionally misheard. British Library Harl. MS 1836, which includes copies of Sir John Davies's epigrams, is a striking example of a manuscript replete with errors seemingly because the scribe was not heeding the sense as he wrote, and a few of them suggest that he might have been working from dictation, and occasionally mishearing. For example, he renders Davies's first epigram, 'Flie merry Muse unto that merry towne', as 'ffly merrie newes unto *tha*t merrie Towne'.[34] The written word 'Muse' would be difficult to misread as 'newes', but certainly could be misheard as such.

Widespread oral transmission has led to widely variant readings, in some cases to the point where in certain lines an original cogent meaning cannot be discerned. Hence, Andrew McRae may be right in arguing that many libellous poems were originally self-conscious literary works;[35] through oral transmission they became both poetically diminished and divorced from an original self-conscious artist.

Inscription and posting of epigrams

In the early stages of mixed and oral and written transmission of topical epigrams, they were often inscribed or posted in significant public locations. Here it is worth recalling Puttenham's description of the epigram: 'an inscription or writing made as it were upon a table, or in a window, or upon the wall or mantel of a chimney in some place of common resort, where it was allowed every man might come'. Although Martial (11:51) distinguishes himself from the sort of poets who wrote on lavatory walls, and Harington mockingly refers to them as 'coal prophets',[36] and a number of writers recall the Italian proverb, '"A wall is the fool's paper," whereon they scribble their fancies',[37] such epigrammatic inscriptions were widely recognized and circulated. Matthew Hodgart's formulation that 'graffiti are meant to be fugitive[;] ... the epigram ... permanent',[38] needs further qualification. While graffiti might be written with that which is erasable, like a coal, it can also be carved into a wooden window frame, a glass window or a stone wall, hence becoming part of the writing surface itself and achieving the lasting quality of that material. In addition, as some of these examples show, that which began as graffiti often moved into the part-oral, part-paper circulation of the epigram culture, and hence borrowed that medium's permanency achieved through the reproduction of copies. These short poems were long-lasting because they were widely read and remembered, not because of the permanency of the original posting. Paper-written political epigrams posted in public places could expect to be taken down by some authority quickly. Coal or chalk would fade, and, while inscriptions carved in wood or stone might have a longer life, true permanency could ultimately be achieved only through wide dissemination and reputation; at which point the original medium became irrelevant. In some cases, the wall was not so much 'the fool's paper', as the 'prisoner's paper', the only medium for verses by one in close imprisonment. In this situation the prisoner-poet's use of wall or window was

often construed as a marker of his or her defiant spirit in the face of persecution, and hence lent a special quality valued in later circulation.

Pasquil: 'noscens omnia, et notus nemini'[39]

The most famous institution for the public postings of epigrams was the
'Pasquil' or 'Pasquin' of Rome, which Thomas Fuller neatly described as
'no particular person, but a successive corporation of satirists'.[40] In 1501
an unearthed ancient statue was set up in the Piazza Navona and became
quickly known as 'Pasquino' or 'Pasquillo'.[41] Unlike most ancient statues, it was not identified with any specific classical figure, mythological
or historical; instead, as an everyman figure, it became the 'voice' of any
and all who might place verses upon it.[42] At first used for the posting of
polished humanist verses on St Mark's Day,[43] it quickly became a favourite site for the posting of anonymous libellous epigrams, particularly on
the failings of major political and ecclesiastical leaders.[44] While still most
heavily used on St Mark's Day, the statue increasingly became a site for
anonymous posting throughout the year.[45] The self-conscious connection
of these poems to the epigram tradition is manifest in the tendency for the
poems pinned on Pasquil to 'recycle phrases and epigrams of Martial'.[46]
The renown of the satiric verses eventually led to the widespread belief
that the figure was named after a particularly outspoken tailor of the fifteenth century named Pasquino who had maligned court and religious
leaders with impunity, and who then became the supposed 'voice' of
others who wished similar licence of censure.[47] A variant legend asserted
that Pasquino had been a schoolmaster who had assigned such verses as
student exercises,[48] which reflects the association of the epigram with
humanist education, as described in the previous chapter.

The popularity of these individual poems ultimately led to annual
anthologies printed by Giacomo Mazzochi,[49] under titles like *Carmina
quae ad pasquillum fuerunt posita* (1509) and *Carmina apposita ad Pasquinum*
(1536). While at first Pasquin was largely used for attacks *within* the Roman
Church, later the name was adopted by collections of Protestant satiric
epigrams in such volumes as *Pasquillorum tomi duo* (1544).[50] Through
these publications and word of mouth, the custom became widely known
beyond Rome as these 'pasquinades' became 'one of those pan-European
institutions that traces its lineage back to an ancient Rome that was filtered
through the Renaissance'.[51] Thus, poems that began as ephemeral verse
mockery, posted for a day in Rome, became established in print for an
audience across Europe and across time.

Sixteeenth-century Rome had a number of other 'speaking statues', but of these only Marforio (or Marphoreus) seems to have been widely known and adopted in England; he, for example, is the fictional voice of *Martins Months Minde* (1589), which mockingly responded to the Martin Marprelate pamphlets.[52] Leonard Barkan describes Marforio as a more straightforward figure than Pasquino, one who 'tends to play the straight man to his crosstown rival, asking for the truth about current events'.[53]

Over the course of the sixteenth century the fame of Pasquin/Pasquil spread across Europe, at least partly promoted by an English church-man: Christopher Bainbridge, Henry VIII's ambassador in Rome and later Archbishop of York. His palace in Rome overlooked the square in which Pasquin stood, and from 1512 to 1514 he orchestrated the collect-ing and publishing of the pasquils.[54] The humanist Richard Pace was his secretary, and was called 'his Master Pasquyll' by Bainbridge.[55] There is evidence for early English familiarity with the Roman custom, as in 1533 John Elyot noted that there were 'Pasquilles in Englande as welle as in Rome'.[56] Puttenham's *Art of English Poesy* refers to

> the two mute satyrs in Rome, Pasquil and Marphorius, which in time of *sede vacante* [when the papal seat is empty], when merry conceited men listed to gibe and jest at the dead pope or any of his cardinals, they fastened them upon those images, which now lie in the open streets, and were tolerated, but after that term expired they were inhibited again. These inscriptions or epigrams at their beginning had not certain author that would avouch them, some for fear of blame, if they were over saucy or sharp, others for modesty of the writer.[57]

However, English adoption of the figure of Pasquil became intense during the Martin Marprelate exchanges, when three anti-Martinist works were published anonymously under the name of Pasquil.[58] Pasquil and Marforio were also deeply associated in the English imagination with the exchange of news. In *The Returne of the Renowned Cavaliero Pasquil of England* (1589) the two meet at a prime newsgathering place, the Royal Exchange. Thomas Nashe offers a lively account of Pasquil:

> I was once a Barbour in Rome (as some report) and everie chayre in my shop, was a tongue ful [*sic*] of newes. Whatsoever was done in England, Fraunce, Germanie, Spaine, Italie, and other Countries, was brought to me. The high and secrete matters of Lordes, Ladies, Kings, Emperours, Princes, Popes, & Monarchs of the world, did ring everie day as shrill as a Bason about my doores. In memory whereof, as *Mercurie* turned *Battus* to a stone for bewraying his

theft, it is thought that one Pope or other, mistrusting the slipprines of my toung, bleast me into a stone to stoppe my mouth.[59]

He jestingly relates how 'in Summer I wore nothing but paper lyveries, which manie great men bestowed upon me to their great cost',[60] and suggests that he came into England after having dangerously mocked Pope Gregory XIII (1572–85) about a girl.[61]

As the decades passed, the term 'pasquil' or 'pasquin' seems to have become increasingly detached from its origins, and was used often in English to mean any written or performed work that indirectly attacked a significant political figure, regardless of whether it was offered through any public posting on a statue.[62] For example, George Gascoigne was accused of composing 'slanderous Pasqualles' in the early 1570s, with no indication that these were posted poems.[63] Hoskins was comfortable enough with the word to transform it into a verb:

If doing nought be like to death,
of him *that* doth Camelion wise
take only paines to draw his breath
the passers by may pasquilize
not here he live: but here he dyes.[64]

John Holles, Earl of Clare, describes Middleton's *A Game at Chess* as a 'vulgar pasquin' in a letter from August 1624,[65] though its length and dramatic nature separate it widely from the verses posted on the Roman statue.

However broadly Holles used the term, some awareness of the more specific meaning of 'Pasquil' continued in England. Fuller's account of Reginald Pole offers a full mid-seventeenth-century perspective on the strength and significance of the phenomenon:

This Pasquil is an author eminent on many accounts. First for his self-concealment, being 'noscens omnia, et notus nemini [all knowing and known to none].' Secondly, for his intelligence, who can display the deeds of midnight at high noon, as if he hid himself in the holes of their bed-staves, knowing who were cardinals' children better than they knew their fathers. Thirdly, for his impartial boldness. He was made all of tongue and teeth, biting whatever he touched, and it bled whatever he bit; yea, as if a General Council and Pasquil were only above the Pope, he would not stick to tell where he trod his holy sandals awry. Fourthly, for his longevity, having lived (or rather lasted) in Rome some hundreds of years; whereby he appears no particular person, but a successive corporation of satirists. Lastly, for his impunity, escaping the Inquisition; whereof some assign this reason, because hereby the court of Rome comes to know her faults, or rather to know that their faults are known; which makes Pasquil's converts (if not more honest) more wary in their behaviour.[66]

Fuller's account is striking in its admiration for the bravado and power of these anonymous postings. This Pasquil, who is no one and everyone, is rendered a formidable mythological figure, enjoying both immunity from persecution and knowledge beyond that of any individual. He has a permanence and power that extends beyond that of popes and cardinals. As with the epigrammatist generally, Pasquil *knows* all the private foibles and sins, and has the boldness to publicize them. Finally, Fuller recognizes the power of Pasquil, if not to change men's hearts, to at least make them more circumspect in behaviour. Perhaps this points to something that is endemic to the epigram tradition: it does not expect conversion of the heart or any real improvement. Instead, it dwells on the social, superficial level of human behaviour, somewhat cynically hoping that it might at least make people *act* better.

Transmission between the Continent and England

Pasquils and epigrams from other European centres, especially France and the Low Countries, often found their way to England. Thus, Henry Wotton, while in Venice during the crisis of the Venetian interdict, wrote to Robert Cecil, Earl of Salisbury: 'I send your Lordship, by a young gentleman of return from hence, divers epigrams, pasquils, and such sport of the time; and his Majesty shall have an accompt of the earnest when it is visible.'[67] Holles noted in a letter to his son how quickly news spread between Paris and London: 'for London, and Paris ar lyk lutes tuned together, tutche the one, and the other sings the same song'.[68] A further example of this frequent transmission between the two cities is found in John Pory's newsletters, where he frequently includes rhymes uttered in Paris: 'The upshot of a French libel now sung at Paris is, that though The Duke of Buckingham be not able to take the Citadel of Rhe, yet is he able to take the Tower of London, which may be construed in many ways.'[69]

The shared culture of Latin facilitated these exchanges through Europe. Widely cited in manuscripts and letters of the 1620s was a jesting Latin epigram on the Valtelline conflict of 1625 that made use of the apostle

Peter's weeping over his betrayal when he heard the cock crow. This account offers some historical context:

> Many peeres of the Valtoline beeing taken by the ffrench from the Spaniard, it was suspected by the Spanish faction in Rome, that the Pope had a hand in it, and favoured the french too much: whereupon the Pope for his greater securitie fledd to his castle St. Angelo: and this Pasquill was sett up, Gallus cantabit, exivit Petrus, et flevit amare [the cock will crow, Peter went out and wept bitterly].[70]

A letter written from London in April 1625 offers a similar account, but with different wording for the Pasquil:

> The Pope hath furthered the French much of late in some designes toward Genoa, but repents now, because he sees his Cardinals are offended at yt. And upon that occasion this motto was set on Pasquine, *Cecinit Gallus, flevit Petrus.*[71]

Clearly, the basic conceit, which aligned France with the cock that crowed and the Pope with Peter's dismay at his infidelity (John 18:27), was in oral transmission, and known far from the original posting in Rome. (France as 'Gallus' was very frequently played on in the Neo-Latin epigrams of the period.)

Like the statue of Pasquin in Rome, certain public places in London became known as sites for posting epigrams. In recalling a late 1590s libel that attacked Sir John Davies, Benjamin Rudyerd writes that 'there was a Libel set up against him in all the famous Places of the City, as Queen-Hithe, Newgate, the Stocks, Pillory, Pissing Conduit, where Three Needle [or Thread Needle Street] merged with Cornhill;[72] and (but that the Provost Marshall was his inward friend) it should not have missed Bridewell'.[73] Mead mentions a libel left on the stairs leading up to the Parliament, with directions that it be delivered to the House.[74] Unlike circulated manuscripts or oral transmission, such postings were truly public rather than limited to a coterie: all could read them. In discussing these urban sites of epigram production and transmission, it is worth keeping in mind Steven Mullaney's argument about the ceremonial and memorial significance of the London cityscape.[75] The royal processions, Lord Mayors' shows, and celebratory masques presented a physical manifestation of the power relations of the time, and one that remained after the ceremonial event ended:

the city at large, in its unadorned streets and conduits, its everyday markets and common places, was a monumental record of the various ceremonies and rituals which had annually shaped and articulated it.[76]

As Mullaney notes, these physical displays usually included mottoes and written devices that called out for interpretation, and these inscriptions often persisted textually in manuscript and sometimes print thereafter.[77] While these displays, and the texts reprinted from them, were largely affirming the powers that be, certain London sites took an inverse role, coming to embody a position of resistance or mockery as libels and epigrams were posted on them. These, like the celebratory verses, also were frequently cryptic, requiring interpretation.

Similar prominent locations were used in towns and villages in the provinces, where both national and local topical verses might be posted.[78] The parish church in particular functioned as a site for public comment on local affairs:[79] church doors, steps, pulpits and the pews identified with significant local figures are mentioned in the libel cases of the period.[80] While local courts generally dealt with libellous epigrams on commoners, attacks on those of higher station would often be brought up before higher courts. Thus, the rector Joseph Batts of Newark, Nottinghamshire, found himself called before the Archbishop of Canterbury for the following epigram on William Cecil (1566–1640), Lord Burghley, which was 'sett vp over the lord Burgleys pew in Newark churche':

A Romane right, then rotten at the kore
      no loyall love wthin his brest resides
Unto his king faire warning given before
      That painted hoodes foule cancred mallice hides
Their volumes vaunt, but leaden are their reasons
      they proffer faire yet would supplant by treasons.[81]

In some cases these were on matters of local concern;[82] in others, more national crises brought forth news and libellous epigrams that circulated and were posted in the provinces. Archbishop Whitgift, in commending Richard Bancroft for a bishopric, noted that in 1583 'At his being at Bury, he detected to the Judges, the writings of a Poesie, about her Majesties Armes, taken out of the Apocalyps, but apply'd to her Highness most falsely & seditiously. It had been sett up a quarter of a year, in a most publick place, without controulment.'[83]

In a November 1599 Star Chamber sitting, Thomas Egerton, Lord

Chancellor, enjoined all present to go into the provinces and deny the libels which maligned the Queen concerning Ireland and catch the libellers.[84] Francis Woodward's account gives some indication of the breadth of circulation: they are 'cast Abroade in Courte, Cittie and Countrey, as also by Table and Alehowse Talke abroade, both in Cittie and Cuntrey'.[85] These examples suggest a desire on the part of central authorities to control libellous and seditious epigrams in the provinces, where local control was wanting. A similar attempt to regulate libels in the provinces is evident from a letter of Christopher Hampton, Archbishop of Armagh, to James Ussher, Bishop of Meath, in the summer of 1623: 'And if your lordship light upon petulant and seditious libels, too frequent now-a-days, as report goeth, I beseech you to repress them, and advise our brethren to the like care.'[86] Presumably these were libels on the Spanish Match, which were at a peak that summer because of Prince Charles's visit to Spain to court the Infanta.

Case studies

The preceding section has attempted to sketch some of the general dynamics of the circulation (both oral and written) and public posting of topical epigrams, particularly of a libellous sort, in the period. However, a review of individual cases will better show the variety of poems so transmitted, and the challenges to questions of authorship, context and meaning brought about by such distribution.

The 'epitaph on the bellows-maker', most often ascribed to Hoskins, offers a rich example of the wide oral circulation of an innocuous non-political epigram. Seemingly written some time in the late 1590s, a typical version of it runs like this:

> Here lyes Tom short ye king of good fellowes
> Who in his time was a mender of bellowes
> But when he came to ye howre of his death
> Hee that made bellowes could not make breath.[87]

Sir John Davies noted that this epitaph was 'in every man's mouth',[88] and that comment is verified by the striking number of versions in which it survives. These begin with such lines as

> Heere lieth John Ellowes the King of good Fellowes,[89]
> Heer lyes John Cob, maker of Bellowes[90]

Here lyes Will: Crooker maker of bellowes[91]
Heere lyeth Thom: Spooner ye maker of bellowes[92]
Here lies John Crinker a maker of bellows[93]
heere lyeth John Goddarde ye maker of bellowes[94]
Here lieth Kitt Craker, the kinge of good fellowes;[95]

Most striking in this example is the extreme variation in the name of
the supposed bellows-maker. Clearly, the epitaph was not simply being
misheard or miscopied: rather the basic conceit and the rhyme on the
pair 'bellows/fellows' were heard, remembered and then reuttered with
different names inserted. Some bellows-maker probably had died, but the
circulation of the poem had nothing to do with him, nor was the poem on
any pressing political matter; instead it was remembered and treasured
for the point, the wit. It seems likely that some of the substituted names
were simply fictional fillers, and in other cases the remembered rhyme was
reapplied to historical bellows-makers, whether living or dead. At least
one name here would seem to be an appropriate fictional one: that of 'John
Ellowes', where the name is made to rhyme internally with the recalled
main rhyme.

A more politically significant epigram on the chief justices of the King's
Bench in 1626 shows a similar variation emerging from oral circulation.
In all versions it concerns the rapid turnover of chief justices: Sir Henry
Montagu had replaced Coke in 1616; Montagu had been promoted Lord
Treasurer in 1620, and Sir James Ley to the same office in 1624; Sir
Ranulph Crewe resigned in 1626, when Sir Nicholas Hyde succeeded.
This poem seems to have been extraordinarily widely known, appearing in
many letters and diaries of the time, mostly from February 1627, as well as
in later (mostly 1630s) manuscript collections of poetry. There is a com-
monality among those whom we can identify as circulating this verse libel:
they are all of East Anglia and tend toward the godly end of the Protestant
spectrum. Mead sent this version to Martin Stuteville in a newsletter:

Learnd Coke and Montagu,
Grave Leigh and honest Crew;
Two preferred, two set aside,
Then starts up Sir Nicholas Hyde.

Mead comments, 'Yet there is a syllable wanting in the second verse, but
I dare not correct the *magnificat*'.[96] John Rous of Suffolk recorded this
version in his diary:

Of 5 Lord Chiefe Justices of the king's bench, living at one time, Feb.
   1626, stilo nto
Lerned Cooke and Montagu,
Sr James Leigh, and honest Crewe,
Two preferd, two put beside,
There's now *in place* sir Nicholas Hide.[97]

In the margin Rous offers another possibility for the italicized words in the final line: 'now skipt in'. He may have heard two versions of the epigram, or had largely remembered the single one he heard but was uncertain about that last line.

The opening of the epigram varies in surviving copies: 'Learned Cooke and Montagu', 'Learned Coke, curt Montague', 'Renowned Cooke, proud Montague', 'Renowned Cooke, proud Montague'.[98] The most distinct version omits Montagu, and offers a new set of rhyme words:

Ould Ned Cooke is putt to a new booke
Learned Crue is putt out for a new
Sage Ley is sett aside, ups Sr Nicolaus Hide.[99]

With this epigram, then, the significance lies not so much in the conceit or rhymes as in the individuals themselves, and Hyde in particular: Coke, Montague, Leigh and Crewes are remembered and a variety of adjectives supplied to describe them. That the adjectives are variable suggests that the public did not perceive the particular qualities of the attorneys-general to be central, but that they, unlike Hyde, were all worthy of the position, and of being commemorated. As such, this epigram is consistent with that loftier understanding of the genre, in that it celebrates the worthy as well as mocking the disreputable. The worth of the four makes all the more ludicrous the arbitrary elevation of Hyde on the part of the Crown, as urged by Buckingham. Hyde had only recently been knighted as well, and both elevations were due to the support of the unpopular Buckingham.[100] Hence the poem is part of a wider unease in the 1620s: that through Buckingham's influence, many were 'starting up' with all the sense of unworthy *parvenus* the term suggests. Furthermore, the 1626 change in the Chief Justice was related to the question of the king's attempts to raise money in legally questionable ways, which was to be a flashpoint of conflict throughout his reign.

Sir Simond D'Ewes includes the verses in his *Autobiography* and offers a detailed context for this epigram that is often lacking. They are presented in relation to the continuing animosity between himself and Hyde. After outlining the origins of the conflict in his father's jest that the presence of both Nicholas and his brother Sir Lawrence Hyde on the Middle Temple bench had left it 'Hide-bound', D'Ewes turns to the context of the verses:

> it was generally wondered at, when, by the Duke of Buckingham's means, in the year 1626, this man was made Lord Chief Justice, being before but plain Mr. Nicholas Hyde.

After further discussion of Hyde's lack of qualifications and experiences, he writes

> some wit of that time, to show the meanness of Sir Nicholas Hyde, and to deliver the four preceding Chief Justices to be remembered by posterity because they were yet living, made this significant tetrastich, which I heard Dru Drury, Esp., repeat at Bury Lent assizes in Suffolk, in 1627, upon the bench, the same Hyde then sitting in his robes there, so loud as I feared he would have overheard him, in the reporting of which I may perhaps mistake a word or two.
>
> Learned Coke, Court Montague,
> The aged Lea, and honest Crew;
> Two preferred, two set aside,
> And then starts up Sir Nicholas Hyde.[101]

Noting that these verses 'do need a little explanation to transmit their meaning to posterity', he then recounts the careers of all four justices preceding Hyde.

A number of things are worth noting about this account. First of all, it offers some precise information about the poem's transmission: the verses were *heard* (or overheard) rather than transmitted in writing, and, like Mead, D'Ewes is thus uncertain if he has exactly captured the wording. Secondly, the lines were repeated in a voice loud enough to be possibly heard by Hyde himself. Hence the verse libel was not just *about* Hyde, whispered behind his back, but used to challenge his position directly. With D'Ewes's account we can also reconstruct an example of the afterlife of such an epigram. He was in fact a close friend of Stuteville (to whom Mead's letter was sent), and recorded these lines as he composed his autobiography in 1638 (presumably from journal notes), and as a further reflection on Hyde's prosecution of him in 1631 for failing to appear to serve on the summer assizes. This suggests that at least for

D'Ewes the identity of Hyde had become fixed by his elevation in 1626 and the responding lines that mocked it. What were very public lines – what all men might say – are in the autobiography put to a much more private purpose: they are a challenge to the very position from which Hyde was prosecuting D'Ewes.

In the process of mixed oral and manuscript circulation, individual epigrams might become reduced from a previous complexity, or grow as further couplets were added. In some cases, what clearly began as separate epigrams on a single topic were conflated into one. An excellent example of some of these developments is the various mock epitaphs on the death of the great Elizabethan financier Sir Horatio Palavicino.[102] In one manuscript the following are presented as two separate epitaphs:

Sir Hor: Palavicino
Here lies a tall thiefe. No theif, thou liest
For tis no theaft to steal from Antichrist.

De eodem [Of the same]
Heere lies Sir Horatio of town of Babram,
Who was taken to the bosome of Abraham.
That cannot be, for Hercules met him with his club,
And beate him downe to Belzebub.[103]

However, in Bodleian Tanner MS 465 these separate epigrams have been conflated into one. That it begins with the typical epitaph opening 'Here lies' confirms that this is a movement of conflation rather than fracturing:

Heere lies a theife. A theife? nay there thou liest:
He is noe theife, yt steales from Antichrist.
Death came to good Sr Horatio at Babram,
And swept him away into the bosome of Abram.
then came Hercules with his club
And beat him downe to Beelzabub.[104]

The last pair of lines is actually a counter-epitaph, which denies the positive eternal destination of the preceding, and is found in a free-standing rebuttal in Bodl. Malone MS 19:

Soft Sir, not soe, for Hercules with his Clubb
Meeting him in ye way beate him downe to Belzebub.[105]

This version is responding to a rather garbled text of the Babram/Abram epitaph:

> Heere lyeth Palabaseen of Babram
> Who is now in the bosome of Abram.[106]

The same mangling of the first line is found in Folger MS V.a.162, which would suggest that one was borrowing from the other in a direct textual transmission.[107] The first epitaph in Bodl. Malone MS 19 illustrates another common phenomenon with widely circulating epigrams of the period: it remains as a more general, unnamed epitaph, entitled only 'An Epitaph on one that robd the Pope'.[108] With this, like some other epigrams from the period, we are left with the unanswerable question of whether this was a general epitaph that was later specifically applied, or a specific one that became generalized.

A mock epitaph from a Cambridge manuscript combines elements of these on Palavicino with a different opening again:

> heere lyeth the knighte w*ith* ye gowty legges
> w*it*h shupped up wheate & bazzelde up egges
> forthe came deathe wth his beesome
> And swepte hym from Babram
> Into the Boosome of olde father Abraham
> At last came hercules w*it*h his clubbe
> And knocked hym downe to Belzebub.[109]

'Sr Horatio Pallavicino' is added in a different hand, which suggests either that the epitaph was recorded and later identified or that the original recorder recognized the figure alluded to but felt it unnecessary or unwise to include the identification. The first printed text offered a different conflated version again:

> **On Sir Horatio Palavozeene**
> Here lyes Sir Horatio Palavozeene,
> Who robb'd the Pope to pay the Queene,
> And was a theife. A theife? thou ly'st:
> For why, he rob'd but Antichrist.
> Him death with his beesome sweept from Babram,
> Into the bosome of old *Abraham:*
> But then came Hercules with his club,
> And struck him downe to Belzebub.[110]

Finally, another mock epitaph picked up on Palavicino's rumoured fathering of an illegitimate son in the late 1570s:[111]

> Heer lyes sir Horatio as it is meet
> for getting a bastard in a white sheet.[112]

Besides serving as a winding sheet, a white sheet was used as part of a ritual public punishment for illicit sexual activity.

These epitaphs on Palavicino also provoked the common phenomenon of counter-epitaphs defending the deceased from libellous attacks. In his biography of Palavicino, Lawrence Stone rejects the long-retold story upon which part of this epitaph is based: that Palavicino had, early in his career, stolen from the Pope while serving as his tax collector.[113] However, as will be seen below, such rumours were current at the time of his death, to the point that his supporters felt called upon to reject them publicly. A number of the poems marking his death in *An Italians dead bodie Stucke with Englishe Flowers* (1600) refer to the envy and malice that had poured forth from his opponents at that time. At least one seems to respond to and rewrite the charges that he stole from the Pope:

> Once Sir *Horatio* from the Pope did steale,
> He stole away into our Common-weale:
> But well and wisely from hence he stole,
> Where still he lived in perill of his soule.
> But ill thou didst to steale the second time
> Away from us, that was no veniall crime.[114]

The opening line reiterates the charge of the mocking epitaph, but, rather than admit to a literal stealing (forgivable because of the identity of the victim), it reinterprets 'steal', using it as an intransitive rather than transitive verb. Hence, all that Palavicino 'stole' was his own person and soul from the threats of the papacy. In this way, the charges against him are reinterpreted as a confirmation of his Protestant commitment and piety.

A further poem by Theophilus Field from *An Italians dead Bodie* seems to respond to both the charges of theft and begetting a bastard:

> If when the partie hath penance done,
> And in a white sheete stood his time,
> For him that lawe and penaltie will shunne,

It is not good once to object the crime.
Deserve not they be taught to rule their tongue,
That now he lies lapt in his winding-sheet,
Stick not to do that noble Knight such wrong,
In saying still (their dove will with them meet.)
He robd the Pope, did other things beside,
Wherein he was the while he lived belide.[115]

The poem seems to admit the first charge, but suggests that penance for this has been done, and hence should no longer be raised, now that his winding-sheet has replaced the 'white sheet' of penance. A longer poem from the same volume, 'The conquest of two Traitors, Envie and Death, by the worthy Knight, Sir Horatio Pallavicino' by one 'P.P.P', relates how Envy

At first an ill opinion she rais'd,
(Oh how much first opinions prevaile!)
She rent her haire when once she heard him prais'd,
And for ones praise, she made a thousand raile.
        He stole from *Rome*, he for no goodnesse fled,
        Coosned the Pope, transported Englands bread.[116]

Once again, the poem is concerned to counter the charges that were circulating widely in libellous epitaphs, in this case by blaming them on envy.

A well-known prophetic distich of the early 1600s that expressed hope for further reformation under Prince Henry shows some of the same dynamics of response and transmission at work:

Henry the 8. pulld down abbeys and cells,
But Henry the 9. shall pull down Bishops and bells.

Harington offers this account of one stage of its circulation:

About the monthe of August last past [1606], his Majestie then being at Windsor, a Londoner of honest credit told me how a preacher in the citty had, with more zeale than discretion, (reprehending the spoylers of the Church, and such as gape for such spoyls) told withall how some lewd person had scatterd in divers places this ryme.[117]

He then goes on to note how Catholics nod their heads at the saying, seeing it as affirmation that Protestantism will ultimately lead to irreligion and atheism; in contrast, Puritans are encouraged by it, as they hope to replace episcopacy with Presbyterianism, and 'malcontents' are simply satisfied with any sort of change. But the 'trew Christian' rushes to 'discover the frawd and resist the mallice of the enemie', which then is what Harington believes he is doing in this work. In Harington's account, by attempting to refute the 'spoylers' the preacher had inadvertently heightened the buzz about the lines, as the 'vulgar auditors' found the memorable distich more intriguing and far easier to carry away than any sermon. Hence, a 'scatterd' written rhyme had achieved a new circulation, one which is ironically built upon a sermon that refuted it, which was then passed along by an auditor of the sermon to Harington, by whom it was then preserved and presented in a manuscript volume he added to Francis Godwin's *Catalogue of the Bishops* to Prince Henry, the very Henry who looked set to become the Henry IX of the prophetic epigram.[118]

The May 1612 murder of an English fencer named John Turner by the Scottish nobleman Robert, Lord Crichton of Sanquhar, prompted a widely circulating epigram:

> They Beg our Lands, our Goods, our Lives,
> They Switch our Nobles, and lie with their wives;
> They Pinch our Gentry, and send for our Benchers,
> They Stab our Serjeants, and pistol our Fencers.[119]

In this case we can trace the development of a rough conceit into a more polished epigram form. William Trumbull had received word of the libel from John Thorys in London: 'This libel is talked of. "Scots switche nobility, pinche gentility and pistoll yeomanry."'[120] The basic concept of the larger epigram is here, but there is no reference to the particular encounter between Turner and Crichton. It would seem likely that one of its readers then took this short circulating libel and produced a more specific and polished version. This is reflected in another letter sent to Trumbull a few weeks later by Abraham Williams in The Hague:

> I received last night a foolish libel from Middelburg, which I will send you just as I had it:
>
> The Scots beg our goods, lands and lives,
> They switch our nobles and lie with their wives.
> They pinch our gentlemen, and send for our benchers;
> They stab our sergeants and pistol our fencers.[121]

Middelburg, as one of the Dutch cautionary towns held by the English, was a major conduit of news and materials between England and the Low Countries. Hence, it seems the lines had been formulated in England, and in early June 1612 were beginning to make the rounds in English-speaking circles on the continent. Sanquhar was tried at King's Bench and executed on 29 June 1612. Most likely the lines were penned within those six weeks, while the feeling was still strong that Scots favourites were abusing the English without any sort of retribution.

Francis Osborne, writing in retrospect, commented on the verses:

> In the mean time this Nation was rooted up by those *Caledonian* Beres, as these homely Verses do attest, which were every where posted, and do contain as many Stories as Lines, which I shall explain, though they may possibly fall out of order, if not suiting the liberty of a Spirit, that walks rather for its own exercise than the instruction of an ignorant and ingrateful State, to be punctual.[122]

While resentment of the Scots at James's court had been ongoing since the 1603 accession, the Sanquhar–Turner incident crystallized English feelings, and thus the polished epigram may have circulated so widely because it captured what so many Englishmen *might say*. The poem offers an accumulation of English grievances at the favoured presence of the Scots at James's court.[123] The first, and most general, line captures the English sense that, through James's court, their wealth was being funnelled to Scottish favourites. The second line, as Osborne notes, refers to the quarrel between Philip Herbert, Earl of Montgomery, and William Ramsay, a young Scottish page of the King's bedchamber, that took place at the Croydon races in 1607. This event, as Osborne puts it, the English did 'draw together to make it a *National Quarrel*'.[124] Osborne explains that the line 'They pinch our gentlemen, and send for our benchers' concerns

> Mr. Edward Hawley, an intimate acquaintance of mine, who coming to Court on a grand day, Maxwell (more famous for this and Wealth, than Civility or Education, not being ever able to read or write) led him out of the room by a black string he wore in his ear, a fashion then much in use. But this had like to have cost warm blood, Hawley appearing of another temper than he at Croydon.

Finally, Osborne explains that the first half of the final line refers to a Scotsman, Murray, who instigated two servants to attack and murder the Sergeant sent to arrest him.

Thus, the poem gathers together in summary, clipped form ('as many stories as lines'), the individual instances that seemed to constitute a pattern of indemnity for Scots guilty of violence and aggression. The poem traces how the full range of English folk, from nobility to mere fencing masters, had suffered. (The version in Bodl. Malone MS 23 more clearly highlights the sense that the Scots have abused *all* English estates, as its fourth line begins 'They kill the Comons'.) Obvious from the high number of manuscripts where it appeared and the level of variation (suggesting oral dissemination), the epigram struck a chord, and Osborne was accurate in saying it was 'everywhere posted'. In one copy, a further comment has been added: 'If this suffred bee / No man shall goe Scot-free.'

Manuscript collections of separates

What happened to those individual epigrams sent near the time of the events to which they responded? Frequently, they were destroyed – or, as it is often put in the letters of the time, 'sacrificed to Vulcan'. Repeatedly, newsletters of the time make reference to verses that are included with the letter as separates, but which do not survive with the letters. They may have been destroyed for their incriminating nature, or simply lost as the letters were collected, moved or bound. It is likely, however, that at least sometimes they were copied into volumes of verse, those manuscript miscellanies that constitute the greatest source of unpublished verse from the period. This process will be more fully explored in Chapter 5. Our awareness of topical (and usually libellous) epigrams depends first of all on letters in which they are passed along and discussed. However, the more formal gathering of single topical epigrams (as opposed to general poetical miscellanies) by individuals is also worth exploring. Many manuscript miscellanies which include such collections survive, but frequently the collecting obliterates the original context, and, in addition, the identity of the compiler is usually unknown. This section will explore three gatherings of libellous epigrams of which the identity is known – or at least suspected – and how this information enriches our understanding of the dynamics of circulation.

John Rous, a priest in Suffolk, copied a significant number of epigrams and other libels into his diary from 1617 to 1643. Most of the manuscript volume (approx. 6 in. by 8 in.) is written in the same colour of ink in a consistent small neat hand; hence it seems that this book was copied with care either from various scraps or from a rougher pre-existing commonplace book or diary. There is some retrospective comment, yet Rous also identifies many items by exact date. The diary is helpful then in establishing when certain political epigrams were in circulation,[125] and in some cases Rous's identification of his source provides insight into the transmission history of the lines.

Rous recorded the epigram on Lambe and Buckingham (discussed above), but this cannot be construed as support for the assassination, or even as antagonism towards Buckingham, as his negative comments on one of them prove: 'Thus foully will the vulgar disgrace him whose greatnes they hate.'[126] However, neither should this necessarily be taken as a completely honest statement: such notes of rejection might have been a cautious gesture to avoid prosecution if the diary were ever to fall into official hands. The uncertainty makes clear that we should be cautious in linking libellous epigrams closely with those who collected them, as Katherine Duncan-Jones does in discussing Bodl. Don. MS c.54, a 1590s commonplace book of Richard ap Roberts, which includes a number of anti-Cecil poems. She concludes that 'Richard ap Roberts' curiosity about Robert Cecil sprang from hostility rather than admiration'.[127] However, such conclusions must be cautiously reached; most often it is difficult to gauge loyalties on the basis of what appears in commonplace books, as they often include poems from both sides in a debate, or indiscriminately record whatever was current.[128] This will become important in a consideration of the poems collected by a member of the Montagu family.

While Rous's diary was transcribed from earlier separates that he had saved, on rare occasions collections of the originally circulated separates survive. Such is the case with PRO C 108/63, a box of papers of the family of Edward Montagu, first Baron Montagu of Boughton (1562/3–1644), deposited in Chancery for some unknown legal cause. This large box contains mostly legal records, but there is also one bundle of poems on separate sheets, in a variety of hands.[129] This particular bundle does not seem directly linked to a Chancery case, and this is confirmed by the inclusion of innocuous love poetry and devotional poetry. However, also collected here are approximately fifteen topical satiric poems, treating subjects from the early 1600s to the 1640s. Some of these are well-known libels, others seem to be unique copies.

The relationship of the poems to the family is confirmed by the details of one devotional poem, found within a letter by Justinian Isham, dated Lamport (Northamptonshire), 23 January 1639. While the letter is simply addressed to 'Madam', within it Isham refers to the recipient's two sisters, 'my Lady Manchester & Lady Barkam'.[130] Lady Manchester was Margaret Crouch, wife of Henry Montagu, first Earl of Manchester, and sister to Anne Crouch who had married Edward Montagu. Thus, the letter was likely written to Lady Anne, and the box would seem to be a collection of family papers, in which poems were received and kept by the Baron or Anne over the years. The variety of paper and hands found among the pile suggests that that these could all be poems *received* by Anne Crouch/Montagu, or perhaps by the family of Edward Montagu more generally.[131]

PRO C 108/63 offers a fairly rare example of a collection in which we know something of the collector(s) and of his or her political opinions. Esther Cope's full-length biography of Edward Montagu presents him as a politically careful man who, while an advanced Protestant, was fully supportive of the monarchy and its prerogative. In all his political actions he demonstrated a respect for law and tradition, and a high regard for order in both Church and state.[132] His principles were supremely tested in the turmoil of the early 1640s, and Montagu, unlike some of his family, ultimately sided with the King. One untitled poem, beginning 'As I about the town did walke', clearly addresses the situation of late 1640, the beginning of the Long Parliament. The other political or libellous poems are from previous decades: there is a folded sheet with six poems ridiculing Cecil, including some of the widely circulated mock epitaphs that followed his death.[133] There is also a widely known libellous poem beginning 'Greate Verulam is very lame, the Gout, of goe out, feeling', on Francis Bacon's fall in 1621.[134]

Thus, PRO C 108/63 seems to show again that the collecting of certain libellous epigrams was not a reflection of commitment to the ideas presented within them. Rather, they were part of the 'news' and of interest to those who were politically engaged. In her biography of Edward Montagu, Cope notes that he was a scrupulous chronicler, keeping 'detailed accounts of public events which were sent to him'.[135] The majority of libels collected here were clearly written after their subjects were no longer politically powerful: that is, those on Cecil were written after his death, and that on Francis Bacon after his loss of office. Certainly, Cope's depiction does not present a man who would idly collect gossipy libels; we must suspect that he saw some political significance in them. Alastair Bellany notes how verse libels were often preserved as part of a broader political discussion, and hence given some legitimacy by being frequently juxtaposed with more authoritative reports on political activities.[136]

To return to Puttenham's definition: epigrams were often what 'all men might say', but sometimes they might be better described as 'what all men might hear'; that is part of the general public culture, to which individuals might ascribe or not, but which was inescapable as they circulated widely in oral and written form.

Notes

1 On the continuing implications of the inscriptional roots of the epigram, right down to the early twentieth-century Greek poet Konstantine Kavafys (Constantine Cavafy), see David Rijser, 'The Practical Function of High Renaissance Epigrams: The Case of Raphael's Grave', in Susanna de Beer, Karl A .E. Enenkel and David Rijser (eds), *The Neo-Latin Epigram: A Learned and Witty Genre* (Leuven: Leuven University Press, 2009), pp. 103–36.

2 Gutzwiller, *Poetic Garlands*, p. 56, notes, 'Even if Hellenistic poets sometimes composed for the stone and sometimes recited their epigrams to friends at social gatherings, they were nevertheless self-consciously aware that their epigrams would ultimately reside with other poetry in a written context.'

3 With some hesitation I use the term 'popular' to describe those epigrams perceived by their authors or readers to be published for a broad audience and with little aspiration to imitation of the classical norms of the genre. At the same time, Michelle O'Callaghan has demonstrated in her study of John Taylor that a poet might appeal to a popular audience while still being fully aware of the literary tradition which he defines himself against ('"Thomas the Scholer" versus "John the Sculler": Defining Popular Culture in the Early Seventeenth Century', in Matthew Dimmock and Andrew Hadfield (eds), *Literature and Popular Culture in Early Modern England* (Farnham: Ashgate, 2009), pp. 45–56. She writes, 'he actively and self-consciously sought to demarcate the boundaries between high and low, learned and unlearned culture, *from below*' (p. 49).

4 See Fox, *Oral and Literate Culture in England*; and Harold Love's chapter in John Barnard, D. F. McKenzie and Maureen Bell (eds), *The Cambridge History of the Book in Britain, vol. 4: 1557–1695* (Cambridge: Cambridge University Press, 2002), pp. 97–121. Harold Love emphasizes 'how many of the key texts of late-sixteenth- and early seventeenth-century England belonged solely or primarily to the oral-aural medium'; *Attributing Authorship: An Introduction* (Cambridge: Cambridge University Press, 2001), pp. 99–100.

5 See Manley, 'Proverbs, Epigrams, and Urbanity', p. 275.

6 Fitzgerald, *Martial*, p. 22.

7 Henry R. Woudhuysen, *Sir Philip Sidney and the Circulation of Manuscripts 1558–1640* (Oxford: Clarendon Press, 1996), pp. 29–203.

8 'Carbones calami stultoru*m*, moenia charta' [Charcoals are the pens of fools, walls are their paper] (Camb. Add. MS 89, fol. 17r). The disparagement of the writer with charcoal is already found in Martial, Ep. 12:61. See Juliet Fleming, *Graffiti and the Writing Arts of Early Modern England* (Philadelphia, PA: University of Pennsylvania Press, 2001), pp. 49–50, on this proverb; she, however, argues that the stigma against such 'parietal writing' may have been no stronger than the 'stigma of print'.

9 Henry Fitzgeffrey, *Certain elegies* (1620); J[ohn] C[ooke], *Epigrames. Served out in 52. severall Dishes for every man to tast without surfeting* (1604).

10 Puttenham, *The Art of English Poesy*, p. 142.

11 Robert Bolwell, *The Life and Works of John Heywood*, (New York: AMS, 1966), p. 134.

12 Hudson, *The Epigram*, p. 130.

13 Fleming, *Graffiti and the Writing Arts*, p. 29. Fleming rather pushes the envelope, however, when she writes, 'I imagine the whitewashed domestic wall as being the primary scene of writing in early modern England' (p. 50). One wonders at first if the emphasis lies on that word 'imagine', and that this is merely a whimsical thought experiment: that she follows this with an example of children writing on walls might suggest that by 'primary' she means 'earliest in life'. However, when she boldly states further down that 'the bulk of early modern writing was written on walls', there is no question of her meaning. Given wall-writing's ephemeral, erasable nature, it is hard to see how it could ever be measured as a basis for this statement.

14 Fleming, *Graffiti and the Writing Arts*, p. 41.

15 Ben Jonson, *Poetaster*, ed. Tom Cain (Manchester: Manchester University Press, 1995), 4.3.111–14.

16 Fox, *Oral and Literate Culture in England*, p. 347. See also Alastair Bellany, *The Politics of Court Scandal in Early Modern England: News Culture and the Overbury Affair: 1603–1666* (Cambridge: Cambridge University Press, 2002), pp. 111–14, on the spread of libels through a wide range of classes.

17 Bellany, 'Railing Rhymes Revisited', p. 1144.

18 Rev. Joseph Mead to Sir Martin Stuteville, 29 June 1628, in Thomas Birch (ed.), *The court and times of Charles the First*, 2 vols (1848), vol. 1, p. 368.

19 29 Aug. 1628, *CSPD, Charles, 1628–9*, p. 273. See also 25 Oct. 1628 in *CSPD, Charles, 1628–9*, p. 360, where the 'baker's boy', Lawrence Naylor, is examined; he could not recall whether he heard the verses before or after Buckingham's death.

20 Edward May, *Epigrams Divine and Moral* (1633), Ep. 79 'To Camelion', mentions the 'Temple Cloysters' as being analogous to St Paul's. On the Royal Exchange as a cosmopolitan meeting place, see Jean Howard, *Theater*

of a City: The Places of London Comedy, 1598–1642 (Philadelphia, PA: University of Pennsylvania Press, 2007), pp. 33–8.

21 See Bellany, 'Railing Rhymes Revisited', pp. 1146–7, for a succinct depiction of news circulation in the period.

22 Bellany, *The Politics of Court Scandal*, p. 108.

23 Mead to Stuteville, 18 Jan. 1622/3 in Thomas Birch (ed.), *Court and Times of James the First*, 2 vols (London, 1848), vol. 2, p. 355. Cf. John Chamberlain to Dudley Carleton, 25 Jan. 1622/3.

24 Woudhuysen, *Sir Philip Sidney and the Circulation of Manuscripts 1558–1640* (Oxford: Clarendon Press, 1996), p. 160. See also Harold Love, *Scribal Publication in Seventeenth-Century England* (Oxford: Oxford University Press, 1993), p. 315, on the effects of oral transmission later in the century; in particular, he notes that 'the astonishing mutability of Rochester's "'I' th'isle of Great Britain" can only be explained on this assumption'.

25 Dudley Carleton to Sir Thomas Edmondes, 25 July 1610, in Thomas Birch and Robert Folkestone Williams, *Court and Times of James the First*, vol. 1, p. 132.

26 Bodl. Rawl. poet. MS 246, fol. 16r. See also *Court and Times of James the First*, vol. 1, pp. 127 and 132.

27 Emily Ross, 'Variations on Andrew Melville's Distich for William Seymour', *Notes and Queries*, 60 (2013), pp. 32–3, notes the significance of the 'regia' here modifying Arabella Stuart, as it emphasizes the scandal of a royal figure being treated in this way.

28 Bellany, 'Railing Rhymes Revisited', pp. 1144–5. Raphael Thorius's lines on Sir Walter Ralegh ('Viderat Acephalos') are another good example of this; see Michael Rudick (ed.), *The Poems of Sir Walter Ralegh: A Historical Edition* (Tempe, AZ: Renaissance English Text Society, 1999), p. 199.

29 Sir John Harington, *A Tract on the Succession to the Crown (A.D. 1602)* (London, 1880), p. 123.

30 BL Add. MS 39829, fol. 93r; Bodl. Sancroft MS 53, p. 47; Bodl. Ashmole MS 781, p. 134, Bodl. MS CCC.327, fol. 24; Bodl. Eng. poet. MS 10, fol. 97; Bodl. Malone MS 23, p. 121; Bodl. Rawl. poet. MS 212, fol. 87v.

31 Mead to Stuteville, 15 Mar. 1622/3 in *Court and Times of James the First*, vol. 2, p. 375. Richard Neile was Bishop of Durham at the time.

32 Mead to Stuteville, 24 Feb. 1626/7, *Court and Times of Charles the First*, vol. 1, p. 199.

33 John Chamberlain to Dudley Carleton, 10 June 1613, *The Letters of John Chamberlain*, ed. N. E. McClure, 2 vols (Philadelphia, PA: American Philosophical Society, 1939), vol. 1, p. 459. Bellany, 'Libels in Action', pp. 102–3, recounts a number of similar examples.

34 BL Harl. MS 1836, fol. 2r.

35 McRae, *Literature, Satire, and the Early Stuart State*, p. 38.

36 Harington, *A Supplie or Addicion*, in *Nugae Antiquae*, vol. 2, p. 140.

37 Fuller, *The history of the worthies* (1840; Rpt New York, AMS, 1965), vol. 2, p. 192. He may have got it from Harington, *A Supplie or Addicion*, vol. 2, pp. 139–40, which offers the following: 'As for the latter predictions or rather post-fictions (since this bishops death [Bp Oliver King of Bath and Wells]) I willingly omit, concerning the successors of this bishop, as things worthier to be contemned then condemned, written by coal-prophets, upon whyted walls, which the Italian calls, *the paper of the fooles, muro bianco charta di matto*'.

38 Matthew Hodgart, *Satire* (New York: McGraw-Hill, 1969), p. 159.

39 [knowing all, and known of none]. Fuller, *The history of the worthies*, vol. 3, p. 129.

40 Fuller, *The history of the worthies*, vol. 3, p. 130.

41 Francis Haskell and Nicholas Penny, *Taste and the Antique: The Lure of Classical Sculpture, 1500–1900* (New Haven, CT: Yale University Press, 1981), p. 291.

42 Leonard Barkan, *Unearthing the Past* (New Haven, CT: Yale University Press, 1999), pp. 210–11. He suggests that its badly mutilated features prevented any likely identification. While some nineteenth-century scholars suggested it represented 'Menelaus with the body of Patroclus', that identification has been since challenged. His study, which draws upon a range of Italian books and articles, is the best guide in English to the phenomenon of the Pasquil or Pasquin of Rome. In addition to Pasquil, Laurie Nussdorfer mentions 'Abbot Luigi, Madama Lucrezia, "il Facchino" (the porter), and Marforio', as well-known Roman 'talking statues' (*Civic Politics in the Rome of Urban VIII* (Princeton, NJ: Princeton University Press, 1992), p. 8). Of these, only Marforio (or Marphoreus) seems to have been widely adopted in England; he, for example, is the fictional voice of Thomas Nashe's *Martins Months Minde* (1589), which mockingly responded to the Martin Marprelate pamphlets.

43 Haskell and Penny, *Taste and the Antique*, p. 291.

44 Other sites in Rome, such as the Goritz chapel in the Church of Sant' Agostino, were also commonly used for the posting of verses (Rijser, 'The Practical Function of High Renaissance Epigrams', pp. 108–10); however, I have not found evidence that English writers were aware of these practices.

45 Reynolds, *Renaissance Humanism at the Court of Clement VII*, pp. 121–3.

46 Fitzgerald, *Martial*, p. 33. See also Anne Reynolds, 'Cardinal Oliviero Carafa and the Early Cinquecento Tradition of the Feast of Pasquino', *Humanistica*

Lovaniensia, 34 (1985), pp. 178–208, on the connections of the Pasquin ritual and humanist consciousness of classical precedents.

47 Barkan, *Unearthing the Past*, pp. 213–14.

48 Barkan, *Unearthing the Past*, p. 216.

49 Peter Partner, *Renaissance Rome, 1500–1559: A Portrait of a Society* (Berkeley, CA: University of California Press, 1976), p. 202.

50 Barkan, *Unearthing the Past*, p. 384n.

51 Barkan, *Unearthing the Past*, p. 212.

52 Barkan, *Unearthing the Past*, p. 291.

53 Barkan, *Unearthing the Past*, p. 223.

54 D. S. Chambers, *Cardinal Bainbridge in the Court of Rome, 1509 to 1514* (Oxford: Oxford University Press, 1965), pp. 121–5.

55 'Richard Pace', *DNB*.

56 John Elyot, *Of the knowledeg [sic] whiche maketh a wise man* (1533), sig. A1v. On Elyot's use of Pasquin, see Pearl Hogrefe, *The Life and Times of Sir Thomas Elyot, Englishman* (Ames, IA: Iowa State University Press, 1967), pp. 116–37.

57 Puttenham, *Art of English Poesy*, p. 142.

58 Joseph Black (ed.), *The Martin Marprelate Tracts* (Cambridge: Cambridge University Press, 2008), p. lxiii.

59 Thomas Nashe, *The Returne of the Renowned Cavaliero Pasquil of England* (1589), sig. A2v.

60 Nashe, *The Returne of the Renowned Cavaliero Pasquil of England*, sig. A2v.

61 See Bellany's 'Railing Rhymes Revisited', p. 1162, on the need for consideration of the connection between the Roman tradition of Pasquin and the rise of the early Stuart verse libel.

62 David Colclough, *Freedom of Speech in Early Stuart England* (Cambridge: Cambridge University Press, 2005), p. 89.

63 Charles Tyler Prouty, *George Gascoigne: Elizabethan Courtier, Soldier, and Poet* (New York: Columbia University Press, 1942), p. 61.

64 'Of ye losse of time', John Hoskins', Chetham MS 8012; ed. Alexander B. Grosart as *The Dr. Farmer Chetham MS. being a Commonplace Book in the Chetham Library*, vols 89 and 90 in the Publications of the Chetham Society (Manchester, 1873), vol. 1, p. 84.

65 Sir John Holles [Earl of Clare], to the Earl of Somerset, 11 Aug. 1624, in *Letters*, ed. Peter Seddon, Thoroton Society Record Series, 3 vols (Nottingham, 1975–80), vol. 2, p. 288.

66 Fuller, *The history of the worthies*, vol. 3, pp. 129–30.

67 Henry Wotton to Robert Cecil, Earl of Salisbury, 14 July 1606, in *Life and*

Letters, ed. Logan Pearsall Smith, 2 vols (Oxford: Oxford University Press, 1907), vol. 1, p. 356.

68 Holles, *Letters*, 4 June 1616, vol. 1, p. 131.

69 John Pory, Mr Pory to Rev. Joseph Mead, 2 Nov. 1627, in Birch and Williams, *Court and Times of Charles the First*, pp. 280–1.

70 Camb. UL MS Gg.I.29, Part II, fol. 33r. Cf. *Cecinit Gallus, flevit Petrus* in *Original Letters Illustrative of English History*, 3 vols (London, 1824), ed. Henry Ellis, vol. 3, p. 244; and BL Harl. 386, fol. 20r.

71 Edward Tilman to Paul D'Ewes, 1 Apr. 1625, in Ellis, *Original Letters*, p. 244.

72 Stow, *A Survey of London*, vol. 1, p. 183.

73 Robert Krueger and Ruby Nemser (eds), *The Poems of Sir John Davies* (Oxford: Oxford University Press, 1975), p. 80, quoting Benjamin Rudyerd, *Prince d'Amour* (1660). 'Provost Marshall' in this context would refer to the municipal officer in London responsible for order in the city, especially with authority over vagrants, hence the authority over Bridewell mentioned here. Having developed from a military office, the provost marshall had the power to execute summary justice. Sir Thomas Wilford was the first provost marshall appointed in London in 1595 (Lindsay Boynton, The Tudor Provost-Marshal', *English Historical Review*, 77 (1962), p. 451).

74 Mead to Stuteville, 29 June 1628, *The court and times of Charles the First*, p. 369.

75 Steven Mullaney, *The Place of the Stage: Licence, Play, and Power in Renaissance England* (Chicago: University of Chicago Press, 1988), pp. 1–25.

76 Mullaney, *The Place of the Stage*, p. 13.

77 Mullaney, *The Place of the Stage*, p. 14.

78 On the vibrant culture of topical verse composed and circulated in towns, see Adam Fox, 'Religious Satire in English Towns, 1570–1640', in Patrick Collinson and John Craig (eds), *The Reformation in English Towns* (Basingstoke: Macmillan, 1998), pp. 221–40.

79 Davies of Hereford, *The Scourge of Folly*, Ep. 121, points to the door of St Mary's Church as an Oxford site.

80 'Suche famous lybells and bills as be sett uppe in night tymes upon Chirche doores' (*OED*, 'libel' 4., quoting Bp. Longland, 1521).

81 Joseph Batts, 'Verses sett up over the lord Burgleys pew in Newark churche for which Mr Batts the preacher there was cited up before the Archbishop of Canterbury, 1606', BL Egerton MS 2877, fol. 88r.

82 For a study of libellous poems on local issues, see C. E. McGee, 'Pocky Queans and Hornèd Knaves: Gender Stereotypes in Libelous Poems', in

Mary Ellen Lamb, Karen Bamford and Pamela Allen Brown (eds), *Oral Traditions and Gender in Early Modern Literary Texts* (Aldershot: Ashgate, 2008), pp. 139–51.

83 Stuart Barton Babbage, *Puritanism and Richard Bancroft* (London: SPCK, 1962), p. 40.

84 Queen's College, Oxford, MS 121, pp. 542–9. See also Rowland Whyte to Sir Robert Sidney, 30 Nov. 1599, Baynards Castle, in Arthur Collins (ed.), *Letters and Memorials of State*, 2 vols (1746; Rpt New York: AMS, 1973), vol. 2, p. 146.

85 Francis Woodward to Sir Robert Sidney, 30 Nov. 1599, Collins, *Letters and Memorials of State*, vol. 2, pp. 146–7.

86 Christopher Hampton [Archbishop of Armagh] to James Ussher [Bishop of Meath], 12 Aug. 1623, in James Ussher, *The Whole Works*, 16 vols (Dublin, 1847), vol. 14, p. 199.

87 Louise Brown Osborn, *The Life, Letters, and Writings of John Hoskyns, 1566–1638* (New York: Archon 1973), p. 170, based upon BL Add. MS 30982, fol. 36r.

88 Sir John Davies, in Krueger and Nemser, *The Poems of Sir John Davies*, p. 423, cites MS Cotton Faustina E.v., fol. 171v.

89 BL Add. MS 15227, fol. 15r.

90 Folger MS V.a.345, p. 150.

91 Folger MS V.a.262, p. 131.

92 Camb. Add. MS 29, fol. 36v.

93 Redding, 'Robert Bishop's Commonplace Book', p. 91.

94 Camb. Add. MS 57, fol. 91v.

95 Krueger and Nemser, *The Poems of Sir John Davies*, p. 303, based upon Bodl. Rawl. Poet. MS 148.

96 *Court and Times of Charles the First*, vol. 1, p. 199. Birch dates this letter February 1626, but it must be 1626/7.

97 Rous, *Diary of John Rous*, p. 8. Rous's diary provides a valuable record of what sort of news and verses typically found their way from London to the provinces.

98 Folger MS V.a.262, p. 38; cf. Birch and Williams, *Court and Times of Charles the First*, vol. 1, p. 199; Walter Yonge, *Diary*, ed. G. Roberts (London, 1848) p. 100; Mead to Stuteville, 24 Feb. 1626/7, in David Cockburn, 'A Critical Edition of the Letters of the Reverend Joseph Mead, 1626–1627, Contained in British Library Harleian MS 390', PhD, University of Cambridge, 1994, p. 663. So dated in Cockburn, but, given its subject, it likely should read 24 Feb. 1625/6. Cf. also John Holles, *HMC*, 2:346; D'Ewes, *Autobiography*, vol. 2, p. 49. A very garbled version is found in Mead to Stuteville, 17 Feb.

1626/7, Cockburn, *A Critical Edition*, p. 656: '*Two were prefer'd, & Two layd aside, / For to bring in Sir Nicholas Hyde*'.

99 Camb. Add. MS 29, fol. 37v.

100 *DNB*.

101 D'Ewes, *Autobiography*, vol. 2, pp. 48–9.

102 Sir Horatio Palavicino died in 1600; born in Genoa, he served as a trading agent for the papacy, but was condemned by the Inquisition in 1584. Already deeply engaged in English trading at that point, he worked with Burghley (William Cecil) and the English court throughout the 1580s and 1590s as a diplomat and financier. He was knighted by Queen Elizabeth in 1587. Babraham in Cambridgeshire was his regular home in England in the years before his death (*DNB*). See Lawrence Stone, *An Elizabethan: Sir Horatio Palavicino* (Oxford: Clarendon Press, 1956), pp. 271–6, on his ownership of Babraham. Stone notes how the 'curious alien household' of Palavicino led to widespread gossip 'about his vast wealth, his usurious money-lending, his speculations in grain, his close connexion with the Cecils, and his hostility to the Essex party' (pp. 282–3).

103 Norman K. Farmer, *Poems from a Seventeenth-Century Manuscript with the Hand of Robert Herrick* in *Texas Quarterly*, Supplement to 16:4 (1973), p. 29.

104 'On the death of Palavicini', Bodl. Tanner MS 465, fol. 62r.

105 Bodl. Malone MS 19, p. 148, 'Another wrott under' ('Heere lyeth Palabaseen'). While it is not certain proof of authorship, these verses appear among some of Hoskins's epigrams.

106 Bodl. Malone MS 19, p. 148.

107 Folger MS V.a.162, fol. 59v. A further variant of this epitaph is found in James Sanderson, 'An Edition of an Early Seventeenth-Century Manuscript Collection of Poems (Rosenbach MS. 186)', PhD, University of Pennsylvania, 1960, p. 234. More literary, and restrained, responses to Palavicino's death are found in two Cambridge collections: *Album seu Nigrum Amicorum* (1600) and *An Italians dead bodie Stucke with Englishe Flowers* (1600).

108 Bodl. Malone MS 19, p. 137. A generalized form of it also appears in Folger MS V.a.262, p. 147. And although the lemma has been partially cropped, the version in Folger MS V.a.162, fol. 33r, also appears to be general rather than specifically on Palavicino.

109 Camb. Add. MS 57, fol. 91v.

110 *Wits recreations* (1640), sig. Bb3v. Cf. BL Add. MS 15227, fol. 14v, where a fragment of this appears, beginning 'Death with his besome did sweepe him from Babram'.

111 Stone, *An Elizabethan*, p. 26, relates, 'in about 1578 Palavicino became the

acknowledged father of an illegitimate son, Edward, who appears to have been educated under his care, and perhaps under his roof'.

112 'sir Horatio Palavasino', Sanderson, 'An Edition of an Early Seventeenth-Century Manuscript Collection', no. 223.

113 Stone, *An Elizabethan*, p. 3.

114 Sig. B1r. Like most of the poems, this is by Theophilus Field.

115 Theophilus Field, *An Italians dead Bodie*, sig. B2r–v.

116 'P.P.P', 'The conquest of two Traitors, Envie and Death, by the worthy Knight, Sir Horatio Pallavicino' in Field, *An Italians dead Bodie*, sig. C1r.

117 Harington, *A Supplie or Addicion to Bishop Godwin's Catalogue of Bishops* in *Nugae Antiquae*, vol. 2, p. 3. From John Nichols, *The progresses, processions, and magnificent festivities of King James the First*, 4 vols (1828; Rpt New York: AMS, 1968), vol. 2, p. 81, it would seem that King James, along with his guest King Christian of Denmark, went to Windsor on 7 August, and returned to London (Greenwich) on 8 August. However, it seems he may have been back at Windsor on 17 August (vol. 2, p. 95).

118 Harington had previously referred to the distich in a letter sent to Sir Thomas Chaloner, governor of Prince Henry (Jason Scott-Warren, *Sir John Harington and the Book as Gift* (Oxford: Oxford University Press, 2001), p. 220).

119 Osborne, *The works of Francis Osborne*, p. 504.

120 John Thorys to William Trumbull, 21 May 1612, *HMC Downshire* (1938), vol. 3. p. 296.

121 Abraham Williams to William Trumbull. 13 June 1612, *HMC Downshire* (1938), vol. 3, p. 315. The poem is also found in Bodl. Rawl. poet. MS 26, fol. 1r, and in Bodl. Malone MS 23, p. 4, where it begins 'They beg our lande, lendinge, and lives'.

122 Osborne, *The works of Francis Osborne*, p. 504.

123 Resentment of such actions by the Scots goes back to the first summer of James's reign, when Dudley Carleton related to John Chamberlain how one who followed through on a vow to kill the first Englishman he met after a quarrel over gaming by slaying an 'old country fellow'; 4 July 1603, Maurice Lee, Jr (ed.), *Dudley Carleton to John Chamberlain, 1603–1624: Jacobean Letters* (New Brunswick, NJ: Rutgers University Press, 1972), p. 35.

124 Osborne, *The works of Francis Osborne*, p. 505. Osborne finds fault with both sides in the dispute, but is especially critical of Philip Herbert, Earl of Montgomery, whose failure to enact vengeance he credits to cowardice rather than virtue. He was quite close to the event, serving as he did in the household of Montgomery's brother, William Herbert, Earl of Pembroke.

125 The 1617–25 diary survives in BL Add. MS 28640 and the 1625–43 diary in BL Add. MS 22959.

126 Rous, *Diary of John Rous*, p. 31.

127 Katherine Duncan-Jones, 'Preserved Dainties: late Elizabethan Poems by Sir Robert Cecil and the Earl of Clanricarde', *Bodleian Library Journal*, 14 (1992), pp. 136–44, p. 142.

128 McRae, *Literature, Satire, and the Early Stuart State*, pp. 42–3, offers a similar argument about the mingling of political views in Bodl. Malone MS 23. Ian Atherton suggests as well that composers of newsletters in the period also collected and transmitted a sampling of opinion without much editorial commenting or selecting; '"The Itch Grown a Disease": Manuscript Transmission of News in the Seventeenth Century', in Joad Raymond (ed.), *News, Newspapers and Society* (London: Frank Cass, 1999), pp. 39–65, p. 51.

129 These pages are all unnumbered. The general catalogue description of the C108 papers notes that they often include a range of family papers.

130 Justinian Isham to 'Madam' ('my Lady Manchester & Lady Barkam'), Lamport (Northamptonshire), 23 Jan. 1639. The poem itself begins, 'O Light of Light, whose Shadow is the Light'; it is a devotional poem with scriptural references in the margins.

131 In his letter, Isham refers to Lady Anne Crouch's/Montagu's own writings: 'tis not strange to you whose writings so abound wt sacred sentences', but there are no poems or prose pieces within this box that would fit this description.

132 Esther S. Cope, *The Life of a Public Man: Edward, First Baron Montagu of Boughton, 1562–1644* (Philadelphia, PA: American Philosophical Society, 1981), pp. 203–5.

133 Some of these are discussed in Chapter 10 below. There is no indication of any antipathy between Montagu and Cecil in Cope, *The Life of a Public Man*.

134 The poem ('Greate Verulam is very lame, the Gout, of goe out, feeling', 1621) is reproduced in *Early Stuart Libels* (www.earlystuartlibels.net/htdocs/monopolies_section/Mii3.html), where it is ascribed to Hoskins.

135 Cope, *The Life of a Public Man*, p. 203.

136 Bellany, *The Politics of Court Scandal*, pp. 113–14.

5

Epigrams in manuscript

Though the word spoken live, the written dye;
Yet that shall end, this live eternally.[1]

As explored in Chapter 4, individual epigrams were apt, after initial oral circulation or as 'separates' on paper, to be recorded in commonplace books or miscellanies that gathered a range of materials on a topic, or that included an unorganized variety of poems. This chapter examines a different sort of gathering, where the manuscript was largely limited to epigrams. These manuscripts can be divided into two main groups: those put together by a collector from a variety of authors, and those of a significant number of epigrams that were prepared by the author. In turn, these surviving author-initiated collections also fall into two main groups: those offered by the author to friends or acquaintances in a limited form of manuscript circulation, and those that were rougher collections developed by the poet as he moved toward publication.

Non-authorial collections

The vast majority of surviving Elizabethan and early Stuart epigrams are found in manuscript miscellanies that preserve a variety of different genres by various poets. Miscellanies were very much at their height in the 1620s and 1630s, and Christ Church, Oxford, was a particularly rich site of collection and dissemination.[2] These miscellanies reflect the interests of the individual collector or at least what was available to him or her as poems circulated. Woudhuysen identifies four groups of private makers of manuscript miscellanies in the period:

- figures at the court
- lawyers and those at the Inns of Court
- students and fellows at the universities
- 'private collectors, especially families living in the country'

Of course, some individuals would straddle a number – even all four – of these groups.[3]

Miscellanies put together by collectors are most often haphazard in organization, with poems appearing in the order in which they were obtained, with only rarely a clear organization of material into generic categories. Although epitaphs are an exception, as they seemed to attract a 'collector' mentality much more sure of what was wanted, few manuscripts consist of exclusively or even largely epigrams. Instead, readers gathered what was popular and came their way. Thus, in the majority of miscellanies, epigrams are sprinkled among other poetic material: love lyrics, satires, verse epistles, funeral elegies etc. While in some manuscripts there are sections of a few consecutive pages of epigrams, in other cases short epigrams have been used to fill in space at the bottom of pages, or even written sideways in the margins. Those manuscripts that are more ordered affairs, with poems organized by genre, and sometimes epigrams divided by subject,[4] are likely second-stage collections – that is, ones put together in a more polished form from a rough volume of immediate collection. These second-stage collections can sometimes be identified by a consistency of handwriting and ink that suggests they were copied in extensive sittings.[5]

Folger MS V.a.345 (ca. 1630) reflects this organizational desire: in addition to the grouping by subject matter in this manuscript, the compiler has added marginal notes pointing to others on the same subject. For example, the well-known lines on Lady Rich, 'One stone contents her …',[6] has the marginal note directing readers to a later page where three further mock epitaphs on her are found. In this case, then, the collector was putting the material together over a period of time from various sources, but still desired to identify the affinities among various poems. He also added occasional marginal notes to explain references.

Gift collections

Gift manuscripts of epigrams are the most straightforward of surviving collections. They fall into two categories: those which are small gatherings (rarely the 'hundreds' or 'centuries' presented in print) offered to a friend or social equal of the poet, perhaps sent with a letter, as evident in the university-based collections of Wheare's circle described in Chapter 3. Less common are more formal (and often larger) 'gift collections' offered to a potential patron. These gifts adopt a humble tone toward the recipient and generally are in a larger paper format and written in a more polished script.

In both classical and Renaissance practice, epigrams might serve as accompanying 'posies' to small gifts, inscribed upon a piece of silverware or attached to some other gift. However, it is already clear with Martial that the poems themselves might be the gifts: 'These distichs you can send to your guests instead of a gift, if a coin shall be as rare with you as with me.'[7] Such were, of course, light and self-effacing gifts, more a token of friendship or an emblem of the poet's poverty than things of substantial worth themselves. Stradling reflects something of this same approach 1500 years later: offering an epigram to his kinsman Thomas Lutterel, he is at pains to assert that it was a casual spontaneous gift rather than one made 'studio praemeditata' [with premeditated effort].[8] As one-time gifts or tokens, single epigrams might also be presented as harbingers of greater works to come, as Luke Roman has suggested (citing Martial 1:107): if the poet had a Maecenas-like patron, 'he would be able to focus on an ambitious, integral work, rather than continuously pursuing many smaller gifts.'[9]

This larger work might be of another genre, or a more substantial gathering of epigrams, where the sheer volume of poems (however slight as individual items) gave the work a literary value. Epigrams of praise (of the dedicatee and his or her family) were common in such collections, but they usually included a high percentage of mocking epigrams as well. The manuscript volume was generally shaped by an understanding of its primary audience, as will be shown in the case of Harington below. The epigrammatist of a manuscript gift collection was somewhat protected in his addressing of a limited, and generally friendly, readership. Political or legal ramifications were of less concern than with a print collection, and a defensive attitude toward the aggressive response of carping critics unnecessary. This relative safety of a manuscript collection is remarked on by numerous epigrammatists. Stradling describes the hostile readership that a printed book might expect:

> Sunt quibus est alium libros cruciare voluptas:
> Impune possunt; res operosa nec est.
> Vae tibi crudeli rapiat si Zoilus ungue:
> Hunc nec blanditiis, nec moveas lachrimis.

[There are those to whom it is another pleasure to torment books:
They can do it with impunity; it is not a difficult thing.
Woe to you if Zoilus seizes you with a cruel claw:
You will affect him with neither flattery nor tears.][10]

In contrast, a gift manuscript of epigrams might find its worst fate was simply being ignored by an indifferent patron.

Manuscript gift collections and dedicated print volumes were not mutually exclusive. Owen had already published two major volumes of Latin epigrams in 1606 and 1607 when he presented a gift manuscript of 105 new epigrams to Prince Henry in 1610.[11] This then formed the foundation for the printed epigrams (in two books totalling 211 epigrams) dedicated to the Prince in 1612; however, only eighty of the manuscript epigrams were included in the new volume. Nicholas Poole-Wilson suggests that some were omitted for their bawdiness or political implications.[12]

Francis Thynne

A typical approach for a gift volume to a potential patron is adopted by Francis Thynne in his dedication of epigrams in manuscript to Sir Thomas Egerton, Lord Keeper (later Baron Ellesmere and Lord Chancellor).[13] The manuscript (Huntington Library EL.34.B.12) is in Thynne's own hand and is the sole surviving copy of his epigrams; the first half of the volume presents sixty-four 'naked emblems' (i.e. without images), and the second half seventy-six epigrams.[14] As an established antiquarian, Thynne had a significant body of more substantial material at hand that he might have offered Egerton instead of epigrams. He had, for example, presented Egerton with a 'Catalogue of the lord chancellors of England', to which he could write that 'Yt nedeth not (my very goode lorde) to lay downe a caise or reasone, why I presente [this work to] your lordship (beinge lorde keper of the greater seale)',[15] and other such works in the 1580s and 1590s.[16]

Epigrams are a quite different gift to present: their frequent low subject matter does not straightforwardly honour the recipient, and thus it is instructive to see how Thynne frames this gift in the dedication. The collection mixes Heywood-like moralizing epigrams with Martialian ones mocking individuals, and Thynne first proffers the common argument that they might fill a moral, instructive purpose. However, this conventional argument is buttressed with a more personal one: the epigrams, which were mostly composed in the 1560s and 1570s, recall a time when

the socially divided Thynne and Egerton, along with others named in the
collection, shared a more equal life as students at Lincoln's Inn. While
the manuscript is now presented as a gift from an underling to a greater
figure, the epigrams invoke a society built upon youthful friendship:
'some of them are composed of thinges donn and sayed by such as were
well knowne to your Lordshipp, and to my self in those yonger yeares
when Lincolns Inn societie did linke us all in one cheyne of Amitie; and
some of them are of other persons yet living, which of your Lordship
are both loved and liked'.[17] However, the volume also includes poems
responding directly to figures of the 1590s, and these too are connected
with Egerton, as they 'of your Lordship are both loved and liked'.[18] Both
Thynne and Egerton were in late middle age when the manuscript was
presented, and in many ways the collection looks back to a time long past,
their days as students at the Inns of Court, and a time when they were
roughly equal in position and power. Egerton after all was the illegitimate
son of a knight, and, while Thynne's father, like him, was an antiquary
and literary scholar, the family claimed aristocratic roots.

Self-deprecation is part of the stance adopted by Thynne: 'you may
Justlie deale with me as Silla did with a badd poet, to whome writing
an Epigram against Scilla [*sic*] of boghed verses, some short and some
longe, Scylla [*sic*] commanded a reward to be given to him, to th'end
he should never after compose anie more verses.'[19] At the same time, as
with a number of epigram collections, Thynne also suggests that these
'hard, harshe and bitter' poems are a foretaste of riper, sweeter fruit;
that is, they are an early stage of an individual's poetic development.[20] It
is worth noting that the late 1590s was also the time when Thynne took
up his father's scholarship on Chaucer, and produced his *Animadversions*
(1599) on Speght's edition of Chaucer, in which he expressed a desire to
produce a commentary on the earlier poet's work.[21] This volume was also
dedicated to Egerton.[22]

Harington

Harington's epigrams offer a much richer and more complex example
of the dynamics of manuscript epigrams as gifts, one that has recently
attracted considerable attention from Jason Scott-Warren and Gerard
Kilroy. Although Harington did print his major works, the translation of
Orlando Furioso (1591) and *The Metamorphosis of Ajax* (1596), he showed
no interest in publication of his epigrams, and a printed edition of them
did not appear until after his death.[23] He wrote occasional epigrams from

the 1580s on, and then from these disparate materials he brought together various select groups of his epigrams as gifts: the earliest recorded was to his fellow epigrammatist Stradling about 1590.[24] However, it was in the first few years of the new century that Harington engaged most heavily in presenting such gifts of epigrams to a number of figures, including his mother-in-law Lady Rogers, King James and Prince Henry. His shaping of these manuscripts is careful and self-conscious; the process of selection is clearly geared to the audience: not all epigrams are for all readers. The controlled manuscript culture allows this fine-tuning for audience in a way not possible for orally transmitted single epigrams or print-published books.

To begin with an example of Harington's use of a single epigram: in his 'Breefe Notes and Remembrances' he records how he will approach the Queen through the Lord Treasurer (presumably Burleigh) and Essex, and that the latter has bid him 'lay goode holde on her Majesties bountie, and aske freely. I will attende to-morrowe, and leave this little poesie behinde her cushion at my departinge from her presence':

> To the Queens Majestie
> For ever dear, for ever dreaded Prince,
> You read a verse of mine a little since,
> And so pronounc'st each word, and every letter,
> Your gracious reading grac'st my verse the better:
> Sith then your Highnesse doth, by gift exceeding,
> Make what you read the better for your reading;
> Let my poor muse your pains thus farre importune,
> Like as you read my verse, so – *read my Fortune.*[25]

This gift of an epigram points away from itself towards the honour that the Queen bestows in reading it and the further gift to Harington's fortune that she has the power to grant. The limitations of the poet's gift are insignificant, as it is the monarch who is the ultimate gift-giver. This poem also functions as a continuing written remnant of the spoken appeal for favour that Harington made directly in her presence, a scene of entreaty that itself reminds the Queen of the closeness of their relationship.

While some of the individual epigrams of Harington originated in specific contexts such as this, he would later package and then repackage collections of them to function as further gifts. These manuscript gift collections were clearly geared to their respective recipients, and served different functions. The major manuscripts are as follows:

- Inner Temple Petyt MS 538, vol. 43 to Lucy, Countess of Bedford, 19 Dec. 1600
- Camb. Univ. Library MS Adv. B.8.1, to Lady Jane Rogers, 19 Dec. 1600
- British Library, Add. MS 12049, a draft of the volume presented to King James, New Year's 1602
- Folger Library, MS V.a.249, to Prince Henry, 19 June 1605.[26]

The first of these, his manuscript gift to the young Lucy, Countess of Bedford, is a limited selection of his epigrams appended to a number of the famous Psalm versifications of Mary Sidney, Countess of Pembroke. As usual, the epigrams are offered in a way that dismisses their significance: Harington's preface nonchalantly suggests that these poems of 'meaner matter, and lighter manner'[27] serve merely to fill up space. While he disparages them thus, he also hopes that they might 'serve to waite, as a wanton page is admitted to beare a torche to a chaste matrone'.[28] This both establishes a social role for Harington as a servant-like figure and asserts that the epigrams do have a function: they may serve as a light with which a godly young woman can see. The epigrams are all at least loosely connected with the topic of religion: hypcorisy, Puritanism and atheism figure prominently, and the poems would thus serve to warn a young woman of spiritual dangers to which she might become prey. As Scott-Warren points out, the epigram section of the manuscript is incomplete: clearly other epigrams were also presented to Bedford at this time, but Harington's preface also indicates that they are a mere selection. If she approves these, he will 'hereafter be embouldned to present more of them, and to entytle som of them to your Honorable name'.[29] That final clause suggests that a further presentation of his complete epigrams might be a more public one, dedicated to the Countess in a way that surpasses this more private gift. As such, this manuscript gathering, as will be true of the others, would function as one step in a more extended series of social exchanges and moments. Scott-Warren argues that this manuscript resepresents 'an important moment in Harington's self-fashioning',[30] as he steps beyond the role of wanton epigrammatist in giving religious direction, something that he will take on more fully in the manuscript epigrams to Prince Henry discussed below. He also plausibly suggests that Harington's gift to the nineteen-year-old Countess was a timely cultivating of a rising young woman of the court.[31]

Cambridge MS UL Adv. B.8.1 is a polished presentation copy of fifty-two of Harington's epigrams.[32] In the prefatory epistle to his mother-in-law, Lady Rogers, dated 19 December 1600, he writes that he presents to her

> as manie of the toyes I have formerly written to you and your daughter, as I
> could collect out of my scatterd papers: supposing (though you have seene some
> of them long since) yet now to revew them againe, and remember the kynde,
> and sometime the unkynde occasions, on which some of them were written,
> will not be unpleasant, and because there was spare roome, I have added a few
> others that were showd to our Soveraigne Lady, and some, that I durst never
> show any Ladie, but you two.[33]

As with Thynne, this collection becomes a sort of remembrancer, pre-
serving the shared social contexts from which the individual poems arose.
As Harington presents it, the manuscript is a record of three relationships: that of Harington with his wife Mary, the more vexed one with
his mother-in-law and finally that of the poet with his godmother, Queen
Elizabeth. The last of these three is strategically important for Harington,
in that he can remind his mother-in-law that she is promoted by him into
a select audience that includes the Queen. Thus, he offers Lady Rogers
not just the poems themselves but the elite royal audience that has also
perused them.

However, as Scott-Warren has argued, this gift of epigrams comes
with a certain sting. He shows that these epigrams (most of which are
addressed to either Harington's wife or mother-in-law) participate in a
tense struggle with Lady Rogers over her daughter and her property
– some arise from 'unkynde occasions'. Unlike most gifts, it is also then a
provocation. In a very thorough and careful reading, Scott-Warren presents the epigrams against the background of Harington's struggles with
Edward Rogers (Mary's brother) and Lady Rogers in the 1590s. Rather
than playing the role of humble gift-giving supplicant, he forces Lady
Rogers to acknowledge his sexual relation with her daughter and taunts
her about her property and his eventual inheritance of it.[34]

No such shared context was possible with the next figure to whom
Harington presented a collection: King James in 1602. This collection
looks *forward* to what Harington hopes will be a future relationship when
James inherits the English throne. In this gathering, Scott-Warren sees a
survey of English life through the 1590s, with an anticipation of reform
under a new King.[35] Harington here can adopt the role of the 'epigrammatist as scourge of villainy'.[36] He concludes his dedicatory poem to James:
'We do but poynt out vices and detect them / 'Tis you great Prince, that

one day must correct them.'[37] In Harington's idealized realm, epigrammatist and king have linked roles, and this manuscript was but one of a number of attempts on Harington's part to find a place under the new king.

Two years into James's English reign, Harington further pressed his appeal to the royal family by presenting a manuscript of his epigrams to the young Prince Henry, which survives as Folger MS V.a.249.[38] This, like the collection offered to Lady Rogers, looks back in time, here to the period 1602–3, as it reproduces Harington's New Year's 1602 gift to James. Harington describes his gift manuscript to Prince Henry as 'this collection or rather confusion of all my ydle Epigrams'.[39] This typical pose of indifference or disdain is belied by a significant degree of organization for a manuscript collection. Jean Humez was the first to recognize that the major Harington manuscripts observe a meaningful sequencing (partly chronological) that is lost in the bungled order of the printed editions that appeared after Harington's death.[40] Humez and Scott-Warren note that mini-sequences on a topic often appear within the volume, and such juxtaposition causes one poem to comment upon another.[41] For example, Harington places his famous distich 'Of treason' immediately before that on the execution of Mary Queen of Scots, entitled here 'A tragicall epigram'.[42] The former offers a cynical view of statecraft that casts a shadow over the specific case of Mary Stuart's 'treason'. In the context of this gift-book, this placement also relegates that attitude to the previous reign, forestalling any application of it to the early years of King James.[43]

Gerard Kilroy goes further than Humez and Scott-Warren, as he suggests an overarching, numbered pattern in Harington's gift manuscripts to Prince Henry and King James. He sees Harington's career as a continuous wrestling with his place as an embattled Roman Catholic in Protestant England, and places the manuscript gifts within that context. The opening of the Latin poem, 'Elegie on the Lanterne' (which explains the material gift to King James in 1602) is the 'key to these four books of a hundred epigrams',[44] where Harington compares himself to Junius Brutus pretending to be a fool before Tarquin, who according to Kilroy represents Elizabeth. This elegy, of course, dates from two and a half years earlier and Kilroy suggests that Harington is asking 'whether these gloriously optimistic readings of the arrival of James ... have materialised'.[45] He goes further, claiming that 'These four decades are definitely the four sorrowful mysteries, the fourth decade being the toughest of all'.[46] From the evidence of the paper used, Kilroy suggests that the fourth book is the last written, and the most vehement in showing the corruption of the English ecclesiastical situation. The manuscript manifests a fascinating process of rewriting; Kilroy points to 4:10 'Of two Religions', a debate between father and son, as the most notable example. Like Donne's 'Satire 3' this poem presents the debate over true religion: as originally written in the manuscript the son concludes,

> a man had neede be crafty
> to keepe his soule and body both in saf'ty.
> But both to save, this is best way to hold
> live in the new, dye if you can in th'old.

However, the last line is overwritten, to read 'die in the new, live if you list in th'old'.[47] The rewriting transforms the poem from an assertion of the ultimate primacy of the Roman Catholic Church (the old faith) into a public acceptance of the Protestant Church (the new). Such points to Harington's willingness to play with the idea of ecclesiastical loyalty and entertain the possibility that the Church of Rome is the one true church, but Kilroy overplays his hand by asserting a more unequivocal commitment and ignoring both the playful (and often cynical) traditions of the epigram as a form, and by focusing on those Harington epigrams which defend Catholicism but ignoring those that denigrate it.

This volume, Kilroy argues, emerged at a time of crisis for English Catholics, as suspicion of Jesuits was leading to heightened prosecution in the summer of 1605, and the manuscript was thus an attempt to show the prince 'the deep corruption that was in the establishment and in the new church, and by implication to see the Catholic cause with more compassion'.[48] Where Scott-Warren sees the collection as another instance of attempting to gain patronage, Kilroy sees it as a 'savage indictment of Elizabethan schism and simony' and one that reflects the fear that the subsequent reign of James has not relieved the Catholic situation in England. Whether the Folger manuscript was ever actually presented to Henry remains unclear: Kilroy summarizes the status and relation of the two manuscripts:

> *BL* [Add. 12049] seems originally to have been the draft text in the hand of a second Harington scribe with autograph emendations. *F* [Folger V.a.249] was a presentation copy for Prince Henry in the italic hand of Scribe *A*. At some point in 'The third booke', the relationship seems to have changed, since both the text and the numbering of the last five 'decades' has been altered in *F*, while *BL* has the final version. By 'The fourth booke' the relationship has settled down again.[49]

This suggests that ultimately *neither* manuscript was actually presented to Henry,[50] and prompts the question of whether the Rosary and Harington's poems on it (which Kilroy takes as the key to reading the epigrams as a hidden 'four sorrowful decades')[51] were ever meant to be part of the presentation, or if they were added when the volume had become something else for Harington. A second question lingers: if the volume simply replicates that given to James in 1602, did Harington have no sense of reshaping the collection for the younger prince? Scott-Warren convincingly argues that in this case there was no political dichotomy between James and Henry, and that Harington is here trying to simply 'relaunch' his career within the Stuart regime.[52] Kilroy has done a great service by redirecting attention to the organizational principles present in the major manuscripts but obliterated by John Budge's printed edition of 1618 (which then served as the basis for N. E. McClure's long-standard edition of 1930). While I cannot follow him all the way in his assertion of a religiously based structure, his work and that of Scott-Warren helpfully demonstrate that epigram collections in manuscript are not always the mere random compilations their authors claimed them to be.

A similar argument regarding the significance of sequencing in epigram collections has been made by Theresa M. DiPasquale about those of John Donne.[53] Following the editor of the Donne *Variorum*, she posits that all three orders in which Donne's epigrams survive in manuscript and all textual variants are authorial, even though they lack the prefatory materials found in Harington, which prove authorial control and choices. Identifying meaningful *sequence* where more cautious readers might see thematic *groupings*, DiPasquale finds anti-Elizabeth satire through many of the epigrams when read as sequence. While she never mentions Harington, she comes to a similar conclusion regarding Donne's epigrams as those offered by Scott-Warren and Kilroy, that the epigrams achieve an enhanced political meaning when read sequentially, and in particular that they explore the tense issue of recusancy in the 1590s. It certainly leads to overreaching at times, as for instance where she finds religious satire in 'Klockius': 'Klockius so deeply'hath vowd nere more to come / In bawdy house, that he dares not go home.' She suggests that he 'is a disillusioned English Protestant who has discovered that his own church is no less tainted than her Roman sister.'[54]

Part of the problem is that DiPasquale's approach reads Donne's epigrams first of all in relation to each other rather than in relation to the immediate moment or figure which prompted each. The latter is largely lost to us, as for many of Donne's epigrams we cannot even establish an approximate date. However, the evidence of the general epigram culture of the period suggests that these epigrams' first readers would have known or plausibly guessed who was meant by 'Klockius', 'Phrine', the 'Liar' etc. Thus, when DiPasquale writes that '"Ralphius" says more as a part of the sequence in which it appears than it does as an isolated fragment of wit',[55] she is omitting to note how our readings are incomplete because we lack the contextual certainty of the poem's earliest readers. As I will discuss in Chapter 6, either the lemma itself or awareness of the immediate topical context of the epigram would guide the understanding of the knowing original reader. Even in its time, such use of the lemma created esoteric and exoteric readers (to borrow Leo Strauss's terminology); scholars now are almost always exoteric ones and no focus on sequencing can overcome that.

Harington: beyond gift manuscripts

Given the number of epigram manuscripts Harington presented as gifts – and it is likely that those surviving are only a remnant of these – it is not surprising that individual epigrams went into more general manuscript circulation. The vast number of manuscripts listed in Peter Beal's *Index of English Literary Manuscripts* that contain at least a few Harington ones testify to the immense reputation he had achieved through manuscript circulation in his own lifetime. Most internal evidence suggests that these were derived from manuscript sources rather than the printed volumes of Harington that began appearing after his death.[56] The most frequently found single epigrams tend to be those that are anti-Puritan or mocking of women. Beal lists a striking total of thirty-sex copies of the bawdy 'A virtuous lady sitting in a muse' and twenty-five appearances of the epigram 'Of swearing' (beg. 'In elder times, an ancient custome 'twas'), which mocks changes in swearing brought about by the Reformation.

The vibrancy of manuscript circulation is attested to by instances where these poems in manuscript were embellished or responded to by others. For example, Rosenbach MS 187 (now MS 1083/16) includes 'Of certain Puritan wenches':

> Six of the weakest sex & purest sect
> Had conference one day to this effect
> To change that old and Popish name of Preaching
> And first, the first would have it called a teaching,
> The second such a common word despisinge

Sayd it were better calld a Catechising,
The third being learned, and in all things wise
Would have it called dayly exercise,
The fourth, a great Magnificates corrector,
Sayd she allowed them best *that* cald it Lecture,
Nay q*uo*d the fift my brethren as I heare
Doe call it speaking in Northampton shire,
Tush sayd the sixt than standing were more fitt
ffor Preachers in the pulpit seldome sitt,
And as these six their matters thus were handling
They all agreed and liked best of standing,[57]

Redding suggests that the final couplet was probably added by another to
'point up the sexual meaning'.[58]

'A Virtuous Lady sitting in a muse' was not printed by Budge in either
the 1615 or 1618 collections of Harington, but John Davies of Hereford
included it in his *Wits Bedlam* (1617):

A Vertuous Lady sitting in a muse,
As oftentimes faire vertuous Ladyes use,
Did leane her elbow on her knee full hard,
The other distant from it halfe a yard.
Her Knight to taunt her with some privie token,
Said, Wife, awake, your Cabinet stands open.
Shee rose, and blusht, and smil'd, and soft did say,
Then looke it if you list, you keepe the key.

However, Davies adds four lines of the imagined husband's response:[59]

But he might have replide; good Wife, you mock;
My Key can open, but not shut the Lock.
Sith tis a Spring; and Kayes in generall
Will doo't, if it so openly to all.[60]

Harington's famous epigram on treason also enjoyed wide manuscript
circulation, surviving in at least seventeen manuscripts: 'Treason doth
never prosper, what's the reason? / For if it prosper, none dare call it
Treason.'[61] Most often it appears next to 'Treason is like a Basiliscus eye /
ffirst seeing kills, first being seene doth dy',[62] an epigram that is similar in
its worldly wise spirit. A poem like this approaches the widely circulated

epigrams discussed in the preceding chapter, which, as what 'everyman might say', moved beyond unique authorship. The 'basilisk's eye' epigram survives in a variant 'Treason is like a Cocatrice's eyes' (MS Tanner 169, fol. 43), which is indebted as well to Fulke Greville's *Mustapha*: 'Mischiefe is like the Cockatrices eyes; / Sees first, and kills; or is seene first; and dies'.[63] Uncommonly, the manuscript actually dates and identifies the source of the couplet: '29 November 1606. Master [John] Clapham from Master Foucke Grevill'.[64] While not published until 1609, *Mustapha* was written in the mid- to late 1590s, and this manuscript quotation shows either that it was known in manuscript before or that the treason couplet was circulating separately. As the composition dates of *Mustapha* are approximately the same as most of Harington's epigrams, at this point it would seem impossible to establish which came first.

Also surviving are a number of composite manuscripts that preserve significant gatherings of Harington epigrams, but do not seem to have been gift collections presented by the poet himself. For example, the Skipwith manuscript (BL Add. MS 25707) has sixty-five, including some unpublished in the 1615 and 1618 editions (these also had appeared in BL Add. MS 12049).[65] While the Skipwith manuscript as a whole dates from after 1649 and much of its material is from the 1620s and 1630s, Harington's epigrams are in a different, and earlier, hand than surrounding material and on a different paper.[66] Without prefatory material we can surmise little about the original function or receiver of this selection of Harington poems.

BL Sloane MS 1889: Thomas Freeman's private, working collection

In surviving manuscripts the rough gatherings made for a poet's own use are usually marked by the evidence of editorial work: frequent changes, additions and deletions. These show something of the process of composition, and, where a final printed volume also survives, comparison may show what effect the pressures and opportunities of print might have. Thomas Freeman, whose published volume, *Rubbe, and a great cast*, appeared in 1614, also produced a manuscript collection of his epigrams distinctly different from the printed work. British Library Sloane MS 1889 is a small (3.5 in. by 5 in.) volume obviously put together as a working copy of the poet, rather than for presentation to another. It has no prefatory material or dedication, and includes a significant number of corrections. Some errors in the numbering of the epigrams in Sloane 1889 suggest that they were all copied from another *already numbered* manuscript version of the poems. Furthermore, the initial numbering in the manuscript has been changed in the same hand to a completely new one: clearly the poet was working towards a deliberate sequence, but it is still not that which appeared in *Rubbe, and a great cast*.

The manuscript seems to reflect Freeman's process of composing, revising and resequencing epigrams over a long span of time. References suggest that some were composed already in the 1590s, while ones further along in the manuscript date from 1605 to 1609 or 1610. A number of epigrams indicate an unsuccessful attempt at publication, probably before 1605. Finally, epigrams in the manuscript (but ones not appearing in *Rubbe, and a great cast*) strongly suggest that Freeman composed some of them during a time in Cornwall and others (probably later) while living in Worcestershire, possibly at or near the home of Lord Windsor, to whom *Rubbe, and a great cast* was dedicated.[67]

About eighty epigrams in the manuscript are not in the book, and about ninety from the book (mostly from Book 2) are not in the manuscript. About two-thirds of the marginal corrections in Sloane 1889 are included in the printed version. Overall, the manuscript seems to represent an intermediate stage in the movement from scattered epigrams to a print collection. It is likely, then, that Sloane 1889 preserves an earlier version of his epigrams, one which underwent significant further reworking before reaching publication. It is nearly certain that there was both a previous manuscript copy of Freeman's epigrams and at least one later one.

While some of the epigrams seem to have been written in the 1590s, they were amended closer to the time of publication.[68] For example, the following poem refers to the well-known hangman Bull:

In Tiburn
Neptune by sea, the hangman Bull by land
each had a trident of no small command
Neptune at thine o how ye waves do shake
and Bull att thine o how ye knaves do quake.[69]

At the bottom of the page a marginal note in a different hand and ink reads, 'now Derrick'; Thomas Derrick replaced Bull as hangman around 1598 and continued in the role until about 1610.[70] Hence the poem was composed some time before 1598, and the manuscript corrected between 1598 and 1610. The manuscript was still being added to as late as 1609, for it includes an epigram on the outbreak of the plague that year in Oxford.[71]

This suggests that the manuscript is at least post-1609, but, as it does not include the epigram on the establishing of Wadham College (founded shortly after Nicholas Wadham's death in 1609),[72] not long after that. Unnumbered epigrams, seemingly entered at a yet later point, appear in the last few pages of the manuscript. These begin with a number on the Gunpowder Plot (likely written shortly after the event) and were among those omitted from the 1614 publication, perhaps having lost their topicality.

While *Rubbe, and a great cast* was dedicated to Thomas, Lord Windsor, there are no poems in Sloane 1889 that refer to him; instead there is an epigram to John St. Aubyn of Clowance, Cornwall, which addresses him as a potential patron and protector. Freeman seeeks his favour as he ventures with his epigrams into a more public realm:

> **Jh: St abin Armigero Cornub:[73]cui rogatas ab ipso, quas plurima conscripsit epigrammata[74]**
>
> Lo what my leasure gave mee leave to write,
> and to your kindest censure I present itt,
> if itt begett your liking and delight
> I shall bee proud my witt did first invent itt,
> but shall itt seeme unsav'ry and distast,
> unto your gentle and iudicious spirrit,
> itt gads no more abroad to bee disgrac'st [*sic*]
> but bides att home to please those friends that heare itt.
> now 'tis no matter though itt passe the pikes,
> and hazard once what fortune may befall,
> or to winne love or entertaine dislikes,
> yet evermore to hope the best in all:
> such is the Hope that now on you depends
> that you like Jove will use a stranger well.
> and bee one of my Muses kindest frends,
> sooth hir but up and see what tales shee'l tell.
>   ever for fashion, if not for desart
> speake a foole faire & you shall have his hart.[75]

The presentation of epigrams to St Aubyn is a 'testing of the waters', as Freeman goes beyond pleasing friends at home to being read by one whose judgement will determine whether the poems 'gad' abroad further, presumably in print publication. The placement of the poem in this manuscript is odd: unlike a typical dedicatory poem, this one is buried in the middle of the volume, and does not seem to conclude or begin a particular collection of poems. Another poem in the manuscript, 'In quenda*m* qui me ex Davis epig. surripuisse dictitabat' [On a certain man who repeatedly said that I had stolen epigrams from Davies], seems to identify this critic of Freeman in the margins: 'Tirack'. I suspect this is one of the Arundels of Trerice, Cornwall, most likely John, born in 1576. The Arundel and St Aubyn families were closely intermarried, and in the mid-1590s these young men were both at the Middle Temple, where they would have encountered Davies's epigrams.[76] All this points to Freeman being in the late 1590s in Cornwall, where he was circulating his epigrams among the local gentry; there is no direct evidence of what he was doing there (or later in Worcestershire), but a number of epigram references to the hard lot of schoolmasters leads one to suspect that he was following this vocation – as discussed in the preceding chapters, he would not be the first schoolmaster-epigrammatist.

Most interesting are the poems in manuscript that do not appear in *Rubbe, and a great cast*. For the most part, these are the more ribald poems, or ones involving a specific element of political or religious satire. For example, 'Supplicatur Puritanus' adopts the voice of a hypocritical Puritan who chastises lukewarm Protestants and celebrates particular acts of iconoclasm at Banbury and Exeter.[77] Similarly, a series of epigrams on two preachers whom Freeman dubs 'Tholus' and 'Rhombus' become very specific. He accuses Tholus of plagiarizing from the popular printed sermons of Henry Smith (Ep. 109),[78] and Rhombus with using those of Edwin Sandys, Archbishop of York, in the same way (Ep. 110). The two plagiarists are brought together in the next epigram:

> **In Rhombum & Tholum**
> I pray you sir, those two *that* preacht to day
> those learned men, whose liveries had they
> why Rhombus ware the Metropolitanes
> Tholus the parsons (sir) of Clement Danes,
> are preachers then allowed liveries[79]
> meddle not with them sir if you bee wise,
> cheefely with Rhombus, itt will not bee tooke
> for hee's a great man in th'Archbishops booke.[80]

A note at the bottom of the page explains the references: 'Edwin Sands his sermons in print and Mr Smiths commo*n* to most ministers as homo is a commo*n* name to al men.'[81] Second judgement and prudence would seem to have kept these explicit attacks out of the published collection. Scott-Warren notes a similar elimination of anti-Puritan epigrams when Harington's epigrams were printed by Budge in 1615 and 1618.[82] Such discretion on Freeman's part may have been prompted by an initial failure to obtain licence for the work: it is clear that this manuscript was prepared after some earlier attempt at publication failed, as it includes an 'Epigram 103', a poem that responds to a licenser's objections to Freeman's ribaldry.[83]

Also included in the manuscript is a striking epigram of savage outburst against a potential patron, with a tone quite unlike that found in Freeman's epigrams or in most others. The subject is spoken *to* rather than *about*, and the usual epigrammatic detachment is put aside in favour of bitter rage:

> **In monstrum horrendum etc. bilinguem assentatorem**[84]
> [On a dreadful monster and two-tongued flatterer]
> In troth I hate thee & I have great reason
> I find thee such a filthy double dealer
> pretending trust where thou intendest treason
> thy tongue is never thy harts true revealer
> thou Janus-face that with thy hot-cold breath
> fedst my Camelion hopes with idle aire
> thou Ambidexter, what still underneath
> shuffle above bord sirra and play faire
> leave (Jugling Jack a both sides) by these pranks
> to cheat mens good conceits for no desart
> to make them think thee kind, and conn thee thanks
> for promisd frendship found not worth a f—
> or run with th'Hare and follow with ye hound
> but seeke some other witts to worke upon
> with mee thy swe'test tunes will harshly sound
> I hate the man whose word and deed's not one
>   the Lapwings cry who list may listen to
>   my eares shall find them something else to doe.[85]

It is plausible that this poem addresses St Aubyn, who has disappointed Freeman's hope for patronage. The 'monster' has fed Freeman's 'Camelion hopes with idle aire' and betrayed him. 'Juggling jack', although not in Tilley, sounds like a proverbial phrase, but would also neatly fit St Aubyn's first name.

And what of the approximately ninety printed epigrams that do not appear in the Sloane manuscript? The better-known ones on other poets, such as Donne, Shakespeare and Heywood, are among those not in the manuscript (though it does include poems on Spenser and Owen). Also missing from the manuscript are poems of praise, such as the ones to the King that open the volume. Generally, it seems that epigrams of praise were usually later additions to an epigram book, meant to give it an air of balance, and this would explain the lack of such in this manuscript.

Thus, BL Sloane MS 1889 is simply one step in what must have been a long process of reworking and reordering the epigram collection, which, while parts were presented to St Aubyn and then Lord Windsor as gifts, also was clearly intended to eventually reach the print market. I would suggest that the most likely scenario is that Freeman produced a volume of epigrams in the late 1590s or early 1600s, during the first rush of printed epigram books in England, which he attempted unsuccessfully to have published as well. He then continued to write further epigrams, gave some to Lord Windsor and was finally successful in reaching print in the second flurry of epigram books in 1613–14. As with Harington, then, Freeman's collection of epigrams was a project that spanned many years, with the poet adapting his poems for new situations. However, Freeman's differed from Harington's in that publication seems to have been the ultimate authorial goal.

Case study: William Percy

William Percy (1574–1648), brother of Henry Percy, ninth Earl of Northumberland, wrote a significant body of unpublished epigrams.[86] While his surviving manuscript plays have attracted occasional scholarly attention over the years for their evidence of stage practices, the epigrams have been largely ignored. For the purposes of this study they are a rare resource in that two complete manuscripts survive, seemingly prepared by the poet himself.

As discussed in Chapter 3, Percy was part of the epigrammatic circles active at Oxford in the 1590s. He seems to have been educated at Gloucester Hall, Oxford, under the tutelage of Dr John Case, and from this scholar the epigram habit may have been developed.[87] As one associated with the Wheare circle, Percy wrote poems venerating the Michelborne brothers and took satisfaction in Fitzgeffry's epigram to him in *Affaniae*.[88] His exclusive use of English for his epigrams, however, sets him slightly apart from this circle. He made an early venture into print with his contribution to the sonnet craze of the early 1590s: *Sonnets to the Fairest Coelia* (1594). Seemingly, it was for this work that Percy was praised as a poet in the late 1590s: William Covell's *Polimanteia* includes Percy in his list of worthy Oxford poets,[89] and Charles Fitzgeffry refers to him as both Virgil and Maecenas, and 'Phaebo decori' [Phoebus' ornament].[90] However, such praise is hard to justify given the poor quality of both his sonnets and his very rough, amateurish epigrams.[91] In the epigrams, Percy repeatedly distorts grammar to achieve ten syllables per line, omits articles, leaves verb tenses incomplete, 'rhymes' on the same word, etc. They thus lack the hallmarks of the epigram as a form: polish and pointedness. Nor is there the consistent topicality that might have made a collection by a member of a significant noble family attract interest. Most are crude jests in cruder rhyme. Hence the chief value of the manuscripts is what they show about author-initiated collections of epigrams.

As the epigrams address figures and events of the 1590s and early 1600s, this would seem to be the likely time of composition, although a few reflect a French setting, and hence may stem from Percy's time in France in the mid-1580s. While Huntington MS 4 was produced in 1647, it is dated 1610 at the end of the epigrams section with the initials of 'W.P. Esq.'. The plays also seem to date from the late 1590s and early 1600s; *The Cuck-queanes* is dated 1601, and *The Faery Pastoral* given a date and location: '1603 Wolves Hill my Parnassus'.[92] ('Wolves Hill' was near the Percy family home at Petworth Manor, north-west of Horsham, Sussex.) Thus, the literary work preserved in these manuscripts seems to be that of a young nobleman at the university. However, the epigrams of Percy survive only in the two late manuscripts described below, and that there are no individual epigrams by him in manuscript miscellanies suggest that he did not circulate them widely around the time of their composition.

Although the poems and plays were written early in his life, the manuscripts all come from much later: the 1630s and 1640s. Whatever literary prominence Percy achieved in Oxford circles in the 1590s, this dissipated as the decades went on, and his life spiralled down into obscurity and relative poverty that led to occasional imprisonment for debt.[93] His fortunes at court were not helped by the complicity of his brother, Henry, the ninth Earl, in the Gunpowder Plot (1605). His time was divided between London and Oxford, but beyond that little is known of his activities through the early Stuart period. With the birth of his nephew, Algernon, in 1602, he was no longer heir to the earldom, although the illness of Algernon and his brother in the late 1630s did raise that possibility once more.[94] Beginning around that time, and continuing into the 1640s, Percy assiduously produced new manuscripts of his plays and poems, but it is not completely clear for what purpose. As Mark Nicholls colourfully puts it, 'What was the old fellow doing, in any event, scribbling away in a city blighted by war [Oxford], forever fiddling with the creative work of his youth?'[95] Thynne returned to the epigrams of his youth in order to foster a social relationship from the past, and Harington reworked earlier epigrams into appropriate gift collections; however, I will suggest that Percy's attempts were of a different nature: that in the mid-1640s, prompted by need and new opportunities, he was attempting to have his literary works belatedly print-published.

Percy's epigrams survive, with the plays, in Alnwick Castle MS F392 509 and Huntington MS 4.[96] The Alnwick manuscript, prepared in 1646, seems to be an earlier draft upon which the Huntington manuscript was based the following year.[97] Corrections and changes made in the Alnwick manuscript are found incorporated in the Huntington copy, and two epigrams added to the margins of Alnwick appear in a regular fashion in Huntington. However, there are also some corrections and marginal notes in Alnwick that are not included in Huntington, and in some cases the marginal corrections are actually carried over from one manuscript to the other.

In one epigram, the two manuscripts show some movement toward explicit topicality. For example, the Alnwick manuscript offers this general epigram on an executed man:

> When *Carbo* had berayne his hose, Before
> The Headsman could reave him of his Heade,
> > Supposing it a Flood, of lukewarme goare;
> > By that great *hand* of his, he fell down dead.

In the margin, next to the underlined name 'Carbo', is found 'Lopez'. This must be a reference to the Queen's physician, Roderigo Lopez, executed in 1594 for allegedly conspiring to poison the Queen. In the Huntington manuscript, the identification of the contemporary figure has been made explicit:

> When Lopez had berayne his hose, Before
> The Headsman could reave him of his Hed,
> > Supposing it a Flood of luke-warme goare,
> > By that greate hearte of his he fell down dead.[98]

A marginal note in both manuscripts then draws the comparison to the classical figure: 'The lyke is reade of Carbo the Roman in Plutarch'. It would seem that an epigram originally based on a classical story has been reapplied to a contemporary. The other possibility is a double change: that it was first written about Lopez, made less topical, and then restored to the original during Percy's 1640s preparation of the manuscripts. At the same time, most of the fictional names are maintained in the Alnwick manuscript by Percy, even though such would not seem politically necessary: the majority of those whom he mocked in the 1590s were likely dead by the time he was revising the epigrams in the 1640s.

The marginal notes in both manuscripts are of two types: those by the author to himself regarding changes, and those intended for a broader readership, as he considers additions or changes. The majority point toward an anticipated readership, one that might not be familiar with specialist terminology or words that are more obscure, some of northern origin, others particular to Oxford, and a few French words. Thus, epigram 205, 'Of Oxford selling Ale', plays on the word 'Caskshier', and Percy explains, 'To send furth in Caskes Caskshier for Cashier which is a Military word when they discard soldiers of a company, signifying to carry away their Town in a Barrill'.[99] Percy is also at pains to explain particularities of Oxford life to a broader audience: the marginal note to epigram 235 begins, 'Here in Oxford ...'.[100] And for the subsequent epigram, 'The Two Hookers', he explains, 'Hookers be a sort of Theeves in Oxford that hooke furth other mens clothes by lower chamber windowes, as they stand toward streete'.[101] Other notes identify the many classical references and reflect what Nicholls calls the 'element of pedantry' in Percy. There are also allusions to late medieval and Renaissance writers such as Chaucer, Rabelais and Spenser, and some of these are glossed by Percy.

Matthew Dimmock follows Patrick Kincaid in suggesting that Huntington MS 4 was a gift manuscript,[102] compiled while Percy 'was trapped in Royalist Oxford', and perhaps meant 'to gain favour in the exiled court'.[103] The problem with this theory is that, as Dimmock notes, this manuscript remained with the two other manuscript copies of the plays (Alnwick MS 508 and 509) until 1796.[104] Thus, a more likely explanation is that all three manuscripts were in the possession of Percy himself at the time of his death. Notes like that to 1:50, where he instructs, 'The word is Guarden not Garden', seem intended to prevent mistranscription or errors in press, directed to a scribe or printer, not a regular reader. Corrections and marginal notes like this are frequent in Huntington 4 and indicate that it was not a gift manuscript itself, but either preparatory to a

gift manuscript to be copied by a more polished scribe or a 1640s preparation for publication. Odd, however, is the number of unquestionable
errors that are not corrected by this hand. It thus may represent a rushed
and desperate attempt on Percy's part to extricate himself from dire poverty, turning to publication in the unsettled world of the 1640s.[105] Such
publication was common in the 1640s: the most famous case is probably
that of Robert Herrick, who, while writing short poems from the 1610s
on, finally published these in London in 1648, a time when he had lost
his church living, and found that his prospects were limited under parliamentary rule. It seems possible that Percy hoped to join these poets who
had found in publication 'a safe haven for their work and a sign of political
resistance to the authority of those who had defeated the king's forces'.[106]
However, Percy's death in Oxford on 28 May 1648 likely prevented the
attempted publication of his plays and epigrams.

Sir John Davies and Thomas Bastard

This chapter concludes with the first two English-language epigrammatists to turn to print in the 1590s: Sir John Davies and Thomas Bastard.
In spite of this step, the epigrams of both continued to have a significant
life in manuscript circulation as well. Davies's epigrams, first published
in a volume with Christopher Marlowe's version of Ovid's *Elegies* in the
mid-1590s, stand at the beginning of the wave of printed volumes that
began in the mid-1590s;[107] however, they were also popular in manuscript
circulation both before and after publication.[108] In most manuscripts they
are found alongside other material emerging from the Inns of Court in the
late 1590s. These same manuscripts often include epigrams by Rudyerd
mocking Davies under the name of 'Matho', and ones by the well-known
epigrammatist John Hoskins, Davies's friend at the Middle Temple.
Some of these manuscripts identify Davies as author, others not, and a
number of sequences of epigrams (on the marriages of Bishop Richard
Fletcher (1595) and Sir Edward Coke (1598)) have been tentatively added
to the Davies canon by Robert Krueger in his standard edition.[109] Overall,
while Davies ventured into print with the main body of his epigrams, he
clearly also continued to rely on manuscript circulation in the mid- to late
1590s. In this he stands in contrast to Jonson, whose epigram composition
began in the 1590s, but who strictly limited circulation of these before
their publication in the 1616 *Workes*.

Thomas Bastard published his *Chrestoleros: Seven Bookes of Epigrames*
(1598) early in the flurry of printed English epigram books, and fairly

soon after their composition: the datable poems in the collection are largely from 1595–97. At first, then, it might seem that his was a body of poems composed with publication in mind; however, it is clear that some enjoyed prior manuscript circulation, and not all epigrams ascribed to Bastard in manuscript appear in *Chrestoleros*. In addition, the evidence makes clear that at Oxford his epigrams continued to be known apart from their print publication. This circulation at Oxford seems similar to what E. A. J. Honigmann has suggested took place with Weever's epigrams at Cambridge at roughly the same time; that is, they circulated amongst a small academic audience that knew the identity of many of the figures mocked.[110]

Bastard suggests that his printed epigram book will circulate at Oxford, because of his already established reputation there:

> My booke, some handes in *Oxford* wil thee take,
> And beare thee home, and lovingly respect thee
> And entertaine thee for thy masters sake:
> And for thy masters sake some will reject thee.
> But to my faithfull friendes commend I thee.
> And to mine enemies, commend thou me.[111]

By the time of *Chrestoleros* Bastard had already achieved a scandalous reputation with his early 1590s libel on various Oxford figures (which came to be known simply as 'Bastard's Libel').[112] This led to the loss of his fellowship in 1591, and his departure from Oxford. Anthony à Wood, who describes him as 'guilty of the vices belonging to poets and given to libelling', offers this account of the work:

> he reflects upon all persons of note in *Oxon* that were guilty of amorous exploits, or that mixed themselves with other Mens Wives, or with wanton Huswives in *Oxon*. Another also, was made after his expulsion, wherein he disclaimeth the aforesaid Libel, beginning thus: *Jenkin why Man? Why Jenkin? fie for shame*, &c. But the Reader must know that none of these were printed.[113]

Such a reputation would have created an audience later in the decade for Bastard's epigrams, the publication of which may have been prompted by poverty-based desperation on Bastard's part.

Bastard's reputation as the epitome of the university epigrammatist is attested to by the play *The Pilgrimage to Parnassus* (ca. 1600), in which the character Madido boasts that he will outgo 'Bastardes Epigrams'.[114]

Similarly, Aurelia's quotation of the stoic concluding lines of Bastard's epigram 4:32 in John Marston's play *The Malcontent* (1604) shows the currency of his poems:

'Life is a frost of cold felicity,
And death the thaw of all our vanity.'
Was't not an honest priest that wrote so?[115]

However, this reference points toward a different aspect of Bastard: rather than the libellous poet, Bastard here is recalled as the wisdom-dispensing priestly epigrammatist.

That he was known through a continuing manuscript tradition is evident in William Twisse's *A Discovery of D. Iackson's vanitie* (1631), which cites his epigram 2:22. The poem appears in *Chrestoleros* thus:

I Mett a courtier riding on the plaine,
Well mounted on a brave and gallant steede;
I sate a jade, and spurred to my paine,
My lazy beast whose tyred sides did bleede,
He sawe my case; and then of courtesie,
Did reyne his horse, and drewe the bridle in
Because I did desire his companie:
But he corvetting way of me doth winne.
What should I doe which was besteaded so?
His horse stoode still faster then mine could go.

However, it is recalled by Twisse some thirty years later as describing an encounter specifically 'on Sarisbury plaine', and the second-last line is reproduced as 'What shold I doe that was bestrided so'.[116] 'Bestrided' makes sense where 'besteaded' does not; hence the latter must have been a printer's error, and Twisse must be reproducing the original that he had seen somewhere other than in the printed edition. Although a decade or so younger, Twisse followed Bastard's path from Winchester College to New College, Oxford, arriving there in 1596, just before the publication of *Chrestoleros*. Thus, he was in a position to have access to Bastard's poems in manuscript. (He was also nephew to the epigrammatist Hoskins.) Ironically, this epigram was then drawn from Twisse's book by Archbishop William Sancroft in 1675, cited with approval, and translated into Latin. Sancroft notes, 'Who this Bastard was I know not: But ye subject of ye Epigram is (me thinks) legitimate, & genuine; & yᵉ sting at last poinant [*sic*] enough: & it past easily into these lat. verses.'[117] This example also serves as an illustration of the continuing life of an epigram, even as its author fades from cultural memory. Similarly, Robert Bishop's manuscript miscellany (compiled in 1630–31) includes a number of Bastard's poems with variants that suggest a continuing manuscript circulation of the poet at Oxford some thirty years later.[118] Such is also found in Folger MS V.a.345 (discussed above),[119] which dates from approximately 1630. It reflects an Oxford provenance and preserves a number of variant readings that would not seem to come from the printed book. Finally, the deeply Oxford-rooted Anthony à Wood, writing in the 1680s, points to manuscript evidence, not the printed *Chrestoleros*, when he celebrates Bastard's accomplishments in the epigram form: 'He was a most excellent Epigrammatist, and being always ready to versifie upon any subject, did let nothing material escape his fancy, as his compositions running through several hands in MS. shew'.[120]

Notes

1 May, 'On Manuscripts', *Epigrams Divine and Moral* (1633), Ep. 2:5.

2 See Hobbs, *Early Seventeenth-Century Verse Miscellany Manuscripts*, Eckhardt, *Manuscript Verse Collectors* and Marotti, *Manuscript, Print, and the English Renaissance Lyric*. For a historical overview of scholarship on miscellanies, see the working paper by Joshua Eckhardt, 'Verse Miscellanies in Print and Manuscript: A Book Historiography' at *Verse Miscellanies Online*, www.academia.edu/3623473/_Verse_Miscellanies_in_Print_and_Manuscript_A_Book_Historiography_.

3 Woodhuysen, *Sir Philip Sidney and the Circulation of Manuscripts*, pp. 163–7.

4 See, for example, Rosenbach MS 187, ed. David C. Redding, as 'Robert Bishop's Commonplace Book: An Edition of a Seventeenth-Century Miscellany', PhD, University of Pennsylvania, 1960.

5 See Marcy L. North, 'Amateur Compilers, Scribal Labour, and the Contents of Early Modern Poetic Miscellanies', *English Manuscript Studies 1100–1700*, 16 (2011), pp. 82–111. Joel Swann also helpfully distinguishes between ad hoc and seriatim transcribing in 'Copying Epigrams in Manuscript Miscellanies', in Joshua Eckhardt and Daniel Starza-Smith (eds), *Manuscript Miscellanies in Early Modern England* (Farnham: Ashgate, 2014), pp. 151–68.

6 Folger MS V.a.345 (ca. 1630), p. 9.

7 Martial, Ep. 13:4.

8 Stradling, *Epigrammatum libri quatuor*, Ep. 2:108 [trans. Sutton].

9 Martial (1:107), in Luke Roman, 'The Representation of Literary Materiality

in Martial's *Epigrams*', *Journal of Roman Studies*, 91 (2001), pp. 113–45, p. 141.

10 John Stradling, BL Add. MS 73542, fol. 1v.

11 Trinity College Library, Cambridge, James MS 767 (8); R.7.23; this has been published as Nicholas Poole-Wilson (ed.), *John Owen's Epigrams for Prince Henry: The Text of the Presentation Manuscript in the Library of Trinity College Cambridge* (London: Bernard Quaritch, 2012).

12 Poole-Wilson, *John Owen's Epigrams for Prince Henry*, p. [5].

13 The most thorough account of Thynne and his manuscripts is David Carlson, 'The Writings and Manuscript Collections of the Elizabethan Alchemist, Antiquary, and Herald Francis Thynne', *HLQ*, 52 (1989), pp. 203–72.

14 An edition was printed from the manuscript by F. J. Furnivall: *Emblemes and Epigrames*, EETS, old series 64 (London, 1876). All quotations are from this edition.

15 Francis Thynne, in Carlson, 'The Writings and Manuscript Collections', p. 234.

16 *DNB*.

17 Carlson, 'The Writings and Manuscript Collections', pp. 2–3.

18 Carlson, 'The Writings and Manuscript Collections', p. 3.

19 Furnivall, *Emblemes and Epigrames*, p. 1.

20 Furnivall, *Emblemes and Epigrames*, p. 2.

21 Carlson, 'The Writings and Manuscript Collections', pp. 214–15.

22 F. J. Furnivall (ed.), in Francis Thynne, *Animadversions uppon the annotacions and corrections of some imperfections of impressiones of Chaucers workes*, EETS, old series, 9 (1875; Rpt London: Oxford University Press, 1965), p. cii.

23 Scott-Warren has explored this well in *Sir John Harington and the Book as Gift*.

24 Harington, Kilroy ed., p. 75. The date derives from Stradling's own poem that mentions them (*Epigrammatum libri quatuor*).

25 Harington, *Nugae Antiquae*, vol. 1, pp. 172–3.

26 The fullest description of the manuscripts is found in Kilroy's edition, pp. 67–73.

27 Sir John Harington, in Scott-Warren, *Sir John Harington and the Book as Gift*, p. 147.

28 Harington, in Scott-Warren, *Sir John Harington and the Book as Gift*, p. 147.

29 Harington, in Scott-Warren, *Sir John Harington and the Book as Gift*, p. 147.

30 Scott-Warren, *Sir John Harington and the Book as Gift*, p. 151.

31 Scott-Warren, *Sir John Harington and the Book as Gift*, p. 153.

32 This manuscript (Cambridge MS UL Adv. B.8.1) is printed in Sir John

Harington, *Epigrams for Lady Rogers*, ed. Simon and Ben Cauchi (Wellington: Pharaoh, 1992).

33 Harington, *Epigrams for Lady Rogers*, p. 3.

34 Scott-Warren, *Sir John Harington and the Book as Gift*, pp. 99–134.

35 Scott-Warren, *Sir John Harington and the Book as Gift*, p. 199.

36 Scott-Warren, *Sir John Harington and the Book as Gift*, p. 198.

37 Harington, 'To James the sixt, king of Scotland', Kilroy ed., p. 94.

38 Prince Henry was also the recipient of a gift manuscript of a selection of Owen's Latin epigrams in 1610 (*John Owen's Epigrams for Prince Henry*).

39 Sir John Harington, *The Letters and Epigrams of Sir John Harington*, ed. Norman Egbert McClure (Philadelphia, PA: University of Pennsylvania Press, 1930), p. 126.

40 Jean Humez, 'The Manners of Epigram: A Study of the Epigram Volumes of Martial, Harington, and Jonson', PhD, Yale University, 1971, pp. 204–5.

41 Scott-Warren, *Sir John Harington and the Book as Gift*, p. 141; Humez, 'The Manners of Epigram'.

42 Scott-Warren, *Sir John Harington and the Book as Gift*, p. 142.

43 Kilroy notes that a copy of this poem in the papers of the recusant Sir Thomas Tresham is given the date 16 July 1603. It is one of three epigrams under the group heading 'Verses Temp. Eliz'. I would thus see it as part of the careful re-articulation of the death of Mary Stuart that went on in the early months of her son's English reign.

44 Gerard Kilroy, *Edmund Campion: Memory and Transcription* (Aldershot: Ashgate, 2005), p. 96.

45 Kilroy, *Edmund Campion*, p. 100.

46 Kilroy, *Edmund Campion*, p. 107.

47 Kilroy, *Edmund Campion*, p. 105.

48 Kilroy, *Edmund Campion*, p. 107.

49 Kilroy, *Edmund Campion*, p. 212.

50 We do know that there was one, as Harington refers back to it in his *Supplie* (*Nugae Antiquae*, vol. 2, p. 44).

51 Scott-Warren, *Sir John Harington and the Book as Gift*, p. 213.

52 Scott-Warren, *Sir John Harington and the Book as Gift*, pp. 204–10.

53 Theresa M. DiPasquale, 'Donne's Epigrams: A Sequential Reading', *Modern Philology*, 104 (2007), pp. 329–78. More detailed information and tables about Donne's manuscript epigrams can be found in *The Variorum Edition of the Poetry of John Donne*, ed. Gary A. Stringer et al. (Bloomington, IN: Indiana University Press, 1995), vol. 8, pp. 14–84.

54 DiPasquale, 'Donne's Epigrams', p. 369.

55 DiPasquale, 'Donne's Epigrams', p. 371.

56 Peter Beal, *Index of English Literary Manuscripts, Volume 1, Part 2* (London: Mansell, 1980–93), p. 124.

57 Redding, 'Robert Bishop's Commonplace Book', p. 51.

58 Redding, 'Robert Bishop's Commonplace Book', p. 51.

59 Redding, 'Robert Bishop's Commonplace Book', p. 19. He also notes that Folger 2071.7, p. 275, has 'A couplet or two fastened to Sr Jo: harrington his Epigram, to doe his Townes knight yeomans service?'.

60 Davies of Hereford, *Wits Bedlam*, Ep. 53.

61 Harington, *Epigrams for Lady Rogers*, Ep. 3:43.

62 This pairing appears in Rosenbach MS 187, p. 146; Bodl. Malone MS 19, p. 40; Bodl. Ashmole MS 36, 37, fol. 145. The 'basilisk's eye' epigram also appears in Folger MS V.a.162, fol. 35v.

63 4.4.116–77 in *Poems and Dramas*, ed. G. Bullough, 2 vols (Edinburgh: Oliver and Boyd, 1939). Variants of the poem are also found in Bodl. Ashmole MS 36,37, fol. 145; Bodl. Eng. poet. MS e.14, fol. 89v; Bodl. Eng. poet. MS e.97, p. 114; Bodl. Tanner MS 169, fol. 43; Folger MS V.a.162, fol. 35v; Rosenbach MS 187, p. 146.

64 Fulke Greville (see *Mustapha*, 1609), in Jason Scott-Warren, 'Reconstructing Manuscript Networks: The Textual Transactions of Sir Stephen Powle', in Alexandra Shephard and Phil Withington (eds), *Communities in Early Modern England: Networks, Place, Rhetoric* (Manchester: Manchester University Press, 2000), p. 27.

65 The 'Skipwith manuscript' (BL Add. MS. 25707) is actually a gathering of 'five separate collections and some loose papers' rather than a unified manuscript (Hobbs, *Early Seventeenth Century Verse Miscellany Manuscripts*, p. 62). It is not clear whether Sir William Skipwith himself compiled the manuscript before his death in 1610, or if it was done by another family member later.

66 Hobbs, *Early Seventeenth-Century Verse Miscellany Manuscripts*, p. 67. On the tendency to overlook how many manuscript miscellanies are in fact later constructions, see Jonathan Gibson, 'Synchrony and Process: Editing Manuscript Miscellanies', *SEL*, 52 (2012), pp. 85–100.

67 Bordesley Abbey near Redditch on the border of Worcestershire and Warwickshire had been the main family estate since the reign of Henry VIII (*DNB*, 'Windsor, Thomas, sixth Baron Windsor 1590–1641').

68 This raises serious doubts about the *DNB* identification of the epigrammatist as the Thomas Freeman born in Burton-on-Water, Gloucestershire in 1590. I would suggest that the Thomas Freeman, 'of Oxon., gent. Magdalen Hall, matric. 23 Apr. 1585, aged 16' is a more likely candidate.

69 BL Sloane MS 1889, fol. 32r, Ep. 151.

70 Brian Bailey, *Hangmen of England* (London: W. H. Allen, 1989), p. 5, suggests that Thomas Derrick was 'active from around 1598 to 1610', and that his role began when Essex (Robert Devereux) had saved him from death after a conviction for rape on a military expedition in France.

71 BL Sloane MS 1889, fol. 32r, Ep. 1:66. In the printed volume the poem is entitled: 'In pestem, Oxonium a duobus Gallis allatum anno. 1609'. The title in manuscript is similar, but the date is cropped (fol. 21r).

72 BL Sloane MS 1889, fol. 32r, Ep. 1:29.

73 Sir John St Aubyn of Clowance (near Penzance in Cornwall), d. 1639, m. Katherine Arundell (1604); he became Recorder of Penzance in 1620, Sheriff of Cornwall in 1635; Diana Hartley, *The St. Aubyns of Cornwall, 1200–1977* (Chesham: Barracuda, 1977), pp. 28 and 106. He also served as MP for the county of Cornwall in 1614, and for the borough of Mitchell in Cornwall in 1620–21. Like a number of other epigrams, this points to Thomas Freeman's residence (if not origins) in the extreme western part of Cornwall.

74 'To John St. Aubyn, armiger of Cornwall, who had requested from him those further epigrams he wrote', in BL Sloane MS 1889, fol. 32r.

75 Fol. 26r, Ep. 122.

76 Arundel entered the Middle Temple in 1594, St Aubyn in 1597.

77 Fol. 11v, Ep. [58]. The reference to Banbury is likely to the 1600 destruction of the market crosses. See Alexandra Walsham, *The Reformation of the Landscape: Religion, Identity, and Memory in Early Modern Britain and Ireland* (Oxford: Oxford University Press, 2011), p. 120.

78 On the sermons of Henry Smith, priest of St Clement Danes, 1587–90, see Walter R. Davis, 'Henry Smith; the Preacher as Poet', *ELR*, 12 (1982), pp. 30–52.

79 I assume these were chaplains of Abp Edwin Sandys and Henry Smith.

80 Fol. 11v, Ep. 111.

81 Smith died in 1591; his sermons were printed that year with many subsequent editions. Sandys died in 1588; his sermons were published in 1585 with a subsequent edition in 1616.

82 Scott-Warren, *Sir John Harington and the Book as Gift*, p. 199n.

83 This poem and its reflection on the licensing procedure are discussed in Chapter 6.

84 Fol. 28r.

85 Fol. 28r., Ep. 130.

86 William Percy (ninth Earl of Northumberland), in Alnwick Castle (Duke of Northumberland) MS F392 509; Huntington MS 4. Of these plays, *The Cuck-queanes* was printed by Joseph Haslewood in 1824, and recently Matthew Dimmock has produced an edition of *Mahomet and His Heaven*

(Aldershot: Ashgate, 2006). A number of theses have also produced edited versions of the plays: *A fforest tragedye in Vacunium*, ed. Caroline Elizabeth Jameson, PhD, University of Birmingham, 1972; *William Percy's Arabia Sitiens*, ed. Clayton Joseph Burns, PhD, University of New Brunswick, 1984. See also Patrick Kincaid, 'John Marston's *The Dutch Courtesan* and William Percy's *The Cuck-Queanes and Cuckolds Errants*', *Notes and Queries*, new series, 48 (2001), pp. 309–11.

87 Among Percy's epigrams is one 'To Mr Dr C. on his Epigramme to mee' (Ep. 3).

88 Huntington, MS 4, Ep. 350.

89 William Covell, *Polimanteia, or, The meanes lawfull and vnlawfull, to iudge of the fall of a common-wealth, against the friuolous and foolish coniectures of this age* (1595), sig. Q3v. Percy's only published work had been from very early in his life, the collection *Sonnets to the Fairest Coelia* (1594).

90 Fitzgeffry, *Affaniae*, Ep. 2:4 [trans. Sutton]. Barnabe Barnes dedicated his 1593 *Parthenophil and Parthenophe* to Percy.

91 Percy, *Sonnets to the Fairest Coelia*, Ep. 1:3.

92 Huntington MS 4, 1647 [1610], p. 190.

93 Harold N. Hillenbrand, 'William Percy: An Elizabethan Amateur', *HLQ*, 1 (1938), pp. 391–416.

94 Hillenbrand, 'William Percy', p. 399.

95 Mark Nicholls, 'The Enigmatic William Percy', *HLQ*, 70 (2007), pp. 469–77, p. 472. While this article is a review essay of Dimmock's edition of *Mahomet and His Heaven*, it provides the most sustained discussion of Percy's epigrams available. See also his 'Lavatory Humour: Two Epigrams Addressed to Sir John Harington', *Notes and Queries*, 51:3 (2004), pp. 303–4.

96 Another manuscript (Alnwick 508), dated 1644, contains some of the plays, but not Percy's epigrams. It does, however, reproduce 'Buckley's Libel' and 'Bastard's Libel', on the same early 1590s Oxford scene from which most of Percy's own epigrams emerge. These too are annotated by Percy.

97 Nicholls, 'The Enigmatic William Percy', p. 473.

98 Huntington MS 4.

99 Huntington MS 4.

100 Huntington MS 4, Ep. 325.

101 Huntington MS 4, Ep. 236

102 Patrick Kincaid, p. 105, in Dimmock, *Mahomet and His Heaven*, p. 48.

103 Dimmock, *Mahomet and His Heaven*, p. 48n.

104 Dimmock, *Mahomet and His Heaven*, p. 48n.

105 On Percy's financial affairs, see M. Hope Dodds, 'The Financial Affairs of a Jacobean Gentleman', *Archaeologia Aeliana*, fourth series. vol. xxii

(Newcastle, 1944), pp. 91–109, and Mark Nicholls, '"As Happy a Fortune as I Desire": The Pursuit of Financial Security by the Younger Brothers of Henry Percy, 9th Earl of Northumberland', *Historical Research*, 65 (1992), pp. 296–314.

106 Marotti, *Manuscript, Print, and the English Renaissance Lyric*, p. 259.

107 Given that the place of publication and date of *Epigrammes and elegies. By I.D. and C.M.* cannot be conclusively fixed, it is not surprising that there is no scholarly consensus on whether Davies had planned the publication of his epigrams. See Susanna Hop, '"What Fame Is This?" John Davies's *Epigrammes* in Late Elizabethan London', *Renaissance Journal*, 2 (2005), pp. 29–42, for a recent discussion. She argues for a Middle Temple context for the Marlowe/Davies publication, and that some of the epigrams were written as late as 1598.

108 Woodhuysen, *Sir Philip Sidney and the Circulation of Manuscripts*, p. 167.

109 Robert Krueger (ed.), *Poems of Sir John Davies* (Oxford: Clarendon Press, 1975), pp. 169–79.

110 Honigmann, *John Weever*, pp. 15–17.

111 Bastard, 'Ad Librum suum', in *Chrestoleros*, Ep. 4:3.

112 This libel survives in the Crawford manuscript, Rosenbach MS 186 (now MS 1083/15), fol. 45v–49r, from which it is produced with extensive notes in Sanderson, *An Edition of an Early Seventeenth-Century Manuscript Collection of Poems*, pp. 440–70. It also appears in Bodl MS.CCC.327, fol. 17v; Bodl. Gough MS misc. antiq. 11, fol. 81; and Bodl. Rawl. poet. MS 212, fol. 123v.

113 Wood, *Athenae Oxonienses* (1691), p. 368. The second poem cited by Wood survives in Bodl. Add. MS B.97, fol. 5. See James L. Sanderson, 'Thomas Bastard's Disclaimer of an Oxford Libel', *The Library*, fifth series, 17 (1962), pp. 145–9.

114 J. B. Leishman (ed.), *The Three Parnassus Plays (1598–1601)* (London: Nicholson & Watson, 1949), vol. 2, pp. 208–12.

115 Bastard, in M. L. Wine (ed.), *The Malcontent* (Lincoln, NE: University of Nebraska Press, 1964), 5.6.44–6.

116 William Twisse, *A Discovery of D. Iackson's vanitie* (1631), p. 216.

117 'To Dr. Wm. Dillingham from Bernes Jan. 24, 1676', Bodl. Sancroft MS 48, fol. 30r. Strangely, Sancroft renders the second-last line 'What sho*uld* I do *that* was besteeded so?'; 'besteed' is not in the *OED*, but makes a sort of sense.

118 Redding, *Robert Bishop's Commonplace Book*. While little definite is known of Bishop, the selections in his miscellany heavily reflect an Oxford context of the 1610s and 1620s (Redding, p. xlviii). This volume also includes an epigram by Bastard that does not appear in *Chrestoleros*. Entitled, 'Tho

Bastard on himselfe having lost his money at the Rackett court', it begins, 'Take up thy Gowne poore Tom, & get thee hence' (p. 245). Redding notes that the poem also appears in Corpus Christi College MS 328, fol. 86v.

119 Folger MS V.a.345, pp. 50–1.
120 Wood, *Athenae Oxoniensis*, vol. 1, p. 367.

6

Epigrams in print

Given that some significant and widely known epigrammatists of the 1590s (Harington, Hoskins, the Michelborne brothers) had achieved fame through manuscript circulation alone, why did others decide to appear in print? And why print publish those individual epigrams whose moment of topical relevance was years in the past? The justification for publishing in these circumstances might be broken down into the 'high' and the 'low' defence. The 'high' defence, alluded to already in Chapter 1, claimed the model of Martial for justification: he had allowed his epigrams to be 'published', in the sense of wide and deliberate distribution of large collections of poems. His precedent, for example, is explicitly adopted by Thomas Campion, who complains of those elitist readers who 'taste nothing that comes forth in Print, as if *Catullus* or *Martials* Epigrammes were the worse for being published'.[1] Beyond these classical precedents, this 'high defence' argued that the individual poems might be insignificant, but that as larger collections the epigram books were noteworthy, and that print ensured continuing fame. Those poets who included epigrams of praise might also see print as broadening the deserved praise of their subjects. The 'low' arguments in support of print publication ranged from a widening of the audience for satiric correction to sheer indifference or financial need. Like all poets of the time, the epigrammatist could expect very limited return: at one point Bastard suggests that the Printer 'buyes my Epigrams at pence a peece'.[2]

The public justification for print was not necessarily the same as the motivation to adopt it. However, once again the figure of Martial is significant: that his epigrams were still known fifteen hundred years later and inviolably bound up with the author himself suggested to English epigrammatists that deliberate authorial publication was the means to poetic fame. Even more than the manuscript publication of Martial's time, the permanence and stability of print seemed to have made it attractive to those authors of the first volumes of the late 1590s. Epigram books themselves provide evidence of resistance to the oral circulation of their contents, and the desire to keep their work distinct from such predominantly oral forms as the jest, the proverbial couplet and the libellous political distich. Printing poems under the author's name established ownership and rescued them from melding with the anonymous flow of popular oral and manuscript epigrams discussed in Chapter 4.[3] The printed word, unlike the spoken, offered to these ambitious poets a longer, perhaps even immortal, life. As one of Owen's books of epigrams concludes,

Sit Verbum Vox viva licet, Vox mortua Scriptum;
  Scripta diu vivunt, non ita verba diu.

[Though words be living voices, writings dead,
Yet these survive, when those are vanished.][4]

The poem enjoys the paradox of the 'dead' written form ensuring future life.

Often epigrams were published only years after composition. While this sometimes stemmed from a poet waiting for a sufficient number of epigrams to make up a 'century' or more, in other cases changing political circumstances finally made the publication of topical epigrams safe. The objects of satiric attack are no longer living, or at least no longer powerful. Such is the case with Henry Parrot's *Cures for the Itch*, published two years after composition, with the accession of Charles I in between. Parrot writes in the preface,

It is now almost two yeares expired when (living in the Country that long Vacation) I wrote these Epigrams, and Epitaphs adjoining, which then, nor since I would consent (nor was it fit indeed they should bee published) till now on times more prosperous opportunity.[5]

Sheer desperation from falling on hard times (as I suggested was possible with Percy in Chapter 5) may also explain a movement into print: Herrick's epigrams (and other poems) were published as *Hesperides* when his personal circumstances radically changed because of the Civil Wars. Up until that point he seems to have kept them close; Ann Baynes Coiro notes that 'not one of Herrick's brief epigrams appears in a manuscript before the publication of *Hesperides*, whereas 39 lyric poems … appear over and over again'.[6] She concludes from this that they were composed relatively late in his career, but at least as probable is that they were earlier poems, kept back by Herrick with some eye to later publication.

Stradling's book of Latin epigrams reflects this unease in a different way; as he writes in his epigram to 'the Honourable Reader' (1:121), 'To sell the treasures of one's wit is a sordid thing, but it would be foolish to scatter them everywhere for free. Do you wish to make a swap with me, candid reader? I give you the poems, you give me your good words.'[7] This epigram is a fascinating mixture of the pragmatic and idealistic: the first part recognizes the inevitability of circulation, and hence accepts print as a more efficient and controlled approach, by which at least the author will actually gain something; however, the following lines deny the usual reward for printing – money – and turns away from the marketplace back to the world of gift-giving. A similar tension between the marketplace and gift culture is evident in the next poem: here Stradling addresses the printer, who hopes that the poems please many, while Stradling wants them only to please a few.

The flurry of the 1590s and the Bishops' Ban

The 1590s fashion of epigram composition led to a spate of published single-author collections towards the end of that decade. While Campion's *Poemata* (1595) included a significant body of Latin epigrams, the first collection whose title identified it as principally a book of epigrams was Bastard's *Chrestoleros: Seven Bookes of Epigrams*, which was entered in the Stationers' Register on 3 April 1598. Throughout this volume, Bastard manifests a degree of self-consciousness about the status of epigrams, and the boldness of his decision to publish his. As he concedes to his dedicatee, Charles Blount, eighth Baron Mountjoy, epigrams are 'a scarse worke: they have ever had but fewe writers, and yet too many'[8] (by 'scarse' he might either mean 'rare' or 'limited in size and scope'). Some five months later appeared Guilpin's *Skialetheia:or, A shadowe of truth, in certaine epigrams and satyres* (1598),[9] and the next year saw a continuing of this trend of printed epigrams, with Weever's *Epigrammes in the Oldest Cut, and Newest Fashion* (which was not entered in the Stationers' Register). It may also be no coincidence that 1598 saw a republication of Heywood's epigrams, which had last appeared in his 1587 *Woorkes*.

This run of publication coincided with the intense period of satire publication, by such writers as John Marston and Joseph Hall, and there was a degree of overlap between the two genres. Guilpin's volume combined both genres in one publication, and the anonymous *Tyros Roring Megge* (1598) entitled its twenty poems 'epigrams', but in their length and narrative approach they are more like satires. These sister genres of epigram and satire were named together in the 'Bishops' Ban' of 1599.[10] Issued by Whitgift, the Archbishop of Canterbury, and Bancroft, the Bishop of London, on 1 June, the ban called for the destruction of a number of named works (including Guilpin's *Skialetheia* and Sir John Davies's epigrams) and ordered 'That noe Satyres or Epigramms be printed hereafter'.[11] Unlike the orders against histories and plays in the same document, the ban on satires and epigrams was complete, not allowing any provision for pre-publication licensing of them. Richard McCabe has argued convincingly that the suppression of satiric libel, rather than obscenity, was the chief goal of the Ban – of course epigrams were frequently guilty on both counts of obscenity and libel. Cyndia Susan Clegg, noting the close relationship between the Earl of Essex and Whitgift, suggests that Essex might have encouraged the ban in response to satiric attacks upon him.[12] The ban was of limited success: Cliff Forshaw notes that both the bishops and the Stationers' Company largely ignored the ban soon after it was enacted, and that it in fact 'ironically gave a new lease of life to formal verse satire',[13] and Honigmann has shown that Weever's *Epigrammes* were published shortly after June 1599, hence in direct defiance of the ban.[14] His conservative didacticism may have allowed him to evade the ban.[15]

While the ban certainly did not fully stop the phenomenon, it may have added to the negative associations of the term 'epigram', and led to epigram books being published that masked their genre. Robert Joyner's *Itys, or three severall boxes of sporting familiars* (*SR* entry 13 Nov. 1598) offers short ribald satiric poems that the prefatory poem clearly identifies as epigrams hidden under another name:

> To speake troth, thy Familiars are nipping grams.
> Yet doe thou conceale, that they be Epigrams.
> *Agrippa* (who knewe Arte Magike forbidden,
> Saide, he wrote but of Phylosophie hidden.
> When a trade is bad, give it a new name,
> And with credit, then one may use the same.
> Epigrams as obscaene [*sic*] vearse each one hates,
> Say then thy vearses are familiar mates.[16]

These 120 'familiars' are epigrams in all but name, sharing all the genre's general features. Similarly, Samuel Rowlands published a series of volumes of epigram-like poems, beginning in 1600 with *The Letting of Humour's Blood in the Head-Vein.*[17] This work was allowed, but then shortly after publication ordered to be burned, and the booksellers fined for carrying it.[18] Fitzgeffry's *Affaniae* (1601) may also have been so titled to mask the clear reality that the poems were in fact epigrams.

The avoidance of the term in the years immediately following the ban is reflected on the title pages of the two editions of Francis Davison's *A Poetical Rapsodie*. The first publication in 1602 was noted in a letter of Chamberlain: 'Young Davison has turned poet, and set out certain sonnets and epigrams.'[19] However, despite Chamberlain's recognition of the epigram-like quality of some of the poems, that first edition made no mention of 'epigrams' on the title page, listing instead simply 'diverse sonnets, odes, elegies, madrigalls, and other poesies, both in rime, and measured verse'.[20] Within the volume itself there is one poem in which 'epigram' appears in the title and a group of poems in 'Phaleuciaks', the eleven-syllable metre often associated with epigrams in the Neo-Latin tradition. However, the next edition of 1608 lists on its title page, 'diverse sonnets, odes, elegies, madrigals, epigrams, pastorals, eglogues, with other poems', and a dozen 'Epigrams translated out of Martiall', and ten original epigrams signed 'F.D.' (presumably Davison's) have been added.

After Weever's book, the term 'epigram' did not appear in the title of a printed volume again until 1602, when it figured in the subtitle of Nicholas Bourman's *An epitaph upon the decease of the worshipfull Lady Mary Ramsey ... Wherevnto is annexed certaine short epigrams, touching the mortalitie of man.* The epigrams included were as advertised: they were a handful of short innocuous poems of a moralistic nature that contravened the ban only in word, not spirit. The next substantial body of satiric epigrams to identify themselves as such on the title page was *Epigrames Serued out in 52. seuerall dishes for euery man to tast without surfeting. By I.C. Gent.* The publication bears no date on the title page, but was entered in the Stationers' Register on 22 May 1604.[21] By 1606-7 any lingering effect of the Bishops' Ban on epigrams seems to have disappeared completely: in that year two prominent Latin collections, by Owen and Stradling, included the Latin form of 'Epigram' on their title pages.[22] Overall, then, the effect of the Bishops' Ban was to limit the entitling of poems as epigrams for the first few years after 1599, but even this effect waned as the years went on. In contrast to the 1590s, when Davies, Weever and *Tyros Roring Megge* were all published outside the usual framework controlling printing, all English-language epigram books of the first decade of the 1600s were entered in the Stationers' Register.

A second intensive period of epigram publication came about in 1613–15, at which time Humphrey King noted that epigrams, along with satires and essays, 'swarm' the press.[23] In these years a number of major epigram volumes appeared: Gamage, *Linsi-woolsie or two centuries of epigrammes* (1613), John Cooke, *Alcilia* (1613), Freeman, *Rubbe, and a great cast* (1614), Richard Niccols, *The Furies. With Vertues Encomium. Or, The Immage of Honour. In two Bookes of Epigrammes, Satyricall and Encomiasticke* (1614), two volumes by Parrot, William Goddard's *Neste of Waspes* (1615) and, most significantly, the first printed edition of Harington in 1615, along with the major gathering of epigrams in Jonson's *Workes* in 1616. Unlike the earlier flurry of epigrams in the late 1590s, there seem to have been few legal problems with the printing of epigrams at this time.

The one exception may be Freeman's volume, which has no printer identified on its title page, although it was entered on 30 June 1614 to Thomas Montforde [or Mountforde], who had just become clerk of the Stationers' Company. As there is no other surviving work entered to him, there may be something irregular about the printing of *Rubbe, and a great cast*. The *STC* identifies it as printed by Nicholas Okes for Lawrence Lisle; in the same year, the latter was responsible for printing Christopher Brooke's *Ghost of Richard III*, Overbury's *Characters* and Overbury's *Wife*, which suggests that he had a willingness to take on controversial work.

Printing formats

While Kathryn Perry suggests that unbound quarto was the most likely format for this type of verse,[24] in fact the majority of epigram volumes from the 1590s to 1610s were in octavo. The books of Weever, Sir John Davies, Guilpin, Bastard, Heath, Gamage, Niccols and Henry Fitzgeffry were all in octavo; although the first (1615) edition of Harington was in quarto, later editions were also in octavo. Freeman's were in quarto, as were the majority by Rowlands and Parrot, but there was also one (*Laquei ridiculosi*) in sextodecimo, and one (*Cures for the Itch*) in octavo. Jonson's epigrams, published not as a free-standing volume but as a section of his folio *Workes* (1616) is the great exception and clearly aspired to a well-off and significant audience. Owen's Latin epigram collections are outliers, being consistently in duodecimo. Marotti notes a tendency to epigram books (including selections of Jonson and More) in the smaller forms in the late 1630s and 1640s.[25]

Gamage comments on the hierarchy of printing format in his second-last epigram:

To his friend the *Printer* of his Booke
Some volumes bring in folio to thy presse,
In quarto some, according to their lore;
'Mongst all the learned, I which am the lesse,
One in octavo bring thee, all my store.
I'le it not fould in sexto decimo,
Least, as the Tome, his count,[26] as little, grow.
    Respect the paper, though a pen'worth small;
    'Twill sixe for one cert's [*sic*] yeeld thee at thy stall.[27]

He admits his humble status of octavo, but fears that anything smaller would be even less esteemed. Either quarto or octavo was relatively cheap: there are repeated references in epigram books themselves to the price of sixpence.[28] Perry suggests that they were the sort of small, inexpensive volumes that might end up in a 'chapman's pack'.

Epigrammatic ambivalence about print

With the more widespread production in the first two decades of the seventeenth century of 'down-market' epigram books that lacked the literary polish and ambition of Davies, Bastard, Guilpin and Weever, a certain discomfort about the print market sets in.[29] This anxiety worked itself out in different ways: Henry Fitzgeffrey washed his hands of his epigrams as they entered the print marketplace, opening his collection with this observation:

These Epigrams thou see'st whose are they? mine!
No! The Book-binders: buy them, they are thine.[30]

His first satire mocks the advancing into print of a range of would-be poets, but is especially critical of epigrammatists – the competitors, of course, with his own work:

Springes for Woodcockes: Doctor Merriman:
    Rub and a good Cast: Taylor *the Ferriman.*
    Fennor, *with his* Unisounding Eare word;
    The unreasonable Epigramatist of Hereford:

> Rowland *with his* Knaves' *a murnivall*
> *Not worth the calling for, a fire burne em all.*[31]

The volumes of Rowland, Taylor, Parrot and Fennor tend toward the 'down-market', and Fitzgeffrey is at pains to condemn Freeman and Davies of Hereford, through association with them, even though they clearly aspire to something more ambitious. Fitzgeffrey's rhetorical strategy is to differentiate his own from the common run of epigrams that had saturated the print marketplace and claim a loftier pedigree. The apology that follows this suggests that other more worthy poets forgo print because they might be grouped with these poetasters.

In contrast, Jonson expressed a reluctance to place his poems in the marketplace at all: in his epigram 'To My Bookseller' he admonishes him not to promote or advertise the book, but let it 'lie upon thy stall till it be sought'.[32] At a number of points he complains of those who misunderstand his epigrams, who laugh at the wrong places.[33] Jonson thus hopes for an elite, knowing readership, one that would be equivalent to the coterie readers of a more closely guarded manuscript work. However, this group would be identified not by mere social connections but by intellectual worth, forming what A. D. Cousins has called a 'feigned commonwealth' of understanders, a fit audience for the 'feigned commonwealth' of virtue presented in the panegyric epigrams of the collection.[34]

That same fear of debasement of the genre is vehemently expressed by Thomas Freeman in his preface to *Rubbe, and a great cast* (1614):

> the very name sticks to him like an *Inustum stigma* [non-burned in brand or tattoo].[35] But how the Comonest? in it selfe; why there, being good (as it is no lesse) it shold be *Melius quo communius* [better because more common] Is it in the Professor? yea there is the misery, it is gone, *ab Equis ad Asinos, Notum Lippis & Tonsoribus* [from the horse to the ass, familiar to the bleary-eyed and barbers], *&* Plaid the Pithagorean pittifully, induring most brutish transmigration, and traveld in as durty wits as the way between Hogsdon and Hounsditch, *Turpe & miserabile* [foul and miserable]: Yet that this shold impeach the ingenuous is meere injustice. But indeed the true cause for which the Epigram suffers, is his liberty and sincere honesty in the search and unmasking vice.[36]

Freeman is suggesting that hostility to the epigram based on its lowness is a mere ruse, that the real reason is the genre's unswerving commitment to revealing vice in a satire-like fashion. Thus, for him, the worthy origins of the epigram coincide with its social purpose, but, as we will see below, he found himself falling short of this loftier role.

Concern over a crowded marketplace is voiced by other ambitious epigrammatists of the period,[37] and the spirit of Martial is frequently invoked as a bulwark against such seepage. Abraham Holland writes:

> Each driveling *Lozel* now
> That hath but seene a *Colledge*, and knows how
> To put a number to *John Setons* Prose,
> Starts up a sudden *Muse-man*, and streight throws
> A *Packe* of *Epigrams* into the light,
> Whose undigested mish-mash would affright
> The very Ghost of Martiall, and make
> Th'Authors of th'Anthologie to quake.[38]

The 'pack' of epigrams suggests the derogation of the genre to mere wares sold by a pedlar – like the ballad-seller epitomized by Autolycus in *The Winter's Tale*. Such sullying threatens the classical inheritance, eroding the epigrammatist's connection to Martial and the *Greek Anthology*.

Ephemerality and fashionability

In addition to the down-market associations of the genre, the epigrammatist also struggled with its seeming ephemerality or topicality. In a repeated conceit epigrams are compared to clothes that are soon dated by changes in fashion. Thus, a heading to a manuscript collection of Sir John Davies's epigrams compares them to an almanac, 'servinge for all England, but especially for the Meridian of the honorable cittye of London calculated by John Davis of Grayes Inne gentleman An*n*o 1594 in November'.[39] This recognizes the ephemeral quality of individual epigrams, but Davies also suggests in his final epigram that the genre as a whole may be a short-lived fashion:

> Besides, this muse of mine, and the blacke fether,[40]
> Grew both together fresh in estimation,
> And both growne stale, were cast away togither:
> What fame is this that scarse lasts out a fashion?

Weever extends Davies's conceit and wonders whether it makes sense to print these ephemeral works at all: 'Epigramms are much like unto

Almanacks, serving especially for the yeare for which they are made, then these, (right judging Readers) being for one yeare pend, and in another printed; are past due before they come from the Presse.'[41] Like Davies, he also draws on the trope of fashion in clothes: his title, *Epigrams in the Oldest Cut and Newest Fashion*, claims an ancient lineage ('oldest cut') while acknowledging the fashionability of the genre in the late 1590s. He follows this in his subtitle with a string of negatives that throws the mere ephemerality into question: they are 'No longer (like the fashion) not unlike to continue'.[42] Ultimately, his point would seem to be that, while epigrams appear to be merely fashionable, there is a literary tradition of which he can claim a part. This same language of sartorial fashion is applied by Thomas Freeman in the second-last epigram of *Rubbe, and a great cast* (1614); he concedes that he has no illusions of immortality for his volume, as 'Epigram's like the stuffs your Gallants weare, / Hardly hold fashion above halfe a yeare'.[43] Freeman also more grimly suggested his epigrams were 'like th'abortive birth / No sooner borne but dead',[44] a conceit picked up on in the title of Sir Thomas Wroth's epigram collection, *The Abortive of an Idle Hour* (1620).

The process of publication

In only a few cases is there evidence of the process of seeing a book of epigrams into print. For Charles Fitzgeffry's *Affaniae*, the surviving letterbook of his friend Wheare, discussed in Chapter 3, provides partial evidence of the process.[45] Fitzgeffry departed from Oxford for the West Country in the spring of 1601, leaving the manuscript with Wheare to oversee publication. There was nothing slipshod or haphazard about this endeavour; Wheare read through the manuscript and sent it to his friends Francis Rous and George Spry in London to do the same.[46] He first sent a partial copy (seemingly the first two books), and promised the rest the next month, 'et tum demum praelo Barnesiano mandare' [and then to commit it at length to the printer Barnes]; that is Joseph Barnes of Oxford. (The vast majority of Latin epigram books by British writers were published, not in London, but in Oxford, Cambridge or Scotland.) There is some suggestion that the third book was printed separately: while Book 1 ends with a cue leading to the beginning of Book 2 on the next page, this is lacking in the transition from Book 2 to 3. The responding letter or letters of Rous and Spry have not survived, but it seems that they suggested some emendations, as Wheare wrote the next month: 'De Fabri et Satyrographi nominib*us* e Caroli poematiis liturâ tollendis cogitabimus'

[We will consider whether the names of Faber and Satyrographus [the writer of satires] should be erased from Charles's poems].[47] The second poem referred to may be 2:58, which in the published text is headless.[48] It is about a nasty fellow who has mocked Charles's one-eyedness, and possibly the most vitriolic in the book. Clearly, there is concern about potential libels in the volume, and precautions were taken even before the book reached the printer.

Also, it seems from this letter that Rous and Spry have asked whether it might be possible to use a foreign printer instead, presumably with the greater licence that such would allow; however, Wheare counters that 'praela transmarina subire no*n* potest hic liber ob causas in superioribus literis allatas' [This book cannot go to overseas presses because of the reasons offered in previous letters]. Thus, it would seem that in a letter that doesn't survive (and perhaps which his friends had not received) Wheare had already rejected this possibility.

Fitzgeffry published *Affaniae* at a time when the Bishops' Ban still had an effect; the licensing of later epigram books seems to follow the general inconsistencies traced by Cyndia Susan Clegg in her books on Jacobean and Caroline publishing. At times, epigrammatists were unable to find a compliant licenser or a printer willing to ignore the licensing requirements. As discussed in Chapter 5, for Freeman's *A Rubbe, and a Great Cast* there is manuscript evidence of the preparation of an epigram book for printing, some time between 1604 and 1610. BL Sloane MS 1889 includes an epigram that comments on a previous attempt to publish his epigrams. The first two lines of the lemma have been scratched out, but the second of these is still partly legible:

N.N. who denyed my ep. printing cause I wrote so oft
meretrices but tould mee if I will write mo common places
as that of fortius est qui se etc. he would privledge them.[49]

Epigram 101
Learning surveing my unlearned Muse
whether she might be priv'ledg'd or no
to licence her did utterly refuse
except I would my Ribaldry forgo
for that I talk't too liberall of a whore
but if I would me Common places take
as I had done of fortitude before
with all his hart hee would their licence make

> well I say nothing, others judge the Case
> whether a Hore bee not a common place.[50]

The lemma and line 7 refer to epigram 1:84, entitled 'Fortius est qui se &c. Ad Labeonem' [Stronger is he who himself, etc. To Labeo], in which Freeman redefines fortitude and valour as moral qualities rather than merely physical ones. Its earnest tone is strikingly different from the bulk of the collection, and recalls some of the lofty and moral epigrams found in the Latin humanist tradition. The epigram and its note in the manuscript suggest that the licenser was encouraging such ethical epigrams derived from the commonplace tradition as a replacement for the more salacious ones. The poems objected to by the licenser could include a number whose titles refer to prostitutes ['meretrices']: 'In duas meratrices litigantes' (2:27) and 'Epitaphium meretricis' (2:35) were both printed, but in Sloane 1889 alone appears 'In Meretricem' (Ep. 34) and a different poem also entitled 'Epitaphium meretricis'.[51] A further unpublished poem near the end of Sloane 1889 addresses the issue of allowing the more licentious poems. It portrays a reader who seeks such epigrams out, and then turns the corner of page down to mark them:

> [Co]me Yonker come, some dreggs her yet remaine
> in few lascivious lines among the rest
> somewhat fitt for thy voluptuous vaine[52]
> some of those lines I know thou likest best
> hast found them boy kin turne a leafe downe qui*ck*
> & might more such stuff have pasd with priviledg*e*
> thou wouldst have hugd my humor bin love-sick
> [...] had those would have sett thy teeth an edge
>   but it is better such sinnes bee conceald
>   some learne to sinne by reading itt reveald.[53]

Here, Freeman seems to accept the role of the licenser, not because of any fault in Freeman himself or his poems but because of the potential depravity of the reader.

Robert Hayman's *Quodlibets* (1628) offers a clear example of the licensing of epigrams early in the next reign, as one poem directly addresses Dr Thomas Worrall as ecclesiastical licenser:

To the Reverend, Learned, and Judicious, Thomas Worall, Doctor in
Divinity and Chapaline [*sic*] to the right Reve. Father in God George,
L. Bishop of London. Of my reprehending Epigrams[54]
It is for one of your gifts, and your place,
To looke *bold-staring-black sinne* in the face,
To *wound*, and *launce* with the two-edged blade,
To *clense*, and *heale* those wounds that you have made:
Yet suffer me, with my *sharp-merry pinne*,
To *prick* the *blisters* of some itching sinne.
And though Divines, justly loose Rymes condemne,
My tart, smart, chiding Lines doe not contemne.[55]

Hayman accepts the role of the licenser and presents himself as sharing
Worall's concern with the moral improvement of the public. As priest,
Worall apprehends major sins by using a 'two-edged blade', with which
he surgeon-like both wounds and heals. Hayman has the parallel, if lesser
task of pricking the mere 'blisters of some itching sinne', which sounds
rather like the pox. Hayman concludes that the chaplain's role of condemning 'loose Rymes' need not extend to his own 'tart, smart, chiding
Lines'. In another epigram Hayman suggests that 'Sermons and Epigrams
have a like end, / To improve, to reprove, and to amend' (4:1). Hayman
may have turned to Worrell as licenser because of his easy-going reputation. Much later Andrew Marvell recalled that Worall was a rather
indiscriminating authorizer: 'Scholar good enough, but a free fellow-like
man, and of no very tender conscience', who was apt to approve and sub-
scribe his name 'hand over head / to any copy submitted to him'.[56] Such
is consistent with Clegg's observation that certain licensers became known
for being more or less lenient, or for being inclined to approve volumes of
particular ideological slants.[57]

The more consistently applied licensing requirements during Charles's
reign may have limited the printing of scandalous and libellous epigrams
in the late 1620s and 1630s. There was a significant decline in published
epigram books in these decades as well: while there had been thirteen
English-language ones published in the 1610s, the 1620s saw only four,
and the 1630s two. An attempt around these controls is found in Edward
May's *Epigrams Divine and Moral* (1633), where the contents have been
arranged to fool the licenser. Despite its title, only the first twelve poems
are 'divine' in any sense and of the rest many more are immoral or amoral
than moral. Overall, it is a strange volume: we have a work, of which a few
of the opening divine poems seem to reflect a Roman Catholic position,

but the satiric poems which follow are clearly and consistently mocking Catholicism.[58] While one explanation may be that the volume is just a collection from disparate writers, with whoever put it together – May or the printer – being unconcerned with consistency, the other, more likely, explanation is that May was primarily concerned with publishing his volume of Martialian epigrams, and slapped on a prefatory group of divine poems (either by himself or by someone else) to get it past the official licenser. Clegg has shown the heavy load shouldered by those authorizing texts and suggests that in practice many works were allowed by the authorizers with a very incomplete sense of their contents. Such would seem to be the case here.[59] That the work was entered in the Stationers' Register on 17 January 1632/3, 'under Hands of Sir Henry Herbert, Master of the Revels', might seem odd at first, but it is not the only case, as 'For about eight months, from June 1632 to Jan. 1633, Herbert also took upon himself the licensing of non-dramatic verse and prose'.[60] In this period, he was responsible for allowing Donne's *Poems* (in which some lines in the satires have been censored) and Fulke Greville's *Certain Elegant and Learned Works*, which ran afoul of Archbishop Laud. As satiric epigrams were consistently more popular than devotional ones, it seems unlikely that May or the printer was attempting to fool the buyer rather than the licenser with this ruse. It is possible that Herbert himself was in on the deception, and that the title and opening poems offered him 'cover' in case of later objections.[61] This strategy of placing serious or even devotional epigrams foremost in a book is also identified by Percy:

> Baldus never built Epigramme Booke,
> But couched one sad, in the Former nooke,
> Lyke to a formall Fidler, that first plays
> One sollume Paven, then his merry layes.[62]

Ultimately, the fate of published epigram books as described above largely confirms Clegg's conclusions that press censorship in the period was far from monolithic or consistent.[63]

Sequencing

Collections of classical epigrams offered two competing organizational approaches. The Greek books of epigrams – from which the *Greek Anthology* was ultimately derived – seem to have offered their poems organized into categories, something of which is still reflected in the

Anthology itself. In contrast, Martial proudly and pointedly adopted unstructured variation.[64] (There were, however, exceptions in Martial, most notably the well-known sequence 'De Spectaculis'.) Classical precedents thus offered two possibilities and left Renaissance epigrammatists with a considerable degree of freedom within which they might still invoke traditional authority. Printed Neo-Latin epigram books of the sixteenth century frequently divided their books up by subject; for example, Buchanan's epigrams in printed form were divided into three books: while the first was an assorted lot, Books 2 and 3 were devoted to epitaphs and epigrams of praise, respectively.[65] The humanist Latin epigrams of the century often embarked on ambitious programmes of poems, for example on the cities or nobility of a nation, and these offered a natural, and often hierarchical, structure.[66] Such is still seen in John Reynolds's massive Latin epigram project: a promised thousand epigrams that he began publishing in 1611; it proceeded in a very deliberate and planned way, in consistent elegiac couplets.[67] The first volume covered the kings of Scotland, Old Testament heroes, Christian martyrs, bishops etc., and he promised further volumes on knights, graduates of the universities etc. Similarly, the first section of Johnston's *Epigrammata* (1632) is arranged by subject: one section includes groups on 'Flores' [Flowers], 'Fructes' [Fruits] and 'Aves' [Birds].

However, Owen's powerfully influential Neo-Latin books rejected this structured approach in favour of a Martial-like miscellaneous approach. The majority of English epigram books follow Martial in proudly presenting their randomness of compilation as part of their nature as epigram books. Such was also adopted by most English-language volumes of epigrams from the 1590s on. At most, they offered rudimentary organization, as in William Goddard's *A Mastiff Whelp*, where the first book contains satiric epigrams on male figures, and the second book on female. Niccols invokes the precedent of Martial to defend this approach:

> Yet I confesse, these to bee Epigrams and but slight; in placing of which, for that I observe no method or order, if his austeritie, out of ignorance, doe cavill with me, I referre him to the Prince of all writers in this kind *Val. Martialis.*[68]

However, there is in fact an order in Niccols that goes beyond Martial: he has offered three books of satiric epigrams and one book of panegyric ones, a ratio he suggests is consistent with the balance of vice and virtue in the world. More common are mini-sequences of perhaps two to five epigrams within the broad mix of an epigram book; Charles Cathcart notes that in

The Scourge of Folly Davies of Hereford 'frequently arranges his poems to named individuals in pairs or groups'.[69]

Prefaces often point to the miscellaneous and unsequenced nature of their collections. In 'To All to Whom I Write' Jonson rejects the hierarchical ordering that might be expected in collections of poems of praise: readers should not look 'For strict degrees of rank or title'.[70] Thus, while he praises a range of elite figures, including King James and the Earls of Salisbury and Pembroke, complete hierarchy is not maintained. However, in spite of this claim and similar ones by other English epigrammatists, the epigrams to the King are usually, as with Jonson, at the beginning of the volume. In what follows there is a new hierarchy of worth, of 'goodness' rather than 'greatness'.[71] The genre itself provides his justification: "Tis 'gainst the manners of an epigram'. It would seem that English epigrammatists pointed to the miscellaneous nature of their work as a way of reinforcing the casual, even indifferent pose they adopted as epigrammatists. And in those cases (as with Freeman) where there are authorial manuscripts to compare with printed volumes, it is clear that a significant degree of editing and ordering occurred. Increasingly, if belatedly, scholarly studies are exploring the significance of the juxtaposition and ordering of those epigram books which might at first seem to be merely arbitrary.

Of printed English epigrams from the period, those of Jonson collected in his 1616 folio *Workes* have attracted the most scholarship on the question of organization.[72] Edward Partridge argues that the preponderance of satirical epigrams among the first sixty is Jonson's way of establishing the corruption of Jacobean England, a corruption to which the epigrams of praise that follow will offer a corrective.[73] Richard Dutton traces significant juxtapositions and sequences in Jonson's epigrams, but acknowledges that the lack of definition 'encourages the reader to keep looking, but never gives him the satisfaction of feeling that he has reached a definitive conclusion'.[74] Most recent scholars have, like Dutton, identified meaningful limited sequences; certainly that Jonson's 'To his Muse', in which he chastises himself for 'for fierce idolatry' towards 'a worthless man',[75] follows two panegyric epigrams to Cecil, suggests a rethinking of his earlier praise.[76] However, elsewhere identification of such is challenged by three problems: intentionality, effectiveness and comprehensiveness. Certainly ironic tensions are manifest, but is this design or coincidence? Furthermore, given the emphasis upon haphazard miscellaneousness in the prefatory materials to epigram books, would the reader of the time be primed to notice such juxtapositions? The identification of a few such significant patches falls short of offering any rationale for the collection as a

whole. James Riddell argues that the antithetical juxtaposition of two epigrams praising Ferrabosco (nos 130 and 131) with one praising Sylvester
(no. 132) is meant to highlight that the latter is unworthy of praise, and
that in the words of epigram 65, 'Who e're is rais'd, / For worth he
has not, is tax'd, not prais'd'.[77] However, the recognition of Sylvester
as unworthy of the praise is dependent upon a comment from Jonson's
'Conversations with Drummond', and would not have been available to
the general reader of the *Workes* in 1616. Furthermore, to say of a cluster
of epigrams that they 'all deal with good and corruption, both public and
private', as Riddell does,[78] is only to find what are the broad subjects of
nearly all epigrams, whether by Jonson or others. Given these subjects,
the mingling of epigrams will invariably lead to the antithetical juxtaposition that Riddell sees as the organizational rationale of the collection.
At times, the overly probing consideration of ironic juxtaposition seems
to serve critics' desire to excuse Jonson for praising those now considered undeserving. The focus on Jonson's sequencing has also led to him
being perceived as exceptional in this regard. Dutton suggests that careful
sequencing of this type is to be expected from a poet who urges his reader
to vigilant reading and discernment, but it is common across a range of
epigram volumes in the period.

Similar extensive work has been done with Harington's epigrams in
manuscript by Scott-Warren and Kilroy, and Ann Baynes Coiro with
Herrick's *Hesperides*.[79] Coiro's argument that *Hesperides* manifests a unity
that is typical of the epigram book tradition has been the strongest and
most thorough offered, but is open to two major objections. Firstly, that
Hesperides is much more than an epigram book in its inclusion of a wide
variety of forms and modes. Secondly, that, while there are epigram
books, both classical and Renaissance, that offer a unity or structure, these
are largely exceptions. Looking back further, Fitzgerald offers a reading
of Martial's Book 1 as a logical whole, suggesting that as a *book* it takes its
place in the world of the marketplace and patronage, and that there are
sequences in Martial, linked by subtle rhetorical techniques.[80] However,
there is no indication that Martial's readers of the 1590s saw this subtle
unity. Thus, I would not argue that a partially hidden ordering was perceived as part of the Martialian model and adopted, but that simply the
impulse at least occasionally to order for significance and effect was too
strong to resist. Epigram collections were often divided into books or
'centuries', and, however disparate and unordered the material within
each century, these usually began and ended with programme poems that
drew attention to the century as a distinct volume.

Telling or ironic juxtaposition of a few epigrams is one thing, an over-arching structure quite another, and comparatively rare. Dana Sutton argues that there is a broad narrative behind Fitzgeffry's *Affaniae*: the first book is largely dedicated to young love – of a woman identified as 'Cordula'; that this segments ends with her death, and a Petrarchan 'farewell to love'. Book 2 concerns non-romantic social relationships and politics. The third book leads to illness and a leave-taking from the world. The volume concludes with epitaphs under the title 'Cenotaphia'.[81] This would seem to reflect the shadowy structure at work in some of the sonnet sequences of the period, but it is exceptional in epigram volumes of the period.

Anthologies, card decks and banquets

Three main metaphors were used to describe this mingling of various material and the accompanying insignificance of order. The 'anthology' itself, of course, in its etymology ('a collection of flowers') bore the conceit of a gathering or bouquet of *various* flowers. This was extended by some epigrammatists to include weeds as well, a gesture typical of the self-disparaging tone adopted by many epigrammatists. However, even from these weeds, the judicious reader might still derive some good ('sucking honey from the weed' as it were). The mingling of weeds and flowers might place upon the reader the responsibility of sorting them out.[82]

Another frequent metaphor applied to miscellaneous epigram books was that of a deck of cards. Francis Quarles presented 'Epigrams, Observations and Meditations' without division, noting that '*Cards*, well shuffled, are most fit for *Gamesters*; And oftentimes, the *Discovery*, adds pleasure to the *Enjoyment*'.[83] Random juxtaposition is thus part of the delightful experience of an epigram book. Parrot uses the same image in the last epigram of *Cures for the Itch*:

> These Rimes you see, unknown, compos'd, conceall'd,
> Had nere by me beene showne, disclos'd, reveald,
> Much lesse at latter Lammas past in print,
> Had not some secret reason since beene in't:
> Which *volens nolens* [willy-nilly] caus'd me afterwards
> Shuffle againe, and deale about the Cards.[84]

This conceit carries with it the claim of absolute randomness and perhaps that readers might also randomly rather than sequentially read the poems.

Finally, the most common trope was that of epigrams as varied food-stuff: it is explicit in the title of J[ohn] C[ooke]'s *Epigrames. Serued out in 52. seuerall Dishes for euery man to tast without surfeting* [1604?] and Peacham's *Thalia's Banquet* (1620), whose title page advertises it as consisting of 'a hundred and odd dishes'. John Taylor presents his volume as a 'hotch-potch, or gallimawfrey of sonnets, satyres, and epigrams'.[85] The 'Epistle to All Readers' in Harington's 1618 edition compares epigrams to the last course in a meal, like fruit or nuts or 'parma-cheese', and it is a given that readers should 'taste but few at once',[86] partaking in a leisurely, savouring way. The variety of epigrams might ensure that all will find at least something to their tastes: 'seuerall pallates require diversity of sawces'.[87] Hayman, in his translation of Owen's epigrams, adopts the food metaphor to suggest that the reader should enjoy only a few at a time:

> For as a Man may surfet on sweet meates:
> So thou maist over-read these quaint conceits.
> Some at one time, some at another chuse;
> As Maidens doe their kissing Confects use.[88]

Like Harington's, this passage places epigrams near the bottom of a literary hierarchy: they are not the main meal but the light course that follows.

Davies of Hereford uses the foodstuff trope to express concern about potential readers' 'consumption' of his epigrams:

> Some foule mouth'd Readers then (which God amend)
> So slop them up, that it would make one spew
> To see how rudely they devoure at once
> More wit then ere their head-peece held perchance;
> As if my wit were minced for the nonce,
> For them with ease to swallow with a vengeance.[89]

Epigrammatic brevity makes them fit for the witless who could not swallow longer works; it also suggests once again how they should be read – one at a time, slowly. The poem is responding positively to Bastard's poem 'Ad Lectorem' (1:40), which similarly complained that 'the Reader soone devoures thy lines, / Which thou in many houres couldst scarce digest'.

From print back into manuscript

Once printed, epigrams were beyond the control of the author: even more than in manuscript circulation, they were frequently borrowed, stolen or reworked by later anthologists. Thus, epigrams could became 'common', both in the sense of widely known among all classes but also detached from the particular authority of the poet. The anxiety over this descent into commonness is articulated in a poem that compares women to epigrams:

> Women are epigrams; epigrams do go
> Once pressed, common to all, do not women so?[90]

Here, the typical epigrammatic cynicism about women is extended to describe the fate of the printed ('pressed') epigram book among a public readership.

Adam Fox has demonstrated how certain printed works that had gathered oral and manuscript materials actually fed further oral and manuscript transmission: 'the boundaries between speech and text, hearing and reading, were thoroughly permeable and constantly shifting'.[91] Folger MS V.a.345 and Bodl. Tanner MS 465 illustrate the phenomenon of a movement of epigrams back into manuscript circulation from a printed source. They both offer a sequence of epigrams drawn from Parrot's *Mastive*, some of which are identified by the Folger manuscript as from that printed work. Both manuscripts reproduce the poems in the same sequence as in the printed text, but the copyist has been very selective, passing over many in taking the few that he presumably liked. It seems likely in fact that the Tanner manuscript borrowed from the Folger, as the latter has a number not included in the former. What this demonstrates is not only an individual reader copying an epigram from print, but from that copying a renewed manuscript-based circulation. BL Harl. MS 1836 offers three 'books' of epigrams, drawn from oral, manuscript and print sources. As noted in Chapter 4, the first book shows evidence of both oral and manuscript sources, whereas Book 2 is a direct reproduction of Henry Hutton's *Follies Anatomies* (1619), including misnumbering, and Book 3 of William Basse's *A Helpe to Discourse* (1619), which had a section described as of 'certaine Epigrams, some olde revived, and some new published'. Such use of printed epigrams rather confirms the anxieties expressed by Jonson and other epigrammatists who aspired to maintain a degree of authorial control in the print realm.

Notes

1 Campion, *Two bookes of ayres*, sig. A2v.

2 Bastard, *Chrestoleros*, Ep. 6:28.

3 This concern with 'authorship' is more fully explored in Chapter 7.

4 Owen, *Ioannia Audoeni Epigrammatum*, Ep. 3:208 [trans. Sutton].

5 Parrot, 'To the courteous Reader', in *Cures for the Itch*, sig. A2r.

6 Coiro, *Robert Herrick's Hesperides and the Epigram Book Tradition*, p. 184.

7 Stradling, 'the Honourable Reader' (1:121), in *Epigrammatum libri quatuor* [trans. Sutton]. Cf. his Ep. 3:1 (also in *Epigrammatum libri quatuor*), where he forbids the printer to use the typical marketing techniques.

8 Bastard, *Chrestoleros*, sig. A3r.

9 *SR*, entry 15 Sept. 1598.

10 John Whitgift and Richard Bancroft, 'Bishops' Ban [June 1]', in Richard McCabe, 'Elizabethan Satire and the Bishops' Ban of 1599', *Yearbook of English Studies*, 11 (1981), pp. 188–93, p. 188.

11 Whitgift and Bancroft, 'Bishops' Ban [June 1]', in McCabe, 'Elizabethan Satire and the Bishops' Ban of 1599', p. 188.

12 Cyndia Susan Clegg, *Press Censorship in Elizabethan England* (Cambridge: Cambridge University Press, 1997), pp. 210–16. Her suggestion also explains the lapsed enforcement of the ban: 'Placing the bishops' actions within the context of the eventful history of Essex, however, goes a long way towards explaining why after the initial flurry of action the ban was largely inconsequential' (p. 216). Cliff Forshaw, '"Cease Cease to bawle, thou wasp-stung Satyrist": Writers, Printers and the Bishops' Ban of 1599', *EnterText*, 3 (2003), pp. 101–31, largely agrees that libel and sedition were the main concerns of the ban.

13 Forshaw, '"Cease Cease to bawle, thou wasp-stung Satyrist"', p. 102.

14 Honigmann, *John Weever*, p. 24.

15 William R. Jones, '"Say They Are Saints Although That Saints They Show Not": John Weever's 1599 Epigrams to Marston, Jonson, and Shakespeare', *HLQ*, 73 (2010), pp. 83–98.

16 Joyner, *Itys*, sig. A4v.

17 It was followed by Samuel Rowlands's *Humors Antique Faces* (1605), *Humors Ordinarie* (1605), *Humors Looking Glass* (1608) and *The knave of clubbs* (1612). The last is better described as a volume of verse characters rather than epigrams. The conclusion of this work promises further 'knaves' of the other card suits: it seems that Rowlands's *The Knave of Hearts* did reach print, as it is mentioned in Fitzgeffrey's *Satyres*, sig. A8v and poems from it are in Folger MS V.a.345, but no print copy has survived.

18 Clegg, *Press Censorship in Elizabethan England*, p. 216; McCabe, 'Elizabethan Satire and the Bishops' Ban', p. 191.

19 Chamberlain to Carleton 8, July 1602. This statement reflects the looseness of the term 'epigram' in the period.

20 Francis Davison, *A Poetical Rapsodie* (1602).

21 The volume was entered in the Stationers' Register on 22 May 1604 as 'Fyftie Epigrams written by J Cooke gent to W. Cotton'.

22 John Owen, *Epigrammatum libri tres* (London: John Windet, 1606); Stradling, *Epigrammatum libri quatuor* (London: G. Bishop, 1607).

23 Humphrey King, *An halfe-penny-worth of wit, in a penny-worth of paper. Or, The hermites tale* (1613), sig. B1r. The revived interest might also be traced back to 1612, when Jonson's epigrams were entered in the Stationers' Register (to John Stepneth on 15 May) and may have been published in a lost edition. William Drummond notes reading them in that year (Jonson, *The Cambridge Edition of the Works of Ben Jonson*, vol. 5, p. 103).

24 Kathryn Perry, '"I do it onely for the Printers sake": Commercial Imperatives and Epigrams in the Early Seventeenth Century', *EnterText*, 3 (2003), pp. 204–26 (www.brunel.ac.uk/faculty/arts/EnterText/3_1_pdfs/perry.pdf), p. 208.

25 Marotti, *Manuscript, Print and the English Renaissance*, pp. 288–9.

26 'count': ''count, an abbreviated form of "account" in the sense of 'reckoning' (*OED*).

27 Gamage, 'Forlorne Hope', Ep. 30, in *Linsi-woolsie or two centuries of epigrammes*.

28 Randall Ingram, 'Lego Ego: Reading Seventeenth-Century Books of Epigrams', in Jennifer Anderson and Elizabeth Sauer (eds), *Books and Readers in Early Modern England: Material Studies* (Philadelphia, PA: University of Pennsylvania Press, 2002), p. 164. In addition to the examples offered by Ingram, see the title page of Rowlands's *Humors Ordinarie* (1605). The price is confirmed by Fitzgeffry's *Affaniae*, Ep. 1:10: 'Tu quem sex modo quatuorve nummos / Nugis perdere non piget iocolis, / Has potes tibi comparare chartas' [You who are not embarrassed to squander fourpence or sixpence on trifling jests, you may purchase these pages] [trans. Sutton].

29 Perry, '"I do it onely for the Printers sake"', pp. 204–26. Perry focuses on the 1610s epigram books of William Goddard and Parrot.

30 Fitzgeffrey, 'Ad Emptorem', Ep. 2 (should be numbered '1'), in *Satyres*.

31 Fitzgeffrey, *Satyres*, sig. A8v. The references are to Henry Parrot's *Laquei ridiculosi: Or Springes for Woodcocks* (1613), *Doctor Merry-man: or Nothing but Mirth* (1616), possibly by Samuel Rowlands, Freeman's *Rubbe. and a great cast* (1614), Taylor's *Sculler* (1612) or *Water-worke* (1614), Taylor's rival

William Fennor whose *Pasquils jestes mixed with Mother Bunches merriments* went through a number of editions, John Davies of Hereford's *The Scourge of Folly* (1611) or *Wits Bedlam* (1617) and Samuel Rowlands's series of books that all had *A Knave of* ... as the opening of their titles. A 'murnival' was a set of four face cards in the game gleek. I am unable to explain the reference to Fennor's 'unisounding eare'.

32 Jonson, 'To My Bookseller', Ep. 3.

33 Jonson, 'To Idiot Groom', Ep. 58 and 'To Person Guilty', Ep. 38.

34 Cousins, 'Feigning the Commonwealth', pp. 27–8.

35 The phrase is from Lev. 19:28.

36 Freeman, *Rubbe, and a great cast*, sig. A2v.

37 Manley, 'Proverbs, Epigrams, and Urbanity', p. 265.

38 Abraham Holland, 'A Continued Inquisition against Paper-Persecutors by A.H.', in John Davies of Hereford, *Scourge for paper-persecutors* (1625), sig. A1v.

39 Davies, *Poems*, p. 377.

40 Black feathers came to be worn by fashionable gallants in the mid-1590s. See Donne, Satire 1, line 55.

41 Weever, *Epigrams in the Oldest Cut and Newest Fashion*, sig. A7r.

42 Weever, *Epigrams in the Oldest Cut and Newest Fashion*, Title Page.

43 Freeman, *Rubbe, and a great cast*, Ep. 2:99.

44 Freeman, *Rubbe, and a great cast*, Ep. 2:99.

45 Wheare, Bodl. Selden Supra MS 81.

46 Wheare [to Francis Rous and Spry], Bodl. Selden Supra MS 81, fol. 19r (7 May 1601).

47 Wheare [to Rous and/or Spry], fol. 21r. The letter is dated 8 Kal. Mai 1601, which would be 24 Apr.; however, it was clearly written later than the letter which Wheare sent on 'Non Mai 1601' (7 May) (fol. 19r) with the first two parts of Fitzgeffry's *Affaniae*. I suspect that it should read 8 Kal. Jun (25 May), and that the error is simply a mental slip on Wheare's part.

48 See Chapter 9 below for a fuller discussion of this poem.

49 'N.N.' likely means 'Nescio nomen' [I do not know the name]; it was occasionally used in the period as a place-holder for a specific identity. Presumably Freeman did know the name of the authorizer, but used this to hide the identity.

50 Clegg, *Press Censorship in Elizabethan England*, p. 12, has shown that the terms 'license and privilege are synonymous in Elizabethan patents', and refer to a special patent conferred by the Crown, and that such 'license' must be distinguished from the more usual 'allowance' offered by bishops' chaplains. However, in common usage, 'license' was frequently used for this allowance.

51 Freeman, *Rubbe, and a great cast*, Ep. 35, fol. 8r. Jonson's 'To a Friend' (Ep. 83) similarly responds to one who has objected to his use of the word 'whore' in the preceding poem 'On Cashierd Captain Surly': 'To put out the word "whore" thou dost me woo, / Throughout my booke. Troth, put out "woman" too.'

52 For this sense of 'voluptuous', cf. Jonson's 'On Sir Voluptuous Beast' (Ep. 25).

53 Freeman, *Rubbe, and a great cast*, fol. 44v.

54 This would be George Montaigne, Bishop of London from 1621 to 1627.

55 Hayman, *Quodlibets*, Ep. 4:13.

56 Andrew Marvell, *Rehearsal Transposed* (1672), pp. 289–90, in W. W. Greg, *Licensers for the Press to 1640* (Oxford: Oxford Bibliographical Society, 1962), p. 101. Greg certainly records many literary works licensed by him, including such potentially controversial ones as translations of John Barclay's *Argenis*, Martial's epigrams as translated by Thomas May and Earle's *Characters*.

57 Clegg, *Press Censorship in Caroline England*, p. 39.

58 See, for example, 'On a shee Papist' (Ep. 2:7) and 'Against praying for the dead' (Ep. 2:13) in May, *Epigrams Divine and Moral*.

59 Clegg, *Press Censorship in Elizabethan England*, pp. 62–3.

60 N. W. Bawcutt (ed.), *The Control and Censorship of Caroline Drama: The Records of Sir Henry Herbert, Master of the Revels, 1623–1673* (Oxford: Clarendon Press, 1996), p. 48. Herbert actually got into trouble for licensing Donne's *Paradoxes and Problems*, for which he was called before Star Chamber. Unfortunately, Clegg's otherwise very thorough *Press Censorship in Caroline England* offers no discussion of Herbert and his role in licensing.

61 If this Edward May is the same who served as a chaplain to Donne in his capacity at Lincoln's Inn early in the 1620s, then through Donne he may have come to know Herbert and found in him a sympathetic licenser.

62 William Percy, Huntington MS 4, Ep. 232.

63 This is demonstrated throughout Clegg's three books, but see, for example, *Press Censorship in Elizabethan England*, pp. 218–24.

64 Fitzgerald, *Martial*, p. 27.

65 Bradner, *Musae Anglicanae*, p. 137.

66 C. A. Upton, 'John Jonston and the Historical Epigram', *Acta Coventus Neo-Latini Bononiensis: Medieval and Renaissance Texts and Studies* (Binghamton, NY: Center for Medieval & Early Renaissance Studies, 1985), pp. 638–44, p. 638. He describes the elder Scaliger (Julius Caesar) as 'a major exponent of epigrammatic sequences' (640) without giving a reference.

67 Reynolds, *Epigrammata* (1611).

68 Niccols, *The Furies*, sig. A3r.

69 Charles Cathcart, 'John Davies of Hereford, Marston, and Hall', *Ben Jonson Journal*, 17(2010), pp. 242–8, p. 243.

70 Jonson, 'To All to Whom I Write', Ep. 9.

71 Partridge, 'Jonson's Epigrammes: The Named and the Nameless', p. 155.

72 See David Wykes, 'Ben Jonson's "Chast Book" – The *Epigrammes*', *Renaissance and Modern Studies*, 13 (1969), pp. 76–87; James A. Riddell, 'The Arrangement of Ben Jonson's *Epigrammes*', *SEL*, 27 (1987), pp. 53–70. Partridge, 'Jonson's Epigrammes: The Named and the Nameless', pp. 153–4, describes earlier scholars' denial of any sequential form in Jonson's *Epigrammes*.

73 In volumes where satiric and panegyric epigrams were divided, the latter usually were placed at the end of the volume. Fitzgeffry's *Affaniae*, for example, placed the panegyric epitaphs in the final book.

74 Richard Dutton, *Ben Jonson: To the Folio* (Cambridge: Cambridge University Press, 1983), p. 92.

75 Dutton, *Ben Jonson*, p. 171.

76 Cousins, 'Feigning the Commonwealth', pp. 35–6. See also Partridge, 'Jonson's Epigrammes: The Named and the Nameless', pp. 172–4.

77 Riddell, 'The Arrangement of Ben Jonson's *Epigrammes*', pp. 53–70.

78 Riddell, 'The Arrangement of Ben Jonson's *Epigrammes*', p. 58.

79 Coiro, *Robert Herrick's Hesperides and the Epigram Book Tradition*, esp. pp. 3–29.

80 Fitzgerald, *Martial*, p. 4.

81 Sutton, 'Introduction to Charles Fitzgeffry', *Affaniae* (www.philological. bham.ac.uk/affaniae/intro.html), paragraph 31.

82 Henry Peacham, *Thalia's Banquet* (1620), Ep. 1.

83 Francis Quarles, 'To the Readers', in *Divine Fancies* (1632), p. 4. Cf. Jonson, Ep. 112.

84 Parrot, 'Coacta ferenda', *Cures for the Itch*, sig. F10r. These lines seem to suggest a non-surviving Parrot volume from the mid-1620s, reordered again in *Cures for the Itch*.

85 Taylor, *Water-workes*, Title Page.

86 Harington, 'Epistle to All Readers', in *Epigrams* (1618), sig. A2r.

87 Harington, 'To the Reader', in *Epigrams* (1618), sig. A3r.

88 Hayman, 'A Praemonition to all Kinde of Readers of these Translations of *John Owens* Epigrams', in Owen section of *Quodlibets*, sig. A3r.

89 Davies of Hereford, *Scourge of Folly*, Ep. 106.

90 Bodl. Malone MS 19, p. 45; this epigram is also found in Folger MS V.a.162, fol. 35v; Bodl. Corpus Christi MS 327, fol. 16v; and Bodl. Corpus Christi MS 328, fol. 48.

91 Fox, *Oral and Literate Culture in England*, pp. 39–40.

7

Authorship

In his introduction to Kipling's poetry, T. S. Eliot wrote that epigrams, like hymns, are 'extremely objective types of verse: they can and should be charged with intense feeling, but it must be a feeling that can be completely shared'.[1] Once again, they are 'what all might say', as Puttenham expressed it. Given such a perception, to whom does an epigram, satiric or otherwise, belong? As explored in Chapter 1, authorial detachment, if not anonymity, lies at the roots of the epigram tradition. Ancient epitaphs and monumentary distichs mark first of all their subjects rather than their author, as the first-person voice is elided or transferred to the stones themselves. They are thus more subject-based than author-centred.[2] While authorial identity becomes more central in the literary epigrams of the *Greek Anthology* and the *Anthologia Latina*, anonymity is still frequent, and not only because of the loss of clear authorship over the centuries. Regarding the 110 epigrams from the *Anthologia Latina* translated by N. M. Kay, William Fitzgerald writes,

> Kay is almost certainly right to argue that they constitute a book written by a single author. But our Anonymous hardly comes across as an auteur. In fact, anonymity seems appropriate to the efficient way he recycles themes and techniques from the long epigram tradition that spans the whole of Classical Antiquity.[3]

This tradition of anonymity or semi-anonymity changed most markedly with Martial, who is stridently manifest in many of his epigrams and strove to maintain authorial control over them. Throughout he shows a desire to achieve a reputation as an epigrammatist, and his ownership of the poems is a recurring theme.

The epigram culture of the late sixteenth and early seventeenth centuries reflects this tension within the earlier tradition, and offers two rival frameworks for understanding epigrams and their authorship: in one, the epigram is free-floating in oral, manuscript and print circulation, open to change and reapplication, and only very lightly connected with its initial author.[4] A genre which depended so heavily on response, imitation and semi-imitation was also likely to raise uncertainties about authorship as a stable entity. The rival framework reflects Martial's approach, in which the epigrammatist strongly asserted his role as author, staking his proprietary claim on all his epigrams. This second approach has been aptly explored by Scott-Warren on Harington and Joseph Loewenstein on Jonson,[5] and it can be argued that Owen pursued a parallel approach in his ever-growing volumes of Neo-Latin epigrams. For these writers, Martial offered a classical legitimacy to what seemed often an ephemeral and frivolous poetic form. His collection of individual epigrams into large books brought a prestige achieved through accumulation, and which bound the author closely with his epigrams.

Two anecdotes illustrate something of the dynamics at work in the epigram tradition between these competing models of anonymity and public recognition of authorship. The first is an oft-cited story about Virgil and one of his distichs, recounted here in Puttenham's *Arte of English Poesie*:

> These inscriptions or epigrams at their beginning had no certain author that would avouch them, some for fear of blame, if they were over saucy or sharp, others for modesty of the writer, as was that distich of Vergil which he set upon the palace gate of the emperor Augustus, which I will recite for the briefness and quickness of it, and also for another event that fell out upon the matter worthy to be remembered. These were the verses:

> *Nocte pluit tota, redeunt spectacula mane:*
> *Divisum imperium cum Iove Caesar habet.*

> Which I have thus Englished:

> *It rains all night, early the shows return:*
> *God and Caesar do reign and rule by turn.*

> As much to say, God showeth his power by the night rains, Caesar, his magnificence by the pomps of the day.
> These two verses were well liked and brought to the emperor's majesty, who took great pleasure in them and willed the author should be known. A saucy

courtier proffered himself to be the man, and had a good reward given him, for the emperor himself was not only learned, but of much munificence toward all learned men. Whereupon Vergil, seeing himself by his overmuch modesty defrauded of the reward that an impudent had gotten by abuse of his merit, came the next night, and fastened upon the same place this half meter, four times iterated. Thus:

> *Sic vos non vobis*
> *Sic vos non vobis*
> *Sic vos non vobis*
> *Sic vos non vobis*

And there it remained a great while because no man wist what it meant, till Vergil opened the whole fraud by this device. He wrote above the same half meters this whole hexameter:

> *Hos ego versiculos fecit tulit alter honores.*

And then finished the four half meters, thus:

> *Sic vos non vobis*   *Fertis aratra boves.*
> *Sic vos non vobis*   *Vellera fertis oves.*
> *Sic vos non vobis*   *Mellificatis apes.*
> *Sic vos non vobis*   *Nidificatis aves.*

And put to his name Publius Vergilius Maro.[6]

The story goes on to recount how Virgil was then rewarded by the emperor.

The story includes a number of features that would come to mark the early modern epigram. The original presentation of the poem is anonymous, but this anonymity is not allowed to rest, and both readers and another potential poet strive to eliminate the anonymity. In this ideal story, where a literal poetic justice triumphs, Virgil manages to have it both ways: while not putting himself forward as a public poet, he nevertheless attains authorial credit and praises the emperor without having seemed to engage in self-serving flattery. The rival poet, or 'poetaster', achieves only public ridicule rather than fame for his attempted theft. This same tension between anonymity and recognized authorship was to be played out in manifold ways in the epigram culture of early modern

England. While literary theft might afflict any sort of poetic work, it was a particular problem with epigrams. Where a plagiarist might steal a choice flower from *Venus and Adonis*, but would never attempt to make off with the whole, an epigram's brevity meant that it might be taken wholesale.

A second story represents a cynical counter-image to that of Virgil above: Anthony Nixon's *Blacke Yeare* (1606) describes an Italian poet

> who having made an *Epigram* which much pleased himselfe, shewed it to some of his friendes, praysing it above the skies: They presently demaunding who was the *Author?* He for very shame of pride would not tell them it was his, but with a fleeting countenance gave them to understand, that the verses and the laughter were Cosin-germaines, and issued both from the same proud heart, Therin discovering both his owne selfe-love and vanitie.[7]

Nixon is suggesting a poetic pride that recognizes the 'shame' of parading itself, and that seeks the glory of both humility and accomplishment. However, unlike in the story of Virgil, here the authorial ruse is seen through. Rather than a truly humble anonymity, this is merely half-hidden anonymity in the service of 'selfe-love and vanitie'. Both stories present an anonymity that is only temporary, where the culture expects that eventually the author will be revealed. While epigrams might circulate anonymously for a time, in this state they were prone to be picked up by an ambitious figure of limited scruples, or to have an author assigned by curious readers, as they fixed it upon a likely or illustrious candidate. While many epigrams were 'what all men might say', readers knew as well that originally some *one* had said it.

Overall, the question of authorship functions differently with epigrams than other genres because of their relatively low status: they were not the sort of works most likely to prompt authorial pride. As trifles they might be denied as much as claimed by their authors. For that reason, those poets who most present themselves as authors of epigrams simultaneously strive to raise the genre's reputation and profile, by pointing to its classical antecedents.

Such were the complicated dynamics of epigram authorship in the early modern period. Some distinction, however, must be made between English and Neo-Latin epigrams. The former were far more likely to be free-floating and anonymous, at least for part of their circulation; for the latter, authorship was often significant and highlighted. Even Neo-Latin epigrams popular in oral and manuscript circulation tend to be spread with an authorial name attached. The massive Neo-Latin epigram collections of the Continent (one of which included 250,000 epigrams) typically divide up the epigrams by author, and in some cases the illustrious nature of the authors (as statesman, poet or scholar) is highlighted. The similar, if somewhat less ambitious, *Delitiae Delitiarum* (1637) compiled by Abraham Wright from books in the Bodleian, also organized material by author. As some of these anthologies were intended as educational models, the assurance that the best authors were represented was important. The more modest English anthologies were significantly different: authorship was less important, or disappeared altogether as a concept. The earliest English epigram collection, Kendall's *Flowers of Epigrams* (1577) borrowed heavily in translation from More's Latin epigrams without acknowledgement.[8] With English epigrams, only in single-volume collections by Harington and Jonson was authorial identity to come to the fore.

Emphatic authorship

Over the fifty years covered by this study (1590–1640), there was an increasing tendency for writers of epigrams to assert and maintain their ownership of these works, and this development is most manifest in the collections of Harington, Owen and Jonson.[9] These poets desired to control their epigrams, both to maintain the prestige of those that they wished to circulate under their own names and to prevent the circulation of those potentially damaging to their reputation or even position. Thus, while anonymity or authorial distancing may have been the most common approach in epigram collections of the period, Harington, Owen and Jonson adopted a more Martialian approach of emphasizing their roles as authors, engaging in what I call 'emphatic authorship'.

Throughout his epigram books Martial identifies closely with his poetry, showing a high level of concern over the circulation of his poems, and a sensitive consciousness of the reception of his work. He often reflects on who is reading his epigrams, in what context, and also what is being done with them once they are made public. Martial passed along epigrams, either singly or in books, to friends before publication, and he shows a willingness for them to be performed orally – within certain limits. Thus, he celebrates that his friend Rufus would quote his poems (6:85), and delights that all the people of Rome are singing them (6:60); however, that Celer recites them draws his censure:

> Ut recitem tibi nostra rogas epigrammata. nolo.
> non audire, Celer, sed recitare cupis.

[You ask me to recite to you my epigrams. I decline. You don't wish to hear them, Celer, but to recite them.][10]

In another he complains about a poet who is mixing his verses with Martial's:

Quid, stulte, nostris versibus tuos misces?
cum litigante quid tibi, miser, libro?

[Why, you fool, do you mix your verses with mine? What have you, wretched fellow, to do with a book that is at odds with you?][11]

Celer's actions obliterate Martial as poet, making the epigrams fully his own. Thus, Martial's epigrams manifest a continuing tension: he moved beyond coterie circulation to a fully published form and yet still wished to maintain control over what was done with his epigrams.

This self-conscious concern on Martial's part was to be echoed by many of his late Elizabethan and early Stuart heirs, such as Campion, Fitzgeffry and Owen among Latin poets, and Sir John Davies, Bastard, Guilpin, Harington, Weever and Jonson among English ones. To varying extents, these all manifest 'emphatic authorship', or 'possessive authorship' as Loewenstein calls it, and to maintain their role as authors they limited circulation of individual epigrams. Instead, they would offer collections or books of disparate epigrams to individual friends and would-be patrons, and then (in most cases) create larger volumes yet for publication. The wiser poets, Harington, Jonson and Owen, allowed for years of gradual epigram composition, but many others failed by trying to become Martial in a hurry. Martial had published fourteen centuries of epigrams over fifteen years, presenting a model that poets like Bastard, Weever and Fitzgeffry sought to emulate; however, while he had accumulated his over a lifetime, adding new volumes as the years went by, these young men, seemingly under the pressure of the fashion, attempted the same in a few years, and at a stage in life when they had little experience. Bastard committed himself to writing one epigram a day (2:37), but found he lacked 'matter and invention'; Weever's title page announced that his were 'A twise seven houres (in so many weekes) studie'. Jonson was more deliberate and astute, carefully holding his back until a bulk of worthwhile poems had been achieved.

Sullivan has suggested that ultimately the English epigram was a melding of two traditions: 'There was a native Anglo-Saxon tradition of brief poems incorporating satire, realism and humour, which tended to rely on subliterary farce, proverbs and folk anecdote. The thinking was simple and direct, but early Elizabethan writing was expansive and rambunctious. The classical formalism of Martial pared down this expansiveness.'[12] It was this merging of two rival traditions that threatened those poets set on being Martialian epigrammatists. If, as Manley suggests, 'it was the destiny of the genre [of epigrams] to wind up in the hands of hacks', and inevitably become a disposable genre,[13] the self-conscious English heirs of Martial would not let it do so without a fight. Their emphatic authorship reflects a desire for the enduring status of their work. Readers as well as rival poets represented a threat: some treated buying a volume of poetry as establishing complete ownership. The epigrammatist Thomas Beedome complained of those who 'gull their Mistris by some Poeme showne / Which, 'cause they paid for, they dare call their owne'.[14] Hence ambitious, emphatic poets struggled against the general tendency for collectors and buyers to treat epigrams they heard or read as their own, and thus erase the author responsible for them.

Martialian authors and stolen verses

While readers today are most familiar with the English epigrams of Harington and Jonson, readers of the early seventeenth century saw Owen as the British successor to Martial, and he was the most noteworthy influence on other epigrammatists.[15] In both prefatory materials and the epigrams themselves Owen draws attention to his authorly status. He also followed a regular programme of publication, one which acknowledged his printer, Simon Waterston's, continuing role in making the epigrams public (4:12). Owen's approach of adding new books to an already printed collection helped maintain the author's prominence, and in the later volumes Owen frequently points back to earlier books. That Owen also includes a large number of epigrams of praise makes his emphatic authorship more understandable. In sending his volume off to the royal court, he hopes that any possible censure will fall on him, not the book (4:15), which is another manifestation of the author's continuing role and responsibility. As Byron Harries has argued, Owen's published epigram books were intended to attract further patronage from the powerful, and his Neo-Latin epigrams of praise offered to celebrate their subjects in an international context.[16] Throughout Owen maintains his prominent image as the author of the whole: he is raised up by the royal and noble names that his epigrams of praise celebrate.

Harington adopted a mixed approach to authorship. While he frequently manifested the Martialian sense of ownership, he (as shown in Chapter 2) also admittedly derived some of his epigrams from widely circulating jests. At other times he distanced himself from epigrams that were fully original to him. (His approach to 'ownership' of his invention of a flushing jakes in *The Metamorphosis of Ajax* shows something of the same playful, ambivalent modesty;[17] however, that invention was offered to all in print, whereas he more carefully maintained control of his epigrams through manuscript circulation.) As detailed above in Chapter 5, his private gift manuscripts exposed his poems to circulation beyond his control, but oral performance also led to dissemination. Individual epigrams at times acknowledge this listening audience: Harington notes that 'The Readers, and the hearers lyke my bookes'.[18] He complains to Sextus that 'thou dost read so harshe, poynt so perverse, / Yt [the epigram] seem'd now neither witty, nor a vearse';[19] in contrast, he praises Queen Elizabeth's oral performance of his poems: '[You] so pronounct each word, and evry letter / your gratious reading, grac't my vearse the better'.[20] However, once epigrams such as these were heard in public settings, they might be used by others, and, like Martial, Harington complains of a reader who has made a practice of memorizing his verses to perform as if his own, a transference into the oral realm which masks authorship.

> I heare that *Faustus* oftentimes rehearses,
> to his chast mistris certaine of my Vearses,
> In which with use, so perfitt he is grown,
> that she, poore foole, now thinks they are his own.[21]

Harington goes on to suggest that he would not mind if Sir John Davies or Samuel Daniel did the same, for then he could retaliate by similar theft. At one point he even distances himself from his most famous epigram, 'On Treason': in a letter to Prince Henry from 1609 he quotes 'Treason doth never prosper' when sending along the verses of King Henry VI, but does not identify it as his own; instead, he introduces the lines with 'thus saith a poet'.[22]

Harington's reputation also created a situation where anonymous epigrams were fathered upon him, as is evident from a late 1590s letter to him:

> Your great enemye, Sir James,[23] did once mention the Star-Chamber, but your good esteeme in better mindes outdid his endeavors, and all is silente

again. The Queen is minded to take you to her favour, but she sweareth that
she believes you will make epigrams and write *misacmos* again on her and all
the courte; she hath been heard to say, 'that merry poet, her godson, must not
come to Greenwich, till he hath grown sober, and leaveth the ladies sportes and
frolicks.' She did conceive much disquiet on being tolde you had aimed a shafte
at Leicester: I wishe you knew the author of that ill deed; I would not be in his
beste jerkin for a thousand markes.[24]

Harington's status as a pre-eminent epigrammatist raises problems for
him: fears on the Queen's part that he will write further epigrams mocking the court, and suspicion that he might be responsible for ones already
circulating. We should not assume from this that Harington was *not* the
author of whatever satiric 'shaft' was in question. Markham might be
wrongly assuming Harington was not responsible, or jocularly pointing
to the trouble into which the poet has got himself. Similarly, Sir John
Davies, in a final epigram (of his published volume), laments that, even
though he will write no more, the libellous epigrams of others will be
ascribed to him:

That from henceforth, ech bastard cast forth rime
Which doth but savour of a Libel vaine,
Shal call me father, and be thought my crime.
         So dull and with so litle sence endude,
         Is my grose headed judge, the multitude.[25]

Such are the perils of epigrammatic fame.

While attribution was more likely (and more reliable) in print, anonymity, partial anonymity and stolen verses could also be factors there. Some
printed compilations, which continued the collecting practice reflected in
the manuscript tradition, often presented their poems with the authors
unidentified. *Alcilia* (1613), whose author is identified on the title page
only as 'I.C.', reproduces a body of Harington's epigrams and offers the
partial attribution of being by 'Sir I.H. and others'. That in both manuscript and print poems often appeared only with authors' initials certainly
widened the possibility of misattribution; three of the best epigrammatists
of the period were 'J.H.' (Harington, Hoskins and John Heath)[26] and,
as will be discussed below, 'H.P.' might point to Henry Peacham or the
slippery 'Henry Parrot'. Richard Brathwaite's *Remains after Death* (1618)
offers a large printed collection of widely circulated epitaphs, and, while
Brathwaite was a poet himself, these were largely by other and usually

unidentified poets. Samuel Pick's *Festum voluptatis* (1639) is an extreme example of outright plagiarism; in a brief 1931 note Hyder E. Rollins makes clear the amount of borrowing at work: it consists 'almost entirely of stolen wares' from published epigram collections of the 1610s (Parrot, Rowlands, Brathwaite, Davies of Hereford, for example).[27]

Jonson

As is so often the case, Jonson stands apart: he not only consistently asserted his authorial status but published his epigrams as part of the ambitious folio *Workes* of 1616. There he described them as 'the ripest of my studies', but what does he mean by that: are they the earliest penned, or, as Marjorie Swann suggests, 'the most lofty of his achievements'?[28] Swann emphasizes how they stand as a collection within a collection: the core work in a group of usually minor genres that was claiming to play a much loftier literary role. Thus, it is not surprising that Jonson guarded his epigrams jealously, and this fear of others stealing them is widely manifest in the epigrams. He complains of 'Playwright', who 'hearing some toys I'd writ', stole five of them for use in a play.[29] Jonson fears similar theft in 'To Prowl, the Plagiary':

> Forbear to tempt me, Prowl, I will not show
>> A line unto thee till the world it know,
> Or that I've by two good sufficient men
>> To be the wealthy witness of my pen:
> For all thou hear'st, thou swear'st thyself didst do.[30]

These lines point to means of establishing ownership of a poem: publication or initial public presentation in an illustrious company. He threatens to make a libel on Prowl to deter him, and, apart from the lack of the real name, this poem itself is that public revealing. An ironic question remains: did he show *these* lines to Prowl, or did he fear that they might they be stolen too? There are no surviving manuscript copies of the poem, so it may be that 'Prowl' saw it only after the printing of the 1616 folio.

Given what we have seen in epigram circulation generally, Jonson's concerns were not merely self-obsessed paranoia. However, Jonson was also at least once concerned about a different type of theft, one where an epigram was physically stolen from him and circulated with his name attached. This situation is described in 'Conversations with Drummond' where he explains how 'That piece of the pucelle of the Court was stolen out of his pocket by a gentleman who drank him drowsy, and given Mistress Bulstrode; which brought him great displeasure'.[31] The episode (and the poem's subsequent history) shows something of Jonson's desire to control the circulation of his epigrams. The poem challenges Cecily Bulstrode (the 'court Pucell'), claiming that Jonson dares to censure her as much as she does him, and to do so publicly:

> Does the court pucelle then so censure me,
> And thinks I dare not her? Let the world see.[32]

Ironically, despite this opening bold claim, Jonson clearly does *not* want the world (or Bulstrode) to see this poem, even after the death of Bulstode in 1609 – otherwise it could have been included in the 1616 'Epigrammes'.[33] However, the details of the episode also suggest that he was willing for *some* to see it or know of it, or that perhaps her death, upon which he wrote a laudatory epitaph, prompted his later reticence, as he adhered to the classical adage 'De mortuis nil nisi bonum' [Of the dead nothing but that which is good]. Seemingly at some drinking spot (one imagines a tavern) Jonson had at the very least revealed the existence of the poem, perhaps had even read it aloud, but wanted it to stop there. Here then, Jonson is concerned not about authorship denied but about authorship proclaimed outside his control.

Jonson's 'An Epigram to my Muse the Lady Digby' serves as an example of the importance of Jonson's profile as poet to his epigrams. Ostensibly the poem praises Sir Kenelm Digby to his wife (Venetia), but, by richly imagining how the poem will be received, Jonson makes the epigram at least as much about his own success as author. He imagines that his muse (Lady Digby) will bring his verses to Sir Kenelm, who will both praise and share them:

> Oh, what a fame 'twill be!
> What reputation to my lines and me,
> When he shall read them at the Treasurer's board!
> The knowing Weston, and that learnèd lord
> Allows them! Then what copies shall be had,
> What transcripts begged! How cried up, and how glad,
> Wilt thou be, muse, when this shall them befall!
> Being sent to one, they will be read of all.[34]

Harold Love uses this epigram to illustrate the passing of a poem from private to public circulation,[35] but does not note how enthusiastic Jonson is about such, in *this case*, in contrast to his earlier epigrams. While he had print-published his epigrams in his *Workes*, and might have been preparing another publication in the 1630s before his death, this late poem (early 1630s) shows Jonson's re-embracing of the older model of coterie manuscript circulation, but with the important distinction that such will involve his name and reputation.[36] The 'all' imagined by Jonson is also not the general public that print publication invited but the elite court circle of Digby and Richard Weston, Lord Treasurer. Ironically, it was Digby himself who by overseeing the posthumous publication of Jonson's *Underwood* brought this poem (and others) to a wider readership yet.

Of bastards and borrowed feathers

Composers of political and libellous epigrams circulating in manuscript might desire anonymity to avoid prosecution for libel, but I would suggest that the authorless nature of these politically charged lines can be a reflection of the perceived communal nature of the verses. It is not so much that a name was suppressed but that the unascribed nature of the epigram was essential to the form, that these were the 'common' thoughts – what was on everyone's lips – and that in the period there was not a significant difference between the first and subsequent utterers of such lines. Even the frequent phrasing 'who first sung it' suggests that the epigram is shared (as well as oral) property, and certainly the authorities saw possession or utterance of a libellous epigram to be criminal regardless of who the author might have been.[37] This communal understanding is consistent with the epigram's roots; as Kathryn J. Gutzwiller notes, 'the authorial disengagement later associated with epigrammatic style is ... an inheritance from the traditional objectivity of earlier inscribed verse'.[38] Detachment in the epigram was sometimes a vehicle for an urbane and even cynical voice, but in the most widely circulated epigrams its more important function was that of a supposed universality. What this highlights is the transferable nature of epigrams: while they might be penned by one, they could ultimately belong to all.

Early modern discussion of authorship drew heavily upon two tropes: that of 'borrowed feathers'[39] and that of paternity. The implications of both are fascinating, and even more when they come together in the series of epigram volumes by Henry Parrot. The first trope partakes of the longstanding tradition of poetry as avian flight, but is most directly derived from a fable going back to Aesop in which a plain bird (variously translated as a crow, jackdaw or chough) dressed himself in the more glamorous feathers of peacocks and attempted to pass in their company. Recognizing him as an imposter, the peacocks 'stript the foolish bird of [his] colours, and whipped him'.[40] This conceit of 'borrowed feathers' was often used in the epigram culture of the seventeenth century to articulate a concern that the goal of legitimate poetic flight has been replaced with that of ostentatious rhetorical flourishes and appearance derived from others. In a poetic culture where deep imitation was valued, 'borrowed feathers' was imitation gone awry. The new author had clumsily plucked the superficial aspects of style, rather than deeply absorbing the essence of the predecessor to become authentically the 'English Martial' or the 'new Horace'. Poets who relied upon 'borrowed feathers' would be unsuccessful in flight and ultimately ridiculous in appearance. Most significantly, no one was fooled. The trope was also used as a polite euphemism for outright theft; here the 'borrower' might fail to live up to his claimed lines, as in the story of the poetaster and Virgil.

Thomas Freeman (see Chapter 5) includes one poem in manuscript (BL Sloane 1889) which uses the familiar trope drawn from Aesop's fable to respond to a contemporary who has accused him of stealing from Davies:

In quenda*m* qui me ex Davis epig. surripuisse dictitabat[41]
[On one who accused me of stealing out of the epigrams of Davies]
No Aesops crow I too too much abhorr thee
to lett my birds have borrowed feathers on
and Davis though I am no fitt match for thee
yet know I write & what I write's mine owne
I fly with mine & not with others wings
nor are they impt with any one strange feather
If I resemble thee in many things
why so most writers do compard togeather
but no brave ribaldry is in my rimes
but itt is Davis one or other cries
yet very fooles speake sentences sometimes
but wott you why I argue on this wise
   onely to prove and that's the only jest
   that I can write as bawdy as the best.[42]

The epigram opens with Freeman distancing himself from the crow or jackdaw of Aesop's fable; while rejecting the charge of theft, he acknowledges a typical literary 'likeness' between himself and Davies. Although he downplays his own abilities, Freeman seems to take pleasure in being mistaken for the more established epigrammatist. His defence is typical, as it invokes the idea that imitation is part of the literary tradition, and in particular that of the epigram, and that such imitation is a sort of flattery or honouring. Freeman thus draws a careful line between admiring imitation and illegitimate 'borrowed' feathers.

The trope of 'fathering' a poem has quite different implications, and the use of it transposes into the poetic realm the complex legal framework of parental and filial rights and responsibilities in early modern England. The metaphor builds upon the relationship and likeness between 'father' and 'son', and the public status and role of bastards, orphans and foundlings. (This discussion, like that of the poets and readers of the time, uses masculine language – the 'mother' of such poems, if mentioned at all, was likely to be the Muse.) A poet who sent forth a poem into the public realm without *fully* acknowledging it was, in a sense, rendering it a bastard. Readers might suspect, or even know, its paternity, but it would not be formally acknowledged by its father.[43] In another scenario a poem that entered manuscript or oral circulation attached to an author's name might lose that attribution as circulation widened. In this case the process of circulation might render a poem a bastard or even an orphan. The latter term fits those poems that went forth or became fully detached from any recognized author, and as such were prone to be adopted as foundlings by other poets. Beyond this, even those poets who published epigrams under their own name would frequently distance themselves from that point on, often using the language of 'bastards' to describe those poems that they no longer recognised as their own. Thus, Guilpin refers to his epigrams as 'Orphants', which 'shal be soone renounced', and 'bastards of my *Muse*' in the concluding poem of his collection.[44] They would seem not to be bastards in the sense of the father not being known but rather the offspring of an illegitimate relationship, and in this sense distanced from their author, who at least pretends to have no further concern for them. Overall, this casual approach to poetic offspring is markedly in contrast to the possessive Martialian authorship of Harington, Owen and Jonson. And it is worth noting that Martial was the first to take the word 'plagiarius' meaning 'plunderer' and then 'kidnapper' and apply it to the thief of writing, and that Jonson was among the earliest to use the term 'plagiary' in English.

In another scenario, a poem might enter circulation without attribution, but its 'paternity' be recognized by comparison to other acknowledged poems. It was expected that there would be some resemblance between 'father' and 'son' – a rough and ready paternity test might be

applied and the poet discovered.[45] In a neat reversal of the direction of
the verbal action of 'fathering', such poems came to be 'fathered' upon
authors, whatever denials they might make.

The tropes of stolen feathers and bastardy could be brought together,
as they were in Goddard's *Mastiff Whelp*, which offers this portrait of one
who stole epigrams:

> Talke you with *Poet-Asse* sitting in's seate,
> You'le heare him ex'lent, *Epigrames* repeate,
> Demaund him whose they bee, they runn soe fine,
> He answers straight, fruits of this braine of myne,
> Yet let a well-read Poet heare the vaine,
> Hee'lle finde they came out of a *Bastardes* braine.
> Dust heare me *Poet-asse?* I'le prophysee,
> That when th'art mari'd, thou't a Cockould bee:
> Thou fath'rest now things got by other men,
> What wilt thou doe when thou art mari'd then?
>> *I pry* [sic] *thee good* Jack-Dawe *give each bird's owne,*
>> *That for a plaine* Jack Dawe *thou maist be knowne.*[46]

Here the focus is not on the original poet who begets the poems – it is not
clear whether they are fully acknowledged here or not – but on 'Poet-asse',
who as a 'Poetaster' willingly adopts them as his own. Such renders him
a cuckold in the extension of the metaphor. As is typical of Goddard's
poems, the final couplet stands apart, here by rendering the same idea
with the conceit of the Jackdaw and his borrowed feathers. (The reference
in line 6 may be to the epigrams of Thomas Bastard, which, as discussed
in Chapter 5, did circulate widely both before and after printing, and
whose unfortunate name rather adds to the confusion surrounding poetic
paternity.)

The trope of the 'father' of a poem is complicated by the fact that occasionally it seems to refer to the subject rather than the author of a poem.
Such a usage seems to lie behind the famous reference to 'Mr. W.H.' as
the 'only begetter' of Shakespeare's sonnets. Similarly, in Harington's
poem 'Of the objects of his satire' he uses the analogy of begetting, and
it seems that revealing the 'father' means identifying the subject of the
poem – not the author:

> Theise rymes are Mungrells gotten on witt and lafter
> My Muse the Nurse that bred them at her breast,

the witt asham'd 'twas occupi'de so lewdly.
By Riballds: faine would have their names supprest,
Save her young Imps father themselves so shrewdly.
that who got some of them, may soone be guest.[47]

Harington here identifies himself with his Muse, the *mother*, and the father would seem to be the subject of the poem. The poem continues with a teasing hint that someday the 'fathers' will be revealed:

But as some Irishe dame that false hath playd
Will not confesse her fact for threats or force
Till death approching makes her soule afrayde
and toucheth her sick hart with sad remorse.
Then wishing she the truthe had uttred rather
She doth her wanton dealings all discover
And makes her children know, and call one father
that none had earst suspected for her lover.
So if my Wanton Muse dy penitent
Perhaps she then may tell you whom she ment.

This threat of revealing is part of the latent power of the epigrammatist, offered here as a warning at the end of Harington's collection.

Henry Parrot

The five volumes attributed to 'Henry Parrot' (*The Mous-Trap* (1606), *Epigrames* (1608), *Laquei ridiculosi: Or Springes for Woodcocks* (1613), *The Mastive – or Young-Whelpe of the Olde-Dogge* (1615) and *Cures for the Itch* (1626)) present a very complicated authorial situation as Parrot's role lies somewhere between that of author and collector.[48] Each of the later volumes except *The Mastive* borrows some epigrams (often revised) from earlier volumes, which are intermingled with new material. All involve a mixture of epigrams clearly by other known authors and ones either original to Parrot or taken from authors who have not to this point been identified. Charges of plagiarism were first laid against Parrot by his contemporaries Davies of Hereford and Brathwaite: most tellingly, Brathwaite completes the trope by suggesting that Parrot has taken on both 'borrowed note and Coate'.[49] Scholars have since confirmed these charges, showing that many of the epigrams in the Parrot volumes were written by others and that he significantly reused original material. He adapted poems by

Rowlands and Guilpin, and Franklin B. Williams most thoroughly shows how Parrot in *Springes for Woodcocks* reproduced epigrams of Harington wholesale, and that such was made possible by the death of Harington the previous year.[50] To this, James L. Sanderson added the recognition that some were likely by Rudyerd.[51] Williams pursues a range of possibilities to explain the plagiarism: that *Springes for Woodcocks* was padded by the printer (John Busby) without Parrot's consent, that some epigrams by others that Parrot had gathered for his own amusement were inadvertently mixed with his own or that ultimately the infraction was minor and typical of poetic borrowing in the period.

Largely overlooked by Williams and Sanderson are the ways in which Parrot's prefatory materials and some of his epigrams play with the question of the origins of the epigrams. For example, in *Springes* epigram 132 he defies those who say he borrows and imitates, and this self-consciousness about what he is doing and the role of such epigrams in the culture of satire and libel in the period need to be considered. It is surprising that most scholars tacitly assume that 'Henry Parrot' was a real name: in the case of *The Mous-trap* we have a book by a *parrot*, dedicated to a *buck*, and intended to catch *mice* rather than *rats*; in *Springes* we have snares set by a *parrot* to catch a *woodcock*: certainly allegorical pseudonyms are at work.[52] Ultimately, I would suggest that the 'Parrot' volumes are not the work of a single, biographical figure named Henry Parrot, but the pseudonym of one or more figures who were gathering and publishing a medley of epigrams from a variety of sources. The whole enterprise was based upon the rich trope of the parrot, which does not offer its own song, but rather merely repeats that of others.[53] Both feathers and song are borrowed.

The prefaces to Henry Parrot's numerous volumes of epigrams show him playing games with his readers: coyly raising the questions of authorship and identity only to leave them unanswered. In *The Mous-trap*, Parrot claims to attempt to 'Onely unfold by way of borrowed rime, / Some few fantasticke humors of our time'.[54] There is no deception here: the epigrams are 'borrowed rime'. His 'To the guilty Coxcome' in *Springes* seems to be playing games with the poet's identity:

Cease gald-backt Gull to question what or whence,
Or who I am that did these lines compose,
Dost thou not privately with shame dispence,
But needes must have it publisht to thy nose?
Will any foole suspect what no man thinks?
Knowst not a T. the more it's stird it stincks?[55]

The address 'To the Courteous Reader' in his final volume, *Cures for the Itch*, talks about his writing of the epigrams, but then, in 'To the Cricicke-seeming Censurer' of the same work, he presents the 'brood' of epigrams as bastards or orphans, as in the trope discussed above: 'so farre unlikely will it be (I know) to finde the owners or fathers [of these epigrams] out, who questionlesse will quite disclaim them to be their Bastards though nere so jumpe a like in qualities as can or may be possibly required'.[56]

The game that Parrot invites his reader to join in is twofold: the usual one of discerning the real subject behind the fictional figures of the epigram, and here the additional game of establishing the paternity of 'bastard rimes'. The implications are significant: a poem without a publicly recognized 'father', like a literal bastard, came to belong to the people; it was in legal terminology 'filius populi'. Thomas Heywood extended this metaphorically to a literary work without an acknowledged author, calling it 'filius populi, a bastard without a father to acknowledge it'.[57] Parrot uses this as well: the unacknowledged poems may 'desperately lye upon the parish for want of shelter'.[58] Parrot's point here is an important one: an epigram whose author would not claim it became public property and could be freely collected and reproduced by compilers like him. Elsewhere in *Cures for the Itch* Parrot addresses the question of the identities behind his epigrams:

> *Magus* a man of artificiall trade,
> Most confident beleeves, and will averre,
> These Epigrams of mine are meant and made
> By persons knowne, in each particuler.[59]

The phrase 'meant and made / By persons knowne' implies that they were both *about* well-known figures, and *by* such figures, which would of course make the collection all the more intriguing for readers as they attempted to discern the identity of both author and subject. While Parrot has raised the accusation as if it were ridiculous, he does not deny it, but simply mocks Magus as a cuckold.

In a poem published in 1617 the epigrammatist Henry Fitgeffrey reverses the blame in castigating those who launch satiric works, but then disowns them out of fear, again likely pointing toward the uncertain paternity of the 'Parrot' epigrams:

> Others have helpes: when their *Invention* faile,
> Straight they begin abusively to raile.

> Then out comes *Whelps of the olde Dog:* for sport:
> Shall barke at Great ones: bite the meaner sort:
> When the On-setters (after all their paine:)[60]
> For feare, woo'd gladly call them in againe.
> And these will *Poets* bee accounted too:
> Because they *Dare* doe more then others doe.
> Though they their *Verses write*, (a man may say:)
> As Clown's get Bastards, and straight runne away.[61]

The passage points particularly to Parrot's *The Mastive – or Young-Whelpe of the Olde-Dogge* (1615), which seems to have stolen its very title from Goddard's *Mastiff Whelp*.[62] However, who are the 'on-setters'? It might be the publishers who come to regret their role, or it may be a reference to the group of figures who have written or collected the Parrot volumes. Such would suggest that 'Parrot' is a pseudonym. He is a fictional front, one who 'parrots', that is repeats, epigrams from a number of poets who have contributed to these volumes. According to Fitzgeffrey, they fall short of being poets, not just because of a lack of compositional originality but owing to their reluctance to claim 'authorship' or responsibility. Was a single collector playing the role of 'Henry Parrot' even behind all these volumes, or did the name become a sort of Pasquil upon whom print-ers fastened poems? Joseph Loewenstein's argument that in the wake of *Venus and Adonis* the printer William Jaggard used the initials 'W.S.' as a relatively innocent pointer to erotic verse ('a brand name for venereal poetry')[63] is suggestive for the Parrot volumes as well. After all, it was only *The Mous-trap* that explicitly identified 'Henry Parrot' as the author on the title page: all the others were by 'H.P.' (although 'Henry Parrot' is given at the end of 'Ad Lectorem' in *Springes*).[64] And as Loewenstein sug-gests of Jaggard, we cannot be certain of whether such use of initials was simply casual lack of concern or deliberate deception on the printers' part.

Illustrious authorship: John Hoskins

Clive James, in noting that it was Hanns Johst rather than Hermann Goering who first made the famous remark about reaching for his revolver at the word 'culture', suggests that it is 'an instructive example of a clever remark floating upwards until it attaches itself to someone sufficiently famous'.[65] This captures well the dynamics of some pseudonymous epi-gram circulation in early modern England. In many cases the perception that an epigram had been penned by a significant public figure greatly enhanced interest and circulation. In those cases supposed authorship was a part of the very *meaning* of the epigram. Such verses were frequently said to 'go under the name of' the great figure, or be 'fathered upon' him, which reflects the unavoidable uncertainty of the legitimacy of such attributions. Those produced in times of hardship or persecution for the 'author' or in response to other widely circulating libels were especially prized. Ultimately, while it may be compare to great things with small, the concept of pseudepigrapha from the fields of classical and biblical studies may be helpful here. While ancient Greek texts were falsely ascribed to Homer to enhance their prestige, and religious texts attached to canonical authors such as Solomon or disciples such as Thomas or Peter to establish their sacred authority, epigrams attached themselves to the name of King James or Ralegh to increase their topical interest and allure.

The reputation of John Hoskins (1566–1638) was based on a number of skills and roles, but in all of them his mastery of language and thought was paramount, and Michelle O'Callaghan has remarked on 'how much of his social and political identity Hoskyns invested in his wit'.[66] An astute lawyer, he achieved renown (and imprisonment) for his outspoken approach in Parliament in 1614. As a rhetorician, his *Directions for Speech and Style* was unpublished, but enjoyed a significant manuscript-based reputation.[67] While a number of his Latin poems (chiefly epitaphs and elegies) were print-published in the period, he never attempted print publication of the widely circulating English epigrams and epitaphs ascribed to him; nor, it would seem, offered gift collections of them in manuscript to friends or patrons.[68] However, his well-known use of the epigram form places him in a line of political English wits running from More to Heywood and Harington.[69]

As one whose reputation was more that of a wit than poet, and since in the area of wit authorship of the original conceit is more significant than the ultimate poetic setting, it is not surprising that Hoskins adopted a casual approach to his poetic offspring. Overall, his status as an English epigrammatist was much based more on the actions of others than on his own. Jonson and Harington offer worthwhile contrasts to Hoskins in this: for Jonson actual poetic authorship was paramount; Harington rather straddled the two public images, at times being a fount of wit, at others a preserver of his own poetic creations in the tradition of Martial. For most poems identified as by Hoskins, either in his own time or by later editors, attribution is particularly vexed. I would suggest that in many cases he became a sort of unwilling Pasquil, a name to which epigrams were fastened. Most surviving copies of poems ascribed to him are from the 1630s, well after his reputation as a witty poet had been established; hence, their authority is not convincing.

As David Colclough points out, Hoskins attended three institutions notably rich in the culture of manuscript circulation: Winchester, New College, Oxford, and the Middle Temple.[70] He became known for his wit early in his student days: John Aubrey recounts one instance, when Hoskins wrote Latin verses underneath a caricature of the 'good servant' at Winchester College.[71] Aubrey adds: 'There were many pretty stories of him when a schoolboy, which I have forgott.'[72] As seen in Chapter 3, Winchester was among those schools that intensively fostered epigrammatic wit, and, like many Winchester students, Hoskins continued on to New College, Oxford (1585). While there he contributed a significant body of Latin verses to *Peplus*, the volume marking the death of Sir Philip Sidney. Ultimately, however, he lost his place as a fellow at Oxford because of some libellous or seditious remarks in his role as 'terrae filius' at the graduation of 1592.[73] His entry into the Middle Temple the following year placed him in a context likely to further his witty inclinations, and a number of facetious epigrams and epitaphs were attributed to him over the following decades. Witty epigrams, increasingly of a political nature, came to be ascribed to him, but it is very difficult to verify his authorship. A number of manuscripts identify him as the author of the famous epitaph on the bellows-maker discussed in Chapter 4, but the majority of versions circulated without attribution to him (and one credits it to Sir John Davies with whom Hoskins had been bound when he arrived at the Middle Temple).[74] Hoskins is frequently identified as the author in manuscript, but, as most of these manuscripts date from the 1610s on, it is difficult to ascertain whether his fame as a composer of mock epitaphs stemmed from poems such as this, or whether this widely known epitaph came to be attached to his name because of that reputation.

By 1605 his reputation for such verses was established in print when the illustrious historian William Camden at the end of his *Remaines* reproduced a selection of 'conceited, merry, and laughing Epitaphes, the most of them composed by maister *John Hostines* [sic] when he was young'.[75] As Camden does not specify which are by Hoskins, he may have been relying on the wit's general reputation rather than any specific information on authorship. Marcy L. North has shown the degree to which epitaphs in manuscript were primarily anonymous;[76] however, Hoskins's reputation for epitaphs is the great exception to this tendency, as so many came to be fathered upon him.

Apart from ascription in manuscript or print, the poems associated with Hoskins can be categorized in this way:

- those whose witty point alone connects them with Hoskins
- those with some specific context shared with Hoskins
- those in his voice

In 1614 Hoskins was imprisoned under the King's orders for his threatening reference to the 'Sicilian Vespers' in a speech in the 'Addled Parliament'. This event prompted a number of widely circulating epigrams, both about and ostensibly by Hoskins.

Soon after his imprisonment, this epigram appeared in wildly varying forms:

> The Counsell by committing 4
> Have sent 8 humors to ye Tower
> Hoskins the poet is merrily sad,
> Sharpe ye devine is soberly mad.
> Cornwallis ye states-man is popishly precise
> And Chute ye Carver is foolishly wise.[77]

The line on Hoskins points to his reputation as a merry wit, but one made 'sad' from the results of that wit. Hoskins himself draws on that public image when he appeals to King James for clemency. He presents his comments in Parliament as being an extension of his usual witty temperament that thus ought to be accepted and forgiven as such; he points to the history of wits such as himself and concludes: 'no man ever suffered for mere witt: but yf he lived not to requitt it hymselfe, yet the witt of all posterity took penaunce on his name that oppressed hym'.[78] At this point he perceives his wit to be protective, that he may as time allows pay back what has been done to him with a verbal attack, or, if he is not able to do so, posterity will for him. He concludes that he would 'rather dy with witt then live without it'. Given his reputation and the public appetite for verses supposedly written by famous imprisoned men, it is not surprising that both Latin and English lines were soon circulating under his name, most of which are epigrammatic.[79] Most famous of these were the lines of advice offered in his epigram to his son, which circulated in both Latin and English:

Sweet Benedict whilst thou art younge
And know'st not yet the use of Toung,
Keepe it in thine thral whilst thou art free:
Imprison it or it will thee.

Dum Puer es, vanae nescisque incommoda Linguae
Vincula da Linguae, vel Tibi Lingua dabit.[80]

The poem, which survives in a wide variety of versions, combines the hard-earned stoical wisdom of so much poetry supposedly written from prison with the typically epigrammatic sharp witty turn of its second half.

A number of manuscripts include a Latin distich supposedly written by Hoskins 'in the windowe when he came out of the Tower':

Sic luo, sic merui; sed quod meruique luoque
Tu poena & meritis ablue Christe tuis.[81]

[Thus I pay and so I have deserved; but the punishment which I have deserved and the sins for which I pay, thou hast washed away with thy merits, O Christ.][82]

Fittingly, a poem in the voice of his wife Benedicta that pleaded for his release also became widely known. At least one manuscript suggests that it was written not by Benedicta but by John for her, and that attribution has been followed by most scholars.[83] It circulated in two states: one was in twenty-two four-line stanzas entitled 'A Dreame',[84] the other this abbreviated six-line epigram version:

The worst is told, the best is hidd,
Kings know not all, I would they did;
What though my husband once have errd?
Men more too blame have beene preferrd.
Who hath not errd hee doth not live;
Hee errd but once, once King forgive.[85]

While addressed and presented to the King, these verses also were repeated in the newsletters of the time, which indicates the high level of interest in Hoskins's situation and the poems that emerged from it.

True to his hope, Hoskins never died for his wit, but some two years later in early 1617 he found himself once again in trouble, seemingly for a rhyme written shortly after his release from imprisonment. Chamberlain reports:

> now for matter of rimes Hoskins the lawier is in a laberinth being brought into question for a rime or libel (as it is termed) made some yeare and halfe agon, yf he find not the bett. friends yt is feared he shalbe brought into the star-chamber and then he is undon.[86]

The identity of the complainant has not been established, but, from the context of Chamberlain's letter, it seems possible that it was a libel on George Villiers (later Duke of Buckingham).[87]

Much later, in the 1630s, the following lines on the death of Walter Pye were ascribed to Hoskins:

> If any aske, who heere doth lie;
> Say 'tis the divells Christmas Pye.
> Death was the Cooke, the divell the urne,
> Noe ward will serve, the Pie will burne.
> Yet serve it in; for many did wish,
> That the divell long since had had this dish.[88]

According to Osborn, the only basis for ascribing the Pye epitaph to Hoskins is that Aubrey records that Hoskins jested upon hearing of the death of Robert Pye that 'The devill haz a Christmas pye'. (It would seem that Aubrey has confused Walter Pye with his younger brother, Robert, who died in 1662.)[89] The witticism may have been Hoskins's, but the poetic rendering another's; or the jest might have been widespread, and Hoskins simply gave it polished epitaph form (as Harington frequently had); or that, penned by another, it came to be ascribed to Hoskins because of his reputation. Hoskins and Pye had longstanding connections: both were of Herefordshire; they were contemporaries at New College and the Middle Temple, and in the early 1620s fellow justices in Wales.

The attachment of Hoskins's name to widely circulating epigrams was based at first upon his reputation for wit, and then in later years his political situation: his firm, at times witty, resistance to the King on behalf of parliamentary rights established a reputation that lasted through the subsequent decades. From the vantage point of later in the century, Antony à Wood writes that Hoskins and his fellows were 'ever after held in great value by the Commons'.[90] In the continuing struggles between Parliament and the early Stuart kings, the short verses attributed to him would function as talismans of resistance. Even much later in the seventeenth century, Hoskins's reputation was intact: Aubrey was to recall that he 'made the best Latin Epitaphs of his time'.[91]

Illustrious authorship: fathered upon the king

The must illustrious author was a king or queen, and, while any poetic form might be so attributed in manuscript circulation, it does seem that epigrams were more likely than other verse forms to be fathered upon monarchs and other illustrious figures. Perhaps their brevity made it more plausible that a busy monarch would have time to dash them off. The other factor is the wide and uncontrolled circulation of epigrams (explored in Chapter 4), which made it more likely that their authors would be forgotten, and the great have their names attached to these orphan children. An epigram by Queen Elizabeth or an imprisoned Ralegh was far more interesting than the same poem in anonymous form. Such enhancement is captured in the following account from 1629:

> One Talboy, a busie prating newsmonger, being desirous to exchange a speech he had pick't up for another which he wanted, he went to a scrivener at Temple Bar, who then traded in such things, who refusing a speech without name to make it currant coin, Talboy stamped on it that of Sir Edward Hailes, and for a while it passed as his.[92]

Here the name of Sir Edward Hales of Kent (ca. 1577–1654), who achieved a high profile through his outspoken opposition to Buckingham in the 1626 Parliament, gives currency and interest to an otherwise neglected piece.[93]

Such attribution to illustrious figures was far from a new phenomenon: Richard Bentley, writing in the late seventeenth century, pointed to this tradition: 'to forge and counterfeit books, and father them upon great names, has been a practice almost as old as letters'.[94] Ernst Curtius notes an epigram from the *Greek Anthology* which was ascribed to Plato (a love one, at that!) and one from the *Anthologia Latina* frequently fathered upon Julius Caesar, Augustus or Germanicus. Fitzgerald recounts an anecdote from Macrobius, where Augustus turns the tables and presents a Greek epigram to a poet expecting patronage,[95] and Suetonius wrote of that same emperor that he had a book of epigrams, 'which he composed for the most part at the time of the bath'.[96]

Fallen royal favourites were particularly likely to have such poems attributed to them. The Earl of Essex was the supposed author of a number of verses, composed 'when he was in disgrace' in the late 1590s.[97] With Ralegh, a well-established literary reputation made such putative verses all the more credible and sought after. As Michael Rudick demonstrates so well in his edition of poems *associated* with Ralegh, through his long imprisonment many short verses were widely circulated under his name, often with the flimsiest of evidence. For example, such widely known political epigrams as 'Heere lyes old Hobinol' on the death of Robert Cecil (1612), and 'I.C.U.R. good mounser Carre' on the Carr–Howard marriage are at least in a few manuscripts assigned to Ralegh.[98] In the months following his execution on 29 October 1618 numerous poems appeared, all said to have been composed by him the night before his execution.[99] While sending along some short verses, Chamberlain reports,

> Yf these papers will not helpe to supplie the want of better matter, I know not how to furnish out a letter this weeke. We are so full still of Sir Walter Raleigh, that almost every day brings foorth somwhat in this kind, besides divers ballets wherof some are called in, and the rest such poore stuffe as are not worth the overlooking.[100]

On New Year's Day 1619 John Holles instructed his son in London, 'I would have yow gather up as many of Sir W. Rawlies verses, and letters as yow can, ex unguibus leonem. I shall easily know the birds of his nest from the invention of others.'[101] Holles's comment points to the widespread circulation of such writings, and his confidence about judging their legitimacy draws upon the familiar trope of paternity, here given an avian twist that suggests the offspring will necessarily reflect the appearance of their progenitor.

Purported royal authorship was a special case: such poems were of great attraction to readers, but also could be dangerous to circulate. They promised contemporary readers an insight into the private world of their monarch (like what Augustus was doing in the bath). *Fragmenta Aulica* (1662) noted the public desire for such relics of the royal court; in a preface 'To the Court', the compiler writes

> These your disports and trifles we poor mortals admire as Oracles, and conceit our discourse highly improved, if we can draw in one of these stories by the head and eares to embellish and set it off.[102]

Ironically, royal trifles became treasured, drawn on by others to embellish their own speech and writing. Many such 'royal verses' were mere jests, but some were embraced because of a deeper political import or the charged context that had prompted them. As with Essex and Ralegh, Queen Elizabeth's best-known verses stem from a moment of persecution. The distich which Elizabeth had been said to inscribe upon the window frame in Woodstock castle during her 1550s imprisonment later achieved wide circulation:

> Much suspected by me,
> Nothing proved can be.
> Quod Elizabeth the prisoner.

This couplet was the kernel in circulation, central and unchanging, and of a length that might plausibly be scratched into a window. However, in some cases the lines were preserved in a fuller version:

> O Fortune, thy wresting, wavering state
> Hath fraught with cares my troubled wit,
> Whose witness this present prison late
> Could bear, where once was joy flown quite.
> Thou causedst the guilty to be loosed
> From lands where innocents were enclosed,
> And caused the guiltless to be reserved,
> And freed those that death had well deserved.
> But all herein can be naught wrought,
> So God grant to my foes as they have thought.
> Finis. Elisabetha a prisoner, 1555
> Much suspected by me, but nothing proved can be.[103]

The longer version of the poem was recorded by a number of German visitors in the late sixteenth century, whereas the recounting of the story with the shorter version by both Foxe and Holinshed helped ensure its fame.[104]

King James's reputation as a poet and his use of the print medium for a range of literary, political and religious works mark him as an exceptional case. His self-acknowledged role as author encouraged readers to link manuscript poems with his name, even as in the period 1610 to 1625 he refrained from the formal issuance of poetry that had marked his Scottish years. He also prepared three manuscript collections of largely unpublished poetry, the last in the late 1610s.[105] However, the last decade of his life was marked by a number of short verses that circulated widely under his name, but were never explicitly authorized by him, and which constitute a range of legitimate attachment to him.

Through the 1590s, as it became likely that James would accede to the English throne upon Elizabeth's death, short verses ascribed to him began to circulate increasingly in England. For example, John Overall, Regius Professor of Divinity at Cambridge (and later a bishop under James), had presented to him a manuscript with Latin epitaphs on Mary, Queen of Scots, ascribed to her son James.[106] Sir Stephen Powle records in his commonplace book a poem that claims in its title to be 'A passionate Sonnett made by the Kinge of Scots upon difficulties ariseing to crosse his proceedinge in love and marriage with his most worthie to be esteemed Queene' (the poem begins, 'In sunny beams the sky doth show her sweet'). However, Powle has later added the note 'Geaven me by Mr. Britton [Nicholas Breton] (as he sayde) in Scotland with the Kinges majesty: but I rather thinke they weare made by him in the person of the Kinge'.[107] His final comment shows an awareness of the distinction between a poem in the *voice* of the King and one actually *written* by him. Steven May notes, however, that until after 1616 such circulation in manuscript tended to be limited to small courtly circles.[108]

The situation changed markedly after 1616, as a small group of topical poems attributed to the King circulated widely and were much commented on. Jane Rickard concludes that the increased circulation of James's poems in the period 1616 to 1625 reflects an explicit willingness on his part to use manuscript circulation 'for poems he wanted to make public to a specific readership'.[109] Thus, she argues that such poems fathered upon him were not merely a manifestation of the public's heightened expectation but a strategy on the King's part. Curtis Perry suggests that public poems attributed to James in these latter years fall into three groups: those fully written by James himself, 'those written by others, vetted by the king, and then fathered upon him', and those 'written for, and authorized by, the king'.[110] The distinction between the latter two types is slight, and I would note that, in the period, the phrase 'fathered upon' generally suggested an unwilling purported father, and, as will be demonstrated below, that some poems under James's name or in his voice were not in any way authorized or accepted by him: such are 'worse than a libel'.[111]

The much noted comet of late 1618 prompted the wide circulation of verses ascribed to King James; in most manuscript versions the poem is titled 'The Blazing Star', and begins 'You men of Britain'.[112] Chamberlain notes about the poem that 'other verses go abrode in the Kings and S.N. [Secretary Naunton?] name'.[113] He does not comment on the King's authorship but on Naunton's: 'I never heard before that he had the vertue of versifieing, and I shold have thought he had not now the leasure.' We cannot be certain that the poem referred to is 'The Blazing Star', but the date matches and Chamberlain mentions the comet later in the letter.

Noteworthy with this poem, as with most of the other verses attributed to James in the later years of his life, is that it represents a direct response to widespread public commentary on state matters. Some of James's subjects were interpreting the comet as a warning to beware of Spain, as negotiations concerning the Spanish Match were ongoing at the time. Other political developments offered further bases for speculation: Sir Walter Ralegh had been executed a few months previously, much to the dismay of many of James's subjects, and the Synod of Dordt had just begun on 13 November. Thus, the poem is not freestanding, but part of a larger discussion, or perhaps an attempt to end it. James exclaims:

> I wish the Curious man to keep
> His rash Imaginations till he sleepe
> Then let him dreame of ffamine plague and war
> And thinke the match with spaine hath causd this star
> Or let them thinke that if their Prince my Minion
> Will shortly chang, or which is worse religion
> And that he may have nothing else to feare.[114]

It would seem that James was provoked into quasi-public poetry by the writings of others, particularly on the subject of the Spanish Match.[115] The King was responding to 'what all men might say': the anonymous quickly circulating *vox populi* prompted a response in the same medium.

Likewise, the death of Queen Anne on 2 March 1618/19 compelled poets, including James, to reconsider the significance of the blazing star. For Corbett it was now 'a Herauld-*Starr*' which 'Did Beckon to Her to appeare', but he downplays any ominous aspect: 'For when such Harbingers are seene, / God crownes a *Saint*, not kills a *Queene*.'[116] In a similar vein, a widely circulated poem attributed to the King reinterprets the blazing star not as an omen but a divine invitation:

> 'Twas to invite this guest God sent the star,
> Whose friends and nearest kin good princes are:
> Who, though they run the race of men, and die,
> It serves but to refine their majesty.
> So did the queen her court from hence remove,

And put off earth to be enthroned above.
She then is changed, not dead; no good prince dies,
But, like this day's sun, only sinks to rise!

This is the version of the poem sent by Sir Thomas Lorkin on 12 April 1619 to Sir Thomas Puckering, who suggests that it is 'the epicedeum [*sic*] that is like to be sung upon the day of the funeral'.[117] These verses on Queen Anne's death survive in a large number of manuscripts, and Craigie notes that 'Not two of the MSS. examined agree exactly in the text they offer'.[118] The variants are significant: some versions end with the line 'but only like the sunne doth sett to rise'; others with 'But onely with the day starr shutts their eyes'.[119] As discussed in Chapter 4, the maintenance of basic sense with varied word order and diction simply cannot be attributed to scribal error, nor does authorial revision seem likely with this sort of topical poem. The wide range of variation suggests that its prime means of circulation was oral,[120] and with free-floating poems like this authorial control of text, let alone meaning, is very limited.

The widely circulated idea that James had composed a poem on his wife's death probably led to the ascription of another poem to him (in this case in the first person) in some manuscripts:

And wilt you goe & leave me heere?
O doe not soe my dearest deare,
The sunnes departure clouds the skie
But thy departure makes me dye,
Thou canst not goe without my hart
And that which is my cheefest part
ffor with two harts thou shalt be gone
And I must stay behind with none
But if that you wilt goe away
Then leave one hart with me to stay,
Take mine, let thine for pledge remaine
Then thou maist quickly come againe,
Meane while my part shalbe to mourne
And tell the houres till thou returne,
Mine eyes shalbe but eyes to weepe
And neither eyes to see nor sleepe.[121]

Later, this poem was revised to fit another departure of a figure close to the King, the Duke of Buckingham: 'And wilt thou goe, great Duke, and leave us heere',[122] a satiric epigram mocking Buckingham's departure for Rochelle in 1627. Once again, the unstable nature of both authorship and subject with such poems is evident.

Another group of short topical poems ascribed to James came in the early months of 1623, during a flurry of controversial epigram circulation; most of these reflected upon the long proposed but now increasingly likely 'Spanish Match'. For the more militant Protestants, the marriage of the English royal heir to a Roman Catholic princess, daughter of the most powerful Roman Catholic king, threatened all the religious and political changes of the previous century. Direct comment on the situation faced prosecution (it was definitely an area that James saw as falling within the *arcana imperii*), but indirect or anonymous comment was widespread. In January 1623, Mead noted the situation in London:

> There is much talk of libels and dangerous books: and that one, this Christmas time, nailed up a libel upon the pulpit in the king's chapel, in sight of all; which boldness made them think he was sent by authority, and he went his way, and escaped.[123]

Neither the contents of this 'libel' nor its author is known, but Mead's comment shows an expectation that there might be officially authorized libels or counter-libels, that the King was adopting the methods of those attacking his policies. Mead goes on to note that

> There is also a great paper of verses, in way of answer to these libels and State meddlers, vulgarly said to be the king's: but a gentleman told me that he will not own it.

Chamberlain also mentions the King responding to libels in a letter from this time (25 January 1622/3):

> And now touching [libels], the report goes there be many abroad; and it should seem the king's verses, I herewith send you, were made in answer to one of them.

A passage from a subsequent letter of Mead illustrates the evolving dynamics of these works in circulation:

> I send you enclosed, as they term them in London, the king's verses; the first in answer, as it seems, to some libel; the latter, 'Good Counsel to Gentlemen to

leave the City'. This latter, some say, the king hath disclaimed expressly; but what he saith to the other, I know not. But, if it be not his, it is worse than a libel; and not to be read. But till that appears, I suppose, there is no danger.[124]

The uncertainty about the poem's status in relation to the King is striking. The King might 'own' a work, deny it or simply leave it in limbo; in that third state it had a semi-official status (rather like a known bastard), but also could be dangerous to hold, if later denied by the King. A few weeks later, Chamberlain was to use similar language: 'The King disclaims those verses I sent you last, and says they are the worst libel of all.'[125] The similarity of his wording to Mead suggests that they were privy to the same rumours about the king's response to his alleged work. One senses from the correspondence of the time public anticipation of royal affirmation or denial, even though such affirmation was more likely to be tacit than explicit. It is also clear that any royal epigram thus circulated was part of a broader public debate.

About a month later James's name was again attached to a widely circulated short poem, this time on the controversial trip to Spain to woo the Infanta undertaken by the disguised Prince Charles and the Duke of Buckingham.[126] Chamberlain reports 'I send you here certain verses made upon Jacke and Toms journy (for the Prince and Lord Marques went through Kent under the names of Jacke and Tom Smith). They were fathered at first upon the King but I learne since they were only corrected and amended by him.'[127] Curtis Perry has used Chamberlain's comment to question James's authorship (as opposed to authorization) of the lines,[128] and it certainly affirms the possibility of such an indirect relationship; however, the Countess of Buckingham (mother of the Duke and a close associate of the King) sent a letter to her son in Spain with the following comment: 'I have sent you some verses of the Prince's Jurney. I thinke you will know the father. You see your best Kinsman doth not forget you.'[129] The reference to the King as 'your best Kinsman' is consistent with Buckingham's familiar epistolary greeting of him as 'dear Dad and Gossip'. This is an affirmation from one very close to the King in his later years, and thus stands as direct evidence in a way that the letters of Chamberlain and Mead cannot. Unfortunately, no copy of the poem being sent with the letter survives. Thus, while from the Countess's letter we may accept with some confidence that James wrote a poem on the Spanish journey, to what extent the many and various surviving copies 'Of Jack and Tom's Journey' reflect the original composition is no more clear. However, the reference does show that such royal verses were circulating on two levels: in the private coterie of the King and the public realm of newsletters and gossip. These verses are then similar to the political tracts of earlier years, but significantly James is relying on the same techniques of wide manuscript and oral circulation as supported that of topical epigrams and ballads. Overall, the circulation of epigrams and other short verses by the King in the last two years of his reign support Rickard's conclusion that he was purposely using these means to enter into the public debate indirectly. Thus, while the epigrams of the period bear out Clive James' neat explanation of texts 'rising' until they attach themselves to the illustrious, it is not the whole story. The cloudiness of authorial legitimacy might be embraced by those illustrious figures themselves.

Notes

1 T. S. Eliot, *A Choice of Kipling's Verse* (London: Faber and Faber, 1963), p. 16.

2 Marcy L. North, 'Anonymity in Early Modern Manuscript Culture: Finding a Purposeful convention in a Ubiquitous Condition', in Janet Wright Starner and Barbara Howard Traister (eds), *Anonymity in Early Modern England: 'What's in a Name?'* (Farnham: Ashgate, 2011), pp. 13–42.

3 William Fitzgerald, *TLS*, 6 Oct. 2006, review of N. M. Kay, *Epigrams from the Anthologia Latina: Text, Translation and Commentary* (London: Duckworth, 2006).

4 Michael Roy Denbo, 'The Holgate Miscellany: The Pierpont Morgan Library, MA 1057', PhD, City University of New York, 1997, p. 22, notes that in manuscripts epigrams are the second least likely type of English Renaissance verse (after complaints) to have an identified author. North, 'Anonymity in Early Modern Manuscript Culture', pp. 13–42, has explored anonymity as the dominant status for early modern libels and epitaphs in manuscript and argued that early modern readers did not seek an author in the ways that contemporary readers do.

5 Scott-Warren, *Sir John Harington and the Book as Gift*, pp. 99–134; Joseph Loewenstein, *Ben Jonson and Possessive Authorship* (Cambridge: Cambridge University Press, 2002), pp. 104–32.

6 Puttenham, *The Art of English Poesy*, pp. 142–3. Whigham and Rebhorn's note supplies this translation of the final verses: 'Thus you, [like] the ox, pull the plow, but not for yourselves / Thus you [like] the sheep, bear a fleece, but not for yourselves. / Thus you, [like] the bee, make honey, but not for yourselves. / Thus you, [like] the bird, make a nest, but not for yourselves.' A slightly different version of the story, where the rival poet is identified as

Bathyllus, is found in C. Suetonius Tranquillus, *The Lives of the first twelve Caesars*, ed. Alexander Thomson (London, 1796), p. 220.

7 Anthony Nixon, *Blacke Yeare* (1606), sig. B2v.

8 Hudson, *The Epigram in the English Renaissance*, p. 67. Thynne also did this in his *Emblemes and Epigrames*.

9 See Loewenstein, *Ben Jonson and Possessive Authorship*, p. 58, on the increasing tendency to emphasize the authors of plays in the first decades of the century: 'The players had always needed authors; now they needed authorship and they began to work steadily to enhance it.'

10 Martial, *Epigrams*, Ep. 1:63.

11 Martial, *Epigrams*, Ep. 10:100.

12 Sullivan, *Martial: The Unexpected Classic*, p. 287.

13 Manley, 'Proverbs, Epigrams, and Urbanity in Renaissance London', p. 275.

14 Thomas Beedome, *Poems, divine and humane* (1641), Ep. 15.

15 See, for example, Freeman, *Rubbe, and a great cast*, Ep. 2:74. Ironically, while there has been a book on the influence of Owen on German epigrams, his role in English literature has been largely neglected.

16 Byron Harries, 'John Owen the Epigrammatist: A Literary and Historical Context', *Renaissance Studies*, 18 (2004), pp. 25–9.

17 See Joseph Loewenstein, *The Author's Due: Printing and the Prehistory of Copyright* (Chicago: University of Chicago Press, 2002), pp. 132–8.

18 Harington, *Epigrams*, Ep. 1:11. Cf. Henry Parrot, 'Ad Momum', *Cures for the Itch*, sig. F9v.

19 Harington, *Epigrams*, Ep. 3:6.

20 Harington, *Epigrams*, Ep. 4:88.

21 Harington, *Epigrams*, Ep. 2:38. This epigram also appears in *Alcilia* (1613), sig. M5v.

22 Harington, *Nugae Antiquae*, vol. 1, p. 385.

23 This enemy has not been identified, but Sir James Croft (the younger, d. 1624), a courtier through the 1590s, is a plausible candidate.

24 'Mr. Robert Markham to John Harington, 1598–9', in Harington, *Nugae Antiquae*, vol. 1, p. 240.

25 Davies, 'Ad Musam', in *Poems*, Ep. 48.

26 There was also a Sir John Heath who translated epigrams of Martial (BL Egerton MS 2982).

27 Hyder E. Rollins, 'Samuel Pick's Borrowings', *Review of English Studies*, 7 (1931), p. 204.

28 Marjorie Swann, *Curiosities and Texts: The Culture of Collecting in Early Modern England* (Philadelphia, PA: University of Pennsylvania Press, 2001), p. 174.

29 Jonson, Ep. 100.

30 Jonson, 'To Prowl, the Plagiary', Ep. 81.

31 Jonson, *Informations to William Drummond of Hawthornden* (or 'Conversations with Drummond'), in *The Cambridge Edition of the Works of Ben Jonson*, vol. 5, p. 390 (lines 50–2).

32 Jonson, Underwood no. 49, in *The Cambridge Edition of the Works of Ben Jonson*, vol. 7, p. 194.

33 Robert C. Evans, *Ben Jonson and the Poetics of Patronage* (Lewisburg, PA: Bucknell University Press, 1989), pp. 76–7. The epigram in question was published only after his death in *Underwood* under the title 'An Epigram on the Court Pucelle'.

34 Jonson, Underwood no. 78, in *The Cambridge Edition of the Works of Ben Jonson*, vol. 7, p. 244.

35 Love, *Scribal Publication in Seventeenth-Century England*, p. 41.

36 Marotti, *Manuscript, Print, and the English Renaissance Lyric*, p. 244.

37 Harold Love, *Attributing Authorship: An Introduction* (Cambridge: Cambridge University Press, 2001), p. 29; North, 'Anonymity in Early Modern Manuscript Culture', p. 27.

38 Gutzwiller, *Poetic Garlands*, pp. 11–12.

39 The conceit is best known from Robert Greene's reference to Shakespeare as an 'upstart crow beautified with our feathers'. For its history, see John Dover Wilson, 'Malone and the Upstart Crow', *Shakespeare Survey*, 4 (1951), pp. 56–68.

40 Aesop, *Esops eables* [*sic*] *translated grammatically* (1617), p. 20. A version of the story is found in Horace, *Epistles*, 1.3.14–19.

41 In the left margin appears the name 'Tirack', presumably the name of the person who had charged Freeman with theft. Given that a number of epigrams in the manuscript point to Freeman living in Cornwall during part of the time of composition, 'Tirack' would seem to be a variant spelling of the Cornish last name 'Tyrack'.

42 Thomas Freeman, BL Sloane MS 1889, fol. 34v.

43 There was also a strong tradition of seeing unfounded rumours and lies as 'bastards': '*Truth* had ever but one *Father*, but *Lyes* are a thousand mens Bastards, and are begotten every where'; Thomas Dekker, *The Seaven Deadly Sinnes of London*, in *The non-dramatic works of Thomas Dekker*, ed. Alexander B. Grosart, 3 vols (London: Hazell, Watson & Viney, 1884–86), vol. 2, p. 34. Similarly, 'A.H.' represents those who spread rumours in the aisle of St Paul's Cathedral as 'scattering their Bastards through the Yard' ('A Continued Inquisition against Paper-Persecutors' in Davies of Hereford, *Scourge for paper-persecutors*, sig. A1r).

44 Guilpin, 'Conclusion to the Reader', *Skialetheia*, Ep. 70.

45 The famous point of Ben Jonson's epitaph 'On My First Son', 'here lies Ben / Jonson his best piece of poetry', offers a self-conscious reversal of the trope: the poem has come to be the vehicle and the son the tenor of the metaphor.

46 William Goddard, *A Mastif Whelp, with other ruff-Island-lik Currs fetcht from amongst the Antipedes* (1616?), Ep. 81. Marston presents in the portrait of Tuscus in 'Satire 11' a similar portrait of a stealer of epigrams, who will present another's epigram as 'his own it, / His proper issue, he will father it'; *The Scourge of Villainy*, in John Marston, *Poems*, ed. Arnold Davenport (Liverpool: Liverpool University Press, 1961).

47 Harington, 'The last Epigram', *Epigrams*, Ep. 4:16.

48 There has also been uncertainty about which volumes are 'Parrot' volumes: *The More the Merrier* was long assigned to Parrot until Margaret C. Pitman showed it to be by Peacham; 'The Epigrams of Henry Peacham and Henry Parrot', *Modern Language Review*, 29 (1934), pp. 129–36.

49 Richard Brathwaite, 'The Parrotts Spring', *Times curtaine drawne, or the anatomie of vanitie* (1621), sig. L8r.

50 Franklin B. Williams, Jr, 'Henry Parrot's Stolen Feathers', *Publications of the Modern Language Association*, 52 (1937), pp. 1019–30.

51 James L. Sanderson, 'Epigrames p[er] B[enjamin] R[udyerd] and Some More "Stolen Feathers" of Henry Parrot', *Review of English Studies*, 17 (1966), pp. 241–55.

52 The prefatory material to this volume strongly suggests it is an act of retribution against 'Woodcock', and John Taylor (also one of Parrot's enemies) in a list of authors mentioned in his satiric work *Sir Gregory Non-sence* includes 'Woodcocke of our side', sig. A5r. Taylor's Epigram 6 suggests a continuing cycle of poetic vengeance: 'MY Muse hath vow'd, revenge shall have her swindge / To catch a Parrat in the Woodcocks sprindge' (*Workes*, p. 263).

53 On our long-standing fascination with the parrot, see Bruce Boehrer, *Parrot Culture: Our 2500-Year-Long Fascination with the World's Most Talkative Bird* (Philadelphia, PA: University of Pennsylvania Press, 2004).

54 Parrot, *The Mous-trap*, sig. A4v.

55 Parrot, 'To the guilty Coxcome', in *Laquei ridiculosi*, Ep. 194.

56 Parrot, 'To the Criticke-seeming Censurer', in *Cures for the Itch*, sig. A3v.

57 Thomas Heywood, 'To the Reader', *The English Traveller* (1633), sig. A3r.

58 Parrot, *Cures for the Itch*, sig. A3r–v.

59 Parrot, *Cures for the Itch*, sig. E7v.

60 In the text this bracket is left unclosed.

61 Fitzgeffrey, *Satyres*, sig. A6r.

62 As the title page of Goddard's volume (*A Mastif Whelp*) is undated we cannot be completely certain that his work preceded Parrot's.

63 Loewenstein, *Ben Jonson and Possessive Authorship*, p. 64.

64 Possibly arguing against this is that the Parrot volumes were produced by a range of different printers, with Thomas Jones being the only figure involved with more than one (*The Mastive* and *Cures for the Itch*).

65 Clive James, *Cultural Amnesia* (New York, London: Norton, Picador, 2007), p. 831.

66 Michelle O'Callaghan, *The English Wits: Literature and Sociability in Early Modern England* (Cambridge: Cambridge University Press, 2007), p. 97.

67 Boutcher, 'Pilgrimage to Parnassus', p. 138.

68 However, Hoskins did seem to maintain a manuscript volume of his poetry; his son Benedict lent out a manuscript of his poetry after his death and never recovered it (David Colclough, '"The Muses Recreation": John Hoskyns and the Manuscript culture of the Seventeenth Century', *Huntington Library Quarterly*, 61 (1998), pp. 369–400, p. 370n). This essay offers the best overview of the many manuscripts that contain poems ascribed to Hoskins; however, his concern is with the process of manuscript compilers rather than Hoskins's own approach to acknowledged authorship and anonymity. Overall, Colclough rather unquestioningly identifies poems as authored by 'Hoskins', side-stepping the issue of how his reputation might gather to itself anonymous witty epigrams.

69 O'Callaghan, *The English Wits*, pp. 97–8.

70 Colclough, '"The Muses Recreation"', pp. 372–3.

71 See Louise Brown Osborn, *The Life, Letters, and Writings of John Hoskyns, 1566–1638* (New York: Archon, 1973), pp. 168–9, for a reproduction of both the caricature and the verses.

72 John Aubrey, *Brief Lives* (Harmondsworth: Penguin, 1962), p. 245.

73 Colclough, *Freedom of Speech in Early Stuart England*, p. 240, suggests that it may have been for comments on the tomb of Sir Christopher Hatton. On the role of the *terrae filius* (a satirical orator) in Oxford, see Mordechai Feingold, 'The Humanities', in Nicholas Tyacke (ed.), *Seventeenth-Century Oxford* (Oxford: Oxford University Press, 1997), pp. 303–5.

74 Davies, *Poems*, p. 423.

75 William Camden, *Remaines concerning Britaine* (1605), p. 56, in Osborn, *The Life, Letters, and Writings of John Hoskyns*, p. 297. She notes that in later editions 'Hostines' is changed to 'Hoskines'.

76 North, 'Anonymity in Early Modern Manuscript Culture', pp. 16–18.

77 Bodl. Malone MS 19, p. 95. The epigram appears in variant forms in many other manuscripts from the period, but usually without the first two lines.

The version in Farmer, *Poems from a Seventeenth-Century Manuscript*, offers a completely different figure in the second-last line: 'Ch: Cox: is popishly precise' (p. 27).

78 Hoskins, 2 March 1614/15, in Osborn, *The Life, Letters, and Writings of John Hoskyns*, p. 71.

79 Osborn, *The Life, Letters, and Writings of John Hoskyns*, pp. 202–8.

80 Osborn, *The Life, Letters, and Writings of John Hoskyns*, p. 203.

81 Osborn, *The Life, Letters, and Writings of John Hoskyns*, p. 208.

82 Baird W. Whitlock (trans.), *John Hoskyns, serjeant-at-law* (Washington, DC: University of America Press, 1982), p. 469.

83 Whitlock, *John Hoskyns*, p. 480.

84 Osborn, *The Life, Letters, and Writings of John Hoskyns*, pp. 206–8.

85 [John Hoskins?],'Verses presented to ye King by Mrs Hoskins in the behalfe of her husband prisoner' (Bodl. Malone MS 16, fol. 20v).

86 Chamberlain to Carleton, 8 Feb. 1617, *Letters*, vol. 2, p. 52.

87 Whitlock, however, suggests that this is unlikely since it was Buckingham who 'helped Hoskyns out of his troubles' (*John Hoskyns*, pp. 490–1). He raises the possibility that the poem was more likely 'He that hath heard a Princes Secrecy', and that James was the adversary at this point. Chamberlain's reference to 'some yeare and halfe agon' would certainly fit the breaking news of the Overbury scandal in the latter half of 1615.

88 [John Hoskins?], Bodl. Tanner MS 465, fol. 62r.

89 Osborn, *The Life, Letters, and Writings of John Hoskyns*, p. 295. Such plays on the surname preceded Walter Pye's death; a letter of 1628 reports that at the election of burgesses at Westminster 'the duke, being steward, made account he should, by his authority and vicinity, have put in Sir Robert Pye. It continued three days; and when Sir Robert Pye's part cried "A Pye! a Pye! a Pye!" the adverse party would cry "A pudding! a pudding! a pudding!" and others "A lie! a lie! a lie!"' (Birch, *Court and Times of Charles I*, vol. 1, p. 327–8, March 1627/8, Mead to Stuteville).

90 Anthony à Wood, in Whitlock, *John Hoskyns*, p. 490.

91 Aubrey, *Brief Lives*, p. 247.

92 Notestein and Relf (eds), *Commons Debates for 1629*, pp. xxxv, xl–xli, in Woudhuysen, *Sir Philip Sidney and the Circulation of Manuscripts*, p. 182.

93 Andrew Thrush and John P. Ferris (eds), *The History of Parliament: The House of Commons 1604–1629* (Cambridge: Cambridge University Press, 2010).

94 Richard Bentley, *Dissertation upon the Epistles of Phalaris*, in Love, *Attributing Authorship*, p. 181.

95 Fitzgerald, *Martial*, pp. 29–30.

96   Suetonius, *The Lives of the first twelve Caesars*, vol. 1, p. 253.

97   Chamberlain to Carleton, 20 Oct. 1598, *Letters*, vol. 1, p. 50.

98   Rudick, *The Poems of Sir Walter Ralegh*, pp. 120–1.

99   See Rudick, *The Poems of Sir Walter Ralegh*, pp. 133–7.

100 Chamberlain to Carleton, 21 Nov. 1618, *Letters*, vol. 2, pp. 184–5.

101 Holles, *Letters*, p. 219 [1 Jan. 1619]. The full proverbial phrase is 'Ex unguibus leonem aestima' [Judge/recognize the lion by his claws].

102 T.S., *Fragmenta Aulica* (1662), sig. A5r.

103 Leah S. Marcus, Janel Mueller and Mary Beth Rose (eds), *Elizabeth I: Collected Works* (Chicago: University of Chicago Press, 2000), pp. 45–6.

104 Marcus et al., *Elizabeth I*, p. 46.

105 Steven W. May, 'The Circulation in Manuscript of Poems by King James VI and I', in James Dutcher and Anne Lake Prescott (eds), *Renaissance Historicisms: Essays in Honour of Arthur F. Kinney* (Newark, DE: University of Delaware Press, 2008), pp. 206–24, p. 207.

106 May, 'The Circulation in Manuscript of Poems by King James VI and I', p. 209.

107 Sir Stephen Powle, Tanner MS 169, fol. 43r, published in the section entitled 'Daffodils and Primroses', in Nicholas Breton, *The Works in Verse and Prose*, ed. Alexander B. Grosart, 2 vols (1879; Rpt New York: AMS, 1966), vol. 1, p. 22.

108 May, 'The Circulation in Manuscript of Poems by King James VI and I', p. 214.

109 Jane Rickard, *Authorship and Authority: The Writings of James VI and I* (Manchester: Manchester University Press, 2007), p. 176.

110 Curtis Perry, '"If Proclamations Will Not Serve": The Late Manuscript Poetry of James I and the Culture of Libel', in Daniel Fischlin and Mark Fortier (eds), *Royal Subjects: Essays on the Writings of James VI and I* (Detroit, MI: Wayne State University Press, 2002), pp. 205–34, p. 212.

111 Chamberlain to Carleton, 10 Feb. 1623, *Letters*, vol. 2, p. 478.

112 On this comet and the poetic response to it, see my 'The Comet of 1618 and the British Royal Family', *Notes and Queries*, new series, 54 (2007), pp. 30–5.

113 Chamberlain to Carleton, 21 Nov. 1618, *Letters*, vol. 2, p. 185. That 'S.N.' refers to Robert Naunton is credible given that he had become Secretary of State in January, 1618, which would explain the reference to his lack of leisure.

114 James Craigie (ed.), *The Poems of James VI of Scotland*, 2 vols (Edinburgh: W. Blackwood, 1955–58), vol. 2, p. 172, from Bodl. Rawl. Poet MS 84, fol. 72. The libel responded to is possibly that referred to in a letter from Rev.

Thomas Lorkin to Sir Thomas Puckering, 18 Dec. 1618: 'There hath lately run up and down an infamous libel, which touches, as they say, most of our great ones; and two gentlemen are committed about it, one Ashfield and another Matthews, either as authors or divulgers' (Birch, *Court and Times of James the First*, vol. 2, p. 114).

115 Rickard, *Authorship and Authority*, pp. 188–9.

116 Richard Corbet, *Poems*, eds J. A. W. Bennett and H. R. Trevor-Roper (Oxford: Clarendon Press, 1955), p. 67. See also the anonymous elegy 'On the death of Queene Anne 2 of March. 1618' in BL Harl. MS 3910, fol. 29r–v, which begins, 'I chide no Blazing Starr *that* did forgoe', and that in the Holgate MS, 'You towringe spiritts whose Art-irradiate eyne' (Denbo, 'The Holgate Miscellany', p. 509). The Oxford volume of Latin elegies marking the Queen's death, *Academiae Oxoniensis funebria sacra Aeternae memoriae serenissimae Reginae Annae* also has a number of poems that allude to the comet (sig. E1r–2r). One in particular, by John Pyt, echoes the King's supposed poem, and suggests that, like the comet at Caesar's death, this one 'excelsam monstret ad astra viam' [would show the high way to the stars].

117 Birch, *Court and Times of James the First*, vol. 2, p. 150.

118 Craigie, *The Poems of James VI of Scotland*, vol. 2, pp. 174–5.

119 Craigie, *The Poems of James VI of Scotland*, vol. 2, pp. 174–5.

120 Raphael Thorius's lines on Ralegh ('Viderat Acephalos') are another good example of this: Rudick, *The Poems of Sir Walter Ralegh*, p. 199, notes that this appears in BL Sloane MS 1768, fol. 76, and 'garbled in places' in BL Cotton Titus MS c.vii.

121 'K. James uppon the death of Q: Anne', in Redding, *Robert Bishop's Commonplace Book*, p. 109.

122 Huntington MS 742, fol. 1v; BL Add. MS 10309, fol. 42r; Bodl. Rawl. poet. MS 26, fol. 80v.

123 Mead to Stuteville, 18 Jan. 1622/3, Birch, *Court and Times of James the First*, vol. 2, p. 355.

124 Mead to Stuteville, 14 Feb. 1622/3, Birch, *Court and Times of James the First*, vol. 2, p. 364.

125 Chamberlain to Carleton, 10 Feb. 1623, *Letters*, vol. 2, p. 478.

126 See Perry, '"If Proclamations will not Serve"', pp. 212–13.

127 Chamberlain to Carleton, 21 Mar. 1622/3, *Letters*, vol. 2, p. 484. The widespread quotation of these verses is attested to by a letter of Mead from the same time, where he writes 'But that I guess I am prevented by others, I would have sent you the King's Sonnet of "Jack and Tom", and other such like tricks' (22 Mar. 1622/3, Ellis, *Original Letters Illustrative of English History*, vol. 3, p. 133).

128 Perry, "'If Proclamations Will Not Serve'", p. 212.
129 The Countess of Buckingham, BL Harl. Ms 6987, in Nichols, *The progresses*, vol. 4, p. 838.

8

The readers of printed epigram books

What readers actually did with texts in the early seventeenth century is largely beyond scholarly recovery, and this is particularly the case with the humble genre of epigrams. While this chapter concludes with a survey of what one reader did with a copy of the 1615 edition of Harington's *Epigrams*, it mostly concerns the imagined or implied reader constructed or addressed by printed volumes of epigrams themselves rather than that which the book in the marketplace would necessarily achieve. I first turn to the general reader addressed by prefatory poems and epistles, and secondly the patron-reader invoked by some volumes. Overall, printed epigram volumes reflect a tension between the disparaging attitude toward both the form and its reader as manifest in these reflections upon the general reader, and a desire to validate the genre as worthy the attention and even protection of a significant public figure as patron.

The imagined general reader

Chapter 4 considered the very public role of the epigram as an expression of what 'all men might say', but what of its reader? The very public origins of the genre (and the continuing of this aspect in the posted libel) would seem to invite a wider readership than many other literary genres, to be also what 'all men might *read*'. The readership was broad, and little claim to exclusivity was possible, in particular with the English epigram. While a few epigram collections, like Jonson's folio *Workes*, were printed in expensive formats, most came out in a 'cheap print' format (see Chapter 6) that would lead to a popular audience. Prefatory material and epigrams to the reader show a recurring expectation of this socially broad audience, with frequent poetic apprehension at the more common elements within it. However, some poets did imagine a variety of reader groups, with distinct interests, ways of reading (or misreading) and levels of interest. Some were better placed to understand the real figure hidden behind a fictional name or trace the progressive crossing of epigrammatic swords by competing poets.

The projected audience might serve a variety of rhetorical purposes: Adam Smyth suggests that many prefaces to collections of ephemeral poems try to evoke a fashionable young male readership that would lend the work a certain cachet.[1] While epigrams fall at least partly within this category of ephemeral poems, the genre's approach to readers often went beyond this: the casual, even disdainful attitude of poets towards epigrams was also frequently extended to their readers. Thus, the profile of the imagined reader was bound up with the epigrammatist's posing or public image. While I show that such is the dominant presentation of readers in epigram books, there were other noteworthy strands: a few epigram books envision at least a partly female audience, and volumes of Latin epigrams generally treated more respectfully what was perceived to be an educated elite audience.

Early in his 1628 volume of epigrams, Robert Hayman suggested that his were for the middling sort, neither scholars nor fools.[2] Others anticipated or hoped for the full gamut of intellectual attainment on the part of readers, while ultimately accepting that there were many more fools than scholars in the reading public at large. For some, a social breadth of audience was positive: Gamage, in the second (1621) edition of his epigrams, points to the use of English to achieve this:

> In the Popes tongue I list not to endite:
> Cause of my time all men should have the sight.[3]

The suggestion here is that the epigrammatist, in the vein of the satirist's moral imperative, offers a picture of his time, one that all should see.

In *Chrestoleros* Bastard reflects upon his readership and his complex relationship with it at a number of points. He asks his book, 'How shalt thou knowe to please thou know'st not whom?',[4] which shows an anxiety over the breadth of the anonymous readership that print allows. Such will also be central to Jonson's wrestling with the question of readership in not just his epigrams but his other poetry and drama as well. Bastard opens Book 3 with an announcement that his epigrams are not for any sub-group but for all:

> My Booke is not for learned men nor wise,
> Nor mery nor conceipted, nor the plaine:

Nor angry, foolish, criticall or nice.
Nor olde nor young, nor sober, nor the vaine.
Nor for the proud, nor for the covetous,
Nor for the Gentle man, nor the Clowne:
Nor for the glutton, nor adulterous,
Nor for the valiant worthy of renowne.
Nor for the thrifty, nor the prodigall,
But if thou needs will know for whom? for all.[5]

This corresponds to the breadth of subject matter he announced in the opening poem of the whole volume. Here he seems satisfied with this concept of the 'general reader', but at the beginning of Book 6 laments the variety of readers that he feels compelled to satisfy:

Some mirth doth please, to some it is offence.
Some will have vices toucht, some none of that,
Some will have sleight conceipt, some deeper sense,
Some wil have this, and some they know not what,
And he which must please all and himselfe to,
Reader, I thinke something he hath to doe.[6]

The disparity is not primarily derived from the social classes represented among his readers, but the variety of readers' understandings on what an epigram *is*. In what might strike us as an anticipation of the required scene with a dog in the film *Shakespeare in Love*, Bastard at one point reflects upon a series of epigrams on animals, which are there to satisfy readers. He apologizes for this relative slumming, claiming, 'I doe it onely for the Printers sake',[7] so that the simple will also buy his book. Kathryn Perry has seen this as typical of the apprehension of the epigrammatist, as he felt compelled to offer that which the printer considered saleable.[8] Hence the poet's relationship with the reader is not a direct or simple one, but rather mediated through the figure of the printer and bookseller, and driven by the needs of the marketplace.

The note of disdain that creeps into Bastard's reflections on the market-based reader is magnified in some poets who followed him, as the indifferent and even cynical attitude typical of the epigrammatist was extended to readers as well. J[ohn] C[ooke] expects that envious readers would have spat even upon 'the choicest flowers', so he has instead sent them nettles,[9] and he ridicules the foolish reader who would be impressed by a bawdy jest.[10] This sort of scoffing, lackadaisical attitude toward the reader seems to have been particularly the fashion of the first decade of the seventeenth century. In *Nosce te* (1607) Richard Turner addresses the reader with a shrug of the shoulders:

> heeres a sixepenie purchase for you; I thinke you may call it *Epigrames*, or a booke of this thing and that thing, and just nothing, if you have better skil, you may scoffe at it, or you may looke and laugh at it, you may buy it and beare it, and then you may eyther reade it, or heare it, or else take it and teare it.[11]

If the work consists of mere trifles, the author may more readily disown it, asserting that once it enters the marketplace it is no longer his, nor does he care about its readers.

Poets jest about epigrams books (usually those of others, sometimes their own) being used in jakes, wrapping peppercorns or lining pies,[12] but what *textual* use was seriously envisioned for such collections? Common in prefaces to the reader are allusions to the limited readerly purposes arising from the triviality of the genre. *Tyros Roring Megge* invites the 'curteous Reader' to read them 'when thou art lazie'.[13] Freeman has even more limited ambitions for his epigrams, suggesting that they might serve as lavatory reading:

> Which though they'l do thy study little grace,
> They'l do thee pleasure in some Privy place.[14]

Robert Hayman hopes his might escape another lavatory use, if only to achieve an only slightly loftier disposable one:

> Doe not with my leaves make thy backside bright:
> Rather with them doe thou *Tobacco* light.
> I'd rather have them up in flames to flye,
> Then to be stiffled basely privily.[15]

All these examples also suggest that epigrams are read a few at a time, as ways of passing away brief moments of idleness, which echoes how poets often presented their *composition* of the same works. As poems written in an offhand way, epigrams would seem to demand a similarly desultory readership. Even Latin epigrams might anticipate such use by readers: Charles Fitzgeffry suggests that his might be used by a theatregoer to while away the time until the actors reappear, or during a dull academic lecture, or while waiting in a tavern.[16] However, that same reader is looked

down upon by the poet as a less than competent Latinist: he mispro-
nounces words and laughs at jokes he does not understand.[17] Similarly,
Stradling captures well the incongruity of 'learned' epigrams entering the
mass market:

Clamant ante fores tuas tyrones
Crebro, Paule: Novum quis, en, libellum
Doctus parvi emat? Est hic expolitus,
Perbellus, novus, et iocis refertus.
Quaestus, qualis es artium magister,
Stultis ingenii ciens acumen!

[his prentices shout over and over before your doors, Paul, 'Hey, will any
learned man buy a slim volume on the cheap? It's refined, elegant, novel, and
crammed with jokes.' There's a profit (for such a master of these arts you are)
in whetting the keen edge of wit for fools.][18]

Overall, then, the majority of both English and Latin epigrammatists
anticipate a broad, if not low-brow, audience, but are ambivalent about
even deserving more given the limited status of the genre itself.

The more complex attitude toward ownership and authorship found in
Harington, Jonson and Owen utters forth a different sort of disdain: the
epigrams are bound up with the author's identity and *together* they are
above the down-market tastes of many readers. Jonson especially harbours
lofty suspicions that his will be misunderstood by readers expecting the
unsophisticated bawdry and vituperation often found in printed epigram
books. His conflicts with readers and theatre audiences (especially in his
late career) have been much noted: Jennifer Brady aptly refers to his
'judicious intimidation of his readers'.[19] He opens his 1616 'Epigrammes'
with a cluster of poems admonishing his reader on how to approach them.
In these Jonson's habitual antagonism towards readers is enhanced by the
genre's own attitude of disdain. Brady identifies the complex dynamics of
this: readers can easily evade Jonson's censure of thieves and prostitutes,
but must struggle to overcome the possible identification of themselves
among these scorned unworthy readers.[20] His concern with audiences and
readers was twofold: that he might be unappreciated and that he might be
wilfully misunderstood. Jonson's attitude towards his epigrams' readers
was exceptional in his desire to construct fully ideal readers as an alterna-
tive.[21] These readers would seek out Jonson's epigrams (rather than stum-
ble upon them in the marketplace) (no. 3), and they would be scholarly

and virtuous, an expectation that would not be out of place with Latin epigrams but is uncommon with English ones. Whereas Martial had banned
the stern moralist Cato from his volume, unless he accepted its licentious
content, he is invited at the end of Jonson's preface to his *Epigrammes* to
serve as a sort of gatekeeper.[22] Jonson's expression of this lofty ideal reader
is mocked in an epigram in the manuscript 'Times' Whistle' by 'R.C.':

> his intret [preface] Cato stands before,
> Even at *the* portall of his pamphlets dore;
> As who should say, this booke is fit for none
> But Catoes, learned men, to looke upon:
> Or else, let Cato censure if he will,
> My booke deserves the best of judgement still.
> When every gull may see his booke's untwitten,[23]
> And Epigrams as bad as e're were written.[24]

By his invocation of Cato as a more worthy representative reader Jonson
has raised himself up above the common run of epigram books, and is
promptly slapped down by 'R.C' for his aspirations.

Male readers and female readers

More so than most genres of the period, epigrams largely anticipated
a male readership, and in the first generation of epigram books there is
little reference to potential female readers, and no dedications to women.
However, after about 1610 both general female readers and female patrons
come to figure more prominently in epigram books, perhaps as a response
to a growing awareness that women *were* reading such volumes. Such a
readership did have a classical history: Donne notes how '*Martiall* found
no way fitter to draw the Romane Matrons to read one of his Books,
which he thinks most morall and cleanly, then to counsel them by the first
Epigram to skip the Book, because it was obscene.'[25]

Frequently expressed in early Stuart epigrams is a mingled praise and
concern for the tender or chaste qualities of female readers; however, this
can also tip over into derision. Hayman, both in his own epigrams and
his translations from Owen, simultaneously mocks and praises potential
female readers. In 'To my delicate Readers' (3:2) he presents his own
rough rhymes as to women's taste, as they are 'Deare and farre fetcht'
(they were composed in Newfoundland): thus, their appeal is less intrin-
sic than based on pleasing women's vain tastes for expensive imports.

Similarly, the preface to his translations of Owen informs female reader that his Muse undertook to bring the wit of Owen, 'Lock'd in a tongue you did not understand' to their eyes. In a playful and humble tone he suggests that his Muse 'hath vailde, or quite omitted what *She* feares might offend your chast eares'.[26] Like those Renaissance editors who had 'gelded' Martial (described in Chapter 1), Hayman has played the role of purging epigrams of that bawdiness that so frequently clung to them. For a female audience he found a need as well to address the high degree of cynical hostility to women in the epigram tradition: 'If *She* [his Muse] speake any thing against your sexe, it is but what malicious men some-times mutter in an unknowne language against your inferior frailties, and hath answered somewhat in your behalfe.'[27] Ironically, he rather uses that same misogynistic language about his own composition: it is presented by 'the ragged, bashfull slut my *Muse*'.

Niccols is also conscious of female readers and addresses them sep-arately. His prefatory poem directed to males adopts the conventional argument that he is only attacking the guilty, and so if his readers 'fault-lesse bee', they need not fear the whipping to come.[28] However, that to women is more nuanced:

> The Furies, by your fingers daintie touch,
> Doe know your gentle sex, and marvell much
> You'le come in danger of their jerking rimes,
> Perhaps they thought to passe your pettie crimes,
> In hope your faire would bring forth no foule deed,
> Yet in faire fruit, since wormes doe soonest breed,
> They bid that you your selves with patience arme,
> A little whipping will doe you no harme.[29]

This establishes the epigram genre as generally outside the female domain, but asserts that women who have entered must be willing to recognize the need for satiric whipping that Niccols's 'Furies' offer, that they, in spite of their fairness, might have a corruption that whipping can cure. Niccols's final section, 'Vertues Encomium', is a set of panegyric epigrams, dedi-cated to Honoria Hay, and, in fact, most of the poems are in praise of her, however limiting the epigram form might be:

> If in what followes you find my stile too harsh for so sweet a subject, my forme to impolish for so faire an image, be pleased to know that I am limited to Epigrams, in which no man can limme so faire a picture as your faire deserves.[30]

Once again, the female reader, in this case a particular (and virtuous) one, is beyond the usual bounds of the epigram tradition.

In *A Mastiff Whelp* Goddard goes further yet in distinguishing between male and female readers, as he divides his collection of satiric epigrams into two volumes, the first directed to male readers and depicting male characters, and the second similarly devoted to women:

> Woemen I've done my worst, to th' worst of men.
> But now I'le occupie on you my penn.[31]

While he assures his female readers that he has returned his 'angrie whelpe' to its kennel in deference to their sensibilities,[32] his aggressive attitude toward the reader – his mastiff definitely bites – largely continues as he presents satiric epigrams on female figures.

The patron as reader

Despite the general tendency of epigrammatists to disparage the significance of their own work and its readers, many printed volumes of epigrams were nevertheless dedicated to friends, family members or significant public figures. Even though they were still less likely to open with a dedication than other volumes of early modern published poetry,[33] in 1610 Rowlands remarks that 'its in use now to have great *Godfathers* though we be never so meane'.[34] Those collections that are strictly satiric or mocking rarely have a conventional dedication, and usually lack as well the commendatory poems that grace more ambitious poetic genres. Collections of Latin epigrams were more likely to include dedications, and those that were divided into books or centuries frequently presented the individual books to different patrons (as in the case of Fitzgeffry's *Affaniae* and Owen's *Epigrams*).

As shown in Chapter 5, individual epigrams might serve as small gifts (or as accompaniments to gifts), and manuscript volumes as more substantial ones; the entry into the print marketplace changed these dynamics. Thus, Stradling questions the importing of dedication into the print realm, suggesting that the bookseller 'Insignem petit eligi patronum' [requests that a distinguished patron be sought out], to make a volume more marketable, and likewise desires poems of commendation.[35] In his view such dedications are not a vestige of the old manuscript gift culture but a demand of the print market, as the printer tries to exploit the perception that epigrams that had circulated in elite coteries were now being made available to the general reader of the marketplace. Thus, Stradling distances himself from the conventional preliminary material, and his work is exceptional as a Latin and literarily ambitious work that forgoes all preliminary materials. Printed volumes of epigrams often noted that the dedicatee had seen at least some of the epigrams earlier in manuscript, thus recalling earlier gift transactions while pointing forward to a potential role of protection on the dedicatee's part. In these pleas for protection, epigram books were like other early seventeenth-century verse, but the poets often struggled to justify the epigram as a genre worthy of such protection. The poems were too nugatory, and, while the same was true of lyric poems, the urbane, detached persona of the epigrammatist was less apt to cringe and apologize than the lyric or pastoral poet. The epigrammatic pose of disdain for the would-be readers was difficult to reconcile with the humility of a poet seeking patronage and protection.

Some volumes adopted a relatively lowly dedicatee: Peacham offers *The More the Merrier* to his ill friend 'M.H.C.' (probably Mr H.C.), hoping that the work might serve as 'physicke'. There were a number of other printed epigram books similarly dedicated to non-illustrious friends and family, such as Goddard's *Mastive-Whelp* to his 'very loving Frends, GF. RN. WS. RG. IF. IG. Gentlemen of the Inner Temple', Henry Fitzgeffry's *Satyres: and satyricall epigrams* (1617) 'to his True Friend Tho: Fletcher of Lincoln's-Inne Gent.'[36] and Joseph Martyn's *New Epigrams* (1621) dedicated to Sir Henry Martyn, Knight.

However, despite the genre's low prestige a significant number of epigram books were dedicated to individuals of much higher public stature. Of the initial wave of printed English epigram collections in the 1590s, while two were undedicated (Guilpin and Davies), the other two were directed to members of the aristocracy: Weever's, because of local associations, to Richard Houghton, Justice of the Peace and High Sheriff of Lancashire, and Bastard's to Charles Blount, eighth Baron Mountjoy, as will be more fully explored below. Weever adopts a balanced, measured attitude toward his epigrams: they are offered to Houghton as 'my not curious nor carelesse studies', which might 'serve you for a jeast, to refresh your wearied mind, continually exrcised [*sic*] in matters concerning the common wealth'.[37] This is an only somewhat loftier expression of the idea noted above of epigrams serving to pass the time: such was often the most that could be said (in a shamefacedly tentative way) in offering epigrams to an illustrious patron.

Classical precedents for lofty patronage of such a humble form were frequently invoked, and thus Weever trots out the obligatory reference to Maecenas. After all, Augustus had accepted not only the *Aeneid* but also *Virgil's Gnat*,[38] Alexander the Great the poems of Chaerilus,[39] and Pliny the Younger the epigrams of Martial.[40] The last in particular, with his poems of praise (or even sycophancy) to Domitian, provided a model for Renaissance epigrammatists' appeals for patronage. Jonson's 'To the Ghost of Martial' (no. 36) invokes that poet's 'nobler epigrams' given to Domitian as justification for his own to King James, but claims to go beyond Martial since his royal subject 'cannot flattered be', as he actually has the virtues celebrated. While Jonson's collection includes three epigrams to King James, its dedicatee proper is the Earl of Pembroke, privy councillor and Lord Chancellor. Jonson notes that Pembroke thus has the 'honour of leading forth so many good and great names as my verses mention on the better part'.[41] This highlights the epigrams of praise within the collection, and thus the appropriateness of such a lofty dedicatee. However, much of the prose dedication to Pembroke involves further defensive gestures towards the misapprehending general reader.[42]

Praising Jonson a couple decades later, Thomas Bancroft recalls this epigram of Jonson, but considers what the favour of King James did for the poet:

> As *Martials* Muse by *Caesars* ripening rayes
> Was sometimes cherisht, so thy happier dayes
> Joy'd in the Sun-shine of thy Royall JAMES,
> Whose Crowne shed lustre on thine Epigrammes.[43]

Bancroft has heightened the ideal nature of the monarch–epigrammatist relationship by identifying Martial's patron, not as the scandalous Domitian but as the more general 'Caesar' – after all, equating a royal patron with Domitian was quite a step down from Augustus. Bancroft's lines also create a neat parallel between Martial and his disciple Jonson, bound as they are by parallel worthy subjects. As a genre that might be read and blessed by monarchs, the epigram's worthiness is raised. (Bancroft's own volume was somewhat less ambitious, being dedicated to 'two top-branches *Of GENTRY*. Sir *Charles Shirley*, Baronet, *AND William Davenport*, Esquire').[44]

After Harington's gifts of manuscript epigrams to royal figures (described above in Chapter 5), the publisher John Budge aimed for illustrious dedicatees close to the King for the posthumous printed editions. The 1615 edition was, like Jonson's, dedicated to Pembroke, and claimed a right to patronage based on the epigrams' worth: 'Better then [*sic*] these, none have yet put on an English habit' – the sort of claim not likely to be made by a living poet on his own behalf.[45] The 1618 and 1625 editions of Harington were then dedicated to the Duke of Buckingham, the most powerful non-royal Englishman in those years.

As explored in Chapter 5, Freeman's manuscript volume of epigrams seems to have been prepared with an eye towards eventual publication; when that took place in 1614, *Rubbe, and a great cast* was offered to Thomas, sixth Baron Windsor of Stanwell. Freeman aspires to show a continuity between the epigrams in manuscript and this print publication, as he reminds Windsor that 'The most part of them have already past your Lordships private liking: they All jointly crave your public protection.'[46] This sheds some light on the different roles of a patron in manuscript and print. A manuscript given to a reader of social standing is primarily a *gift*, whereas the same figure addressed as the dedicatee of a printed work is construed as having the additional role of a protective guardian. Further, the print dedicatee receives the 'gift' of printed recognition rather than the poems themselves, which by being printed are given to all, and are hence of lesser value. Thus, in the dedication of the second volume Freeman makes a virtue of celebrating Windsor's name not just in writing but in print.[47] Freeman still claims to be giving something to Windsor, but now it is public fame rather than private amusement. However, like many epigrammatists, he admits to qualms about offering such trifles to one of high estate: 'It was much against my mind, to entitle your worthy Lordship to these worthlesse toyes.'[48]

Only a few epigram books were dedicated outright to British royal figures, and most of these were Latin ones of relatively lofty ambition. Gordon Craig's *Specimen epigrammatum Iacobo Primo Britanniarum Regi dicatum a G. Cragio I.D* (1624) carries its dedication to King James in its very title; its exceptional brevity for an epigram book raises the question of whether it might have been a volume printed only for limited presentation rather than general sale. John Owen's ever-expanding epigram volumes began with an illustrious series of royal dedicatees, before turning humbly to friends and family members: Lady Mary Neville (Books 1–3), Arabella Stuart (Book 4), Prince Henry (Books 5–6), Prince Charles (Book 7), Edward Noel (Book 8), William Sidley (Book 9) and Roger Owen (Book 10). Both John Vicars's and Robert Hayman's translations of Owen's epigrams were presented to Prince (and then King) Charles, which likely reflects the widespread esteem enjoyed by Owen's work. In Hayman's case, both his own epigrams and Owen's were part of a larger publication in which Hayman was very much espousing the benefits of the colony of Newfoundland, where he had composed the work, to the King:

these few bad unripe Rimes of mine (coming from thence) are in all humility presented with the like intendiment to your Majestie, to testifie that the Aire there is not so dull, or malevolent, but that if better were transplanted thither, neither the Summers heat would dilute them, nor the Winters cold benumme them, but that they might in full vigour flourish to good purpose.[49]

However (as noted in Chapter 6) in the poem to the licensers, Hayman had a fairly lofty sense of his epigrams' social role, suggesting that they, like kings, 'reprove those that *offend*' and commend the virtuous.[50] Similarly, Freeman's original disparagement of the form gives way to defence: the satiric epigram is worthy because it speaks naked Truth; it suffers because of its 'liberty and sincere honesty in the search and unmasking vice'.[51]

Dedications to women

Noted above was epigrammatists' ambivalence about female readers; such, however, did not prevent a number of volumes being dedicated to them. Owen dedicated his first three books (1607) to Lady Mariam (Mary) Neville, whom he calls 'patronam suam'. She was the daughter of Thomas Sackville, Earl of Dorset (famous as a poet himself). However, in this dedication and that of Book 4 to Arabella Stuart, there is no discussion of them as distinctly *female* patrons or readers. Both editions (1614 and 1621) of Gamage's *Linsi-woolsie* are dedicated to Katherine, Lady Mansell, daughter of Robert Sidney, and niece of Sir Philip.[52] While there is probably a family connection as Katherine's mother was Barbara Gamage of Coety, Glamorgan,[53] the Sidney family's poetic reputation also encouraged the poet in his dedication. He uses the language of battle and soldiery in reference to his poems and the dedication, hoping that they will 'Passe the Muster' and that Lady Mansell will deign to protect them. Once again, in the dedication itself there is no explicit comment on the issue of dedicating epigrams to a female, but an opening epigram acknowledges that 'This stuffe of mine, I grant, is overcourse, / For your fine wearing, Loadstarre of our Clime'.[54] However, uncommonly for an English-language collection, the majority of the epigrams are panegyric or addressed to friends, and his mocking ones are less licentious than most. Hence it would have been a more fit volume than most to be dedicated to a female reader.

Two case studies: Bastard's *Chrestoleros* and John Heath's *Two Centuries of Epigrams*

Dedicated to Charles Blount, eighth Baron Mountjoy (and later Earl of Devonshire), Bastard's *Chrestoleros* is among the more ambitious epigram collections of the 1590s. As an already ordained priest within the Church of England, Bastard was in a different position from most epigrammatists, who were more likely to be students at one of the universities or Inns of Court, or newly launched from those places as they made their way in the world. It may be that this atypical entry into print was a result of his tumultuous career through the 1590s. Bastard had received the church living of Bere Regis in his home county of Dorset from Thomas Howard, Earl of Suffolk, in the early 1590s. However, in 1591 he had been expelled from his fellowship at Oxford for writing and circulating a libel in which he exposed the vices of various Oxford men. Thus, his career was under a cloud through much of the 1590s, and his disappointed expectations are noted in some of his epigrams. Suffolk is not mentioned at all in *Chrestoleros*, which may be a reflection of some bitterness on Bastard's part towards him. Epigram 7:12 is on 'Carus', a patron who has presented a living to 'Morus' with the condition that the latter only receives one-tenth of the tithe, but then decides that even that is too much. Later in his career, Bastard was once again to turn to Suffolk, to whom he dedicated his *Twelve sermons* (1615). However, in 1598 Bastard turned to Blount when he came to publish his epigrams.[55]

Blount and Bastard, of roughly the same age, probably met at Oxford in the late 1580s, and in the early 1590s Bastard served as Blount's domestic chaplain.[56] As a rising military figure of the time, prominent in the defence of southern England from anticipated Spanish attacks, Blount would have appealed to Bastard, whose epigrams show a repeated concern with the perceived Spanish threat, which was at a high point in early 1598. He adopts abject humility towards Blount, presenting himself in Epigram 1:8 as one from whom Blount may learn 'what th'unknowne vulgar saies', and how much the lowly love him. Bastard's dedication to Blount, then, is an attempt to further ingratiate himself with a rising courtier and soldier, and this must be considered within the climate of late 1598.[57] At that time rumours were rampant that Blount was about to be named viceroy of the Queen in Ireland, a post ultimately given to the Earl of Essex,[58] to whom there are also epigrams scattered throughout the volume. That Blount remained on good terms with both Essex and Robert Cecil, the secretary of state, rendered him a very safe and likely potential patron for Bastard.

What exactly did Bastard want from Blount, and what purpose might *Chrestoleros* serve in achieving this? The bid for patronage seems to have been borne partly out of desperation. He notes that 'audacious neede' has led him to present the poems to Blount, and he hopes that 'If neede have well done, I am glad therfore, / But I beseech you lett her do no more'.[59] The last comment seems to point away from further similar material. In this epigram near the end of *Chrestoleros* Bastard is hoping that Blount will relieve him from his need, thus making further epigrams unnecessary. Like many in the period, Bastard wrote for patrons not to establish himself as a poet but ultimately to achieve some non-poetic end. This need-based production is reflected in the epigrams themselves, and, more than most epigrammatists, Bastard dwells upon his personal situation. Such poems are concentrated in the later books of *Chrestoleros* and come to a climax with a most unepigram-like poem near the end of the work:

> Such was my griefe upon my fatall fall,
> That all the world me thought was darke withall.[60]

Bastard continues by describing how he showed his wretched state to the various heavenly bodies, none of whom is in any way concerned with it. He concludes with an address to himself on his isolation in the universe:

> Go wretched man, thou seest thou art forlorne.
> Thou seest the heavens laugh while thou dost mourn.

The self-pitying quality of Bastard's appeal did not go unnoticed: Dudley Carleton wrote to Chamberlain:

> having at this time no better thing to send, I send you the Epigrammes (which I often tolde you of). The authors name is Bastard, who hath the name of a verie good libelling wit; but as yt seemes by these, yt lies not this waye. For in the Epigram he doth botch up his verse with variations, and his conceites doe soe withowt varietie runn uppon his povertie, that [in my conceit – *inserted above line*] his poore witt is rather to be pitied, then commended. howsoever because he showeth his good witt to the sport of Epigram-making I send him to you. and happilie he may come at such a time that having nothing else to do yor leisure may bid him welcome. I will detaine you no longer from reading his badd verse with my worse prose.[61]

Bastard could only hope to find a more sympathetic reader in Blount.

Bastard himself recognizes the incongruity of a priest publishing such work, as he writes to Blount, 'I faine object to my calling this kinde of writing: in other things I woulde be glad to approve my studie to your good Lordshippe.'[62] As with those who published pastoral poetry and collections of lyrics, Bastard offers the present work as a humble experiment that might lead to more ambitious poems, which also will be offered to the patron. This thought is returned to in the verse conclusion of Bastard's dedication:

> If I my pen an higher taske should set,
> Great Lord, what better matter could I finde,
> Then of thy worth and vertue to entreate,
> Of thy heroicke spirit and noble minde:
> Now take my gnatt, and try me in a toye,
> Whether hereafter I may sing of Troye.[63]

In this way, Bastard aligns his epigrams with Virgil's 'Gnat', the short, light poem that Renaissance readers believed the great Roman poet had composed early in his career.[64] Bastard, like Virgil, might then move on to an epic poem of military valour, one which would highlight the significant role of Blount in the defence of England against the Spanish or in the suppression of the Irish rebels. Hence, the dedication presents epigrams as merely a stage in a writing career, not a continuing role for an 'epigrammatist'.[65] Blount's role as patron-reader of epigrams then is likewise secondary to his main public and military role.

While Bastard's dedications reflect his future aspirations, those in John Heath's *Two Centuries of Epigrammes* (1610) reflect more the origins of the epigrams within an academic setting. Heath's main dedication is to his peer Thomas Bilson, with whom he had attended New College, Oxford. However, Heath focuses more on Bilson's father (also named Thomas), the Bishop of Winchester, whom Heath describes as his 'singular Maecenas'.[66] Bishop Bilson had strong connections to Winchester School and New College, having been educated at both, and then having been warden at the former until 1596.[67] Heath's education followed the same path, and having entered Winchester in 1600 he would have experienced the direct supervision of the Bishop. Thus, he indirectly presents his epigrams to a figure closely connected with the educational context in which he likely composed many of the epigrams. He presents them as chaste, suitable even for the eyes of a Lucretia (or by implication even a bishop as chaste as Lucretia).[68] They are also of a literary ambition that

exceeds most English collections: Heath is clearly part of the Oxford epigram scene and writing 'literary' epigrams that are frequently reminiscent
of the humanist collections, but in English rather than Latin. The commendatory poems reflect this same academic milieu – all are in Latin by
fellow scholars at Oxford, especially his own New College. Heath offers
a wide-ranging mix of epigrams: laudatory, semi-political, scoffing and
ethical; they are far better than most, displaying a poised rhythmic variety.
Ultimately, they were suitable for a bishop (or at least a bishop's son), and
constituted the most decorous of English epigram volumes published to
this point.

While the poems mostly recall his life at Oxford as a student, Heath,
like Bastard, also uses the volume to point toward further poetry. As the
trifles of youth, they are offered to Bilson as an earnest of more ambitious
work to come: 'The favourable acceptance of these my first endeavours,
who knowes whether it may set my head a working in times to come, to
thinke on some other subject, better worthy your Patronage, and mine
owne fathering.'[69] Like many epigram books, these were published when
the author was at a crossroads – he had received his BA in 1609, and just
begun a fellowship at Oxford; a couple of years later (1612) he was to be
ordained.[70] Apart from a Latin epitaph on the death of Sir Thomas Bodley
in 1613, no further poetry of his reached print. *The Oxford DNB* certainly
errs in suggesting that *The House of Correction* by 'J.H.' (1619) might be
by Heath: 'J.H.' is designated as 'gent.' and seems to be of the Middle
Temple, whereas Heath went on to a career as scholar and churchman.[71]
Furthermore, *The House of Correction* is far more down-market and full of
the bawdy and cynical epigrams that Heath rejects.

The friend or fellow poet as reader

Chapter 3 described the small gatherings of epigrams sent to friends as
part of the dynamics of epigram composition. However, in printed volumes epigrams addressed to a friend or fellow poet served a somewhat
different function: that of a public judge and potential guarantor of the
worthiness of the collection. Such is the case with Jonson's epigram to
John Donne, where his poetic colleague's approbation of even a single
epigram will satisfy Jonson:

> Who shall doubt, Donne, whe'er I a poet be,
> When I dare send my *Epigrams* to thee?
> That so alone canst judge, so alone dost make;

Any in thy censures evenly dost take
As free simplicity to disavow
As thou hast best authority t'allow.
Read all I send, and if I find but one
Marked by thy hand, and with the better stone,
My title's sealed. Those that for claps do write,
Let puisnes', porters', players' praise delight,
And, till they burst, their backs, like asses, load:
A man should seek great glory, and not broad.[72]

In a print collection such a poem serves two rhetorical functions: it offers epideictic acknowledgement of Donne as a poetic authority, and, perhaps more importantly, subjugates the general reader to a higher judge. If even one epigram is affirmed by Donne, the judgements of others are without consequence: on what grounds might they reject what Donne has approved? The inclusion of such a poem, an invocation of a sort of anti-Momus, also signals to the reader that Jonson is hostile not to judgement but rather to those unfit, self-appointed judges of the world.

An actual reader of epigrams

Prefaces and epigrams themselves present what an author would hope or perhaps fear readers will do with his works, but this is not solid evidence of what actually was done. For this, we turn to marginalia that provide some insight into a reader's response to and use of a printed epigram book.[73] One rich example is a copy of Harington's *Epigrams* (1615) in the Huntington Library[74] that has marginal annotations by the same hand throughout, seemingly from the 1630s.[75] These marginalia do not identify individuals or give further information; nor for the most part do they respond *against* the text. The bulk of annotations point to other epigrams and proverbial bits that the poems reminded the reader of. The greatest tendency is to return to the general proverb from which Harington had derived his conceit. For example, next to 'Of the Warres in Ireland' (1:6)[76] is placed, 'Dulce bellum inexpertis' [war is sweet to those who have not experienced it], putting back in the proverbial Latin what Harington has paraphrased and made particular. Similarly, 'Of Milo the Glutton'[77] attracted a fair amount of marginalia, including the familiar proverb 'Pone gulae metas, ut sit ti*bi* long aetas' [to live long place boundaries to gluttony], and a scriptural reference to Genesis 43:16 where Joseph feasts at noon. So once again the reader has brought forth a proverbial response to a personal attack, and he then offers three separate English couplets on gluttony.[78] The Harington volume in this way has become something of a commonplace book where the reader encapsulated wisdom from a variety of sources. This is similar to what Smyth describes as the tendency for readers to treat printed verse miscellanies, which reprinted many epigrams and mock epitaphs, as 'incomplete collections to which more should be added'.[79]

In the epigram 'Of two that were married and undone' the reader underlined 'Without their parents will, or friends consent', and next to the bottom of the poem, which jests about 'undone', is presented the well-known couplet:

> John{
>   Donne
> Ann {
>   undone[80]

Was the reader identifying the unnamed figures in the poem, or did the joke about 'undone' simply remind him of the 'John Donne' tag?

At times, the reader attempted a Latin version of a part or the whole of an epigram; at other times he added epigrams by others of which Harington's put him in mind. For example, next to 'Of a toothlesse Shrew'[81] the reader has penned an epigram that likewise mocks an old woman with no teeth but an active tongue: it begins

> Sylla is toothlesse: yet w*he*n shee was younge
> she had teeth enough, & tongue.

The reader has recognized the jest and added another manuscript-circulating epigram based on the same.[82] Clearly, this reader had some education, and was far from the ignorant reader drawn only to salacious poems so often feared by the epigrammatist. Thus, the connections of the epigram book to the common-placing tradition are re-established in the reading process. They are not merely isolated topical poems (whose prompting events at this point would be thirty years in the past) but part of a web of inherited wisdom and mockery.[83]

Notes

1 Adam Smyth, *Profit & Delight: Printed Miscellanies in England, 1640–1682* (Detroit, MI: Wayne State University Press, 2004), pp. 33–6.
2 Hayman, *Quodlibets*, Ep. 1:2.
3 Gamage, 'To the Readers of his Epigrams', *Linsi-woolsie or two centuries of epigrammes* (1621), Ep. 2:99.
4 Bastard, *Chrestoleros*, Ep. 1:39.
5 Bastard, *Chrestoleros*, Ep. 3:1.
6 Bastard, 'Ad Lectorem', in *Chrestoleros*, Ep. 6:1.
7 Bastard, *Chrestoleros*, Ep. 3:18.
8 Kathryn Perry, '"I do it onely for the Printers sake"', pp. 217–18.
9 C[ooke], *Epigrames*, sig. A3v.
10 C[ooke], 'To the Judicious, Envious and foolish Reader', *Epigrames*, sig. A3r.
11 Richard Turner, *Nosce Te* (1607), sig. A3r.
12 Joyner, *Itys*, Ep. 2:2.
13 Tyro, *Tyros Roring Megge Planted against the walles of Melancholy*, sig. A2v.
14 Freeman, *Rubbe, and a great cast*, Ep. 1:100.
15 Hayman, 'To my Readers. An Arsee-versee Request, to my Friend *John Owen*', *Quodlibets*, Ep. 3:70.
16 Fitzgeffry, *Affaniae*, Ep. 1:10.
17 Fitzgeffry, *Affaniae*, Ep. 1:10.
18 Stradling, *Epigrammatum libri quatuor*, Ep. 3:1 [trans. Sutton].
19 Jennifer Brady, '"Beware the Poet": Authority and Judgment in Jonson's Epigrams', *SEL*, 23 (1983), pp. 95–112, p. 95; George E. Rowe, 'Ben Jonson's Quarrel with Audience and its Renaissance Context', *Studies in Philology*, 81 (1984), pp. 438–60; Ranjan Ghosh, 'Ben Jonson and His Reader: An Aesthetics of Antagonism', *Comparatist: Journal of the Southern Comparative Literature Association*, 37 (2013), pp. 138–55.
20 Brady, '"Beware the Poet"', p. 110.
21 Rowe, 'Ben Jonson's Quarrel with Audience and Its Renaissance Context', p. 459.
22 Winner, 'Ben Jonson's *Epigrammes* and the Conventions of Formal Verse Satire', p. 75.
23 The *OED* cites this as the only example of 'untwitten' and suggests its meaning is obscure. However, it would seem to mean 'uncarved', as Elisha Cole, *English Dictionary* (1677), defines 'twytten' as 'carved'.
24 R.C., in Cowper, *The Times' Whistle*, p. 132.
25 Donne, 'To Sir G[eorge] M[ore]', *Letters to Severall Persons of Honour*, p. 93.
26 Hayman, *Quodlibets*, sig. A2r.

27 Hayman, *Quodlibets*, sig. A2v.
28 Niccols, *The Furies*, Ep. 1:3.
29 Niccols, *The Furies*, Ep. 1:4.
30 Niccols, *The Furies*, sig. D5v.
31 Goddard, *A Mastiff Whelp*, Ep. 2:3.
32 Goddard, *A Mastiff Whelp*, Ep. 2:1.
33 Ingram, 'Lego Ego', pp. 163–4.
34 Samuel Rowlands, 'To the Reader', *Roome, for a messe of knaues* (1610), sig. A2v.
35 Stradling, *Epigrammatum libri quatuor*, Ep. 3:1 [trans. Sutton].
36 Fitzgeffrey, *Satyres*, sig. C2v.
37 Weever, *Epigrams in the Oldest Cut and Newest Fashion*, sig. A2r–v.
38 See Bastard, *Chrestoleros*, sig. A4v.
39 Freeman, *Rubbe, and a great cast*, sig. A2v.
40 May, *Epigrams Divine and Moral*, sig. A4v.
41 Jonson, *The Cambridge Edition of the Works of Ben Jonson*, vol. 5, p. 221.
42 Brady, '"Beware the Poet"', p. 106.
43 Bancroft, 'To Ben Jonson', *Two bookes of epigrammes*, Ep. 1:21.
44 Bancroft, *Two bookes of epigrammes*, sig. A1r.
45 Harington, *Epigrams both pleasant and serious* (1615) [sig. A2r].
46 Freeman, *Rubbe, and a great cast*, sig. A2r.
47 Freeman, *Rubbe, and a great cast*, sig. F4v.
48 Freeman, *Rubbe and a great cast*, sig. A2r.
49 Hayman, *Quodlibets*, sig. A2r.
50 Hayman, *Quodlibets*, Ep. 3:1.
51 Freeman, *Rubbe and a great cast*, sig. A2v.
52 The most extended discussion of Gamage and his family is found in the annotated edition of *Linsi-woolsie* by Glyn Pursglove, available at www.phil ological.bham.ac.uk/gamage. See also *Welsh Biography Online* (http://wbo. llgc.org.uk/en/s1-GAMA-GEC-1176.html).
53 Pursglove, *Linsi-woolsie*, paragraph 5, suggests that Gamage, being of a minor and illegitimate branch of the family, was quite distant from the family to which he dedicated the work.
54 Gamage, *Linsi-woolsie*, Ep. 1:1.
55 Suffolk (Thomas Howard) was named by Charles Blount as a trustee for his will (Cyril Falls, *Mountjoy: Elizabethan General* (London: Odhams, 1955), p. 236), so it is possible that Bastard came to know Blount through Suffolk.
56 Foster, *Alumni Oxoniensis*, provides no matriculation date for Blount, but he received an MA in June 1589.

57 It is clear that the volume (Bastard's *Chrestoleros*) was published after November 1598, as Ep. 7:13 concerns the fortieth anniversary of Elizabeth's accession on the 17th of that month.

58 *DNB*. Falls, *Mountjoy*, pp. 105–6, makes clear that it was not a completely enviable position, as it was removing the figure from the court, and possibly setting him up for military catastrophe.

59 Bastard, *Chrestoleros*, Ep. 7:39.

60 Bastard, *Chrestoleros*, Ep. 7:37.

61 Dudley Carleton to Chamberlain, 13 Sept. 1597[?], PRO State Papers 15/33/90.

62 Bastard, *Chrestoleros*, sig. A3r.

63 Bastard, *Chrestoleros*, sig. A4v.

64 This is the poem 'Culex' which forms part of the 'Appendix Virgiliana', a larger body of poems long attributed to Virgil.

65 The loftiest surviving poetic work by Thomas Bastard is *Serenissimo potentissimoque monarchae Iacobo Magnae Britanniae* (1605) (a presentation manuscript copy of this also survives as BL Royal MSS 12 A.xxxvi and 12 A.xxxvii).

66 Heath, *Two Centuries of Epigrammes*, sig. A3r.

67 *DNB*. Thomas Bilson, who was about six years younger than Heath, matriculated at New College, 28 Nov. 1606, the year after Heath. Bishop Bilson himself had a reputation as a Latin poet (Wood, *Athenae Oxonienses*, vol. 1, p. 344). Sir John Harington, *A briefe view of the state of the Church of England as it stood in Q. Elizabeths and King James his reigne* (1653), pp. 72–3, also notes Bilson's interest in poetry.

68 Heath, *Two Centuries of Epigrammes*, sig. A3v.

69 Heath, *Two Centuries of Epigrammes*, sig. A3v.

70 According to the *Clergy Database Index* Heath was ordained deacon of Newnham Courtney by Bishop Bridges of Oxford in 1612, and priest in the same parish in 1613.

71 I suspect that he was the John Heath who was granted the living of Clanfield in the Diocese of Winchester in 1616.

72 Jonson, *The Cambridge Edition of the Works of Ben Jonson*, Ep. 96. A puisne was a junior judge.

73 The best overview of readers' marginalia in printed books of the period is found in Smyth, *Profit & Delight*, pp. 40–59.

74 Harington, *The Epigrams of Sir John Harington* (1615) (Shelf-mark 61291).

75 On sig. C3r is found the note, 'Though London for a good Deane once had John Donne', which makes clear that the hand is from after Donne's death in 1631.

76 In this 1615 edition the numbering of epigrams in Book 1 is inconsistent.

77 Harington, 'Of Milo the Glutton', in *The Epigrams of Sir John Harington* (1615), sig. D2v.

78 Harington, *The Epigrams of Sir John Harington* (1615), sig. D2v.

79 Smyth, *Profit & Delight*, p. 45.

80 Harington, 'Of two that were married and undone', in *The Epigrams of Sir John Harington* (1615), sig. F3r.

81 Harington, 'Of a toothlesse Shrew', in *The Epigrams of Sir John Harington* (1615), sig. D1v.

82 It is found in BL Add. MS 15227, fol. 2r; BL Add. MS10309, fol. 135r; Westminster Abbey MS 41, fol. 49r; Folger MS V.a.319, p. 2, among other places.

83 Similarly, a Folger Library copy of Heywood's *Workes* (1576) has underlining of passages in his *Epigrams*, which are then reproduced at the back of the volume (I am indebted to the anonymous reader of the present book for this reference).

9

Two facets of the epigram: names and responsiveness

Names and naming

Because of epigrams' topical emphasis on individuals, names are central to the genre: those of praise highlight the real name of the figure and some-times find appropriate meaning embedded within it;[1] mocking epigrams typically hide identity with a fictional name, but often in a way that hints at the real person. There was a sense that tradition did allow for the use of a real name even with satiric epigrams, even if in practice there was little of this. Pontanus reflects upon the use of real names in epigrams by invoking the example of Old Comedy; such works had used real names in their vituperation of individual folly, and the epigrammatist was free to do so as well, but might for the sake of caution use feigned ones as Martial had:

> In Comoedia prisca, Poëtae homines impunè nominatim accusabant, irride-bant, contemnebant. Quae materies, probrosa & ridicula scilicet, convenit etiam Epigrammatis, quorum auctores aliena peccata patefaciunt, insectantur, atque rident. Nec nominibus abstinent, quod reprehendit praelatione lib. 2. Mart. quamvis ea saepius commutent, aut pro veris ficta supponant: rem enim ipsam intelligi ab omnibus nihil vetat, pudori autem & famae hominum consulendum est, si consuli adhuc potest.[2]

> [In Old Comedy poets accuse men by name with impunity, they mocked, they despised. Such subject matter, while certainly shameful and ridiculous, is indeed fitting to the epigram, in which authors bring to light, reproach and mock others' sins. Nor do they abstain from names, which Martial, Book 2 corrects in preference, although they more wisely change them, or they supply fictitious ones for the true. Truly I know from all nothing that forbids this, but the shame and fame of men is to be considered, if it is possible to consider.]

However, while some early modern satiric epigrams in manuscript use real names, the vast majority of printed ones involve a fictional one, and found ample warrant in Martial for doing so.[3] For Campion, feigned Latinate names are an essential component of the epigram:

> You ask why I am laying an accusation regarding a true crime, but using a false name, not employing your titles or any mark of your identity. No poem that does not indulge in fiction can be called an epigram and, Matho, there is scarcely anyone who takes pleasure in the unvarnished truth.[4]

The phenomenon also takes its bearings from the related context of personation on the stage in late Elizabethan and early Stuart England. Overall, there was a strong desire on the part of audiences and readers to look beyond the fictional name for the real individual. As Richard Middleton puts it, 'application now is growne a trade, / And by construction, best the worst is made'.[5] ('Application' was the applying of a fictional figure or situation to a real-life equivalent.)[6] Middleton's opening clause is in fact a direct echo (or theft) from the Dedicatory Epistle of Jonson's *Volpone* (1607), where he complained that 'Application is now grown a trade with many, and there are that profess to have a key for the deciphering of everything'.[7] Jonson and Middleton share the fear that their fictional figures will be applied by readers to actual individuals, and that thus they will control the meaning of their works. Certainly, however, one wonders whether such prefatory complaints actually invited readers to look for personation.[8]

Most epigrams of the period, like Campion's, drew upon a common stock of Latinate names most often derived from Martial: Paulus, Priscus, Bassa, Gellia etc. Jean Humez notes that 'Fifteen of Harington's fictional names are borrowed from Martial, and all but one of his eight major characters bear Martialian names.'[9] English epigrammatists also coined new names that were Latin-based and seemed like they might come from Martial. These have the characteristic inflections -us and -a, but have no basis in the classical tradition. The real-life identity of the subjects is complicated by the fact that over the span of an epigrammatic career, the same feigned names might be used for more than one real-life figure. D. R. Shackleton Bailey suggests that there are very few continuing characters through Martial's epigrams, and that 'To track Lesbia or Galla through their numerous manifestations would be a waste of time'.[10] Given this variance of identification even within Martial, and this widespread indebtedness to a stock of Martial-based names, we need to be chary of assuming that a certain character in one English epigram book represents the same historical figure as one of the same name in another volume. Harington himself might use the name 'Paulus' to depict two different individuals, and neither might have anything to do with the 'Paulus' mentioned by Percy or Parrot. More evidence than a shared name is required.

Newly invented names may be merely arbitrary constructions, or as with many in Middleton's *Epigrams and Satyres* (1608) have etymological significance based on the characteristics of the figure: for example, 'Vesicanum' (from 'vesica' – bladder) is used for one who has grown fat. Others are nonce names built on the English base of the name with a Latinate 'us' or 'a' ending added, or a translation of the English name into a Latin equivalent. Some instances of substituted names would be examples of 'paragrams'; that is, name or word replacements that share certain sounds with the original. Most extensive in exploring these possibilities is E. A. J. Honigmann's edition of Weever's *Epigrammes* in which he offers possible identification of most figures, largely based upon the names of students at Cambridge from Weever's time there.[11] Hence, he ventures 'Robert Rudd, sizar at Queens' as a possible identification of 'Rudio', 'John Otter of Corpus' for 'Otho' etc. In other cases, Honigmann suggests that Weever draws upon the meaning rather than sound of the Latin name. Thus, he wonders whether 'Charis' might represent 'John Grace, at St. John's', and 'Pontus' might represent 'John Seaman'. Honigmann offers these tentatively, and any certainty is difficult to establish. As evident below, however, authors of published volumes seem to have been very careful to avoid this rather obvious naming approach, fearful of prosecution. Rare is the use of initials in satiric epigrams to identify the subject.[12]

Despite the appearance that they were depicting a real individual under a fictional name, some epigrammatists insisted that, like satirists, their attacks were on general vices, and not individuals. In this they could find a precedent in Martial, who had claimed that his poems endeavour 'to spare the person, to denounce the vice' ('parcere personis, dicere de vitiis'),[13] a position that became a satiric commonplace. By this claim, the use of a particular name was merely conventional, not a masking of a known individual. Sir John Davies's first epigram is typical of this defence. He dismisses those who think that he 'do[es] to privat Taxing leane' as not understanding the epigram as a genre. It is that 'Which Taxeth under a particular name, / A generall vice that merits publique blame'.[14] In his *Mastiff Whelp*, William Goddard claims that he is only describing general human sins and foibles, but that some might ask then, 'why men I doe pertick'larize'; he answers that 'I onely faine a name; / All knowes this kinde of vayne requires the same'.[15] Davies of Hereford defends himself by claiming to use 'namelesse names',[16] ones which point to that elusive figure, 'Nobody'.

Despite such claims, there are far more suggestions within epigram books that real individuals were being glanced at, and the reading culture generally expected that such 'personation' was at work. As an example of this expectation, an opponent of epigrammatists rejected this defence of only attacking general vice as disingenuous: 'And verily you ['Signior Epigrammatist'] have greatly troubled your selfe in naming certaine particular persons. Such a one you call Fabius, and another Felix, anon comes me Rufus and Clodius.'[17] The prefatory material to *The More the Merrier* (1608) points to the dangers of too obvious personal satire: 'As for Satyrick inveighing at any mans private person, (a kind of writing which of late seemes to have beene very familiar among our Poets and Players to their cost) my reader is to seeke it else where.'[18] The parenthetical statement suggests that the steps taken against playwrights and poets in the Bishops' Ban has caused him to be more circumspect. However, the poet does not actually deny specific satiric intent, but that readers are 'to seeke it else where'. The book claimed to offer 'head-lesse epigrams, shot, (like the fooles bolt) amongst you, light where they will', but these epigrams have lemmas in the common vein of fictional Latinate names.

While Jonson claims in the preface to his epigrams that 'I have avoided all particulars, as I have done names',[19] the fact that he could and did use epigrams as instruments of personal attacks seems to belie this. In 'To Fine Grand' (no. 73) he describes one who 'take[s] an epigram so fearfully, / As 'twere a challenge, or a borrower's letter'. Why might 'Fine Grand' be fearful? He has solicited Jonson to pen a variety of minor poetic works, but not paid him, and so Jonson ends with a threat: 'pay me quickly, or I'll pay you'. From the beginning it is clear that 'Fine Grand' would be 'paid' with a satiric epigram – he does have reason to fear Jonson's epigrams, because *they can be personal*. In 'To Person Guilty' he criticizes 'Guilty' for going to the opposite extreme in laughing uproariously when he himself is 'touched', and concludes that if 'Guilty' continues to wrongly respond to Jonson's epigrams, 'I'll lose my modesty, and tell your name'.[20] Implicit here is a social contract in which the subject and poet share responsibility for keeping the real subject hidden, but the poet holds the stronger hand in being able to threaten revelation.[21] At the same time, both undermine the claim that the poet is merely depicting general vice. Naming of this sort (that is, where the attribute itself is used rather than a Latin-based fictional name, like 'Lord Ignorant', 'Don Surly', 'Captain Hungry' or 'Court-Worm') recalls the characters in Jonson's comedies.

Partridge argues that part of Jonson's strategy is the *denying* of a name beyond the negative attribute to the person under attack, thus turning him wholly into a type.[22] The same approach is adopted by Herrick in the satiric epigrams scattered throughout *Hesperides*.

In *52 Epigrams* J[ohn] C[ooke] acknowledges the contemporary influence of the Roman tradition, which he believed used real names, but adopts his own way:

> the Romanes in their Epigrames did use the true names of those they write of, and our Epigramitists do borrow their names of them, but I have used bastard names, such as my fancie was father of, not waying whether they were proper to the nature of the Epigrame, as indeede there is no such necessitie.[23]

His second-last clause seems to hint at an awareness of traditions in naming, but he has, perhaps, in the casual attitude typical of the epigrammatist, tossed aside any such burden of tradition. Cooke's epigrams actually show a mixture of English names with more typical Latinate epigrammatic names.

The threat of revealing

As seen in Jonson's 'To Person Guilty', the use of feigned names in epigrams sustained a further threat: that the epigrammatist might later reveal the figure's identity. For example, in the second of two mocking epigrams on a bishop, Thomas Pestell warns,

> Jeast on: & thinke I do but jeast in these!
> I vowe the next, shall name your Diocese.[24]

Guilpin also wittily refuses to reveal his subject in the third of a series of epigrams mocking one 'Naevia' who attempts to be merchant, lawyer and gentleman:

> Pardon me (Reader) I will not bewray
> Who *Naevia* is, not that I feare to say,
> But that he should be punished I am loth,
> For engrossing occupations as he doth.[25]

These instances reflect the power and prestige of the epigrammatist, who assumes that even to be defamed in his poem would be a sort of privilege or honour. They might all be ultimately indebted to Martial, 12:61, which reassures one Ligurra that he will not write verses on him, because Ligurra is not important enough; he should beware instead of 'nigri fornicis ebrium poetam, / qui carbone rudi putrique creta / scribit carmina quae legunt cacantes' [some dark cellar's sottish poet, one who with coarse charcoal or crumbling chalk scrawls poems which people read in the jakes]. A gesture like this can be made only by an epigrammatist with an already well-established reputation.

John Owen asserts his power in a different way, refusing to identify the subject he has labelled with the fictional name 'Momus' (which always represents a carping critic), for that would establish the very public recognition that his enemy sought. He has defamed Owen's epigrams in order to make a name for himself:

> Incendit Triviae sacra templa, ut nomen haberet,
>   Quidam, nescio quis; nec puto nomen habet.
> Sic tu dente nigro carpis mea carmina; speras
>   Forsan in hoc quarto nomen habere libro.
> Usque licet per me rodas mea carmina, carpas
>   Usque licet; fallam spes ego, Mome, tuas.[26]

> [One, whom I know not, infamous by Fame
> Diana's Temple burn'd to get a Name:
> So with black Teeth thou dost my Verses bite,
> Hoping to have thy name in what I write:
> But bite, backbite thy fill, I will deceive
> Thine hopes, and thee without a name will leave.][27]

The opening lines refer to Herostratus, an ancient Greek, who infamously burned the Temple of Artemis in Ephesus in a bid to achieve fame. However, as part of his resistance to Momus, Owen refuses to even name Herostratus – he is simply 'One, whom I know not', thus erasing the success of this illicit attempt at renown. The poem also indirectly aligns Owen's epigram books with the Temple, one of the seven wonders of the ancient world.

Riddling the reader

Epigrams and epitaphs, in both manuscript and print, occasionally will engage in a playful game that might be called 'riddling the reader'; that is, withholding the full identification of the subject by name, but offering enough information to invite speculation. Thus, Martial 9:95 toys with one reader's curiosity on this score:

> Nomen Athenagorae quaeris, Callistrate, verum.
> si scio, dispeream, qui sit Athenagoras.

> [You ask Athenagoras' real name, Callistratus. Damned if I know who Athenagoras is.][28]

In an epigram entitled 'Of the objects of his satire', Harington acknowledges pressure from an unnamed 'Lord' to reveal 'who are meant/By *Cinna, Lynus, Lesbia*, and the rest', but suggests that 'if my wanton Muse dy penitent, / Perhaps she then may tell yow whome she ment'.[29] There's no record he did any such thing – perhaps he died before his 'wanton muse'. Epitaphs generally include the real name of the deceased in the lemma; however, a series in BL Harl. MS 1221, fol. 72ff., are headless, and some, like this one, clearly 'riddle the reader':

> Heere under lyes a Counsellor of state,
> a deepe divine, a stout & grave prelate;
> a Bishopp, and an Alcymist; who ist?
> he is not; & in him is veryfied,
> This trueth, yt all thinges must be Nullified.[30]

Most readers at the time were likely able to identify this as Bishop Thomas Bilson (d. 1616), who was commonly referred to as 'Nullity Bilson' because of his role in the nullifying of the Essex–Howard marriage.

At the end of his manuscript epigrams, many of which had mocked a figure named Lun (an unusual feigned name), Percy writes:

The Conclusion
> To shewe, who you be, now gentle Sir Lun,
> you may uncase you, For my Playe is done.[31]

There is the tantalizing possibility that the final line plays on 'uncase' and points toward Dr John Case, Percy's tutor. Case's interest in music is reflected in his *Apologia musices* (1588), and another Percy epigram on Lun had referred to his music-making:

> Lun to learne, on sweet Instruments, from Brune,
> Did chuse the Pipe because he could not tune.[32]

Overall, such 'riddling' encouraged readers to seek out real-life subjects who lay behind the fictional names throughout the epigrams of the period.

In epigrams of praise the custom was of course to name, but even in these an occasional degree of riddling is found. One epitaph by Jonson identifies the subject only as 'Elizabeth, L.H.', and the abbreviation is deliberate, as Jonson notes in the mysterious final lines:

> One name was Elizabeth,
>   The other let it sleep with death:
> Fitter where it died to tell,
>   Than that it lived at all. Farewell.[33]

Nor did all subjects of praise want to be named, which is the sole conceit of Jonson's 'To One that Desired Me Not to Name Him':

> Be safe, nor fear thyself so good a fame
>   That any way my book should speak thy name:
> For if thou shame, ranked with my friends, to go,
>   I'm more ashamed to have thee thought my foe.[34]

Here the reader is left wondering if there is any praise at all: the subject has rejected inclusion in what Jonathan Z. Kamholtz has neatly called Jonson's 'magic circle of his collection of *Epigrammes*'.[35] In doing so, has the subject raised himself above it or foolishly excluded himself from a most worthy company that includes such eminent figures as the King and the Earl of Pembroke?

Punning on names

One significant body of exceptions to the avoidance of real names is the group of epigrams and epitaphs that pun upon the subject's name or play upon its literal meaning, finding ironic significance in the process. (A few poems also jest on the *inappropriateness* of a name.)[36] This playing on the appropriateness of a name stretched back to the classical epigram. Certain names of public figures seemed to invite epigrammatic wit. Chief Justice Edward Coke (1552–1634), whose fortunes at the hands of epigrammatists is considered in Chapter 10, had a name (usually pronounced 'Cook')

that few could resist. While nearly any political figure might find his name
the basis of punning epigrams, in a few instances the stars seemed to align
to bring forth a rich crop of names for epigrammatic use. For example,
the appointment of a new Justice to the Court of Common Pleas in 1634
prompted the following lines based on the names of those involved:

> Noy's floods are past, the Banks appear,
> The Heath is cropt, the Finch sings there.[37]

Attorney General William Noy had recently died, and Robert Heath had
been removed from the bench; the two were replaced by Sir John Bankes
and John Finch. While there may be a political dimension to these lines,
as both Bankes and Finch were perceived as strong advocates of the royal
prerogative, the epigram may also be little more than a whimsical observation based on the meanings of the names.

A figure whose name was played on might respond with the same
punning practice; such is the case with Barten Holyday, who responded
to attacks on his Oxford play *Technogamia* (performed before the King in
1621) in this way:

> Tis not my Person, nor my Play
> But my surname Holliday
> That does offend her, thy complaints
> Are not against mee, but her saintes.
> So ill dost thou endow my name
> Because her church doth like the same
> A name more awfull to the puritane
> Then Talbot unto france or Drake to Spaine.[38]

Here the poet proudly embraces the meaning of his name, recognizing it
as that which divides the Puritans from the Church of England. His argument extends his opponents' attacks as being against the Church itself,
and presents those attacks as irrational and fearful. The final lines take
the further step of casting his enemies into a parallel situation with the
traditional enemies of England.

The lemma

Given the significance of naming, it is not surprising that the title, or
more precisely, the 'lemma', of an epigram bears so much importance.[39]

A *lemma*, that is the title or that on which the epigram stands, is central, and takes the place of the monument or building on which the epigram proper is inscribed.[40] By a large margin, epigrams feature the name of an individual within the title; in some books nearly every epigram is so titled, and even the more innovative Jonson constructs over a hundred of the 133 epigrams in his *Workes* (1616) in this way.[41] In Latin titles, the heading usually takes the form '*In* ...', except in epigrams of praise, where '*Ad* ...' is typical.[42] (In English lemmas these are replaced by 'On ...', and less commonly '*Upon* ...', '*Of* ...', or '*To* ...') Scaliger suggests that, as the epitaph genre was transferred from its original inscription in stone, the lemma came to take the place of the statue or monument upon which it had been inscribed:

> Exempli gratia, Rufi rhetoris statuae inscripsit lepidum illud poematium Ausonius. His ipsum poematium inscriptum, Epigramma est. quum verò illud in libro descripsit, statuae imaginem, id est Rufi nomen inscripsit sic: In Rufi statuam. [43]

> [For example, Ausonius inscribed a short poem on the stone of the statue of the rhetor Rufus. This inscribed poem was an epigram. Truly when it was copied into a book, the image of the statue, it is the name of Rufus that is thus inscribed: 'On the statue of Rufus.']

A rare exception is Parrot's *Cure for the Itch*, where the two-word titles are in Latin but do not include the name of the subject; instead they include an adjective and noun or two adjectives, or two adverbs. However, the names almost invariably appear in the first line.

Fiddling with the lemma

Often an epigram that survives in both manuscript and print has a different lemma or name in each medium: this may indicate an attempt to better mask the identity of the subject in print, or may show a reapplication (by author or reader) of the lines to a new individual. The irregularities of many lemmas also raise questions about authorial origins: in an article on Donne's epigrams M. Thomas Hester suggests that while their headings may not be Donne's they do show how readers interpreted and applied the poems and something of the circulation of the epigrams in manuscript.[44] In the movement from manuscript to print often one feigned name is substituted for another; thus, a published epigram of Parrot has the first line

'Dacus doth daily to his Doctor go',[45] but it survives in two manuscripts as 'Chus doth soe often to the Doctor goe'.[46] Dacus is a conventional name in epigrams, but 'Chus' is an unlikely Latinate construction and it seems likely that the epigram has been reapplied to another individual whose name was being quite closely echoed. Such would then reflect a movement from print to manuscript. Another explanation would be that an original had 'In Chas.', but this was mistranscribed at some point during manu-script circulation.

As the lemma was frequently the only identifying marker of a satiric epigram, if circulation were to take place without it, or if the lemma was changed, the epigram might be radically reapplied.[47] This phenomenon was described already in Chapter 4 with the epitaph on the bellows-maker; in that case, the individual identity of the subject seemed less important than the conceit upon his occupation. However, with prominent figures such as princes and court favourites, the reapplication of an epigram was much more significant, as it connected an old subject with a new, and presented folly or corruption as part of a repeated historical pattern. An epigram on an individual might be reapplied by a simple name change, or a general or even proverbial epigram fitted to a particular situation. For example, John Rous records the following in his diary regarding a distich about the Duke of Buckingham in oral circulation:

> It was reported that the dole for the duke was farthings; and an ould rime was rehearsed:
>
> > *Brasse farthings in charity are given to the pore,*
> > *When all the gold pieces are spent on a whore.*[48]

This example also shows how in diaries and newsletters a lemma was replaced by a sentence leading up to the verses, which establishes the con-text. Similarly, Harington took a Latin epigram by the early Hungarian humanist Janus Pannonius, 'written of Pope Paulus and his daughter', and reapplied it to Bishop William Chaderton and his granddaughter, Elizabeth Sandys:

> Cum sit filia, Paule, cum tibi aurum,
> Quantum pontifices habere raros:
> Vidit Roma prius, patrem non possum
> Sanctum dicere, sed possum beatum.

Which I thus translated, when I thought not thus to apply it:

> Thou hast a daughter Paulus, I am told,
> And for this daughter store thou hast of gold:
> The daughter thou didst get, the gold didst gather,
> Make thee no holy, but an happie father.

But if the bishop should fortune to heare that I applie this vearse thus sawcily, and should be offended with it, I would be glad in full satisfaction of this wrong, to give him my sonne for his daughter, which is a manifest token that I am in perfect charitie with him.[49]

In this case, the original lemma (fully identified by Harington) adds sting to the reapplication of the epigram. After all, any daughter of Pope Paul was illegitimate, and a Protestant English bishop who tended toward the godly end of the spectrum would not relish a parallel drawn to the pontiff. Harington seems to be pursuing one of his frequent satiric concerns: the way in which the new-found family commitments of English bishops led them to garner dynastic accumulations of wealth.

The rapid rise of King James's favourites, Somerset and Buckingham, seemed to follow a pattern, and Wotton's epigram 'Dazzled thus with height of place', seemingly first written about Somerset, was later reapplied to Bacon and Buckingham.[50] In a couple of manuscripts it is lifted out of historical specificity entirely and becomes 'On the sudden restraint of a favorite'.[51]

Bellany notes how certain verse libels were recopied decades after their political moment, or found their way into printed collections of jests in the 1640s and 1650s.[52] This encouraged a reapplication of conceits to fit the new political or social situation. For example, the familiar distich threatening Buckingham's life, 'Let Charles and George do what they can, / The Duke shall die like Dr. Lambe', was rewritten in 1640 by those opposing Archbishop Laud: 'Charles and Marie do what they will, we will kill the archbishop of Canturbury like Dr Lambe.'[53] The would-be assassins seem not to have been concerned with the uncouth rhythm and loss of rhyme their reapplication brought about.

Case study: Personation in Fitzgeffry's *Affaniae*

The first wave of English published epigram books coincided with the fashion of 'personation' in the 'Wars of the Theatres' (1598–1601). Like the epigrams of Weever, Bastard and Davies, such plays as John Marston's *Histriomastix*, Thomas Dekker's *Satiromastix* and Jonson's *Poetaster* used lightly fictionalized versions of their contemporaries.[54] Matthew Steggle identifies the strong convention of using such disguised figures:

> At no point during the entire War do the participants name their opponents by their real names: the strongest taboo of all on personal satire, the reluctance to name names as Aristophanes had done, remains strong. As will be seen, even this decorum was sometimes breached in later satirical drama.[55]

Such fictionalized names were also an extension of the humanist tradition where scholars and writers adopted Latinate names.[56] Such an approach certainly primed audiences and readers of these years to discern the real individual behind the fictional veil.

Chapter 6 considered the letter of Degory Wheare concerning the publication of his friend Charles Fitzgeffry's *Affaniae*. One passage where Wheare considers the lemmas shows something of the dynamics of fictional naming in epigrams of the time and how they was intertwined with the 'Wars of the Theatres'. He writes:

> De Fabri et Satyrographi nomini*bus* e Caroli poematiis liturâ tollendis cogitabimus: interim tamen ne vos lateat, priorem istu*m* non honoris causâ nominatu*m* [de] sed deridiculi et joci: quod si aliter intellexistis false fuistis. lepide enim fungu*m* perstrinxit inanis gloriolæ et immortalitatis (si diis placet) cupidissimu*m*; quod ex secundo versu (licet obscuriuscule) perspicere est. neq*ue* fingit quicqua*m* poeta noster Revera enim nasutus iste ffaber ad me quonda*m* veniebat et obnixe rogabat ut hanc gratia*m* a Carolo impetrarem nempe ut quædam Epigra*m*mata nomini suo inscriberet: meruimus sane inquit tum quod Carolum amamus, tum quod Musis etia*m*[57] favemus: præterea curavim*us* semper ut cresceret eius fama, apud Daniele*m*, Draitona*m*, Ionsoniu*m* et alios. ridebam herclè Asinu*m* blandiente*m* et nescio quid auræ aucupantem, dicebamq*ue* me facturu*m*: hinc ortu*m* est illud carmen De grege versificum etc. Sed si homo minus placeat removebimus e choro; locu*m* tamen sortitus est suo dignu*m* ingenio, videlicet inter præstigiatore*m* et Bardu*m*.[58]

> [We will consider whether the names of Faber and Satyrographus [the writer of satires] should be erased from Charles's poems: meanwhile, however, it should not be concealed from you that the first one is named not because of honour, but as an absurdity and a joke, but if you thought otherwise you were wrong. For, he charmingly offends the fool, most desirous of a little empty

glory and immortality (if it pleases the gods); a thing which is ascertained out of the second line (although slightly more obscurely). Nor does our poet in fact imagine anything, for that long-nosed (*or* clever) craftsman came to me once and vigorously asked that I entreat this favour from Charles: truly that he should write certain epigrams on his own name. He said, 'surely I have deserved (this) both because I love Charles and also because I support the Muses. Moreover I have always taken care for his fame to grow, among Daniel, Drayton, Jonson and others.' By Hercules I laughed at the Ass, flattering and snatching at some bit of gold, and I said that I would do (it): hence arises that song 'Of the flock of versifiers', etc. But if the man should be less pleasing we will remove him from the troop; however, he has received a place worthy of his cleverness, between a juggler and a bard (*or* a stupid man).]

Wheare's first reference is to the Fitzgeffry poem entitled 'Ad Fabrianum' (2:63) in the printed text:

De grege versificum quidam, quem dicere nolo
(Tu, Fabriane catus, quem volo, coniicias)
Flagiciis a me crebis contendit, et instat
Ut libris vivat carminibusque meis.
Victuram ergo aliis ausint promittere famam,
Quam mihi, quam nequeant carmina nostra sibi?
At si tantus amor sit in ora venire nepotum,
Inque libris vatum carminibusque legi,
Davisios laedat mihi, Ionsoniosque lacessat,
In Nashum dicat turpia quaeque trucem.
Haud aliter speret vatum per carmina famam,
Haud aliter meruit scilicet ille cani.

[There is a certain member of the versifying flock, whom I do not wish to name (You, clever Fabrianus, can guess whom I mean), who pesters me with frequent entreaties, and begs that he might live in my poems. So shouldn't others promise him enduring fame, rather than me, whose poems cannot achieve this for themselves? But if he has such a desire to be in the mouths of our descendants, and to be read of in poets' verses, as far as I am concerned he may bother the Davises, injure the Jonsons, and slander savage Nashe. Scarce otherwise might he aspire to fame in poetry, scarce otherwise has he deserved to be sung about.][59]

The poem itself is playing with the question of naming the ambitious poet, who had hoped to be celebrated under his own name among the many panegyric poems in *Affaniae*.[60] Instead, Fitzgeffry had exercised his power as epigrammatist to depict him with a feigned name in a satiric epigram. However, it is clear from Wheare's letter that Francis Rous and George Spry felt that 'Faber' – the fictional name originally employed – was too obvious; so, in the final printed version, Fitzgeffry has changed the name to 'Fabrianus', and slyly suggests that they both know his identity. Who was Faber? The Latin word is a fairly general one for craftsman or worker. The most likely candidate is Weever, who was heavily involved in the topical satire of the period 1598 to 1601 and who is believed by Honigmann to be mocked as Simplicius Faber in Marston's *What You Will*.[61] This play, which some scholars have dated to April 1601, was a central one in the 'Wars of the Theatres'.[62] Hence, it may be that Rous and Spry recognized that Fitzgeffry's poem too closely built upon Simplicius Faber and that the identity would be dangerously obvious. Further support for identifying this figure with Weever is the reference to him as 'Asinum blandientiem': Asinius Bubo in Dekker's *Satiro-mastix* has long been recognized as another depiction of Weever.[63] That play has usually been dated to the second half of 1601, but this echo suggests either that an earlier date for *Satiro-mastix* is possible or that the play was influenced by Fitzgeffry.[64]

'Faber's' desire for poetic fame has been frustrated by Fitzgeffry, both because he is left unnamed and because his poem is placed amongst other mocking epigrams – literally between poems to the 'impostor' Martin and the slow 'Bardus' – rather than among the English poets celebrated by name in *Affaniae* 2:11–25, such as Daniel, Drayton and Jonson. Fitzgeffry has even taunted Faber–Fabrianus on the whole business of personation in the second line, to which Wheare particularly points. He also suggests that Faber will achieve immortality only by being satirized by such well-known writers as Sir John Davies, Jonson and Nashe.[65] The claim may be a disingenuous one: actually to name the fellow when he is being mocked would tend towards libel, and Wheare's correspondents, Rous and Spry, had obviously raised the issue amongst a host of similar concerns.

The example of Wheare and Fitzgeffry suggests that the development of a name or lemma might come late in the compositional process, and it is plausible that early versions of a satiric epigram would use the real name, with the feigned one replacing it later. Among Sir John Davies's unpublished epigrams are a couple that name individuals directly: 'In Bretton' and 'In Mundayum', presumably on Nicholas Breton and Anthony Munday. [66] One suspects that if these had been printed, or even entered wider manuscript circulation, Davies would have substituted feigned names in keeping with the norms of the epigrams and to avoid libel charges.

Epigram and counter-epigram

Chapter 3 explored how epigram composition in the grammar schools was based upon responsiveness: students were expected to compose in relation to an assigned biblical passage, maxim or other text. Such responsiveness is one of the hallmarks of the epigram in the period. It takes its bearing immediately from a specific subject or moment, or even another written work (often someone else's epigram). The very etymology of the word reflects this: it is literally something written (γράφειν, *graphein*) upon (ἐπί, *epi*) something else, and the lemma is the hinge that joins the two. Deep in the history of the genre, the event was most often a death or the construction of a building or artefact to which the epigram attached itself through inscription. Over time the elements directly responded to became broader. The term 'occasional poetry', which accurately describes so much Renaissance verse, is not quite sufficient here, as it does not capture those epigrams that respond, not to a specific public event but to the fixed and continuing properties of an individual who is praised or blamed, or a literary work. Overall, responsive epigrams are not as time-based as occasional poems.[67] The slender quality of the form requires a pre-existing situation or text upon which the epigram can build or develop. Put another way, the brevity of the genre does not allow it to be self-generating: it must rely upon the established reality of its subject as the basis for its wit. A variety of this responsiveness was dominant in the early history of the English epigram, as John Heywood's mid-sixteenth-century 'Epigrams upon Proverbs' were just that: poems that took a well-known saying as a starting point for a more witty turn.

In some cases another's epigram was itself the starting point, and thus we have epigram and 'counter-epigram'.[68] S. K. Heninger, Jr, posits that, while companion poems were known in the medieval period, they were a more 'distinctively Renaissance phenomenon'.[69] However, his definition of these as 'two relatively brief metrical compositions each of which is semi-autonomous, even though they are meant to be read together',[70] does not completely fit the phenomenon of 'epigram and counter-epigram'. The secondary, responsive epigram is wholly dependent on the first, but it cannot be said that the first anticipated the composition of the second. (In fact, Heninger's opening example, 'The Passionate Shepherd' and 'The Nimphs reply' may also fall short: there is no evidence that the first 'was meant' to be read with the second. More accurately, it has *come* to be usually read with the second. His use of the passive voice here – 'are meant' – probably points to the uncertainty.) E. F. Hart's term 'answer-poem' better fits the unidirectional relationship usually found between two epigrams:[71] the original provocatively elicits a response, which, in reusing something of the original's language or form, offers a corrective or at least different perspective. Hart sees these as being firmly rooted in the court and musical context of the period,[72] and, while this is accurate for lyric examples and some exchanged epigrams, many 'answer-epigrams' seem more to emerge from the broader public sphere of dialogue and exchange. Also, the more courtly lyric answer-poem 'sometimes amounts to gentle satire, but it never goes beyond the bounds of friendly chaff',[73] whereas responsive epigrams were often downright vitriolic. The use of epigrams to mock individuals easily led to exchanges wherein epigrams of ever-increasing vehemence were thrown back and forth, often involving *tu quoque* responses.

The cultivation of such epigram exchanges could draw on the classical legacy by pointing, for example, to the well-known conflict of Naevius and the Metelli in ancient Rome (late third century, BC).[74] Of this exchange, only two lines survive, where Naevius is quoted as saying, 'Fato Metelli Romae fiunt consules'. This can be translated as either 'The Metelli became consuls at Rome through fate' or 'The Metelli became consuls to Rome's sorrow', and the double meaning would seem to have been the epigram's very point.[75] Lucius Caecilius Metellus supposedly responded: 'Dabunt malum Metelli Naevio poetae' [The Metelli will bring misfortune to the poet Naevius]. The fulfilment of this prophecy in Naevius's exile to Utica would seem to have fostered the fame of the exchange, and, despite its flimsiness, by the Augustan period it was frequently being cited.

The majority of epigram exchanges of the Renaissance are relatively insignificant in comparison to the Naevius–Metelli epigrams. The following trivial example is typical: a man named Glascocke wrote this mock epitaph on a certain Henry Anderton:

> Heere lyes one, the mo*re* the pitty
> His name was Henry Andertitty
>> because Towne would not stand in the verse.[76]

That is, 'Anderton' provided no workable rhyme. Preserved in the same manuscript is Anderton's bawdy reply:

Heere lyes one proper & well shapen
Whose name was Willia*m* Glascapon
  because Cocke would not stand in the verse.[77]

Such exchanges were legion, but our interest is drawn towards those involving more illustrious figures, or at least more wit.[78] On the same page in Bodl. Malone MS 19 appears the widely circulating exchange between Sir Walter Ralegh and Henry Noel:

Raw-ly
The offence of the stomach, & the word of disgrace,
Is the name of the man with the brazen face.

Reply
The word of Deniall, the figure of fiftye,
Is the Gentlemans name *tha*t will nev*er* be thriftye.[79]

Michael Rudick suggests that 'By the late seventeenth century (if not before), the verses had evidently become part of oral tradition'.[80] The wit here is no finer than that in the exchange on Glascapon, but the association with Ralegh, as with supposed epitaphs on his death, seems to have ensured the epigrams' fame.[81] This exchange seems to be more courtly playfulness than serious vitriolic, in keeping with other verses ascribed to Ralegh.

 Such witty responses seemed to have been valued for how they epitomised the learning or character of a well-known individual. Thus, Thomas Fuller recounts the following exchange about Bishop John Jegon (1550–1618):

Whilst master of the College [Corpus Christi], he chanced to punish all the under-graduates therein for some general offence; and the penalty was put upon their heads in the buttery. And because that he disdained to convert the money to any private use, it was expended in new whiting the hall of the college. Whereupon a scholar hung up these verses on the screen:

 'Doctor Jegon, Bennet College master,
 Brake the scholars' head, and gave the walls a plaister.'

But the doctor had not the readiness of his parts any whit impaired by his age; for, perusing the paper, *extempore* he subscribed,

> 'Knew I but the wag that writ these verses in a bravery,
> I would commend him for his wit, but whip him for his knavery.'[82]

Evident again is that dynamic where the effrontery of an underling is to an extent forgiven because of the accompanying wit. At the same time, Jegon triumphs by extemporaneously answering with corresponding wit (and double rhyme) to the original.

Peacham recounts an instance of convivial if mocking epigram exchange in his *Thalia's Banquet* (1620):

A Lattin distich which a Frier of *Shertogen Bosch* in *Brabant* wrote in my Greeke Testament, while I was busie perusing some bookes in their Library, intituled,

Ad Angliam vestram.
Epigram 108
Angelus indiderat, dicas, anne Anglia nomen,
Spirituum siquis Lucifer ille fuit.

Thus in English.

Say England, did an Angell christen thee?
If any, surely *Lucifer* was he.

His back being turn'd, I left this behind me, in the first printed page of a faire *Arias Montanus* bible,[83] to requite him.

Ad Sylvam Ducis.
Epigram 109
Dicere Sylva Ducis cur falso nomine, sylva
Cum carcas, sterilis stagnet et omnis ager?
Fallor, an in divos arbor mutatur adseos,
In Monachum stipes quem stipe vulgus alis.

Which is in English,

Why falselie art thou call'd the Dukes-wood, when
Thou hast no woods, and all thy feildes are fenne?
Thy Trees (I ghesse) are turn'd to sainted stocks,
And begging Friers have robb'd thee of thy blocks.[84]

Both poems play with the names of places, once more finding an inherent incongruity in the name that allows for a quick jest. The pun on 'Angelus/ Anglia' had a long history going back to Gregory the Great; the play on Hertogenbosch was also widespread, made repeatedly, for example, by Donne in his Latin epigrams (as translated by Jasper Mayne). As a Spanish-controlled Dutch city repeatedly under siege by Protestant forces in the period, it was prominent in the English imagination. In Peacham's account, one jest provokes the other, and an air of spontaneity hangs over the whole episode, even while the individuals draw on a tradition of bantering. The incident also gives some indication of how randomly epigrams might be recorded on surfaces that have little to do with their content.

The examples above involve complete epigrams that were then responded to by others. There is at least one famous example where an epigram was created by the witty rhyming response to a single line. Fuller records the story:

> [Sir Walter Ralegh] comming to Court, found some hopes of the Queens favours reflecting upon him. This made him write in a glasse Window, obvious to the Queens eye,
> *Fain would I climb, yet fear I to fall,*
>
> Her *Majesty* either espying, or being *shown* it, did under-write,
> *If thy heart fails thee, climb not at all.*[85]

The original line is a hesitant appeal for favour; the response, with a playful firmness, does not respond with favour, but mock pragmatic advice along the lines of the familiar proverb 'Fortune favours the brave'. The Queen's wit is manifest with the literary satisfaction of 'capping verses' in rhyme, and it is her addition that turns the text into an epigram. By no means were all exchanges so courtly, and it seems that the nastier exchanges are frequently obscured by the use of personation and the absence of any clear context.

These examples reflect situations of relative intimacy: the poets know each other by name, and the identity of the two parties is in fact part of the meaning of the poems. In other cases, a poem, often anonymous, attracted responses in the course of circulation. Here what the poets share is a focus on the same subject, but they offer distinctively different judgements upon it. Unlike the examples above, there is no element of social interaction.

Such pairs were most often found in multi-author manuscripts, but on some occasions published epigrammatists included the poems by others to which they were responding. Henry Fitzgeffrey's *Satyres: and sat-yricall epigrams* (1617) includes a poem headed 'Incerti Authoris / Of a Bald-man' (generally attributed to Donne):

> Thy *Haires,* and *sinnes,* no man may aequall cal
> For as thy *Sinnes increase* thy *Haires* doe *Fall.*[86]

It is followed by his own 'An Answer to the same':

> Yes: If thy *Haires fall,* as thy *Sinnes increase,*
> Both will ere long prove *aequall, Numberlesse.*[87]

The broad respect and fame of Owen's Latin epigrams also compelled responsiveness. In the course of translating some of Owen's epigrams, Hayman was sometimes moved to reply and correction. Where Owen writes

> **Much Preaching. To Preachers**
> 'Tis signe of much ill, where much preaching needs,
> For what needs preaching, where you see good deeds?[88]

Hayman adds,

> **A reply to mine Author**
> Yes, preaching may doe good, where goodnesse growes,
> T'incourage, to confirme, to comfort those.

Thus, Hayman is offering a more Protestant corrective to the position adopted by his model.[89] The most complicated instance is at 4:182, where there is an eight-line 'Addition' to the Owen poem, 'A fearefull Soules flesh-farewell'. His translation of the original reads:

> Why should the immortall soule feare bodies death?
> Feares shee to expire with the bodies breath?
> Or feares she going hence, she must resort
> To long long punishment, but judgement short?
> Cold, shaking feare of the hot fire of hell,
> Makes this sad soule loth bid the flesh farewell.

To this, Hayman responds with three epigrams of his own:

Addition. A good Christians Soules Flesh-farewell
A thought so base hath not that soule surpriz'd,
Who knowes the flesh shall be immortaliz'd:
He feares no punishment, who is assur'd
Before he dye, his pardon is procur'd.
Body and soule thus chear'd by Gods grace,
Part like friends, pointing a new meeting place:
Therefore who hopes for Heaven, and feares not Hell,
May chearefully bid the fraile flesh farewell.

An Epigram on both these
Hee feares not death, who hopes for Heavens glory;
He may feare Death, that feareth purgatory,
Or he that thinkes this life shall end his story.

A Prayer hereupon
Good dreadfull God, though I live fearefully;
Yet when I dye, make me dye cheerefully.

As translator, Hayman feels bound to reproduce accurately the epigram-matist whom he reveres; however, his religious sensibility compels him to offer correction also: he rejects both the fear of death and the dismissal of the body in the original, as he looks forward instead to the Final Resurrection.

The political realm also saw significant examples of responsive epigrams. For example, an epigram satirizing the influence of Buckingham on the King enjoyed widespread manuscript circulation:

Rex and Grex are of one sound
but Dux doth Rex and Grex confound
if Crux of Dux might have his fill
then Rex of Grex maie have his will.
three subsedies to five would turne
and Grex would laugh *tha*t nowe doth mourne
O Rex thy Grex doth much complaine
that Dux beare Crux, and Crux not Dux againe.

However, in one surviving manuscript it appears with this response:

An answere to ye late leud libell of Lex and Grex Dux and Crux
Greate is the blemish laide upon the Dux
And wretched wishers crave no lesse then Crux,
But if a mischeife fall on Rex and Grex
Let Grex thanke onelie breathe of humane Lex
Leave Grex) thy prate and turne it into praye
Least all thinges goe the cleane contrary waie
The greatest Dux that ever dyed on Crux
for ever save our Rex our Grex, our Dux. ffinis.[90]

The original poem finds a correspondence between king and people based upon the similarity of their Latin names ('Rex' and 'Grex'), and this is then extended in the version from BL Add. MS 44963 (used in *Early Stuart Libels*) when the final rhyming word 'Lex' is added. King, people and law are all one side, and the Duke ('Dux') is then brought together with the rhyme word 'Crux': punishment 'naturally' goes with him. The sixth line, however, suggests that the relationship between 'Dux' and 'Crux' has been inverted: he ought to be the punished, not the punisher.

The response poem begins by laying out plainly what the original has implied: that 'wretched wishers' desire the crucifixion of the Duke. It then exploits the Biblical language that lies behind 'Crux', reminding readers that the pre-eminent leader who suffered the 'Crux' was Christ ('The greatest Dux that ever dyed on Crux') and that all are dependent on him for release from 'Lex'. The conceit of the original thus once again provides the starting point for the response, as the latter identifies the unintended irony of aligning 'Dux' with 'Crux'. Line 5 engages in typical epigrammatic wordplay: 'prate' is to be replaced by the like-sounding 'praye', a manoeuvre that furthermore reminds readers of a more significant religious reality. And line 6 turns back on itself the satiric language applied to the Duke of Buckingham, not in 'Rex and Grex' but in the widely circulating ballad, 'Come heare, Lady Muses',[91] in which the conventional refrain line, 'The cleane contrary way' was applied to the Duke's aspirations and roles.[92]

The attribution of epigrams to illustrious figures as discussed in Chapter 7 could also take a role in responsive epigrams. The famous highwayman John Clavell had verses attributed to him, which were then supposed to prompt a clever royal response. The lines of Clavell are preserved in a number of manuscripts:

I that so oft have robt am now bid stand,
Death and the lawes assault me & demand
My life & goods, I never usd men soe,
But having taken their money let them go:
What must I dy and is there no releife.
The king of kings had mercy on a theife,
[So may our gracious King too, if he please.]
Without his counsel send mee a release
God is his president, and men shall see
His mercy passing his severity.[93]

The original poem adopts a similar rhetorical strategy to 'Greate is the blemish', as it invokes Christ's mercy on the cross as a model for his own forgiveness. If Clavell is like the thief on the cross, then he invites King Charles to play a Christ-like role of forgiveness. The epigram of royal response picks up on the sixth line, and reuses the 'relief/thief' rhyme:

The king of kings did once a theife forgive
His sinne, but did not suffer him to live,
Whom law condemnd for taking many a purse,
Least living, mercy might have made him worse
Which mercy doth, when as it lends releife,
To him *that* hath been a notorious theife,
Be pleasd most gratious soveragne now therfore
To let him hang for this heel rob no more.[94]

The poem is successful (and popular in its time) because it neatly turns the argument of 'Clavell' back upon himself. The same invocation of the situation of the thief on the cross is used to deny his appeal for clemency. The biblical thief had his sins forgiven, but not his sentence reprieved, and the response recovers the distinction between earthly kings, who wield the power of corporal punishment, and the heavenly King's role of forgiveness. These poems would seem to date from early 1626, when Clavell was captured and sentenced to death. He was spared, not through any particular poetic appeal but by the General Amnesty that accompanied the King's coronation in February 1626.[95] The popularity of the exchange seems to reflect a public appreciation of witty firmness on the part of the monarch.

Case study: Sir John Harington and responsive epigrams

The responsive nature of epigram culture is particularly manifest with John Harington, as his widely circulating poems attracted response and he himself responded to others. His bawdy 'Of a lady musing'[96] elicited a number of answers, including a published one by John Davies of Hereford.[97] His 'A Certaine Woman' is paired in Rosenbach MS 187 with its come-uppance. Harington's poem reads,

> It was not certaine when a certain Preacher
> That having never learned would be a teacher
> And having thus in Latine read his Text
> Of Erat quidam homo: much perplext
> He seemd the same with diligence to scanne
> In English thus, There was a certaine Man,
> And now sayd he, good people marke you this
> He saith there was, he doth not say there is,
> ffor in this age of ours it is most certaine
> Of Promise, word, deed, oath, theres noe man certaine,
> Yet by my text its cleerely brought to passe
> That surely once a certain man there was.
> But this I thinke, in all the Bible, noe man
> Can find this text, There was a certaine woman.[98]

It elicited this response in defence of women:

> That noe man yet could in the Bible find,
> A certaine woman, argues men all blind,
> Blind as the preacher, who had little learninge
> The certaine cause of his soe ill discerning:
> A Certaine woman of the Multitude
> Said, Blest be'th paps *that* gave our Saviour food,
> A certaine woman too, A milstone threw
> And from the wall Abimeleck shee slew,
> Nay more (by men though it be overswaid
> The Text records there was a certaine mayd.
> Which prooves directly certaine woman then,
> And certaine too, more certaine far then men,
> Your preacher then, may well stand much perplext
> To see how grossly he belide the Text,

And blusht that's sermon was noe better suted
Then by a woman thus to be confuted
Yet for his comfort one true note he made
When there is now noe certaine man he sayd,[99]

Redding describes this second epigram as 'an embroidering of the original epigram by another 'wit' of the early seventeenth century',[100] but this rather misses that the epigram is a corrective *response*; instead of continuing the conceit of the original epigram, the poem challenges it. Also, it is a female wit who has offered this riposte, by finding the phrase 'a certain woman' recurring in scripture.

Harington also shows a deep interest in the circulation of distichs by others. While he seems to dismiss the work of 'coal-prophets, upon whyted walls',[101] his works repeatedly reproduce such verses and engage with them. Thus, he records this example of one of these 'coal-prophets':

> the best I remember was this, written by an English gentleman, since the 43d yeare of Queene Elizabeth, on the church wall [of Bath Abbey] with a charcoale.

> O Church! I waile thy wofull plight,
> Whom king nor card'nall, clerke nor knight
> Have yet restord to auncient right.
> Subscribed *Ignoto*.

> Whereto a captaine of an other contrie wrate this for the comfort of this church; and I wish him to prove a true prophet, though perhaps he dyed rather a martir.

> Be blythe, fair kerk, when Hempe is past,
> Thine Olyve, that ill wynds did blast,
> Shall flourish green, for ay to last.
> Subscribed *Cassadore*.[102]

Some history of Bath Abbey is necessary here: its rebuilding had begun just before 1500, and was nearly completed at the time of the Dissolution of the Monasteries, when it was abandoned. Harington vigorously promoted the renewal of work on the Abbey in the latter decades of his life.[103] The first epigram finds a situational irony in the names of the bishops involved in the restoration: 'King' refers to Oliver King (Bishop of Bath and Wells, 1495–1503); he was followed by two cardinals (Adriano Castalessi (1503–18) and Wolsey (1518–23)), John Clerk (1523–41) and

William Knight (1541–47).[104] Thus, a 'king', a 'clerke' and a 'knight' were all involved in this rebuilding project. The response epigram depends upon a complex set of associations and plays upon words. 'Hempe' was a widely used acronym in prophetic writings of the time for the Tudor monarchs after Henry VII; in *A Tract on the Succession to the Crown (A.D. 1602)*, Harington cites another prophecy regarding 'Hempe': 'After Hempe is sowen & growen, / Kings of England shalbe none'. Harington explains that the letters represent Henry VIII, Edward, Mary, Philip and Elizabeth.[105]

The second line refers to a famous depiction of an olive tree on the north wall of Bath Abbey, which with the Abbey itself will be restored. However, it is also allegorically applying Jotham's parable of the trees in Judges 9:7–21 to the contemporary political situation. By implication, Henry VIII and his offspring (HEMPE) are like the bramble in that story, which is illegitimately made king over the trees; the olive would then represent the rightful king who will restore the nation.[106] The 'olive' reference may also glance at Bishop Oliver King, who famously initiated the rebuilding of the Abbey in 1499 after a dream vision in which a voice said 'Let an Olive establish the Crowne, and let a King restore the Church'.[107] The original sense of that dream would have understood the olive as Henry VII, a king of peace after the Wars of the Roses, but, in the late Elizabethan context, it may also anticipate another monarch famous for peace-mongering: King James.[108] The responsiveness here is of a different sort from most described above – as the counter-epigram does not negate the original, but rather offers hope in response to its despair. Part of the success here lies in the response's use of the voice and form of the original.

John Britton recognizes the possibility that Harington was not merely the *recorder* of these verses, as he speculates that Harington wrote the first epigram himself,[109] but I would go further and suggest that he may in fact be the author of both. The restoration of the Abbey and the coming of King James were both objects of deep interest to Harington around 1600. His sentence introducing the second quotation at the very least affirms this desire, while lamenting the possible fate of those who express such things. Harington may be hinting that in the last years of Elizabeth he had been daringly outspoken by anticipating the coming reign of James, as he did by sending a gift manuscript to James with the request, 'Remember me when thou comest into thy kingdom'. Of course, Harington wrote *A Supplie or Addicion* a few years after James's reign had safely arrived, and offered the volume in manuscript to Prince Henry.[110] These poems, then, may be in fact a feigned scenario of epigram and counter-epigram, with Harington using the conventions of such exchanges to indirectly comment upon the political situation and the state of the church.

Notes

 1 See, for example, Heath, Ep. 1:62, 'Ad D. Georgium Ryves', which begins, 'Your name it jumps with your profession right / A husband-man sent from the God of might'.
 2 Pontanus, *Poeticum institutionem*, pp. 475–6.
 3 See D. R. Shackleton Bailey (ed.), *Epigrams* (Loeb), vol. 3, pp. 323–6, on Martial's use of names.
 4 Campion, 'To Matho', Ep. 2:150 [Sutton's trans.].
 5 Richard Middleton, *Epigrams and Satyres* (1608), sig. A3r.
 6 *OED* 4.a.
 7 *Volpone or the Fox*, ed. Alvin B. Kernan (New Haven, CT: Yale University Press, 1962), p. 30.
 8 For a recent reassessment of the significance of personation in the Wars of the Theatres, see Charles Cathcart, *Marston, Rivalry, Rapprochement, and Jonson* (Aldershot: Ashgate, 2008), pp. 1–14.
 9 Humez, 'The Manners of Epigram', p. 168.
10 Shackleton Bailey (ed.), *Epigrams* (Loeb), vol. 3, p. 325.
11 Honigmann, *John Weever*, pp. 120–6.
12 Parrot does this in 'Secreta Necessitas', *Cures for the Itch*, sig. D3v.
13 Martial, Ep. 10:33.
14 Davies, *Poems*, ed. Krueger, p. 129.
15 Sig. G3v. The words 'particular' and 'particularize' frequently come up in this context in the writings of the time.
16 'Againe [Of the Booke]', *Scourge of Folly*, sig. A7r.
17 John Weever, *The Whipping of the Satyre* (1601), sig. A3v.
18 Sig. A2v.
19 *The Cambridge Edition of the Works of Ben Jonson*, vol. 5, p. 221. On the question of names in Jonson, see Partridge, 'Jonson's *Epigrammes*: The Named and the Nameless', 190–8; he gives the most attention to the significance, even 'magic', of the use of names in the panegyric epigrams.
20 Jonson, Ep. 38. See also his Ep. 115, 'On the Town's Honest Man', and his dedication to the Earl of Pembroke, where he notes that 'everyone thinks another's ill deeds objected to him'.
21 Wykes, 'Ben Jonson's "Chast Book"', p. 80, argues that 'the threat is an idle one, for Jonson aims at the whole class of fools represented by Guiltie, not at one alone', but his discussion focuses on those of Jonson's epigrams that

use 'character-type names' rather than the typical fictional names. He also neglects the broader phenomenon of personation both in epigram culture and in the Wars of the Theatres.

22 Partridge, 'Jonson's *Epigrammes*: The Named and the Nameless', p. 192.

23 J[ohn] C[ooke], *52 Epigrams*, sig. A3v.

24 'Ad Eundem ['*Bishop* Guilty. of Keeping Promise']', *The Poems of Thomas Pestell*, ed. Hannah Buchan (Oxford: Blackwell, 1940), p. 51.

25 Guilpin, 'Of the same [Naevia]', *Skialetheia*, Ep. 42.

26 Owen, 'In eundem [quendam Momum, priorum Epigrammatum Censorem iniquissimum]' [On the same, one Momus, the most hostile censor of his earlier epigrams], *Epigrammatum*, Ep. 4:51.

27 Harvey, *John Owen's Latine epigrams* (1677), p. 79. It seems not to have been included in either Vicars or Hayman's selection of translations from Owen.

28 Martial (Loeb ed. 1993).

29 Harington, 'The last Epigram', transcribed from Folger MS V.a.249, by Kilroy, *Edmund Campion*, p. 236.

30 BL Harl. MS 1221, fol. 72v. Bodl. Rawl. poet. MS 160 also has some headless epitaphs, in which the lemma has been left incomplete.

31 Huntington MS 4, Ep. 357.

32 Huntington MS 4, Ep. 125.

33 Jonson, Ep. 124.

34 Jonson, Ep. 77.

35 Kamholtz, 'Ben Jonson's *Epigrammes* and Poetic Occasions', p. 92.

36 See N. M. Kay (ed.), *Epigrams* (London: Duckworth, 2001), p. 121.

37 *CSPD, 1634–5*, p. 221.

38 'To the Puritan Dispensers', Westminster Abbey MS 41, fol. 25v.

39 In the classical studies tradition, the lemma is frequently called the 'superscription' On the relation between superscription and poem, see B. J. Schröder, *Titel und Text: zur Entwicklung lateinischer Gedichtüberschriften* (Berlin: Walter de Gruyter, 1999). Peter Hess, *Epigramm* (Stuttgart: Metzler, 1989), has argued for the significance of titles (lemmas) for the epigram tradition, a view that is challenged by Enenkel, 'Introduction: The Neo-Latin Epigram', pp. 13–14, who suggests that in the Neo-Latin tradition, at least, it usually merely repeats what is evident from the poem itself. While I would agree that epigrams of praise (whether of the living or of the dead) often make clear the identity of the subject apart from the title, I hope that this chapter demonstrates that, with satiric epigrams, the lemma was of central significance.

40 Hudson, *The Epigram in the English Renaissance*, p. 11.

41 Wykes, 'Ben Jonson's "Chast Book"', p. 77.

42 Bastard, *Chrestoleros*, Ep. 5:11, notes that Severus has complained that 'he findes lesse ads then ins', among Bastard's poems, by which he means that there are too few of praise.

43 Scaliger, *Poetices*, p. 170.

44 Hester, 'The Titles/Headings of Donne's Epigrams', *ANQ*, 3 (1990), pp. 3–11.

45 Parrot, *Laquei ridiculosi*, Ep. 1:162.

46 *The Dr. Farmer Chetham MS*, vol. 1, p. 100; Sanderson, *An Edition of an Early Seventeenth-Century Manuscript Collection*, p. 48.

47 In reference to eighteenth-century jest-books, James Osborn has identified what he terms 'Joe Miller's Law' where 'a good name (of a well-known personality, living or dead) tends to replace a less known one'. The reference is to the long-popular volume, *Joe Miller's Jests* (1739) (Joseph Spence, *Observations, Anecdotes, and Characters of Books and Men*, ed. James M. Osborn, 2 vols (Oxford: Clarendon Press, 1966), vol. 1, p. xxxii). The dynamic is similar to that found with 'illustrious authorship' as discussed in Chapter 7.

48 Rous, *Diary*, p. 31. Rous adds, 'Thus foully will the vulgar disgrace him whose greatnes they hate', and in the margin, he notes, 'Older than the duke's death'. In spite of his describing it as 'an ould rime', I have not been able to trace it.

49 Sir John Harington, *A Supplie or Addicion to Bishop Godwin's Catalogue of Bishops* in *Nugae Antiquae*, vol. 2, p. 116. The bishop left a dowry of £2000 to Sandys. The original epigram can be found at http://mek.oszk.hu/04200/04297/04297.htm. Harington does not identify the author of the original poem.

50 Marotti, *Manuscript, Print, and the Renaissance Lyric*, p. 103.

51 Bodl. Rawl. poet. MS 147, p. 97; Bodl. Tanner MS 465, fol. 61v.

52 Bellany, 'Railing Rhymes Revisited', p. 1159.

53 Curtis Perry, *Literature and Favoritism in Early Modern England* (Cambridge: Cambridge University Press, 2006), p. 11. (He quotes the lines on Laud from Keith Lindley, *Popular Politics and Religion in Civil War London* (Aldershot: Scolar, 1997), p. 34.)

54 On the general fashion for personation in the theatre of the time, see Matthew Steggle, *The Wars of the Theatres: The Poetics of Personation in the Age of Jonson* (Victoria, BC: English Literary Studies, 1998), pp. 11–20. 'Code names' went well beyond these literary contexts: both official government correspondence and newsletter writers such as Chamberlain engaged in this sort of naming because of fears that letters might be intercepted.

55 Steggle, *Wars of the Theatres*, pp. 51–2.

56 See David Friedrich Strauss, *Ulrich von Hutten: His Life and Times*, trans. G. Sturge (London, 1874), pp. 15–18.

57 'Etia*m*' has been added above the line.

58 Bodl. Selden Supra MS 81, fol. 21r. The letter is dated 8 Kal. Mai 1601, which would be 24 Apr.; however, it was clearly written later than the letter which Wheare sent on 'Non Mai 1601' (7 May) (fol. 19r) with the first two parts of *Affaniae*. I suspect that it should read 8 Kal. Jun (25 May), and that the error is simply a mental slip on Wheare's part.

59 [Trans. Sutton] The Philological Museum (www.philological.bham.ac.uk/affaniae/2eng.html).

60 A similar situation is played with in John Russell's manuscript epigram 'De Quodam anonymo':

'Me rogitat quidam, vix nomime dignus amici,
Ipsum versiculis imposuisse meis.
Iudex lector eris: nulla hic tu nomina cernis:
Huic plane imposui versibus ergo meis'

['Of a certain anonymous one':
A certain one begs me, scarcely dignified with the name of a friend, to have himself placed among my little verses. Reader you will be judge: here you do not discern any names: here openly therefore I have placed him in my verses] (BL Add. MS 73542, 3:78).

61 Honigmann, *John Weever*, p. 40. Another, slighter, possibility would be the similarly named Robert *Joyner* (author of *Itys*, which appeared in 1598), but he did not have the high profile of Weever in the Wars of the Theatres. Thomas Campion also mocks one 'Faber' who pathetically seeks the favour of a great lord: see his *Poemata* in *Works*, ed. Percival Vivian (1909; Rpt Oxford: Clarendon Press, 1966), vol. 1, p. 196.

62 Roscoe Addison Small, *The Stage-Quarrel between Ben Jonson and the So-Called Poetasters* (1899; Rpt New York: AMS Press, 1966), pp. 101–7.

63 Small, *The Stage-Quarrel*, p. 126, identifies him with Simplicius Faber, but does not make the connection of either with Weever.

64 Steggle, *Wars of the Theatres*, p. 23.

65 Nashe had died by the time *Affaniae* was published, as he is commemorated in a later epigram in the collection, *Cenotaphia*, Ep. 29.

66 Davies, *Poems*, ed. Krueger, pp. 156–7.

67 See Kamholtz, 'Ben Jonson's *Epigrammes* and Poetic Occasions', p. 79, on how Jonson's epigrams begin with time-based occasions but then move beyond them.

68 The term 'counter-epigram' for this sort of responsive, secondary epigram

is my own; while I have not found this exact term used in the period, the similar term 'counter-ballad' is used in Bodl. Rawl. poet. MS 26, fol. 95v, to describe an instance in that genre.

69 S. K. Heninger, Jr, *The Subtext of Form in the English Renaissance: Proportion Poetical* (Philadelphia, PA: Pennsylvania State University Press, 1994), p. 119.

70 Heninger, *The Subtext of Form*, p. 120.

71 E. F. Hart, 'The Answer-Poem of the Early Seventeenth Century', *RES*, 7 (1956), pp. 19–29.

72 Hart, 'The Answer-Poem', p. 21.

73 Hart, 'The Answer-Poem', p. 22.

74 The fullest English discussion of the exchange is given in Henry T. Rowell, 'The "Campanian" Origin of C. Naevius and Its Literary Attestation', *Memoirs of the American Academy in Rome*, 19 (1949), pp. 17–34. The main source of the story is in Pseudo-Asconius.

75 Tenney Frank, 'Naevius and Free Speech', *American Journal of Philology*, 48 (1927), pp. 105–10, p. 108.

76 Bodl. Malone MS 19, p. 53. The subject of the verse cannot be identified certainly; there was a portrait painter of the name Henry Anderton, 1630–67, but this poem seems likely to date from the 1620s or earlier. A variant of the exchange is found in BL Sloane MS 1489, fol. 12.

77 Bodl. Malone MS 19, p. 55.

78 See Fleming, *Graffiti and the Writing Arts*, pp. 56–7, for further examples of epigram-like answer poems written on walls and windows.

79 Bodl. Malone MS 19, p. 53. The same exchange (with variations) is found in Redding, 'Robert Bishop's Commonplace Book', p. 195, and Folger MS V.a.162, fol. 64r, among other places. Rudick (ed.), *The Poems of Sir Walter Ralegh*, p. xlii, traces the history of these lines. That version preserved in Manningham's diary, 'Shewes the gent. name with the bold face', is rhythmically inferior and unlikely to be authentic. As it is recorded in a diary entry five years after Noel's death, it would seem to show that the lines continued in oral circulation until at least that time.

80 Rudick (ed.), *The Poems of Sir Walter Ralegh*, p. xlii.

81 The lesser known Henry Noel (d. 1597) was a rival courtier who enjoyed some reputation as a wit and gallant.

82 Fuller, *The History of the Worthies of England*, ed. P. Austin Nuttall, 3 vols (1840; Rpt New York: AMS, 1965), vol. 1, p. 506.

83 This was a polyglot Bible, first published, 1568–72.

84 Peacham, *Thalia's Banquet*, sig. D2r–v.

85 Fuller, *The History of the Worthies of England* (1662), sig. 2M1.

86 Fitzgeffrey, *Satyres*, Ep. 51.

87 The same pair is included in a gathering of Fitzgeffrey's poems in Folger MS V.a.97, p. 63.

88 Owen, Ep. 3:110, in Hayman, *Quodlibets*.

89 At another point where Hayman questions Owen's religious position, he simply adds a note that the sense of the poem is 'Contrary to the Prayer of the Apostles, Luk. 17.5' ('An argument against sleeping', Ep. 3:140).

90 Chetham MS A.3.47, fol. 32r.

91 *Early Stuart Libels*, Oi16.

92 Alastair Bellany, 'Singing Libel in Early Stuart England: The Case of the Staines Fiddlers, 1627', *HLQ*, 69 (2006), pp. 177–94.

93 Folger MS V.a.345, p. 16. The line in square brackets is supplied from a letter of Mead to Stuteville (BL Harley MS 390, fol. 11v, as quoted by J. H. P. Pafford, *John Clavell, 1601–1643: Highwayman, Author, Lawyer, Doctor* (Oxford: Leopard's Head, 1993), p. 28).

94 Folger MS V.a.345, p. 25.

95 *DNB*.

96 Beg. 'A vertuous Lady sitting in a Muse', Harington, Ep.4:57.

97 Marotti, *Manuscript, Print, and the English Renaissance Lyric*, pp. 141–2.

98 Redding, 'Robert Bishop's Commonplace Book', p. 16.

99 Redding, 'Robert Bishop's Commonplace Book', p. 16. There seems to be no closing parenthesis, and, despite the passage concluding with a comma, this does seem to be the end. The reply is also found in BL Add. MS 10309, fol. 108v; Folger MS V.a.345, p. 245; BL Add. MS 15227, fol. 16r, BL Sloane MS 1792, fol. 4v. The biblical references are to Luke 11:27 and Judges 9:53.

100 Redding, 'Robert Bishop's Commonplace Book', p. 17.

101 Harington, *A Supplie*, in *Nugae Antiquae*, vol. 2, p. 140.

102 Harington, *A Supplie*, in *Nugae Antiquae*, vol. 2, p. 140. Another prophetic epigram involving 'HEMPE' is preserved in Merlin Ambrosius, *The Whole Prophecies of Scotland, England, France, Ireland and Denmarke* (1617): 'When HEMPE is come, and also gone, / SCOTLAND and ENGLAND shalbe all one. / Praised be God alone, for HEMPE is come & gone, / And left us olde ALBION, by peace joyned in one' (sig. A2r); and another in Thomas Heywood, *The Life of Merlin* (1641): 'When Hemp is ripe and ready to pull, / Then Englishman beware thy scull' (p. 361), which is also ascribed to Merlin.

103 John Britton, *The History and Antiquities of Bath Abbey Church* (London, 1825), p. 41.

104 Fuller, *History of the Worthies* (1662), p. 19.

105 Harington in Scott-Warren, *Sir John Harington and the Book as Gift*, pp.

174–5. Fuller, *History of the Worthies* (1662), pp. 83–4, offers this variant: 'When HEMPE is spun / England is Done.' Tilley lists it as H414, and cites Bacon who writes that he heard it 'when I was a child', and that it suggested 'that after the princes had reigned which had the principial letters, of that word hempe … England should come to utter confusion' (*Works*, ed. James Spedding, vol. 12, p. 204).

106 On the various attempts at rebuilding Bath Abbey, see Britton, *The History and Antiquities*, pp. 32–47.

107 Harington, *A Supplie* in *Nugae Antiquae*, vol. 2, p. 137. An inscription alluding to King was also formerly on the west front of the Abbey: 'The trees going to chuse their king / Sayd bee to us that Oliver King' ('Oliver King', *DNB*).

108 Some later seventeenth-century writers took the 'olive' of the prophecy to be fulfilled in Oliver Cromwell (G.S., *Anglorum speculum* (1694), p. 741).

109 Britton, *The History and Antiquities*, p. 38. On Harington's interest in prophetic verses, especially those regarding King James, see Scott-Warren, *Sir John Harington and the Book as Gift*, pp. 154–76.

110 Scott-Warren, *Sir John Harington and the Book as Gift*, pp. 219–30. It was published only in 1653.

10

The epigram and political comment

Through the period 1590 to 1640 epigrams of explicit political satire were widespread in manuscript and oral circulation, but limited in printed epigram books,[1] where they were by necessity either more general or oblique. A consideration of epigrammatic libels on great figures could be a book of its own; thus, this chapter explores the political dimensions and possibilities of the epigram in the period through a number of limited focuses. The first is the flurry of manuscript political epigrams that appeared in the late 1590s, particularly those concerning the career (and eventual downfall) of the Earl of Essex. Following this, a consideration of Bastard's *Chrestoleros* (1598) from roughly the same time shows the stricter limits of political comment in printed books. I then turn to the epigrams written in response to the political role of a single prominent legal and political figure, Edward Coke, across the span of his long career. The epigrams on Essex and Coke are most often highly partisan: the last section of the chapter turns to a number of epigrams (both print and manuscript) that attempt a more nuanced approach to politics, one that was in fact more consistent with the traditional urbane and even cynical attitude of the epigram as a genre.

Late Elizabethan and early Stuart epigrammatists were well aware that their engagement in political and religious controversy was an extension of a tradition reaching back into the late Middle Ages. Often recalled was William Collingbourne's epigram on the favourites of Richard III:

The Cat, the Rat, and Lovel our Dog,
Do rule al England under a Hog,[2]

In *The Mirror for Magistrates* this epigram is presented as an example of the danger in an overly explicit poetic attack, and the need to season such assaults with humour: poets must

> mixe their sharpe rebukes with mirth,
> That they may pearce, not causing any paine,
> Save such as foloweth everye kindely birth,
> Required straight, with gladnesse of the gayne.
> A Poet must be pleasaune,[3] not to plaine,
> Faultes to control, ne yet to flatter vice
> But sound and sweete, in al thinges ware and wise.[4]

Harington invokes the same verse as he hesitates about translating one of More's epigrams ('Te Crepitus perdit ...'):

> for I will tell you true, my Muse was afraid to translate this Epigram: and she brought me out three or foure sayings against it, both in Latine and English: and two or three shrewd examples, both of this last poet, who died not of the collicke, and of one Collingbourne, that was hanged for a distichon of a Cat, a rat, and a dogge.[5]

In *The Mirror,* Collingbourne complains that his words have been misconstrued, which points to a continuing, integral aspect of the epigram as a form: its brevity encouraged a cryptic style (what Owen called 'steganography'), which both encouraged readers to supply the context and significance of the brief utterance and allowed the poet the opportunity to deny a topical reading. Collingbourne found, however, that the King's was the final authoritative reading.[6] The epigrammatist Samuel Rowlands recognizes the same precedent: 'And as King Richards *Collinbourne* for ryming, / Did end his dayes, (so they may do) by clyming.'[7]

Harington recalls a well-known story about the epigrammatist Heywood and King Henry VIII to illustrate the political danger of epigram writing, but in his case the same wit that led to the poet's troubles also saved him in the end:

> [Heywood] scaped hanging with his mirth, the King being graciously and (as I thinke) truely perswaded, that a man that wrate so pleasant and harmlesse verses, could not have any harmfull conceit against his procedings, & so by the honest motion of a Gentleman of his chamber, saved him from the jerke of the six stringd whip.[8]

The story of Heywood reinforces the idea found in *The Mirror for Magistrates* that the satiric epigram could be rendered safe through its subtle wit, that it must be 'pleasant and not too plain'.

Many epigrammatists of the period eschewed political matter in favour of what might be called the social or domestic: they were concerned with the foibles and sins of ordinary men rather than the great. They mock debt-ridden young men, proud fools, avaricious churchmen, rakes, mistresses, prostitutes and cuckolds. Parrot notes in the introduction to his first collection of epigrams, *The Mous-trap*, that he is only concerned to catch the 'silly Mouse', leaving larger vermin 'to the cunning Rat-catcher, (my little trap being much too weake and unable to hold them)'.[9] While Parrot does not explicitly mention politics here, by 'larger vermin' he would seem to mean either those guilty of greater wrongs, which would include abuse of political power, or the great who wield political power. Those who might wish to use the printed form for political comment usually found themselves stymied, most of all by the prevailing publishing climate, but also by the expectations associated with the genre. The challenge of maintaining a political focus is considered by Freeman:

> But when I would this indigested heape
> Reduce (more seemely) into severall;
> In steed of one; in, *All* together step.
> That when I would tell *Sylla's* tyranny,
> Or *Nero's* cruelty, and *Caesars* stabing,
> Straight interrupts me *Druso's* letchery,
> *Lucullus* drudging, or *Lucilla's* drabbing.[10]

For Freeman any intention to produce and gather political epigrams is overcome by the proliferation of individual sexual wrongs that are the epigram's more usual subject. Freeman's sorting (and editing) of his epigrams (discussed in Chapter 5) led to an elimination of overly political material: of the approximately ninety poems in the manuscript (BL Sloane MS 1889) that were not printed, the majority have some political or scandalous dimension. Thus, Freeman's statement above is somewhat disingenuous, masking a process of self-censorship. It was not only the prevalence of sexual immorality that shaped Freeman's collection, but the inability to print more politically contentious poems. Like satire more generally, epigrams faced the danger of sliding into libel or sedition and their legal consequences. Epigrammatists might recall that not all were as fortunate as Heywood: Niccolo Franco, a notorious Italian satirist of the mid-sixteenth century, was famously tried and executed by the Inquisition for a series of satiric epigrams against Pope Paul IV.[11]

There is not always a clear dividing line between the general epigram of social satire and that which can be called 'political'. Those directed at public figures often point as much to their more private failings as any political misdeeds; as will be shown with the epigrams on Coke below, sometimes it is only the status and role of the individuals which makes the epigram 'political'. The rhetorical techniques and tone of explicitly political epigrams are the same as those of the genre in general; Thomas Cogswell has convincingly argued that political libelling was simply taking the mocking of rivals at universities, Inns of Court and the royal court into a broader sphere.[12] The 'found irony' of puns, anagrams and situations was exploited as a brief means to a memorable, if often unprobing, political comment. As Arthur Marotti points out, however, in reference to such material, 'Even when the interest seems to have been frivolous, more a matter of gossip and humorous satiric backbiting than of serious political analysis, these manuscripts nevertheless bring to light social and political relations and conflicts, even "constitutional" struggles'.[13]

Stylistically, the manuscript political epigram was most often set apart from the broader genre by its cryptic quality. The reasons for this are at least twofold: a desire to avoid damningly direct references, and the creeping in of changes as the epigram circulated widely (as demonstrated in Chapter 4). For this reason, full explication of political epigrams is not always possible, but I have chosen here to include some of this sort, nevertheless, to give a fuller picture of the range of political epigrams at the time.

Intense periods of political and libellous epigrams

John Rous, whose diary has been quoted a number of times already in this book, preserved short 'railing rhymes' as they served as a 'precedent of the times';[14] by 'precedent' he means 'example' or 'illustration' (*OED* 5). In his *Table-talk* the great early Stuart jurist John Selden offered a more extended explanation of libels as a slight, but significant, guide to the times: 'Though some make slight of *Libels,* yet you may see by them how the Wind sits: As take a Straw and throw it up into the Air, you shall see by that which way the Wind is, which you shall not do by casting up a Stone. More solid Things do not shew the Complexion of the times so well, as Ballads and Libels.'[15] In some seasons the wind blew more than others, and certain years or spans of years can be identified as 'libel-rich', where the sheer quantity of libellous epigrams offers some indication of the public temperature. On the basis of the surviving materials in the State Papers, Adam Fox identifies the late 1530s as one such period (which he connects to the controversy surrounding Thomas Cromwell), then the late 1590s, and the early 1640s.[16] Others have recognized other brief libel-intense periods: McRae sees the libel as a new form that 'flourished in the reign of James, providing perhaps the single most important textual site for interaction between political and literary cultures',[17] and Cogswell explores the 1620s and 1630s as a period rich in poetic libels that fostered an underground political forum.[18] Political epigrams of an earlier time were often remembered, echoed and reworked during these 'moments' of heightened activity. These most often coincided with periods of resentment of favourites or other powerful figures, culminating in an outpouring at the point of that figure's death (Cecil and Buckingham being the most notable examples), or at other times of political crisis (the Essex rebellion, the attempted Spanish Match). While any such conclusion is based on the uncertainties of rates of survival (i.e. epigrams from the 1620s are more likely to survive than ones from the 1590s), I would suggest that the circulation of these political epigrams were at their highest level from the beginning of the Palatinate crisis in 1619 to the death of Buckingham in 1628. In a letter of 1628, John Holles, the Earl of Clare, presented this explanation for such libels:

> Lybells are suntomes of ill government, that things be amis and none to complayne unto, and if any by interest or impatience will nevertheles fynd fault [and] such be punished, which lerning others a more warei sylence, sum vent themselfs thus in the dark, as yow style it rightly by a chargable wit, witnes Tacitus unde [*sic*] Tiberius, Nero and the other few Caesars, yet that Minister's punishment proportions not with Mannering's, though Mannering's misdeamenor in the ey of Justice cann not be exceeded.[19]

Holles's assessment recognizes libels as a reflection of a general problem: an unresponsive government that discourages frank complaint and thus drives individuals to 'vent themselves in the dark', an allusion to the anonymous dimension of libel culture.

The Earl of Essex, 1598–1601

In particular, the rise, rebellion and execution of Robert Devereux, second Earl of Essex, in the years 1598–1601 prompted a wide variety of political epigrams, largely circulating in manuscript. These reflect a range of attitudes towards the then rising man, some seeing him as a valiant figure in contrast to other courtiers, and others as an illegitimately ambitious man who meets his just end for threatening the Queen. Of the former type is 'A libell scattered abroad in tyme of the Earle of Essexes Trouble':

> Admireall weaknes wrongeth right
> honor in Generall looseth lighte.
> Secret ar ever their designes,
> through whose defect true honor pines.
> A warde in worth *that* is esteem'd
> by vertues wracke must be redeemd.
> pride spite and pollicie taketh place,
> in stead of vertue valour and grace.
> no Cob am I *that* worketh ill,
> or frame my tongue to deride will.[20]

This version, from Bodl. Eng. hist. MS c.272, includes marginal notes that identify some of the allusions:

> next to line 1: 'Howard Lo: admirall'
> next to line 2: 'Essex lieutenant generall of England'
> next to line 3: 'Secretary Cecill'
> next to line 4: 'ye Court of wardes promised to Essex given to Sir Ro: Cecill'
> next to line 9: 'Lord Cobham'

This manuscript seems to date from the 1620s, when presumably some of the poem's topicality had been lost and needed to be thus spelled out.[21] A copy of the poem in BL Add. MS 5956, fol. 23, dates it to 20 December 1599,[22] which gives us a far more specific original context than with most political epigrams. In late December 1599, Essex was imprisoned in York House, and was believed to be near death, 'prompting several churches in London to ring their bells or offer special prayers for him – infuriating both the queen and the council'.[23] This epigram, along with other widespread libels and murmurings, represents a similar, if less respectable, expression of public sympathy for the Earl. It lashes out at his perceived enemies, such as Charles Howard, Earl of Nottingham; Robert Cecil and Henry Brooke, eleventh Baron Cobham, obliquely referring to them by name. It partakes of the longstanding epigram tradition of playing on names, but here the individuals' roles provide a pun where the name does not. Its popularity, as reflected in the large number of surviving copies, would seem to reflect a commitment to (or respectful memory of) Essex rather than an admiration of wit or sophistication in the poem. The circulation of such libels at this time was officially responded to by Star Chamber.[24]

In Bodl. English hist. MS c.272 this epigram is followed by another poem with similar marginal identifications, entitled 'A libell in tyme of ye Earle of Essexes troubles':[25]

Gods Ordinance must governe all.
Let no man smile att vertues fall,
Care you *that* list for Carye not
By Crooked ways true worth to blott
Nor will I stand upon ye ground
Wher such impietie doth abounde.
but basely clothed all in Gray
       unto ye Courte Il' take my waye,
Wher thoughe I can no eagle see,
A Cubbe is good enoughe for me.
Whose mallice swelling over his minde
Will frame his will Apish by kinde.
or make a choice of present tyme,
and by Ridiculous wayes to clime:[26]
Ther may I see walke hand in hande
the polititians of the lande.
That Robbe artes glorie with a tongue
dipt in water ffrom Lymbo sprunge.
These bussards imp't with Eagles plumes
to wrong true noblenes presumes.
ffamous actons now we ffinde.
they *that* see nott this, ar very blinde.

Once again Bodl. English hist. MS c.272 has marginal annotations:

next to line 1: 'Lieutenant of ye Ordinance'[27]
next to line 3: 'Sir George Carew. Carye Lo: Hunsdon.'
next to line 4: 'Sir Ro: Cecill Crooked.'
next to line 7: 'Lo: Gray of Wilton'
next to line 12: 'Sir Ro: Cecill'
next to line 19: 'Sir Robert Cecill'

While awkward and unsophisticated, these verses exploit the potential meanings within names that I identified as typical of the genre in the preceding chapter.

A further example with the same rhetorical strategy of a list of prominent figures with their actions dates from a couple years later:

> Essex prayes, Southampton playes:
> Rutland weepes, Sandes sleepes
> Crumwell quaffes, Mounteagle laughs.
>   And amongst all this treachery
>   They brought in L. Pembroke for his lechery.[28]

While this poem mocks the Essex circle, its main point is to defend William Herbert, third Earl of Pembroke. It reflects on the situation in the early months of 1601 when Pembroke had antagonized the Queen by his affair with Mary Fitton, a young woman of the Queen's court. (The poem must have been written between 7 February, the date of Essex's rebellion, and 25 February, the date of his execution.) Fitton was pregnant by Pembroke, but he refused to marry her: the episode put an end to Pembroke's possibilities at Elizabeth's court.[29] The poem implicitly supports Pembroke by comparing his punishment for lechery to that of those guilty of the far more serious challenge to the court represented by Essex's rebellion, which took place in 1601. The Earls of Southampton and Rutland; William, Lord Sandys; William Parker, Baron Monteagle; and Edward Crumwell were among Essex's co-conspirators.[30] 'Essex prayes' could mean two things: that Essex is still praying to Elizabeth, hopeful of forgiveness (which would suggest the poem reflects on the situation in the few days after the insurrection, probably before Captain Lee's attempt to enter the court on 12 February), or that he prays to God, mindful that he is facing his imminent execution. The flavour of the comments on the other figures suggests that it is not yet clear that there will be full punishment for the rebellion. Ultimately, the epigram works in two ways: first it attempts to dismiss the charges against Pembroke as frivolous, given the far more serious treachery at hand; secondly, it shows concern that Essex and his followers might once again be forgiven their actions against the Queen.

Thomas Bastard

Of the printed epigram books of the late 1590s, Bastard's *Chrestoleros* most frequently turns in a political direction, and he largely reflects a pro-Essex position, while it was still safe to do so. His longstanding reputation for satire (or even libel, for which he had been expelled from Oxford in the early 1590s) likely only heightened the expectation of controversial material in his published epigrams. While the first four books of *Chrestoleros* largely avoid political controversy apart from some unremarkable mockery of Spain and the papacy (2:29–30), the latter three books manifest an increasing number that seem to touch upon it, and this shift seems to be signalled in the first epigram of Book 5:

Ad Do. Mountjoy
Mountjoy if I have praised worthy men,
And with safe liberty contented me,
Touching no states with my presumptious pen:
If from all secret biting I am free:
I hope I shall not loose thy patronage,
If I doe lawfull thinges and voyde of feare,
If hunt the Fox if bring the Ape on stage,
If I doe whip a curr or baite the Beare,
    For these are exercises of such sorte,
    As ly alike to earnest and to sporte.

Bastard claims to have taken the safe, non-political approach, but this odd poem also suggests that Mountjoy may have wanted more; that is, by being apolitical ('touching no states') and avoiding libel Bastard might lose the patronage of Mountjoy. The first four lines are fully ambiguous: they could mean '*although* I have avoided political topics, I hope that I will not lose your patronage' or '*since* I have avoided political topics …'. The second half of the epigram claims that some of his poems of seemingly harmless mirth about animals (which in 3:18 he had claimed he included only to increase sales to the vulgar) are in fact double-written, involving both 'earnest' and 'sporte', and these must be considered within the framework of the widespread political allegories based on animals in the period.[31]

This prefatory epigram may particularly concern a series of cryptic poems, Book 6:12–14. The first complains of how 'The wicked wound us', comparing the people of England to the captive Israelites in Egypt: it concludes

And these not *Pharoahs* out of *Aegypt* sponge,
But our owne *Israelites* which doe this wrong.
    And we from stranger countries having rest,
    In our sweete *Canaan* are thus opprest.

The poem suggests political division and even oppression within England that far outweighs any foreign threat. The next poem, which defies my interpretative abilities, ostensibly concerns fishing:

> There is no fish in brookes little or great,
> And why? for all is fish that comes to nett.
> The small eate sweete, the great more daintely.
> The great will seeth or bake, the small will frye.
> For rich mens tables serve the greater fish.
> The small are to the poore a daintie dish,
> The great are at their best, and serve for store.
> The small once tane, keepe or you catch no more.
>> We must thanke ponds, for rivers we have none.
>> The fowle swim in the brooke, the fish are flowne.

This must be more than culinary advice; perhaps it glances at the figure of Cobham, Lord *Brooke*. The next epigram, 'De Piscatione', also complains of the lack of fish: 'Fishes decrease, and fishers multiply'. As a sequence, these seem to involve some indirect political commentary, possibly on the topic of monopoly, taxation and other burdens on the people. The evasive and cryptic approach adopted by Bastard is quite understandable given his earlier expulsion from Oxford for his libels.[32]

An earlier poem, 'Ad Aulicos' (2:17), had complained about courtiers – not all, but those 'upstart courtiers' who were 'unworthy of a peerelesse princes port'.[33] He then goes on to name them: 'courtier leather, courtier pinne, and sope / And courtier vinegeer, and starch and carde, / And courtier cups'.[34] These lines reflect frustration with the increasing number of monopolies on everyday things that were being granted to courtiers, a concern that came to a head with the 1597–8 Parliament, which brought forward a petition to the Queen to overthrow them. This poem had been proceeded by another in which he reflected on the nature of his epigrams – here as well he claims there is 'no biting' and 'no cause of offence', only to concede in the next lines that there is typical epigrammatic saltiness: 'Such are my Epigrams well understood, / As salt which bites the wound, but doth it good.'[35] Presumably, the much-complained-of monopoly on salt did not extend to the epigrammatic variety.

Epigrammatic balance is reflected in a pair of poems (7:13–14) that mark the fortieth anniversary of Elizabeth's reign in November, 1597.[36] The first straightforwardly praises her accomplishments, noting how each year adds 'more sweetnes to thy sweetest reigne'. However, 7:14 also addressed directly to Elizabeth, remarks that this 'golden peace' is marred by conflict and corruption. Bastard puts aside jesting and indirection to make a direct complaint to the Queen about the state of the nation:

> *Eliza*, thou hast spread a goolden peace,
> Over thy land thrise blessed be thy raigne.
> And were it that some civill wars did cease,
> Which in our selves devided we sustaine:
> Betweene the patron and poore minister,
> Landlordes and Tenants, raigning more and more.
> Betweene the borrower and the usurer.
> Betweene so fewe rich, and so many poore:
> Ours were the golden age, but these home jarres,
> Houses, and fields and states have overthrowne.
> And spoyled us no less then foreyne wars.
> Thanke we this idle mischefe of our owne.
> But who did heare, or who did ever read,
> Peace without wars, or something else in stead.

The poem, an epigram-sonnet, simultaneously celebrates the long foreign peace enjoyed under Elizabeth as a golden age and laments the recent internal divisions. The complaints are of specific economically based social conflicts in England. However, the final couplet goes beyond lament to something potentially more threatening: Bastard takes the proverbial concept that there is never 'Peace without wars',[37] and applies it to the English situation. To bring about social peace within England, some 'war' is necessary: the final elusive half-line seems to stand in apposition to 'wars'. If civil peace does not come about through war, it must arise through 'something else in stead'. Here the very vagueness conveys a threat; it posits an unspoken and unspeakable crisis in the state that would correct the abuses of the present and bless England with a blemish-free golden age. Given the extensive support of Essex throughout *Chrestoleros*, one wonders if Bastard intends an allusion to some act on the Earl's part. In addition to the dedication and numerous other poems to Lord Mountjoy, who had served as a lieutenant under Essex in the Azores expedition, *Chrestoleros* celebrates a range of English military heroes, particularly of the West Country (where Bastard made his home) and associated with the more aggressive foreign policy represented by the Earl of Essex. Books 2 and 3 include a number that seem to allude specifically to the Cadiz expedition of 1596.

Sir Edward Coke

The political epigrams touching on the Earl of Essex were largely a phenomenon of the late 1590s and very early 1600s. In this section I trace
those epigrams written on Sir Edward Coke, a figure whose zenith was
never as high as that of Essex, but who for over three decades was centrally
and often controversially involved in English politics in a variety of legal,
judicial and political roles. Coke enjoyed a long and tumultuous public
career, which included stints as Solicitor General, Attorney General,
Chief Justice (of the Court of Common Pleas, and then of King's Bench),
and an outspoken member, and then Speaker, of the House of Commons,
consistently supporting the traditions of the English common law and
Parliament. He was among those public figures whose very name seemed
to call out for epigrammatic use, as they brought with them found ironies
irresistible to poets.[38] His name was usually pronounced, and sometimes
spelt, 'cook'; hence, frequently applied to him was the fictional Latinate
name Cocus (meaning 'cook'), or sometimes 'Caecus' (meaning 'blind'),[39]
and punning could also connect his name with 'cuckold'. Given this,
and his frequent role as prosecutor in trials, especially of such prominent figures such as Essex and Ralegh, it is not surprising that he was
frequently subject to the attack of satiric epigrams. While the majority of
poems mocking Coke were epigrams, my survey also touches upon some
that extend beyond the genre in length and in adopting a more narrative
approach.

Typical of this sort of epigram is one by Harington lengthily entitled, 'To Master Cooke, the Queenes Atturney, that was incited to call
Misacmos into the Starre-chamber, but refused it; saying, he that could
give another a Venue,[40] had a sure ward for himselfe'. Misacmos was the
name adopted by Harington for his *Metamorphosis of Ajax*, which stirred
considerable scandal in 1596. The epigram itself is somewhat cryptic:

> Those that of dayntie fare make deer provision
> yf som bad Cookes marr it with dressing evill
> Are wont to say in Jest but just derision,
> the meat from good the Cookes came from the devill
> But yf this dish, though draffe[41] in apparision,
> Were made thus sawst, a service not uncivill,
>> Say ye that taste, and not digest the Booke,
>> The Dee'le go with the meat, God with the Cooke.[42]

It seems that Coke, as Attorney General, declined to prosecute Harington in Star Chamber, and Harington's title claims it was from fear of his sharp wit. The epigram plays with the common expression that with an ill meal, 'The meat from God, the Cookes came from the divell': here the 'dish' is presumably Harington's book, *A New Discourse*, and the question then turns upon how Coke (the 'Cook') will treat it. This early epigram responding to Coke's legal work is the first of many that will play upon his name in this way.

However, the greater number of epigrams written on him stem from his marriage to the young, rich and dynamic Lady Elizabeth Hatton, both at its beginning in 1598 and at later points of violent strife between husband and wife in the 1610s. This perhaps shows something of what Freeman suggested in the quotation which opened the chapter: that, however political the epigrammatist's desire and impetus, the form's traditions led it back to more domestic issues such as cuckoldry, shrewish wives and mercenary marriages. At the same time, both the marriage itself and the couple's later struggles over the marriage of their daughter were part of political dynasty building.

Coke had already established himself as a prominent lawyer and parliamentarian when on 7 November 1598 he wed Lady Elizabeth Hatton, who continued to be known by that name. As the niece of Robert Cecil she brought with her very important family connections, and her first marriage to Sir William Hatton, the heir of Sir Christopher Hatton, had left her a wealthy widow in 1597. She had inherited her husband's properties, including Ely House, which under the compulsion of Elizabeth had passed from the hands of the Bishop of Ely to Christopher Hatton. This combination of family connections and wealth rendered her a much-sought-after young widow, and even six weeks before the Coke–Hatton marriage there were rumours of another possible match: 'There is speech of a match between my Lord of Pembroke's [son], Ld. [William] Herbert and Lady Hatton.'[43] However, Coke, a widower only since June of 1598, had a long association with the Cecils, and by the late 1590s had a very substantial income as well; thus, from a political and legal perspective he had much to offer.

Nevertheless, many public comments suggest a sentiment that he was unfit for her. As a May–December relationship (she was twenty; he in his late forties), it attracted the usual smirking remarks. That the marriage was first conducted in violation of the marriage laws (without banns, in a private house and at night rather than in the morning) also attracted attention, including that of Archbishop Whitgift, before whom Coke had to appear. More sinister, however, were the rampant rumours that at the time of the marriage she was already pregnant by a servant,[44] which were seemingly belied by the birth of a daughter, Elizabeth, in late July 1599, more than nine months after the marriage.[45]

The most significant group of satiric epigrams on the early years of the Coke–Hatton marriage is a series of eleven ascribed to Sir John Davies by his twentieth-century editor Robert Krueger.[46] This series of 'sonnet epigrams', which must have been written between the announcement of the marriage and the birth, dwells largely on the pregnancy rumours: 'Beleeve me Cooke, thou art not much beguild, / Thy Lady trulye sweares its a Cookes childe.'[47] The octave of 'Cocus the pleader' (the first in the series) describes Coke's rage and humiliation at the scandal of his new wife's supposed pregnancy. The final six lines offer a cynical mock reassurance to him: he might be cuckolded, but through the marriage he has achieved his real goal – property. The poem concludes with a biting couplet: 'Toil not so much, resigne her half thy cares; / Buy thou the land, let her provide the heires.' Similarly, the second epigram offers an ironic consolation: Coke's wife may, like Asturian mares, have been impregnated by the wind, or like 'Olympias' mated with Zeus; these comparisons render Coke a figure like Philip the Great, who can expect a 'heavenlye heire'. Once again, the sting in the tail traduces Coke's hoarding of land: his son may be like Alexander the Great in conquering all lands, 'Unlesse before his tyme thou purchase all'. Subsequent epigrams draw on dense legal analogies, the card-game Primero and Coke as a horned Actaeon figure. In his edition, Krueger treats all eleven as a series, even though they appear as such only in one manuscript, and in the others only the first six are found. The sixth also seems to mark an ending and turning away from mocking Coke to the man who had cuckolded him:

> Holla my muse, leave Caecus in his greife,
> And turne the force of thy two edged penne
> To punishe Meochus as a arrand theife,
> Filcher of ladyes, murtherer of men.[48]

These first six share a sophistication and polish of both conceit and sound unmatched by the other five, the first two of which are variations on the 'Coke–cooke' conceit. Here Coke is mocked simply for being a cuckold, and not for the greed that led him to accept the situation.

Coke and Hatton, 1616

In 1616–17, Coke again found himself at the centre of public controversy, one involving both his legal role and his private family life. In November 1616 he was dismissed from his position as Chief Justice of King's Bench owing to a struggle over the jurisdiction of the courts and King James's prerogative, commonly called the 'Case of Commendams'. A plaintiff had charged that the king had no right to grant a *commendam* (an extra stipend from a vacant church living granted to a bishop), and the King had responded by ordering the court, through Bacon, to halt the case. The judges, led by Coke, refused, saying it was their duty to the law to continue. When the judges were called before the Privy Council over the matter, Coke would not completely back down. Brought as well before the court of Star Chamber, Coke was finally removed from his seat in King's Bench. At that point, John Chamberlain passed along 'a prettie epigram upon the Lord Cooke', and added that 'no doubt more will follow; for when men are downe, the very drunkards makes rimes and songes upon them'.[49]

Coke's political problems at this time overlapped with increasing estrangement from Lady Hatton. Chamberlain notes in the same letter that even her friends and family were 'grieved at' her failure to support him in his troubles. She had 'disfurnished his house in Holburn and at Stoke of whatsoever was in them, and caried all the moveables and plate she could come by God knowes whether, and retiring herself into obscure places both in towne and countrie'.[50] By early 1617 the two were openly fighting over property and appearing before the Privy Council. This conflict was further complicated by the question of a marriage between their daughter, Frances, and John Villiers, Buckingham's brother, which had already been mooted during the November struggle over Coke's place on the King's Bench. The match was opposed by Lady Hatton, who made off with Frances, holed up at Oatlands (being leased by her relations Edmund and Frances Withipole), and attempted a match with Henry Vere, eighteenth Earl of Oxford. She had her daughter write an *Obligation*, condemning herself to burn in Hell if she did not wed the Earl. The struggle within the family also split the court and Privy Council: Lady Hatton had notable supporters of high rank, including Francis Bacon and Lord Chancellor Ellesmere, but Coke could count on the support of his friend Sir Ralph Winwood, Secretary of State, and, ultimately, Buckingham as well. In July 1617 he went with an armed troop of servants and kin, including his son 'fighting Clem Coke', and broke down the doors of Oatlands to seize Frances. As a result, both husband and wife were called before the Privy Council. With the help of Bacon,

the momentum seemed to be in Lady Hatton's favour, until Winwood
turned the tables by revealing that the King and Buckingham desired the
Villiers match. Bacon was left scurrying and Coke returned triumphantly to
favour and a place on the Council. The wedding took place on Michaelmas,
29 September 1617, with the King's full involvement. Lady Hatton had
been imprisoned in the house of Alderman Bennett, and, although she was
invited to the wedding, she begged sickness and remained away. Later the
same year, the King was making amends to her and unsuccessfully attempting a reconciliation of husband and wife.

All this scandalous behaviour of the great (and not so good) provided
rich material for satiric epigrams; those which survive show the responsive dynamic typical of the genre. Holles, out of animosity towards Coke,
took Lady Hatton's side in the quarrel, and sent Latin lines mocking Coke
to one Bond, the secretary of Lord Chancellor Ellesmere.[51] Both his verses
and the introduction to them build upon earlier jests and libels. He introduces the lines in this way: 'Mean while I have sent yow the ravings of
an obsolet faded poet [himself?] in exchange of your distike, to intertaine
yow a little with this divell Cook, whoe sumtyms hath marred our dinner,
uppon condition that yow communicate them not to others, least they
mock me who am yours'. The 'divell Cook' echoes the proverbial saying
used years earlier by Harington:

10 November 1616

Quae tibi Coce fuit Chancerum causa ridendi.
Alteriusque loquax, carpere jura foci.
Has tibi condignas insana superbia poenas
Scriptaque non oculis conspicienda tuis
Struxere, at semper vetitum sine Voeste [*sic*][52] Dianam
Actaeon, sed tu Lucifer alter eras
Heu nimium miserando luxuriavit iniqua
Sanguine magnanimi lingua cuiusve viri
Sic vermis, pestis*que* ferox invadit amaenos
Fructus, ac homines, sed mala nulla volunt
Justitiae est nobili vitiosos scindere ferro
Ast omni probos arte nutrire viros
Idcirco pereat Cocus, pellexit amorem
Qui populi, nullo tempore faustus erit

[Coke, for what cause was Chancery laughed at by you. And gossiping about
another, to mock the laws of the hearth; Insane pride and writings not to be

beheld by your eyes have devised for you these worthy penalties, but Diana was always forbidden to Actaeon without a covering; but you were another Lucifer. Alas, indeed, your perverse tongue took pleasure in the blood of that magnanimous man that ought to be pitied. In this way the worm and the fierce pest invade the delightful fruit and men, but they did not will any evil. It is just and noble to rend the vicious with a sword, but with all art to foster righteous men. Therefore, Coke would perish, he enticed love, who will be favourable to the people at no time.]

As with many Latin epigrams of this period, the sense is difficult and the reading here a tentative one. However, a number of features are clear: while Holles's main charge is that Coke attacks the noble and righteous, and thus part of the ongoing political and legal controversy surrounding Coke in 1616, Holles still looks back to libels from the late 1590s by comparing Coke to Actaeon, thus bringing the notorious matter of his marriage into play.

The recipient of the epigram is significant as well: as secretary to the aged Lord Chancellor, Bond was at the centre of this controversy, and it is clear from the letter that he had sent a distich on the matter to Holles. The struggle was widely perceived as one over the relative jurisdictions of the common law and Chancery, and Ellesmere was generally perceived in his time as an enemy of the common law; thus, tension between him and Coke would be expected. It seems quite possible that the distich sent by Bond was this widely circulated one:

Jus condire cocus potuit! Sed condere Jura
non potuit; potuit condere Jura Cocus.

[A cook can pickle/season the law/a sauce! but he is not able to dispose of the laws/sauces; Coke is able to dispose of the laws.]

If such were the case, the allusion by Clare to 'this divell Cook' would be picking up on its jest. In Folger MS V.a.345 another version of this poem is ascribed to Sir Edward Hoby,[53] a courtier and writer:

Condit iura cocus: quid ni condire peritus
Iura cocus, sed non condere iura potest.[54]

[Coke hides the laws, why may not a skilled cook season sauces? But he is not able to dispose of the sauces/laws.]

The same basic sense and punning is at work here, dependent upon the found ironies in a cluster of Latin words. The familiar play on Coke/cook appears once more, but that 'jura' means both laws and sauces fits perfectly with the play on 'cook'; to this is added the distinct verbs 'condire' (to season) and 'condere' (to hide, dispose of) that share the third person singular form 'condit'. That the two epigrams share a common conceit but have radically different syntax suggests recalled oral circulation, as in the examples from Chapter 4.[55] In the Folger manuscript the distich is followed by an English response by Sir John Herbert (d. 9 July 1617), a noted civil lawyer and privy councillor:

> Who bites a cooke and leaves his wonted grasse
> Of a proud Hobby may becom an asse.

This response uses the same technique as the epigram that prompted it, playing upon the name of the individual to ridicule him.

The complicated antagonism of Coke and Lady Hatton in 1617 over the marriage of their daughter seemed to have spilled over into poetic attacks on figures connected to them. These epigrams served in a struggle that was partly a factional dispute of the court and partly a division within the marriage of Coke and Hatton itself. John Villiers was ailing bodily, which became the subject of a circulating libel that Coke and his associates attempted to prosecute. Holles relates:

> These busines [Lady Hatton] ar full of consideration, and every one therin interested from the King to the favoritt, and from him to the ferriman of Putney, and a women [*sic*] that sells chickens who have been examined for some scandalous words of Sir Jhon Villars soar legg, is full of consequence, and heavily will it fall at the last.[56]

Presumably, the reference to Villiers's 'soar legg' is a euphemism for another body part.

A couple of weeks later, Holles reported further:

> Winwood, with Coke, is 'busie in examining 2 men of Lady Withipols, concerning the slaunderous speeches of Sir Jhon Villars soar legg, and though the authority be to the more part of the Commissioners, yet he undertaketh it alone, and commits the felloes close prisoners, as in point of treason.[57]

The two servants were connected to Lady Hatton, as Lady Withipole had assisted in the abducting of Frances Coke.[58] The most likely candidate to be the 'ferriman of Putney' mentioned in the first letter is John Taylor, the Water-Poet, as he had written and published an epigram on a lecher with a bad leg some years before ('Looke how yon Letchers Legs are worne away').[59] (The one difficulty about this identification is that Taylor's residence in the 1610s, while not definitely known, seems to have been in Southwark rather than Putney.)[60]

> Looke how yon letchers Legs are worne away
> With haunting of the Whore-house every day:
> He knowes more greasy Panders, Bauds, & Drabs,
> And eats more Lobsters, Artichockes, and Crabs,
> Blew roasted Egges, Potatoes, Muskadine,
> Oysters, and pith that growes i'th Oxes Chine:
> With many Drugs, Compounds, and Simples store,
> Which makes him have a stomacke to a Whore.
> But one day heele give ore, when tis too late,
> When he stands begging through an iron grate.[61]

Since this was published in 1612, it was not originally written about Villiers by Taylor, as the future favourite's brother was on the continent for the three years leading up to 1612. However, it seems plausible that the lines had been reapplied to Villiers by the 'chicken monger' in the summer of 1617, and, thus, Taylor's 'authorship' of it was not culpable.[62] In a letter to the Privy Council (penned by Holles) Lady Hatton denied having anything to do with the libel:

> nevertheless my intent heerby is rather to informe yow a truthe, then to fault him [Coke], yet seeing his passion so extendeth, as the poor woman your Lordships committed upon the slanderous words is threatned with Brydwell, if shee accuse not a greater person to be the author of them: I leave to your wisdoms what suche terrifyings, and punishments may worke with suche a captive to the injurie of any: as for myself I am so free from this foule part, that I detest both the words, and that unworthy boddy soever, that shall think guilty of them.[63]

Worthy of note is that Lady Hatton seems to be associated with the libel through her servants, or at least is believed to be so by Winwood and Coke. This provides another example of the crossing of social boundaries by libellous poetic materials. Servants, scullers and chicken vendors come to partake in the affairs of the elite, as they are used by the superior powers in their struggles. The possible connection to the Taylor poem also illustrates how epigrams might be reused and reapplied.

Coke and Bacon had been legal and personal rivals over many decades: already in 1594 they had competed for the office of Attorney General, and Bacon had been among the unsuccessful suitors of Lady Hatton a few years later. Then, in the crisis of 1616–17, Bacon, as Attorney General, was the King's main instrument against Coke. While Coke lost his judicial positions, he led the Commons in the 1621 attack on Bacon.

These very public conflicts and the inviting coincidence of their names provided easy work for poetic wits; this epigram playfully presents the Parliamentary attacks as the 'nimble Cooke' slicing 'from thy gammon [bacon]':

On Fran. Ld. Verulam Keeper of greate seale
Stand fast thou shaking quaking Keeper
    A tent[64] thou must endure,
For feare in time thy wounds grow deeper,
    And so become past cure.
Into thy past life see thou looke,
    For if thy faults grow common,
Thou soone wilt find a nimble Cooke
    Slice rathers from thy gammon.
Patient hee is like Job, I wis
    And poore, you need not doubt him,
Butt most of all like Job in this
    Hee hath such scabbs about him.
Meazly Bacon is quite forsaken
    And none thats heere care for it,
The Parliament with one consent
    I oft have heard it spoke
Hath made a law to singe it with straw
    And hange it up in smoake.[65]

Here the mockery is mostly of Bacon, and it lightly characterizes the proceedings that he must endure.[66] Coke is nimble and Job-like in patience, but the depiction is double-edged, and, in the typical epigram spirit of cynical detachment, he is also Job-like in having 'scabbs about him', which may be an unsupported allusion to venereal disease, or, based on the sense of 'scab' as 'scoundrel',[67] referring to the supporters of Coke in Parliament. A variant of these four lines circulated as well:

Solon[68] would needs be rich as he was wise,
And just as Job in all his qualities:
And to be Job least men might doubt him
He had a[s] many a scabs about him.[69]

The maintaining of the basic conceit and one rhyme in conjunction with a completely different syntax again suggests that this was an orally circulating epigram about Coke, which was then incorporated into the longer poem on Bacon. Curiously, the copy of the shorter poem identifies the Job-like figure as 'Lo: B', presumably Bacon himself.

Coke's parliamentary triumph in 1621 was short-lived, however; after the dissolution of the House in November, he himself was sent to the Tower, which prompted the following poem:

De Domino Edwardo Cooke in Turrim immisso. 1621
Clauditur in Turri mandato Principis albâ:
    A populo causam pratereunte rogor.
Non Domini, sed Coce tuo servire palato,
    Regibus insipidum ius populare soles.
Liber adhuc esses, unum hoc si dogma teneres;
    Nempe Cocus Domini debet habere gulam.

[Of Lord Edward Coke, sent to the Tower, 1621
He is shut up in the white tower by order of the Prince:
I am asked the cause by the people passing by.
Cook, to serve your own palate, not that of your Master,
You are accustomed to ruin the insipid/tasteless law/broth for kings.
You are still free, if you hold on to this one tenet:
Certainly the Cook ought to please the taste of the Master.][70]

The last line is a direct quotation from Martial 14:220, but it is put to a new use. Martial's original had suggested that skill was not sufficient for a cook: he must also fulfil his master's taste.

The life and career of Coke presented a perfect storm for poetic wits to play upon: an ambitious, rising man, busy in the prosecution of the great, in conflict with royal power, married to a wealthy but scandalous wife, and, by the time of his death, fabulously rich. Hence, it is not surprising that, even after death, epigrams and jests continued to circulate. Even in the later seventeenth century, John Aubrey recorded jests that echoed those found in epigrams much earlier. In one, Henry Cuffe, the Earl

of Essex's secretary, during the proceedings against him for the rebellion, tripped Coke into identifying himself with the horned Actaeon; in
another, he records a final play on Coke as cook:

> His second wife, Elizabeth, the relickt of Sir William Hatton, was with Child
> when he maried her: laying his hand on her belly (when he came to be) and
> finding a Child to stirre, What, sayd he, Flesh in the Pott. yea, quoth she, or els
> I would not have maried a Cooke.[71]

Epigrams of more stoic and nuanced political comment

Cogswell and Bellany stress the oppositional nature of political epigrams, and, while certainly the majority would be categorized as such,
Ian Atherton accurately argues that in discerning an opposition tradition
Bellany ignores the pro-Whitgift, pro-Buckingham tradition.[72] However,
it must be noted that attacking epigrams had far higher rates of circulation, and epigrams of political praise were written only in response to
widespread ones of attack and derision, as with the satiric epitaphs that
greeted the deaths of Salisbury and Buckingham.[73] McRae also holds back
from identifying the tradition as an 'oppositional' one, as a term that is too
binary, and devotes a chapter to the responses of the 'authorized' poet,
Corbett.[74] In addition, as seen in the Coke epigrams of 1616–17, the political struggle was not always between court and opposition but between
two factions within circles close to the centre of power, and the epigrams
reflect this divide.[75] These Coke poems also demonstrate Cogswell's point
that few of the widely circulating political epigrams of the early Stuart
period 'analysed issues in a cool, dispassionate manner', but instead were
'wildly partisan' in their attacks on prominent individuals.[76] Nevertheless,
there was still a spectrum of both literary sophistication and urbane
detachment, and partisanship did not render such attributes impossible:
Harington often uses epigrams to support King James's title to the Crown
and further his own political ends, but generally with a degree of wit and
polish that render the approach palatable.

In addition, while admittedly rare, there were moments when the wry
urbane tone of the Martialian epigram tradition lent itself well to a more
detached and stoic, sometimes even cynical, political attitude, one found
most prominently in the epigrams of Harington, and to a lesser extent in
Herrick and John Heath. Certainly the best known of these, and among
the most famous epigrams in the period, was Harington's on treason, discussed in the opening section of this book. Scattered amongst the better

known Anacreontic and Martialian epigrams in Herrick's *Hesperides* are a fair number of what can be best described as political distichs, some verging on the proverbial, others offering a sharpness of ironic insight similar to that of Harington's 'On Treason'. Besides Herrick's better-known and more direct poems on King Charles and the trans-shifting times of the 1640s, these political epigrams of general reflection convey the dynamics of the political world without explicit basis in particular events or moments. His epigrammatic comment on treason offers a straightforward warning:

Treason
The seeds of Treason choake up as they spring,
He Acts the Crime, that gives Cherishing.[77]

Here, the identity of treason is clear, and Herrick uses a vegetative metaphor (possibly drawing on the Biblical parable of the sower) to urge the need for vigilance at the first sign of treason's growth. Furthermore, it suggests that one who treats emerging treason mildly ('gives Cherishing') is culpable of the crime itself.

A number of Herrick's epigrams take the form of advice to princes:

Strength to support Soveraignty
Let Kings and Rulers, learne this line from me;
Where power is weake, unsafe is Majestie.[78]

Patience in Princes
Kings must not use the Axe for each offence:
Princes cure some faults by their patience.[79]

Others advise how subjects are to thrive under a monarch:

Caution in Councell
Know when to speake; for many times it brings
Danger to give the best advice to Kings.[80]

Collectively, these poems offer a vision of the royal court as a place of wariness for both king and courtiers. They manifest a memorable brevity, but with a sharpness and polish that sets them apart from proverbs in verse.

While the Herrick poems just cited were general rather than situational, there are also surviving epigrams of specific events that offer a more nuanced perspective than those on Essex and Coke explored above. The following poem on Ralegh, preserved in a collection of separates concerned with his execution in 1618, offers a far more probing understanding of the realities of political life than most:

> Hope flattered thee though lawes did life convince
> *Tha*t thou might'st dy in favour of thy prince[81]
> His mercy & thy liberty at last
> did sealle beleife, and make opinion fast
> In truth when time had puld thee out of jayle
> and newe hopes had sett againe new saille
> As many of this world as held free will
> Thought thou wert safe, & had'st escapt thy ill
> But nowe wee see, that thou wert bay'ld by fate
> To live or dy, as thou could'st serve our state
> And then wert lost, when it was understood
> Thou might'st doe harme, but could'st not doe more good.[82]

The poem successfully questions the optimism of both Ralegh and his supporters when he was released from the Tower in 1616 for a final expedition to the New World. Unlike many poems that lamented his death, this one recognizes the inescapable political reality: that Ralegh was allowed to live and take this final journey only as long as he was still useful. He was redeemed from prison not by King James but by 'Time'; this was misread, however, by those naive figures who believed in 'free will'. Subsequent events offered a corrective: Ralegh had been 'bayl'd' by Fate, and his fatal (and useful) role now passed, the political situation (or Fate) required his death. The poem challenges not merely Ralegh's hope but those of the author and his reader as well. Their perception of the insistence of political reality has clarified their vision, leading them to a far more stoic perspective. More than most topical epigrams, this one offers a nuanced and polished analysis of a particular moment.

The same can be said of an epigram that circulated following the birth of Prince Charles in 1630:

> When private men get sonnes, they gette a spoone,
> Without eclipse or any starre at noone;
> When kings get sonnes, they get withall supplies,
> And succours farre beyond five subsidies.
> Welcome, God's loane, great tribute of the state,

Thou mony new come in, rich fleete of plate;
Welcome, blest babe, whom God thy father sent
To make him rich without a parliament.[83]

The poem functions by playing with the much celebrated new star that supposedly appeared at the time of the prince's birth in late May, noted for example in the widely known Latin epigram, 'Dum Rex Paulinas'.[84] Rather than straightforwardly celebrating the advent of this star as a harbinger of good to come with this new member of the royal family, the poem bathetically compares it to the more usual nativity gift of a spoon. A new star may be wonderfully prophetic, but the poem goes on to recognize that King Charles has also received immediate material reward, which far exceeds the spoon of other fathers: he has received 'supplies'. A recalcitrant House of Commons that had resisted providing the expected parliamentary supply had now been rendered superfluous by the happy arrival of a royal son and the material gifts that followed. The balanced final four lines welcome both 'God's loane' and the 'blest babe', but the phrasing suggests that the event is more significant for its immediate financial repercussions than the usual continuing of the royal line offered by a first-born son. The poem is polished, balanced, and witty: like a number discussed in this section it is most typically epigrammatic in its worldly wise attitude toward politics, neither strongly praising or blaming, but shrewdly identifying the reality of the political moment.

The longstanding attribution of the poem to Corbett complicates his position as a staunch royalist; as McRae suggests, it is 'an extraordinarily prickly piece of praise' and seems 'a poem motivated more by embittered resentment than joyous triumphalism'.[85] At least one contemporary had doubts about ascribing it to the bishop: in recording the poem in his diary, Rous first added the ascription, 'Finis. qu*o*d Rich. Oxon.' [meaning Corbett, Bishop of Oxford], but some pages later he notes that 'Rich. Oxon. may be subscribed by some other, and it may be by such an one as is in the former [another poem by Corbett] termed Puritan'.[86] It certainly is very different from his more straightforward panegyric on the event, 'Was Heav'n afray'd to be out-done', where he reads the star and eclipse as 'Prognosticks of a rare prosperity'.[87] However, in a third poem on the occasion, 'What Joy that Shunamite did once inherit', Corbett makes similar jesting reference to the King–Parliament relationship: among his predictions for the reign of the future Prince is that it will bring 'That Peace, rich warlick Peace, I meane Consent / Between the closet and the Parliament'.[88] I would suggest that the poem is most of all reflecting epigrammatic wit, one that is less concerned with ideological or factional sides than with wryly identifying the irony of the political situation.

Also willing to reflect ironically (if less playfully) on the royal situation from an 'insider' perspective is Robert Ayton, a prominent courtier and secretary to Queen Anna. One of his poems from 1620–21 scolds King James quite directly for his failure to intervene on his son-in-law's behalf in his struggle for the Bohemian Crown. English and Latin versions of the poem appear together (but in different hands) in Bodl. MS Malone 19:

> Whiles thy sonnes rash unluckye armes attempt,
> ffrom the Austrian yoake Bohemian necke t'exempt,
> Thow dost condemne his plott K. James; & that
> The world may thinke thee no confederate,
> Thou leavst thy sonne to fates, & wilt not ayd,
> Though but with prayers alone his case decayde
> Nay with unwatered, undew'd cheekes canst see,
> Throwne out of house & home thy progenye.
> Rare proofe of justice! yet lett me but utter,
> With thy good leave what all the world doth mutter.
> This way perhapps a just Kinge thou mayst seeme,
> But men a cruell ffather will thee deeme.[89]

The poem is not, like some in the years 1620–21, fully celebratory of Elector Frederick: his acceptance of the Bohemian Crown is described as 'rash' and a 'plott'. Further, the epigram acknowledges James's lofty motivation: to disassociate himself from his son-in-law's action and appear as the impartial advocate of peace and justice in Europe. His political decisions are not distorted by emotion. Yet even while Ayton describes this state of affairs in the first nine lines, he quietly raises questions. King James may perhaps be too concerned with what 'The world may thinke', and he is described as unmoved by a violent action against his family: they are 'Thrown out of house & home'. Thus, the turn in the final three and a half lines is not fully unexpected, as the poet suggests that, in being 'a just Kinge', James is also being 'a cruell father'. The poem ultimately appeals to that concern with opinion identified in line 4: he is reminded of how he will be judged. Only the 'world' ('orbis') of the international community in line 4 has been replaced with the world of his own subjects. There is no appeal here to the rightness of the cause, but only to the expected emotions of a father/king and the judgement upon him of his subjects. Ayton, if he is the poet, stands as an intermediary between the common *filius populi* and the close adviser to the King.[90] He asks the King to 'lett me but utt*er*, / With thy good leave w*ha*t all the world doth mutter'.[91] The epigrammatist again plays the role of expressing in verse what all men might say, but he is also a courtier offering *parrhesia* (frank council) to aid the King in his decision-making.[92] This plain-speaking poem to the King circulated widely enough to have its final two lines embraced as a sort of 'vox populi' by the more radical supporters of Frederick's cause; first in the outspoken pamphlet *Tom Tell Troath* (1622?), and then in the margin to a passage in John Russell's *The Spy* (1628) that chastises the King directly for his willingness to ignore his offspring in bending to Spanish will.[93]

Finally, George Herbert's poem on King James's visit to Cambridge on 19 March 1623, which took place while Prince Charles was in Spain courting the Infanta, is a further example of a witty epigram that subtly conveys something of general public sentiment:[94]

> Dum petit Infantem Princeps, Grantamque Iacobus,
> Quisnam horum maior sit, dubitatur, amor.
> Vincit more suo Noster: nam millibus Infans
> Non tot abest, quot nos Regis ab ingenio.

> [While Prince to Spaine, and King to Cambridge goes,
> The question is, whose love the greater showes:
> Ours (like himselfe) o'recomes; for his wit's more
> Remote from ours, then Spaine from Britains shoare.][95]

While this, to my knowledge, has always been read positively as a poem extolling King James's wisdom and love, the text in fact sustains just as well the opposite reading. All that the poem explicitly notes is a great distance between the wisdom of the King and that of Cambridge: it does not say which is greater. I suspect that the poem's popularity at the time stemmed partly from this clever ambiguity: Herbert, as orator of Cambridge, had produced a double-written work that in its negative form quite fully conveyed popular sentiment at Prince Charles and Buckingham's quixotic journey into Spain: the King was a fool for having allowed it. There are also indications that the King was willing to tolerate such jesting critique when cleverly presented: from the same political crisis comes the story of Archie Armstrong, the court fool, who suggested that the event showed that he and James ought to exchange hats.[96]

Collectively, these examples illustrate how the epigram could be used for subtle political comment, firmly based in the detached ironic tradition of Martial. While the more starkly vituperative and partisan epigrams attacking Coke found a broad audience, the same networks of circulation could foster the sophisticated epigrammatic reflections of Corbett, Ayton and Herbert, as they touched upon issues of great topical interest.

Notes

1 Marotti, *Manuscript, Print and the English Renaissance Lyric*, p. 75.
2 *The last part of the Mirour for magistrates* (1578), fol. 154v.
3 *Sic*, but presumably a printer's error for 'pleasaunte'.
4 *The last part of the Mirour for magistrates*, fol. 155v.
5 Harington, *The Metamorphosis of Ajax*, p. 100.
6 See Sherri Geller, 'What History Really Teaches: Historical Pyrrhonism in William Baldwin's A Mirror for Magistrates', in Peter C. Herman (ed.), *Opening the Borders: Inclusivity in Early Modern Studies: Essays in Honor of James V. Mirollo* (Newark, DE: University of Delaware Press, 1999), pp. 163–4, on *The Mirror*'s framing of the Collingbourne episode.
7 Rowlands, *A Fooles Bolt is Soon Shot*, sig. C3r.
8 Harington, *The Metamorphosis of Ajax*, p. 102.
9 Henry Parrot, *The Mous-trap* (1606), sig. A3r.
10 Freeman, *Rubbe, and a great cast*, sig. F4r.
11 Paul F. Grendler, *Critics of the Italian World (1530–1650); Anton Francesco Doni, Nicolo Franco & Ortensio Lando* (Madison, WI: University of Wisconsin Press, 1969), p. 48.
12 Thomas Cogswell, 'Underground Verse and the Transformation of Early Stuart Political Culture', in Susan D. Amussen and Mark A. Kishlansky (eds), *Political Culture and Cultural Politics in Early Modern England: Essays Presented to David Underdown* (Manchester: Manchester University Press, 1995), pp. 277–300, p. 281.
13 Marotti, *Manuscript, Print and the English Renaissance Lyric*, p. 82.
14 Rous, *Diary*, p. 109.
15 John Selden, *Table-Talk* (Freeport, NY: Books for Libraries, 1972), p. 93.
16 Fox, *Oral and Literate Culture in England*, p. 338.
17 McRae, *Literature, Satire, and the Early Stuart State*, p. 8
18 Cogswell, 'Underground Verse and the Transformation of Early Stuart Political Culture', pp. 277–300.
19 John Holles, Earl of Clare, to Wentworth, 15 Nov. 1628, *Wentworth Papers, 1597–1628*, ed. J. P. Cooper (London: Royal Historical Society, 1973), p. 309.

Clare seems to be referring to the impeachment of Dr Roger Manwaring by the 1628 Parliament, for his sermons proclaiming the King's authority over Parliament. In spite of Charles's concurrence in Manwaring's punishment, by the latter half of 1628 he was rewarding him with new church livings.

20 Bodl. English History MS c.272, fol. 41r.

21 Versions of the poem also appear in Bodl. Don. MS c.54, fol. 7r, and Bodl. Rawl. poet. MS 26, fol. 20v.

22 Crum, vol. 1, p. 33.

23 *DNB*.

24 See the record of Speeches in Queen's College, Oxford, MS 121, pp. 542–9, and BL Add. MS 40838, fol. 13ff.

25 Bodl. English hist. MS c.272, fol. 41v. In Bodl. Don. c.54 these lines had simply been a conclusion to 'Admire-all weakness'.

26 This couplet is not in Bodl. Don. c.54.

27 Essex was Master of the Ordnance; on 10 Dec. 'he sent his patents as Master of the Horse and Master of the Ordnance to the Queen. She sent them back.' G. B. Harrison, *The Life and Death of Robert Devereux Earl of Essex* (1937; Rpt Folcroft, PA: Folcroft Library, 1973), p. 254.

28 Bodl. Rawl. poet. MS 26, fol. 2r.

29 *DNB*.

30 Roger Manners, fifth Earl of Rutland; Edward Crumwell, third Baron.

31 See Anthony G. Petti, 'Beasts and Politics in Elizabethan Literature', *Essays and Studies*, 16 (1963), pp. 68–90.

32 *DNB*.

33 Possibly sense 5 in *OED*: 'customary or legal contribution or payment; rent paid in kind or money; a tribute, *esp.* a tribute rendered by a religious house to its parent institution'.

34 Some of the courtier monopolists mocked by Bastard can be identified: Sir Edward Dyer held a monopoly on leather, Sir Walter Ralegh on wine.

35 Bastard, 'Ad Lectorem', *Chrestoleros*, Ep. 2:16.

36 Harington's Ep. 3:70 (Kilroy ed.) marks the same anniversary with such outspoken criticism that Kilroy 'wonders how this godson of the Queen dared to circulate it, even in manuscript' (p. 45).

37 Tilley, P153.

38 A similar instance, on the names of Lord Keeper Finch and Matthew Wren, Bishop of Ely, is traced by Cressy, *England on Edge*, pp. 334–5.

39 A similar-sounding pejorative term was 'cokes', meaning a fool or simpleton, which Jonson plays on in the character Bartholomew Cokes in *Bartholomew Fair*.

40 'Venue': the primary sense here is from the field of swordplay, where a 'venue'

is an attack. It seems likely that a play on the legal sense of the place where an action is laid is also at work.

41 'Draffe': dregs, swill. (Kilroy has 'drass', which would seem to be a misreading; other manuscripts and printed editions have 'draffe'.)

42 Harington, Ep. 1:87 (Kilroy ed.).

43 Tobie Matthew to Dudley Carleton, 15 Sept. 1598, *CSPD*. In February of that year there were rumours that she was to be married to 'Mr. Grivell' (Fulke Greville?) (Rowland Whyte to Sir Robert Sidney, 2 Feb. 1597/8, Collins, *Letters and Memorials of State*, vol. 2, p. 88).

44 One of these rumours is evident from an affidavit of Mary Berham concerning one William Dennis, servant to the Countess of Warwick, who had said that Lady Hatton was delivered of a son ten weeks after her marriage.

45 Chamberlain to Carleton, 4 Aug. 1599, *Letters*; Bowen, *The Lion and the Throne*, p. 109, mistakenly has this daughter identified as 'Frances'. The International Genealogical Index shows Elizabeth Coke, born to Edward and Lady Hatton, 6 Aug. 1599 at Hatton House, Holborn. Frances Coke, the daughter whose marriage to John Villiers sparked the 1617 crisis between Coke and Lady Hatton, was born in 1601.

46 I have serious doubts that these epigrams are by Davies, which I hope to unfold fully in a subsequent article.

47 *Poems of Sir John Davies*, ed. Krueger, p. 174

48 *Poems of Sir John Davies*, ed. Krueger, p. 174. 'Meochus' would seem to be an error or variation of 'moechus', adulterer.

49 Chamberlain to Carleton, 23 Nov. 1616, *Letters*, vol. 2, p. 40. The epigram does not survive with the letter.

50 Chamberlain to Carleton, 23 Nov. 1616, *Letters*, vol. 2, p. 38.

51 'To Mr Bond my Lord Chancellors [Egerton] Secretary', 10 Nov. 1616, BL Add MS32464, fol. 130r–v. The transcription in Holles, *Letters*. ed. Peter Seddon, vol. 1, p. 146, contains many errors. Coke later brought a bill against Holles (Bowen, *The Lion and the Throne*, p. 354).

52 'Voeste' here would seem to be a variant of 'veste'. The line echoes Ovid's description of the Actaeon–Diana story: 'in vultu visae sine veste Dianae [in the cheeks of Diana as she stood there in view without robes]' (*Metamorphoses*, Loeb ed., 3: 185).

53 The manuscript gives the title as 'A Distick on ye Lord Cooke by Sr E: Ho:'; the identification of Hoby depends on the reference in the following poem to 'a proud Hobby', and by that poem's title, which has the name 'Hobby' scratched out in the title; the copyist must have had Edward Hoby's name in mind as he began transcribing the response. Hoby was related to Lady Hatton through his mother, a daughter of Anthony Cooke.

54 Folger MS V.a.345, p. 149. Another copy is in Folger MS V.a.162, fol. 27.
55 A similar play on 'Jus' and 'Coquus' is found in Owen, *Epigrams*, Ep. 4:59.

>   Ex quo caelestum terras Astraea reliquit
>   Ultima, signifero legit in orbe locum.
>   Templum Iustitiae, legumque evertimus aras:
>   Scitque fere solus ius dare cuique coquus.

['E're since *Astraea*, last of heav'nly Race, / Abandon'd Earth, and took in Heav'n her place, / Laws Altars, Justice Temples are forsook, / And t'each his *Jus* * to give, sole knows the Cook.'
* *Jus signifies Pottage.*]
[trans. Thomas Harvey, *John Owen's Latine epigrams* (1677)].
56 Holles to Sir Tho. Lakes (*sic*), 26 July 1617, *Letters*, vol. 2, p. 180.
57 Holles to Sir Tho. Lakes (*sic*), 6 Aug. 1617, *Letters*, vol. 2, p. 188.
58 Letter of King James in *HMC Buccleugh and Queensberry*, 16 July 1617. John Campbell Baron Campbell, *The Lives of the Chief Justices of England*, 3 vols (London, 1858), vol. 1, pp. 298–9.
59 Taylor, *The Sculler* (1612), Ep. 32.
60 Bernard Capp, *The World of John Taylor the Water-Poet, 1578–1653* (Oxford: Clarendon Press, 1994), p. 9n.
61 Taylor, *The Sculler*, Ep. 32.
62 The epigram was not reprinted in either the 1614 *Waterworkes* or the 1630 *Workes*. There is no indication of any hostility on Taylor's part towards Villiers or his family in the 1610s, and he dedicated his account of his 1618 trip to Scotland, *The Pennyles Pilgrimage* (1618) to the Duke (Capp, *The World of John Taylor*, p. 22).
63 15 Aug. 1617, Holles, *Letters*, vol. 2, p. 191.
64 'Tent': a surgical probe.
65 *Early Stuart Libels*, Mii2, based on BL Add. MS 22118, fol. 42v. Bellany and McRae note further copies in *Trevelyan Papers*, 3.163; BL Add. MS 61481, fol. 99r; Beinecke Osborn MS b.197, p. 182. The poem is an expanded version of a more general one on monopolists and the 1621 Parliament, beginning 'Oyes, can any tell true tideings' (*Early Stuart Libels*, Mi5), discussed in McRae, *Literature, Satire, and the Early Stuart State*, pp. 38–40.
66 There are also many satiric epigrams on Bacon that play on his name without reference to Coke.
67 *OED*, 4.a.
68 Jonson praised Coke by comparing him to Solon, the Athenian law-giver (d. ca. 651 BC), in 'An Epigram on Sir Edward Coke, When he was Lord Chief Justice of England', *Underwood*, no. 46.

69 'On a Lo: Ju:', Farmer, *Poems from a Seventeenth-Century Manuscript*, p. 27. The poem also appears in Folger MS V.a.262, p. 156; Yale MS c.50, p. 133.

70 Bodl. Rawl. poet. MS 26, fol. 39r.

71 Aubrey, *Brief Lives*, p. 162.

72 Atherton, '"The Itch Grown a Disease"', p. 57.

73 Cogswell, 'Underground Verse', p. 286, also notes that many poets rushed in to defend those being libelled.

74 McRae, *Literature, Satire, and the Early Stuart State*, pp. 49–50.

75 Alastair Bellany, 'Libels in Action: Ritual, Subversion and the English Literary Underground, 1603–42', in Tim Harris (ed.), *The Politics of the Excluded* (Basingstoke and New York: Palgrave, 2001), pp. 99–124.

76 Cogswell, 'Underground Verse', p. 284.

77 Herrick, *Poetical Works*, ed. F. W. Moorman (Oxford: Oxford University Press, 1921), p. 10.

78 Herrick, *Poetical Works*, p. 295.

79 Herrick, *Poetical Works*, p. 302.

80 Herrick, *Poetical Works*, p. 311.

81 Rudick (ed.), *Poems of Sir Walter Ralegh*, reads 'Y^t' as 'Yet', but it must be an abbreviated 'That'.

82 PRO SP 14/103/61. The poem is reproduced in Rudick (ed.), *Poems of Sir Walter Ralegh*, pp. 192–3. It records no other copy.

83 Rous, *Diary*, p. 54, 27 June 1630.

84 The poem has been variously ascribed to Sir Robert Ayton or John Hoskins; in some versions it begins, 'Rex ubi Paulinas'.

85 McRae, *Literature, Satire, and the Early Stuart State*, p. 180.

86 Rous, *Diary*, p. 55.

87 Corbett, *Poems*, ed. Bennett and Trevor-Roper, p. 85.

88 Corbett, *Poems*, ed. Bennett and Trevor-Roper, pp. 85–6. Cf. Bastard's reference to 'civil jarres' discussed above. The biblical prophet Elisha raised from death the son of a Shunamite woman (2 Kings 4:8–37).

89 Bodl. Malone MS 19, fol. 20v.

90 If Ayton was not truly the author, this is another case of a controversial poem being 'fathered upon' an illustrious figure.

91 Bodl. Malone MS 19, fol. 20v. This manuscript offers both the Latin poem and an English translation. This translation also appears in Harvard MS Eng. 686, fol. 17.

92 On the significance of the concept in the period, see Colclough, *Freedom of Speech in Early Stuart England*, chapter 1; on its role in the Parliament of 1621 (the seeming time of this poem), see p. 184.

93 John Russell, *The Spy* (1628), sig. F4r.

94 Nichols, *Progresses*, vol. 4, pp. 835–8.

95 *Works of George Herbert*, ed. F. E. Hutchinson (Oxford: Oxford University Press, 1941), pp. 438–9.

96 R. Malcolm Smuts, 'Archibald Armstrong', *DNB*.

11

The feigned epitaph

Then base report, ware what thy tongue doth spred,
Tis sin and shame for to bely the dead.[1]

Among the sub-genres of the Renaissance epigram, the epitaph has been best served by recent scholarly attention. Joshua Scodel's *The English Poetic Epitaph* (1991) offers a valuable survey of the function and dynamics of the form over a number of centuries, and Scott Newstok's *Quoting Death in Early Modern England: The Poetics of Epitaphs Beyond the Tomb* (2009) astutely explores the movement of epitaphs from tombs to other contexts, and non-inscribed scenarios. Both Scodel and Newstok are primarily concerned with conventional epitaphs; that is, ones of praise written for the truly dead. This chapter instead explores variants of the sub-genre, in particular parodic or 'feigned' epitaphs that mockingly commemorate both the living and the dead. In a further type of indirect satiric epitaph, the central subject is not the deceased but those in positions of power, who might control any official inscribed epitaph. Finally, epitaphs were occasionally composed for those who for political reasons lacked a grave. These sub-genres of the epitaph share one quality: they defy the levelling effect of the genre, which treats all deceased with the same limited terms of conventional praise. These varieties of epitaph also on occasion prompted poems of response that attempted to redirect the poetic discussion towards the panegyric norms of the genre. Overall, these poems represent a rich and complex dimension of the broader epigram culture of the time.

The term 'feigned epitaph', which is used throughout this chapter, is derived from Ralph Johnson's *Scholar's Guide* (1665), where he defines such poems in contrast to 'Epitaphs of friends, or relations': 'In feigned Epitaphs, or upon vitious persons, 1. We merrily and wittily play upon the name, manners, lineaments, manner of death, or other memorable events affording matter of witty conceit.'[2] Most literary epitaphs (as distinct from inscribed ones) might be construed as parodies; however, the majority of these lack only inscription: they fully adopt the tone, style and matter of those on tombs. In this way, they are markedly distinct from the feigned epitaph as defined by Johnson.

The function of the feigned epitaph is strikingly different from that of the parent genre, offering a counter to official versions that praised the deceased. The feigned epitaph suggests implicitly its fictionality, its prioritizing of form over reality. Because of their widespread oral and manuscript circulation, many of these have survived, ironically triumphing over the seemingly more permanent official epitaphs engraved in stone. Mock epitaphs of political figures in the early Stuart age are of particular significance, as they contributed to the intense political and factional struggles explored in the preceding chapter. While scholars such as Alastair Bellany and Pauline Croft have considered individual instances of such poems,[3] hitherto lacking has been a study that considers them within the theory and conventions of the epitaph as a genre in the period. While this chapter focuses on the English use of mock epitaphs, it was a more widespread European phenomenon of the seventeenth century; the death of Pope Urban VIII (d. 1644), for example, was marked by a tremendous outpouring of such verses.[4]

Engraved, pinned and feigned epitaphs

While a Renaissance tomb would generally be the site only of a single engraved epitaph, many literary epitaphs that were fully removed from the physical site of the body were composed and, in some cases, published. However, in the funerary customs of the time there was also a tradition of temporarily pinning epitaphs and elegies to the hearse; this represents a half-way step between the literary and the inscribed epitaph. Such a practice was common with more illustrious figures whose corpses (of often wax effigies) would lie in state upon a hearse for a period of time before burial. These pinned epitaphs and elegies were originally and primarily ones of praise, and examples were known across Europe. For example, the tomb of the Neo-Latin epigrammatist Giovanni Pontano (1426–1503), in his funerary chapel in Naples, was famously adorned with the contributions of his fellow poets.[5] Surviving collections of funerary poems (for example, some of the published Latin compilations produced in Oxford and Cambridge) seem to have emerged from this practice. However, there are also cases where feigned epitaphs were fixed upon the hearse or placed on the tomb; the satiric attacks against Archbishop Whitgift that took this form have been explored by Bellany,[6] and the final part of this chapter explores how the tomb of the epigrammatist Owen became the site of competing epitaphs in 1623. Unlike inscribed epitaphs, these feigned epitaphs never aspired to brazen permanence, or even that offered by inscription in print; instead, their immortality was based upon multiplication of copies, encouraged by brevity and memorability.

These feigned epitaphs were parodic, in that they reflected the conventions of other texts; in this way, they reflect Margaret Rose's understanding of parody as deriving its comic effect from some 'incongruity between the original and its parody'.[7] However, these feigned epitaphs were, for the most part, parodying the conventions of a genre rather than the details of individual works. Despite the responsive nature of so many epigrams, feigned epitaphs usually could not *respond* to original official ones, as the public display of the latter was usually delayed by the long period required for the building of the tomb. (The Owen examples below are an exception to this.) Instead, they rewrote the conventions and norms that were widely associated with the genre, hence offering a pre-emptive parody of what might eventually be inscribed upon the tomb. Thus, this sub-genre functioned significantly differently from most parodies, and, in fact, some laudatory epitaphs and elegies respond to the satiric parodies that preceded them.

Rhetorical functions of the feigned epitaph

Renaissance discussion of epitaphs generally recognizes the potential for the form to disparage as well as praise. Thus, Puttenham defines the epitaph as

> but a kind of epigram, only applied to the report of the dead person's estate and degree, or of his other good or bad parts, to his commendation or reproach, and is an inscription such as a man may commodiously write or engrave upon a tomb in few verses, pithy, quick, and sententious, for the passerby to peruse and judge upon without any long tarriance.[8]

Francis Osborne noted that it was 'the fashion of the Poets all my days, to sum up great mens Vertues or Vices upon their Graves'.[9] However, in practice both inscribed and print-published epitaphs largely omitted the 'bad parts' or vices of the deceased, while in manuscript circulation castigating or satiric ones generally dominated. In a poem entitled 'To the D. of Sar: Stilo novo' [To the Dean of Salisbury, new style], Thomas Pestell treats the mocking satiric epitaph as the 'new stile':

> Persist to bee & doe good; So shall I
> Still date your Prayses stylo veteri [in the old style].
> Delude; & at yow Living I will laugh
> Out, in new stile, some Vengeful Epitaph.[10]

Pestell anticipates possible ill behaviour that will provoke mocking epitaphs while the Dean is still alive.

An expressive theory to explain the popularity of parodic epitaphs is not hard to formulate: the pent-up frustrations and opposition find an outlet in a safer political environment brought about by the great figure's death. But what of their rhetorical function? In a letter regarding the feigned epitaphs on Robert Cecil, Earl of Salisbury (d. 1612), Donne argues that such verses can have no justifiable purpose:

> there may be cases where one may do his country good service by libelling against a live man; for where a man is either too great, or his vices too general to be brought under a judiciary accusation, there is no way but this extraordinary accusing, which we call libelling, and I have heard that nothing hath soupled and allayed the Duke of Lerma in his violent greatness so much as the often libels made upon him. But after death it is in all cases unexcusable.

Donne finds such parodic epitaphs empty of satiric purpose, but he overlooks how they might serve as a warning to the living to change their ways to avoid a similar legacy.[11] In this vein, Dekker describes the despised figure 'Politick Bankrupt': 'those that goe over thee, will set upon thee no Epitaph but this, *Here lyes a knave.*'[12] Osborne, in recording a feigned epitaph on Cecil, also points to this function: '[it] came from so smart a Pen in the Kings sense, that he said, *he hoped the Author would die before him*: who it was God knows'.[13]

Richard Brathwaite, whose 'Remains after Death' (1618) offers an extensive discussion of the genre, brings together Donne's rejection of satiric epitaphs with an understanding of their power:

> *Epitaphs* of this sort we have too frequent, being forged out of the braine of unseasoned Satyrists, that without distinction bend their wits to asperse imputation

upon the deserved memorie of the dead: men of basest nature, defaming such whose silence gives them freer scope and priviledge of detraction.[14]

Brathwaite suggests their cowardly nature, in that they are attacking the silently defenceless. None the less, he also acknowledges that by tradition epitaphs could depict vices as well as virtues, and affirms what might be called 'mixed epitaphs' – those that in celebrating the deceased's virtues subtly instruct the living by identifying vices as well:

> these Descriptions are to bee shadowed and suited with modest allusions, equally disposed Allegories as their vices, though in part discovered, yet that discovery so intangled as may minister matter of observation to the judicious, and leave the ignorant in a continuall suspense. (sig. E5r)

This is a fascinating argument for a sophisticated approach to epitaphs, dependent upon a double audience of the judicious and the ignorant. Brathwaite then opens the door a crack further, opining that, while the authors of 'these prophane *Epitaphs* sinisterly aiming at the detraction of such obliquities should be severely censured', nevertheless 'sin should in some sort be unmasked' in 'prophane epitaphs'.[15] Seemingly, his objection was to those crude libellous epitaphs that lack subtlety in their method and discernment in their targets. Ultimately, Brathwaite does include a selection of such 'prophane epitaphs' in his collection, which he suggests 'modestly discover vice in her nativest colors'.[16] He then presents six examples of acceptable satiric epitaphs ('some invented, others translated and traduced from others'). Of these examples, only one appears in other works from the time: the widely popular epitaph (in both Latin and English) on the drunken Thomas Elderton, the ballad-maker.[17]

Conventions adapted for satiric epitaphs

Feigned epitaphs use the same rhetorical techniques that were widespread in the parent genre (the conventional opening, 'Here lies'; the direct addressing of the passer-by; the cataloguing of qualities; the cause or situation of death; the tension between the fate of the body and soul; the playing upon the deceased's name), but the content is shifted from eulogy to sharp rebuke and blame. Implicit is that this particular figure does not deserve the usual rhetoric or epitaphic praise.

Frequent in the epitaph tradition (going back to classical Greece) were poems that imagine an interaction between the reader passing by and the tombstone or grave. The passer-by is often implored to 'stay', or briefly pause, a tradition that goes back to the classical epitaph. The addressees are typically the public at large: 'all ye who pass by'. This dynamic imagines a reader who has not come to pay homage or mourn, to whom the deceased is of no prior interest. The reader is enjoined to appropriate honouring or mourning of the deceased.

Such addressing of the reader may also be a component of the feigned epitaph, as the reader is invited to engage with the tomb in a very different way. A striking example of this is found in 'On old weymarke the rich & coveteous usurer', which actually encourages physical disrespect of the grave; it begins, 'Stampe on hym Reader; under this Clode / Rich Weymarke Lyes, that made his gould his god', and, after much further abuse, concludes, 'Here the old Fox is catch't, and lett hym lye / The Curse and scorne, of all that pass hym bye.'[18] This hostile epitaph is followed immediately in the manuscript, however, by another that, while acknowledging Weymark's sins, cautions against such disrespect:

> Forbeare rashe frind, and add not to thyne owne
> By pressing Weymarks sinns; lett hym alone
> To wormes and Judgem*ent*, lett his memorye
> Together *with* his Bodye buryed lye.[19]

This reflects the rhetorical approach of offering silent oblivion as the most appropriate marker of the unworthy; yet even here, as with Brathwaite's examples above, a certain moral purpose, based upon a typically epitaphic play upon the name, is derived from the circumstances:

> when thou seest this; Condole the Tragedye
> Of mortall Riches; and Congratulate
> The happye Calmness; of a meane estate
> And as some Marriners, beehoulding are
> To sea-markes that advise them to beware
> Of Rockes and Quick-sands; soe lett weymarke bee
> In this lifes sea, A way-marke unto thee.

In this way the dead Weymark serves as a sombre object lesson for a pensive reader.

A large number of epitaphs (especially those on children) address the visitor to the tomb with some variant of 'Tread softly, passenger'. One feigned epitaph inverts this convention as it begins,

> Nay tread and spare not Passenger,
>   My sence is now past feeling,
> Who to my grave a wound did bear
>   Within, past Physicks healing.

The second stanza inverts the usual exhortation for the passer-by to read the epitaph – at least if that passer-by is planning to wed – for such might compel him instead to 'creep into my cold bed [of the grave] / rather then live to marry'.[20] Here the epitaph is not satirizing the diseased but participating in conventional mockery of wives and the state of marriage.

The use of the epitaph to list the attributes of the deceased, all of which lie buried in the tomb, was common.[21] It could be used for praise, as in this poem on Queen Elizabeth:

> Spaines Rod, Romes Ruine, Netherlands Reliefe,
> Earths Joy, Englands Jem, Worlds Wonder, Natures chiefe.[22]

However, such a convention could also be adapted in the feigned epitaph. A number of those on the death of Buckingham in 1628 suggest that the grave holds not the Duke but his attributes, positions or manifold oppressions of the nation. Like the panegyric epitaph, this could be concluded with the conceit that this small tomb wondrously held all these elements:

> Fortunes darling kings Content
> Vexation of the parliament
> The Flatterers deity of State
> Advancer of each merrie mate
> The Devills factor for the purse
> The Papists hope the Commons Curse
> The saylors crosse the Soldiours greefe
> Commissions blanke, and Englands theefe
> The Coward at the Isle of Ree
> The bane of noble Chivalrie
> The Nightworke of A painted dame
> Confederate with Doctor Lambe.
> All this lies underneath this stone
> And yet (alas) heere lyes but one.[23]

The basic structure of these mock epitaphs was maintained in circulation, but the listed attributes varied, and it is quite possible that such poems slowly accumulated their catalogues of vices.

Another parody of the epitaph's summing up of accomplishment is found in a well-known one frequently ascribed to Hoskins, the acknowledged master of the sub-genre in the period: 'Here lyes the man was borne and cryed / tould three score yeares, fell sick and dyed.'[24] This poem invokes and then undermines the convention of the epitaph to briefly provide an overview of the life. This man did nothing – in sixty years – but be born and die; ironically, the epitaph in its brevity is a more fit form for such a subject than for a life of accomplishment that defies the narrow boundaries of the form.

The feigned epitaph shared with the main genre a fondness for finding an ironic appropriateness in the death: a correspondence between the name, character or occupation and the circumstances of death. Typical is the epitaph on the first Earl of Dorset (Lord High Treasurer), who in 1608 died in the midst of a case at Whitehall:

> Discourteous Death that wouldst not once confer,
> Or daign to parly with our Treasurer:
> Had he been Thee, or of thy fatal Tribe,
> He would have spar'd a life to gain a bribe.[25]

The exceptional situation of his death allowed for a witty comment that summed up the whole of his corrupt public life. This particular example is also very nicely polished, all leading to the balanced phrases of the last line and the final sharp point on the rhyme word 'bribe'. In some feigned epitaphs the individual name and identity are omitted completely, as the social role or occupation becomes the sole focus.[26]

It must be said that a strict dividing line between laudatory and mocking epitaphs cannot always be maintained. For example, the play upon the dead person's name was widespread: even inscribed epitaphs frequently employ what might seem to us a frivolous or facetious approach. This is part of what distinguished the form from the more sorrowful expression of the elegy. Even a largely laudatory and serious epitaph on one Mary Mudd could not resist a final play on her name:

> Thus earth to earth, her Creator thought it good
> To shew, that by her name, she was but Mudd.[27]

Even in the face of death, the epigrammatic witty point is paramount. Readers of the period also might fail to distinguish between earnest and feigned epigrams. For example, the feigned epitaph on the Elizabethan poet Thomas Churchyard enjoyed wide circulation:

> Come, *Alecto,* and lend me thy Torch,
> To fynde a Church yard in a Church porch.
> Povertie and Poetrie, this Tombe doth enclose
> Therefore Gentlemen, be merry in Prose.[28]

However, Weever, in his massive collection of epitaphs, *Ancient Funeral Monuments* (1631), takes it in earnest and pedantically asserts in correction, 'in the Quire [of St Margaret's, Westminster], *Thomas Churchyard,* that old Court-Poet lieth interred, and not in the Church-Porch, as these rimes following would approve'.[29]

Pre-emptive epitaphs

A feigned epitaph need not wait for the actual death of its subject: composing such epitaphs on one's friends seems to have been a common exercise of wit in the literary circles at the Inns of Court. It might also be put to more public satiric purpose, as in these widely circulating lines from 1619 on Mary, Lady Lake, who did not die until 1642:

> Heere lyes the breife of badnes vices nurse
> The badge of Usurie the Clergies curse.
> The shame of weomen kind, tradsmens decay
> The patronesse of pride, Extortions high way
> The forge of slaunder, and each wild action
> ffrend to romes whore, Spy to the Spanish faction
> A bitch of court, a common slincking snake
> Worse then all these, Heere lyes the Ladie Lake.[30]

The subject is the wife of Sir Thomas Lake, secretary of state from 1616; she found herself at the centre of scandal in 1617 over her daughter's tempestuous marriage with William Cecil, Lord Ros (grandson of the Earl of Exeter), which led to Lady Lake and her daughter being charged with fraud and slander in Star Chamber. It seems likely that the epitaph emerges from that time, obviously penned by someone who sided with the family of Ros.[31] There is a religious dimension to the attack as well: Sir Thomas's suspected Catholicism and inclination to favour closer relations with Spain are reflected in 'ffrend to romes whore, Spy to the Spanish faction'. Like the epitaphs on Buckingham, this is a catalogue of the vices of its subject, only finally named in the concluding couplet, which also suggests that her name and reputation already surpass all the listed vicious roles.

Written about a living figure, a feigned epitaph may point to the legacy that the subject will leave on his or her actual death. William Fennor and Taylor, the Water-Poet, engaged in an ongoing poetic conflict through the mid-1610s; as part of this, Fennor feigned an epitaph on his enemy:

> Here lyes a Carkasse in this Grave,
> Who while he liv'd, would rayle and rave;
> Borrow his wit from others worth,
> And in his owne name set it forth:
> He row'de from Tyber to the Thames,
> And there his tongue himselfe proclaimes
> The luster of all Watermen,
> To row with Scull, or write with Pen.[32]

The poem continues, but after this point with a decreasing sense of being an epitaph; instead it simply becomes satire by another means.

Case study: 'Here lies Hobbinol': feigned epitaphs on Robert Cecil, Earl of Salisbury

Further manipulation of conventions can best be considered in a few specific examples written on the death of powerful figures in the period. When Robert Cecil, Earl of Salisbury, died in 1612, after two decades of ever-increasing political power, there was the usual immediate composition and publication of official elegies.[33] However, more remarkable was the mass of mock epitaphs and other forms of libellous abuse, which has been identified as the largest outpouring of libellous abuse up to that time.[34] Donne wrote, 'Nothing in my Lord Salisbury's death exercised my poor consideration so much as the multitude of libels';[35] Simond D'Ewes noted the 'infamous libels' that were written on him instead of funeral elegies;[36] and the Earl of Dorset wrote that Cecil was 'More ill-spoken of and in more several kinds, than I think ever anyone was'.[37] Such was the public expectation of libellous epitaphs that John Donne (playfully I believe) speculated that friends of Cecil had circulated 'tasteless and flat' poems to draw attention away from those more polished ones that 'would take deep root': 'For when the noise is risen that libels are abroad, men's curiosity must be served with something, and it is better for the honour of the person traduced that some blunt, downright railings be vented, of which everybody is soon weary, than other pieces which entertain us long with a delight and love to the things themselves.'[38] Regrettably, Donne gives no indication of which libels he had heard.

However, from surviving manuscript evidence, it would seem the most popular was that which in mock pastoral form treated Cecil as 'Hobbinoll':

> Heere lies Hobbinoll our Shepheard while ere
> Who once a yeere duely our fleeces did sheere,
> To please us his curre he chaynde to a clogg
> And was himselfe after both Shepheard and dogg
> For oblation to Pan his order was thus
> Himselfe gave a trifle and sacrifizde us
> And so with his wysedome this provident swayne
> Kept himselfe on the mountayne and us on the playne
> Where many a fine Hornepipe he tund'e to his Phillis
> And swetely sunge walsingham to Amarillis
> Till Atropos payde him, a pox on the drabbe
> In spight of the tarbox, he died of the scabbe.[39]

Like panegyric epitaphs, this sums up the life, only here one of greed and misuse of power; the conclusion's reflection upon the cause of death is also a common feature. Serious epitaphs frequently reflected upon the corpse that the grave contained, offering some variant on the concept that 'the bones lie here, the soul is in heaven'. In the mock epitaphs on Cecil this focus on the body is maintained, but not as a mere empty shell which has been surpassed. Instead, the body's corruption is presented as a marker of the corruption of Cecil's body *during* his life, it being widely bruited that he had died of the pox. Such is the case in both 'Heere lyes Hobbinol', and 'heere lyes enterred lyttle robyn ye woorthie',[40] a much rarer feigned epitaph on Cecil. This latter poem also includes a facetious portrayal of his soul's arrival not in Heaven but in Hell.

Case study: Hatton's tomb and the epitaph for Sidney and Walsingham

Only a short list of exceptional figures enjoyed widely circulating cele-bratory epitaphs: Sir Philip Sidney, Essex, Prince Henry and Ralegh. Many of these poems still have a satiric element, as they criticize those who survive, either for their neglect of the dead or for their failure to match his or her accomplishments. A variant of this is found in a widely known poem on the relative treatment after death afforded three major figures of the late Elizabethan court: Sir Christopher Hatton (d. 1591), Sir Francis Walsingham (d. 1590) and Sir Philip Sidney (d. 1586). From the 1560s to the 1580s Hatton had risen to prominence and great wealth through the personal favour of the Queen; he reached his zenith in the late 1580s as Lord Chancellor. Shortly after his death, his nephew Sir William (husband of the Lady Hatton discussed in the preceding chapter) had erected an ornate tomb in St Paul's Cathedral. It attracted much attention in the 1590s: in one of his epigrams Sir John Davies mocked 'Titus' as unsophisticated because 'Yet my lord Chauncellors tombe he hath not seene'.[41] Given its grandeur and Hatton's envied favour under Elizabeth, it is unsurprising that it became the object of mock epitaphs:

> Here lyes in gold, and not in brasse
>> at least a man and halfe.
> Who living was a silver asse
>> Now dead a golden calfe.[42]

In this slight epitaph, the ornate tomb has become an idol of worship. Similarly, in his widely circulated elegy on Thomas Ravis, Bishop of London (d. 1609), Corbett mocks how Hatton's tomb has been raised 'Above the host and altar' (36).[43]

In describing the tombs in St Paul's, John Stow's *Survey of London* notes the proximity of those of Sidney and Walsingham to Hatton's:

> Sir *Philip Sidney* above the Quire, on the North side the Quire, 1586. Sir *Francis Walsingham* knight, principall Secretarie, and chauncelor of the Duchie of *Lancaster* 1590. Sir *Christopher Hatton* Lord Chancelor of *England*, knight of the Garter, above the Quire, 1591 under a most sumptuous monument, whereof a mery Poet writ thus.

> *Philip* and *Francis* have no Tombe,
> For great *Christopher* takes all the roome.[44]

This couplet circulated widely and is connected with a more extended, and less explicit, epigram published in Bastard's *Chrestoleros*:

> Sir *Francis* and sir *Philip*, have no Toombe,
> Worthy of all the honour that may be.
> And yet they lye not so for want of roome,
> Or want of love in their posteritie.

> Who would from living hearts untombe such ones,
> To bury under a fewe marble stones?
> Vertue dyes not, her tombe we neede not raise,
> Let them trust tombs which have outliv'd their praise.[45]

The herald Augustine Vincent records both the two-line and eight-line version, and then a Latin translation.[46] Presumably out of caution, a later hand very carefully and completely crossed out the lemma.[47] However, the eight-line version in the Vincent manuscript maintains a line found in no other copy that makes the identity clear and drives home the point much more strongly than in the *Chrestoleros* version: 'Sr Christoper hath tomb ynough for three'.[48] The likely explanation is that the College of Arms copy preserves something close to Bastard's original, which, like much of his other poetry, presumably circulated in manuscript. As he moved towards publication in *Chrestoleros*, the general (and really quite weak) line, 'Worthy of all the honour that may be', was substituted to avoid trouble.

Bastard's poem adopts a rhetorical strategy that Scodel associates with the humanist tradition: the virtuous deceased need no lavish tomb, as their honour and fame have already been achieved through their deeds.[49] In this way, Hatton's tomb manifests an attempt to make up for deficiencies in his life, while Sidney and Walsingham are appropriately entombed in surviving loyal hearts and celebrated by this uninscribed poem, which is needed to explain the absence of a lavish monument. The poem is consistent with the pro-Essex stance of Bastard described in the preceding chapter, as Essex was widely seen as the inheritor of Sidney's mantle, both for his military role and his marriage to Frances, the widow of Sidney and daughter of Francis Walsingham. While this was a rare case where authorship was claimed in print, its two-line version enjoyed wide circulation but with no manuscript indicating Bastard's authorship. It seems most likely that this rougher four-beat version was derived from Bastard's original rather than the other way around.

Case study: 'Dallying with false surmise': epitaphs for the tombless

Bastard's poem on Hatton, Sidney and Walsingham reflected on the relative impressiveness of their three tombs; in other cases, the lack of any tomb whatsoever became the focus of epitaphic reflection. Thomas Washington, a page to Prince Charles, died during the much-maligned

1623 voyage to Spain to promote the Spanish Match: he was apparently denied a tomb there, which provided an opportunity for comment on the politics of the moment in the form of a widely circulated elegy. In many manuscripts it concludes with an imagined epitaph, beginning 'Knew'st thou whose these ashes were'.[50] The epitaph opens with a familiar trope from elegies on those who die young: they were ripe in maturity or virtue, but not in years. However, it takes an abrupt political turn in the fourth couplet while engaged in the conventional consideration of the cause of death: 'Inquire not his disease, or payne: / He dyed of nothing but of Spayne.'[51] The death is supernatural in that it is caused by political circumstances rather than any illness. The lines following offer another role for this epitaph: it circulates and acknowledges Washington's death in a way that no literal epitaph is allowed to do.

> Where hee is not allow'd to have
> (Unlesse by stealth) a quiet grave
> Hee needs no Epitaph, nor stone
> But this: Here lyes lord Washington.

Here the content of a potential epitaph is less important than there be at least *some* epitaph, however brief. The political circumstances of Charles and Buckingham's situation in Spain had led to an Englishman of good birth being denied the bare essentials of a tomb and simple epitaph marker. The poem then offers an imagined one in its place, written with tears upon the dust of Washington's own body, which will be reinscribed by those of subsequent mourners. Those readers would be mourning the general folly of the Spanish Match, as well as the death of the young Washington.

John Felton, the killer of Buckingham in 1628, is another whose unburied body was commemorated in a variant of the conventional epitaph. That his executed corpse was left hanging in chains as a warning to other political assassins provided the central conceit for this poetically successful and widely circulating epitaph:

> heere uninterr'd suspends (though not to save
> Surviving frends th'expenses of A grave)
> Feltons dead earth which to the world must bee
> Its owne sadd monument, his Elegie
> As large as Fame, but whether badd or good
> I say not; by him selfe 'twas writt in blood:
> ffor with his bodie is intomb'd in ayre

Arch't ore with Heaven, sett with A thousand faire
And glorious Diamond starres. A Sepulchre
that Tyme cann never Ruinate, and where
Th'impartiall worme (which is not brib'd to spare
Princes corrupt in Marble) cannot share
his Flesh, which oft the Charitable skyes
Embalme with teares: doeing those obsequies
Belonge to men shall rest, till pittying fowle
Contend to beare his Bodie to his Soule.[52]

This is among the more clever of parodic epitaphs, and it has recently attracted a great deal of scholarly attention, with most finding in it an articulation of political opposition, or even incipient republicanism, that fits a post-revisionist historiography of the period.[53] My concern is more with its poetics and playful status as an epitaph for one who has no tomb to mark. Its opening overthrows the convention of 'here lies' with its 'heere uninterr'd suspends', and it highlights the irony of Felton's 'earth' not fulfilling the usual returning of the dust of the human body to the dust of the earth. The norms of the natural elements have been turned upside-down, with the 'earth' suspended in the air.

The poet refrains from identifying this as either a 'good' or 'bad' elegy – that is, a panegyric or feigned epitaph – but he directs the reader to the 'elegy' that Felton wrote for himself: the slaying of Buckingham. This pointing to an act or accomplishment on the part of the deceased as the ultimate epitaph is itself a conventional rhetorical step in the epitaph tradition.[54] Here the gesture enables the poet to evade ultimate responsibility for his affirmation of the act: it speaks for itself. The lines that follow recreate a funerary scene, but the usual marble and candles are replaced by the natural elements, thus becoming a divine affirmation of Felton's act. This 'sepulchre', unlike marble and 'gilded monuments', will be eternal, achieving that which many epitaphs strove to establish for their subjects. The final reality of vermiculation, suffered even by 'Princes corrupt in marble' (a warning to King Charles?) is also avoided by this 'heavenly burial'. David Norbrook argues that this echoes the famous passage in Lucan on the sky as the ultimate covering for the unburied: 'caelo tegitur, qui non habet urnam',[55] and that the allusion to Lucan is significant in directing attention towards King Charles himself, rather than Felton or Buckingham. The King is no longer simply an innocent figure misled by a bad favourite.[56] Ultimately, the poem, like that on Washington, offers a compensation for the tombless who will receive no inscribed epitaph.

The poem's words likewise float in the air, unengraved, unpublished, passed by word of mouth and manuscript, a fitting marker of the unburied Felton, who was left to hang in chains.[57]

Reactions against satiric epitaphs

In Chapter 4 we saw how hostile epitaphs on Palavicino were countered by poets more sympathetic to him; the same dynamic is found with more prominent public figures like Cecil or Buckingham. However maligned they might be, there were always some supporters who would step forward to offer a response to the abuse of feigned epitaphs. The section above noted Donne's dismay at such treatment of the dead, and a similar observation was made by Richard Johnson in his commemoration of Cecil's death. Rather than appropriate memorials, he finds that poetry 'carelessly gives way to envy (that canker-worme to greatnesse) to eate out all remembrance of mortallitie'.[58] However, in some cases the response to satiric epitaphs took the form of *counter*-epitaphs. In Cecil's defence, William Herbert, Earl of Pembroke, wrote an epitaph that survives in a number of manuscripts. It draws on standard features of the epitaph tradition, beginning with its direct (if awkward) addressing of those who pass by the tomb: 'You that reade passing by / Robert, Earle of Salisburye', and concludes with the common consolation that, while the grave holds his corpse, Heaven has his soul. Here, however, Pembroke adds a detail to the usual rhetoric: 'Heaven *and friends* preserve the rest' (my italics). This points to the role of Pembroke in defending Cecil against the 'dogs' that had 'snarled' after his death.[59] In such exchanges survivors struggle to control the legacy of the deceased. No single poem might triumph by being physically inscribed on the tomb, but they vied to be pre-eminent in circulation and memory: to become known as *the* epitaph.

While vastly outnumbered by the feigned epitaphs that triumphed over Buckingham's death, there were some that poetically responded to them. Most noteworthy is the extended poem 'Thalassiarchiae Manium Vindiciae' [The Claims of the Shade of the Admiral], which turns against those who have defamed the dead Buckingham. Like Pembroke's defence of Cecil, it presents the poetic attackers as 'snarling' figures, whose response is based upon the distorted tendency of the satirist to disparagement:

Yee snarling Satyrs, cease your horrid yells
O're this sad hearse, all such prodigious knells

> Be hush't, and tongue-ty'd; but yet if your rymes
> For issue itche, goe lash the petulant tymes
> With whipps in salt, and sulphur steep'd the need
> A scorge to urge them either blush, or bleed.[60]

This is similar to Brathwaite's objection, discussed above, that feigned epitaphs were 'forged out of the braine of unseasoned Satyrists'. Their poetic work is also ridiculed by pointing to its down-market circulation: they

> Shall pace the suburbes with aspurgal'd newes
> And sprinckle Pasquills in the Burse, or Stewes
> Alas! those gloewormes, elfe-fire flashes shall
> But like faint sparkles, on danke tinder fall.

Once again, the widespread dissemination among the lower classes surfaces as a potential basis of dismissal, and the suggestion is that the brief flame of their popularity will not translate into any lasting significance. Their 'producer', because 'he never showes / The spurious issues Parent', will be forgotten. 'Thalassiarchiae Manium Vindiciae' assumes that authorial recognition is the motive for poetic composition, but, with these verses on Buckingham and Felton, anonymity was essential to avoid prosecution. For another pro-Felton poem, 'Enjoy thy bondage', Ben Jonson was questioned, and ultimately Zouch Towneley, the likely author, fled England under the threat of Star Chamber charges. Ironically, given the poem's emphasis on authorial fame, the two copies of 'Thalassiarchiae Manium Vindiciae' survive in manuscript with no identified author.

Similarly, Felton's epitaph discussed above, 'heere uninterr'd suspends (though not to save …)', was closely responded to in a parody:

> Here uninterd suspends, (doubtles to save
> hopefull, and freindles, th'expences of a grave)
> Feltons curst corps, which to the world must bee
> I'ts owne fowle Monument his Elegie
> wider then fame, which whether badd or good
> Judge by himself, bee-smear'd in faultles blood,
> For which his bodie is intombd i'th Aire
> Shrowded in Clowds, blacke as his Sepulchere
> Yet time is pleas'd; and thine partiall worme
> Unbribd to Spare, this wretches wretched Urne

His fleshe which ever memorable Skyes
Enbalme, to teache us and Posterities
T'abhorre his fact: shall last till Harpies fowle
through Stix shall dragge, his Carkas to his sowle.[61]

Like some of the responsive epigrams discussed in Chapter 9, this one
borrows much of the language of the original, including the majority of
the rhyme words. The 'dead earth' of Felton becomes a 'curst corpse', and
the 'monument' of his hanging in chains is a 'fowle' rather than 'sad' one.
Most significantly, the upward motion of the original's conclusion, where
the body of Felton is borne by the birds to join his soul in Heaven, is here
replaced with Harpies tearing his 'Carkas' to join his soul in Hell.

Finally, Robert Gomersall confronted the 'detractors' of John Deane of
New College upon his death:

Deane, (then [*sic*] which no other name
Is of better, of more Fame)
Sleepe in quiet: if there be
Tongues of that Malignity,
That will dare to wound thy grave
And not suffer thee to have
Slumber here, Ile say no more;
May they when they have plai'd ore
All their scenes of life, but know
The same Rigor, that they shew
That 'tis not generous, nor scarcely safe
To make a Libell, for an Epitaph.[62]

The very defenceless condition of the dead has implications for the com-
posers of feigned epitaphs: all must die and, hence, the maligners of
Deane may one day face the same treatment: to be given 'a Libell, for an
Epitaph'.

Case study: Owen's tomb

The death of the epigrammatist John Owen prompted a host of self-
conscious epitaphs and epigrams – of both the sincere and the feigned
sort. In late 1622 Chamberlain records that 'Little Owen, the maker of epigrams, died not long since of a cold, and was buried in Paul's; whereupon
divers poets, his countrymen, have made epitaphs in his commendation'.[63]

Laudatory epitaphs on him ripple through collections of the 1620s and 1630s, frequently making connections among Owen's small stature, the brevity of the poetic form for which he was known and the subsequent brevity of the poems celebrating him.[64] The most noted epitaph was that which was 'ingraven in a plate of Brasse, and fixed under his monumentall Image, formed and erected by the most exquisite Artist, M. *Epiphanius Evesham*'.[65] This epitaph was by a notable figure: John Williams, Bishop of Lincoln and Lord Keeper, patron to Owen for a number of years; he also paid for the much derided monumental effigy.[66]

> Parva tibi Statua est quia parva statura supellex,
> Parva volat parvas magna per ora liber:
> Sed non parvus honos non parva est gloria quippe
> Ingenio haud quicquam est maius in orbe tuo.
> Parva domus texit Templum sed grande poetae
> Tum vere vitam quum moritura agunt.[67]

> [Small was thy state and stature, which doe claime
> Small statue, through great lands thy small Booke flies,
> But small thine honour is not, nor thy fame,
> For greater wit then thine the world denies:
> Whom a small house, a great Church shelter gives,
> A Poet when he dies then truly lives.][68]

That the tomb and epitaph were established by one of the most powerful churchmen and statesmen of the time points to Owen's cultural stature.[69] An epigram directly echoing Williams survives in the manuscript collection of John Russell. It takes the tomb as a place of veneration:

> Te quoties, sortemq*ue* tuam contemplor Owene,
> Qui faelix volitas docta per ora virum:
> AEmula conflagrant et viscera, cordaq*ue* flammis:
> Aut tibi par, similis vel tibi Owene forem.
> Quae si non potui; magnis sic exridit ausis,
> Efflebunt tumuli marmora nigra mei.

> [Owen, how often I contemplate your Fate, you who happily fly through the learned mouths of men: and their envious hearts and bowels burn in flames, either to be your equal, or similar to you, Owen. Who, if I were not able, so he would laugh at these great attempts, the black marble of my tombs would weep.][70]

However, in the year following his death, Owen's tomb, like that of Hatton, became a flashpoint for a very different sort of verse, as feigned epitaphs challenged both Owen and his patron Williams:

> The poet Owens monument in Powles begins to serve for a Pasquin to any merrie or malicious companion that fasten daylie some odde rime or other foolish paper upon yt, and yt is doubted there wilbe some further disgrace don yt in time, for yt is much maligned as an honor far beyond the mans merit; among many other bald rimes I send you here one that was thought to be the cause that the Lord Kepers name was blotted out the last weeke from under an epitaph *Parva tibi statua est* which you had from me almost a yeare since.[71]

A few weeks later, Chamberlain wrote again to pass along another poem mocking Owen: 'The verses upon Owen paint out his blacke brasen face somwhat handsomly, and the elegie upon Washingtons death is not behind hand with Spaine.'[72]

At least some of these Pasquils or satiric epitaphs posted on Owen's tomb survive in manuscript collections.[73] One is found in Rosenbach MS 187, with the lemma 'Uppon poor Poet Owen whose effigies & Epitaph was set up in Paules wth verses by ye By:[74] of Lincoln, & Lord keep of &c':

> Heer have I many tymes lost my dinner
> walking by this bawdy court like such a sinner
> but out of this pillar now I am a peeper
> & my Epitaph was made by ye Divine Lo: Keeper.[75]

This seems to find its irony in the contrast between Owen as a walker of St Paul's, and the inappropriately dignified position of his tomb. The compiler of the manuscript notes that 'ye Lo: Keeper heer upon caused his verses to be defaced.' Whatever blotting (if any) took place was obviously not permanent, as both Henry Holland and William Dugdale recorded the epitaph in their later descriptions of the cathedral.

Another Pasquil on Owen is a much longer Latin poem by Alexander Gill the younger, entitled 'In dissimilimam Oweno Owen statuam. In aede D: Pauli London' [On the statue of Owen, most unlike Owen, in St Paul's Cathedral, London].[76] Gill was a notable figure of the 1620s and 1630s, a friend of Milton who clashed publicly with Jonson and who was imprisoned in the late 1620s for his enthusiastic response to Felton's assassination of Buckingham. He published a set of Latin epigrams in *Parerga* (1632), but this poem was not included. The epitaph takes the effigy of Owen as its starting point, finding it incongruously large and dark: 'Territat infantes facies monstrosa' [The hideous face frightens the children]. It is mocked for being like the famed brazen head of Friar Bacon. Then, in a way typical of the genre, it attempts to find a witty and appropriate explanation for this incongruity:

> An quod eras nigrae (vir iucundissime) famae
> Est facies fama concolor erga tuae?

> [Or (most happy man) because you are of black fame is your face of the same colour as your fame?]

This is just one of a number of 'explanations'. Overall, the poem mocks the inappropriateness of the effigy without directly maligning either Owen himself or Williams as his patron. Instead, near the end its satire is redirected towards others hostile to Owen: Jonson and Abraham Holland, as the poet imagines their faces enshrined with Owen's in St Paul's:

> Quid si hinc Hollandus? quid si Johnsonius illinc
> Ponatur, lauro cinctus uter*que* satis.
> O quantus[77] risus, populo spectante, moveret
> Doctorum capitum tam bene iuncta trias?
> Tres vates, tres Caenipetae, tres ingeniosi
> Sunt vultu, cultu, more, lepore, gula:

> [What if Holland is placed here, or Jonson placed there, and either fairly bound with a laurel?
> O how much laughter is brought about with the people watching, so well joined are the three learned heads.
> Three poet-prophets, three filth-seekers, three ingenious faces, with refinement, fashion, wit and a gluttonous appetite.]

Gill's suggestion is that *in life* Holland and Jonson have faces as swarthy and hideous as that of Owen's sculpture.[78] His maligning of Jonson is consistent with their later conflicts and he may be ridiculing Jonson here as well by an unwelcome association of him with Owen. In his *Conversations with Drummond* Jonson derided Owen as 'a poor pedantic schoolmaster, sweeping his living from the posteriors of little children, and hath nothing good in him, his epigrams being bare narrations'.[79] As Jonson and Owen were the most renowned of English and Latin epigrammatists at the time, some rivalry is understandable, and Gill is pulling both them and Holland down a notch: while they aspire to be 'vates' [poet-prophets], as epigrammatists they are 'Caenipetae' [filth-seekers].

Abraham Holland, a minor poet who died in 1626, figures in Gill's poem because he had been accused of posting one of the feigned epitaphs on Owen's tomb. In a poem published in 1626 Holland defends himself against those who 'did falsely accuse him, to the late Lord Keeper, of a Libell against John Owens Monument in Pauls'.[80] In this aggressive defence he denies that he could have posted such verses, as he was in Coventry (where he too was a schoolmaster) at the time:

> strange that I
> Should stretch a Line from *Coventry*
> And make it reach to *Pauls*, and place
> It under OWENS *brazen face.*

He suggests that he who has 'fathered' the verses upon him was in fact the culprit, and the references point clearly to Taylor, the Water-Poet.

What we have, then, is a complicated scenario involving an epitaph and responding mock epitaphs that illustrate some of the dynamics of epigrammatic satire. Clearly, Owen's contemporaries saw his tomb as an appropriate venue for Pasquils, and this illustrates physically the merging or overlapping of the culture of the popular Pasquil and the more elite Martialian epigram. Evidently, there was some desire to pull Owen down a level, but at least in this case the deceased is not the chief object of the mock epitaph's satire, which is reserved for Bishop Williams, whose attempt to commemorate the poet lavishly has prompted the reaction. Chamberlain's letter implies some incongruity in a bishop and Lord Keeper penning lines on a mere poet and schoolmaster: it is 'an honor far beyond the mans merit'. (There is some suggestion from dedications by Robert Aylett to Williams that the bishop did maintain an interest in poetry during these years.)[81] In the same year, Donne was criticized by some for penning lines on the death of the far more illustrious Marquess of Hamilton.

It is possible that the merry attacks on Owen's tomb and Williams's epitaph mask hostility toward the Lord Keeper for other, more political, reasons. Opposition to Williams's support of the King's policy of peace towards Spain was very strong, and the December 1623 reference by Chamberlain is followed immediately by one to the widely circulating elegy and epitaph on Washington discussed above. For some, there may have been inescapable irony in that a faithful Englishman was denied a tomb by the Spanish, while an epigram-writing schoolmaster was so celebrated by the Lord Keeper.

Notes

1 Robert Greene, *A Maidens Dreame* in *Plays & Poems*, ed. J. C. Collins, 2 vols (Oxford: Clarendon Press, 1905), vol. 2, p. 232.

2 Johnson, *Scholar's Guide*, p. 39. In an earlier article from which this chapter grew I used the term 'parodic epitaph', but I now prefer the term that originates from close to the period itself ('"A Libell, for an Epitaph": The Parodic Epitaph in the Early Stuart Period', *Appositions: Studies in Renaissance/ Early Modern Literature & Culture*, 1 (2008) (http://appositions.blogspot. com/2008/05/james-doelman-parodic-epitaph.html)). Richard Brathwaite, in his large collection *Remains after Death* (1619), calls them 'prophane epitaphs' (sig. E4r), and Taylor the Water-Poet playfully refers to them as 'epiknaves' (*I Marry Sir, heere is newes indeed* [1623?] (1642), p. 5).

3 Alistair Bellany, 'A Poem on the Archbishop's Hearse: Puritanism, Libel and Sedition after the Hampton Court Conference', *Journal of British Studies*, 34 (1995), pp. 137–64; Pauline Croft, 'The Reputation of Robert Cecil: Libels, Political Opinion and Popular Awareness in the Early Seventeenth Century', *Transactions of the Royal Historical Society*, sixth series, 1 (1991), pp. 43–69.

4 See Laurie Nussdorfer, *Civic Politics in the Rome of Urban VIII* (Princeton, NJ: Princeton University Press, 1992), pp. 245–51.

5 David Rijser, 'The Practical Function of High Renaissance Epigrams: The Case of Raphael's Grave', in Susanna De Beer, Karl A. E. Enenkel and David Rijser (eds), *The Neo-Latin Epigram: A Learned and Witty Genre* (Leuven: Leuven University Press, 2009), pp. 103–36, p. 112.

6 Bellany, 'A Poem on the Archbishop's Hearse', pp. 137–64.

7 Margaret A. Rose, *Parody: Ancient, Modern and Post-Modern* (Cambridge: Cambridge University Press, 1993), p. 45.

8 Puttenham, *The Art of English Poesy*, p. 144. Puttenham goes on to complain of an overly long epitaph that caused him to be locked in a cathedral.

9 Osborne, *Works*, p. 537.

10 Thomas Pestell, *The Poems*, ed. Hannah Buchan (Oxford: Blackwell, 1940), p. 51. Presumably the figure addressed is Richard Bailey, who became Dean of Salisbury in 1635, and to whom Pestell directed a number of other poems.

11 This is an argument widespread in the satiric tradition: that a satiric attack on an individual was not likely to change that figure's behaviour, but might improve others' out of fear of a similar public ridiculing.

12 Thomas Dekker, *The Seaven Deadly Sinnes of London* (1606), p. 8.

13 Osborne, *Works* (1673), p. 514.

14 Richard Brathwaite, 'Remains after Death' in *The Good Wife: or, A rare one amongst women* (1618), sig. E4r–v.

15 Brathwaite, 'Remains after Death', sig. E5v.

16 Brathwaite, 'Remains after Death', sig. E5v.

17 Brathwaite derives his copy from Camden, who attributes it to Hoskins.

18 Bodl. Ashmole MS 38, p. 204. This also appears in BL. Harl. MS 6917, fol. 82r.

19 'Another on the same man [Weymarke]', Bodl. Ashmole MS 38, p. 205.

20 Thomas Jordan, 'An epitaph supposed to be written by a gentleman on himself, who died of a disease, called by the name of a bad wife', *A nursery of novelties* (1663), p. 72.

21 McRae, *Literature, Satire, and the Early Stuart State*, p. 47.

22 [Anon.,] *The life and death of Queene Elizabeth* (1639), sig. C7r. The poem is found in many other manuscript and print sources from the period; in a few it is attributed to Joshua Sylvester. The same rhetorical technique is used in the epitaph on the Earl of Essex beginning, 'heere lyes great Essex deerelinge of mankinde' Cambridge Add. MS 57, fol. 87r.

23 Bodl. Malone MS 23, p. 143.

24 'An Ep: one a man for doyinge nothinge', Osborn, *The Life, Letters, and Writings of John Hoskyns*, p. 171.

25 Osborne, *Works*, pp. 536–7; Osborne wryly notes that he was 'called to answer at a higher Tribunal'. Variant copies are found in Bodl. Don. MS d.58, fol. 18r; Hunt. MS 116, p. 25; BL Add. MS 10309, fol. 153r; Redding, *Robert Bishop's Commonplace Book*, p. 114; Bodl. Ashmole MS 781, fol. 136r; Folger MS V.a.345, p. 33; Folger MS V.a.262, p. 154.

26 North, 'Anonymity in Early Modern Manuscript Culture', p. 22.

27 BL Add. MS. 37719, fol. 208v.

28 John Weever, *Ancient Funerall Monuments* (1631), p. 497.

29 *Ancient Funerall Monuments* (1631), p. 497.

30 Bodl. Malone MS 23, pp. 5–6. It also appears in Folger MS V.a.345, p. 260; Camb. Add. MS 9221, fol. 109v; Camb. Add. MS 4138, fol. 47v. Redding, *Robert Bishop's Commonplace Book*, p. 99; Huntington MS 116, p. 174 (in the latter two the figure is identified as 'Lady Wake').

31 A fuller account of the scandal can be found at *Early Stuart Libels* (www.earlystuartlibels.net/htdocs/lake_roos_section/J0.html).

32 William Fennor, *Fennors defence: or, I am your first man* (1615), sig. B5r.

33 Cecil was buried relatively quietly in St Etheldreda's Church, Hatfield; the fine tomb by Maximilian Colt still survives, but I have not yet been able to

learn what epitaph (if any) is upon it. See Erna Auerbach and C. Kingsley Adams, *Paintings and Sculpture at Hatfield House* (London: Constable, 1971), pp. 111–12.

34 Bellany, *The Politics of Court Scandal*, p. 100.

35 John Donne, *Life and Letters*, ed. Edmund Gosse, 2 vols (Gloucester, MA: Peter Smith, 1959), vol. 1, p. 312).

36 Simond d'Ewes, *Autobiography*, vol. 1, p. 51.

37 BL Stowe MS 172/319, 22 June 1612, qtd in Algernon Cecil, *A Life of Robert Cecil, First Earl of Salisbury* (Westport, CT: Greenwood, 1915), p. 343.

38 Donne, *Life and Letters*, vol. 1, p. 313.

39 *Early Stuart Libels* reproduces BL Egerton MS 2230, fol. 34r, and offers a list of many of the places where this poem is found. McRae, *Literature, Satire, and the Early Stuart State*, p. 36, sees it as a successful poetic work.

40 Camb. Add. MS 57, fol. 95r.

41 'In Titum', Davies, *Poems*, ed. Krueger, Ep. 6.

42 Camb. Add. MS 4138, fol. 47v. It is also in Bodl. Firth MS d.7, fol. 154.

43 'An Elegie written upon the death of Dr. Ravis Bishop of London', *Poems*, ed. Bennett and Trevor-Roper, p. 4.

44 Stow, *A Survey of London*, p. 263. Henry Holland, in his *Monumenta Sepulchraria Sancti Pauli* (1614), notes Stow's quoting of the lines and surmises, 'no doubt but the merry Poet was the merry old man Stow himselfe' (sig. C4r).

45 Bastard, *Chrestoleros*, 4:31.

46 College of Arms MS 218, p. 249.

47 A similar suppression is found in a copy of the two-line version in Camb. Add. MS 9221, fol. 99r, where the second line reads: 'for great xxair [*sic*] hath all the roome'.

48 College of Arms MS 218, p. 249.

49 Scodel, *The English Poetic Epitaph*, pp. 17–49.

50 Bodl. Eng. poet. MS e.14, fol. 91v–2v. See James Doelman, 'Claimed by Two Religions: The Elegy on Thomas Washington, 1623, and Middleton's *A Game at Chesse*', *Studies in Philology*, 110 (2013), pp. 318–49.

51 Folger MS V.a.262. It also appears in Huntington MS 198, vol. 1, p. 22; BL. Add. MS 25303, fol. 136r; Folger MS V.a.345, p. 102; BL Add. MS 15227, fol. 10v; Bodl. Rawl. poet. MS 26, fol. 76v; Howard H. Thompson, 'An Edition of Two Seventeenth-Century Manuscript Poetical Miscellanies (Rosenbach MSS 188 and 191)', PhD, University of Pennsylvania, 1959, p. 192.

52 Bodl. Malone MS 23, fol. 210v. Manifold manuscript copies of the poem survive; see the version and accompanying discussion in *Early Stuart Libels*.

The final couplet is problematic; I have chosen the Malone version as it shows the work of the copyist in attempting to make sense of the lines. In that manuscript, they are originally written, 'Belonge to men shall last, and pittying fowle / Contend to beare his Bodie to his Soule', which is commonly found in other manuscripts, but it has then been amended as it reads above. For discussion of the potential authorship of the poem, see James Holstun, *Ehud's Dagger: Class Struggle in the English Revolution* (London: Verso, 2000), p. 184.

53 A thorough and perceptive reading of the poem is offered in Holstun, *Ehud's Dagger*, pp. 184–6, but it is treated more as an elegy than a parodic epitaph on a non-existent tomb. See also McRae, *Literature, Satire, and the Early Stuart State*, p. 72; Thomas Cogswell, 'John Felton, Popular Political Culture and the Assassination of the Duke of Buckingham', *Historical Journal*, 49 (2006), pp. 357–85; and Alastair Bellany, '"The Brightnes of the Noble Lieutenants Action": An Intellectual Ponders Buckingham's Assassination', *English Historical Review*, 118 (2003), pp. 1242–63.

54 Famous examples would include that on Christopher Wren in St Paul's, 'Lector, Si Monumentum Requiris Circumspice', and Milton's epitaph on Shakespeare. The conceit goes back to Cato, who would have no shrine or monument 'supposing his vertues to be sufficient annals and records to eternise his name' (Brathwaite, *Remains after Death*, sig. D1r).

55 David Norbrook, *Writing the English Republic: Poetry, Rhetoric, and Politics, 1627–1660* (Cambridge: Cambridge University Press, 1999), p. 55.

56 Norbrook, *Writing the English Republic*, pp. 35–6.

57 *DNB*.

58 *A remembrance of the honors due to the life and death of Robert Earle of Salisbury* (1612), sig. A2r.

59 *Dr. Farmer Chetham Manuscript*, p. 188.

60 *Early Stuart Libels*, Piii6. Their text is based upon Bodl. Malone MS 23, pp. 128–30.

61 *Early Stuart Libels*, Pii16. Their text is based upon BL Add. MS 15226, fol. 28.

62 Robert Gomersall, 'To his [Mr John Deane of New College] Detractors', *Poems* (1633), p. 9.

63 Chamberlain to Carleton, 21 Dec. 1622, *Letters*, vol. 2, p. 469.

64 See, for example, John Russell, Ep. 1:93, 'In Joannem Owen epigrammaticum': 'Es brevitatis amans Owen argute poeta: / Laudarem te, sed sum brevitatis amans' (BL Add. MS 73542, fol. 12v).

65 Penkethman, *The epigrams of P. Virgilius Maro*, sig. D3v.

66 Ambrose Philips, *The life of John Williams* (1700), pp. 256–7.

67 Henry Holland, *Monumenta sepulchraria Sancti Pauli* (1633), sig. G2r.

William Dugdale, *History of St. Pauls Cathedral* (1658), p. 55, also reproduces the epitaph, with this location description: 'Adhuc in navi Ecclesiae, Super columnam, gradibus Consistorii proximam, occidentem versus' [A verse still in the nave of the church, on the western column near the consistory steps]. See also Ian Laurenson, 'A Pasquinade for John Owen', *Notes and Queries*, 26 (1979), pp. 403–5.

68 Penkethman, *The epigrams of P. Virgilius Maro*, sig. D3v.

69 It is also possible that common roots or family connections contributed to Williams's support of Owen. They both came from Caernarvonshire, but I have been unable to discover any closer link. Chamberlain's comment that 'his countrymen' were responsible for the poems celebrating him suggests that his Welsh origins were an element in the epitaphic struggle over his memory.

70 John Russell, 'De Joanne Owen Cambrobritanno epigrammatico celeber-rimo', BL Add. MS 73542, fol. 15v.

71 Chamberlain to Carleton, 25 Oct. 16[2]3, *Letters*, vol. 1, p. 518. (The letter is misdated as 1613 in McClure.)

72 Chamberlain to Carleton, 6 Dec. 1623, *Letters*, vol. 2, p. 532.

73 In addition to those discussed here, see also Sir John Roe's 'Viator, hic situs est' and Hoskins's response to Roe, both found in BL Harl. MS 3910, fol. 57r.

74 [*Sic*] for 'Bp. [Bishop]'.

75 Sanderson, *An Edition of an Early Seventeenth-Century Manuscript Collection of Poems (Rosenbach MS. 186)*, p. 198. In the margin adjacent to the poem are Williams's original verses.

76 Huntington MS 172, fol. 3v–4r; and Bodl. Rawl. poet. MS 62, fol. 24r. Only the latter identifies Gill as the poet.

77 Bodl. Rawl. poet. MS 62: quantos.

78 I have identified the Holland of the poem as Abraham on the basis of his involvement in the controversy over the tomb; however, Hugh Holland, another minor poet who moved in the circles of Donne and Jonson, is also a candidate: he mocked his own dark face in *Pancharis* (1603).

79 Jonson, *Conversations with Drummond*, 166–7.

80 'Holland his Hornet To sting a Varlet', *Hollandi post-huma* (1626), sig. G2r.

81 Similarly, Philips, *The life of John Williams*, p. 216, notes that the bishop 'diverted himself when alone sometimes with writing Latin Poems' while imprisoned.

12

The religious epigram

Religious epigrams were a significant sub-genre across Renaissance Europe, one marked by two quite different streams: the epigram of religious devotion and that of religious controversy. Neo-Latin, French and German religious epigrams were widespread, with a tradition going back well into the sixteenth century.[1] This is considerably earlier than English-language attempts at the genre, which reached their high-water mark in the early to mid-1630s.[2] The cultivation of this sub-genre at that time stems from both direct imitation of the continental religious tradition and the adaptation of the secular English tradition by Harington, Jonson and Owen in the early part of the century. Also clear is that religious epigrams in England were very much a manifestation of the university culture of Oxford and Cambridge: they were most often written and collected by students and scholars, and published by university printers.

The expurgated versions of Martial (described in Chapter 1) helped to edify the form, making possible the original religious epigrams of the period. But Richard Crashaw, the most significant English poet of the sub-genre, also laments at length that the 'seed of Idumaea' had grown in the soil of Bilbil, the Spanish home of Martial.[3] He is wishing, vehemently, that Martial had been a Christian poet. While the goal of Crashaw and others was to sanctify and reclaim the genre, to achieve a Christian parody of it, often the result feels closer to burlesque. While Ruth C. Wallerstein writes, 'To characterize them [Crashaw's epigrams] in a word, they translate the Bible into Ovid',[4] I would suggest that he translates the Bible into Martial, if anything. The epigram as a form does not have the breadth for the lavish descriptions of Ovid, and the witty point is paramount for Crashaw as with all others who follow Martial.

A number of early seventeenth-century epigrammatists directly mark their reorientation of the form in programme poems, using the language of repentance and conversion as they adopt religious subject matter. Thus, John Saltmarsh in a prefatory poem to his *Poetices libri septem* (1636) forsakes the Catullan practice of praising Lesbia's cheeks, eyes and hair, to fly with a more innocent feather ['Sed penna calamus iam candidore volavit'].[5] He will return to her as subject to compose an epitaph for her tomb, which ironically is a retrieval of the origins of the epigram tradition. This places Saltmarsh's epigrams in relation to the lyric stream of Catullus rather than the more detached and ironic stream of Martial. Crashaw pointedly rejects the tradition of *both* Catullus and Martial, commanding Cupid to leave him and find refuge in their poems.[6] Both Saltmarsh and Crashaw have adopted the typical explanation for abandoning the love lyric and applied it to the conversion of the epigram.

This conversion of the form to a religious purpose was similar to what Donne, Henry Lok and Barnabe Barnes did with the sonnet; Herbert with the lyric; and Tasso (and, later, Milton) with epic. However, such 'baptizing' was simpler with these other genres: love and glory might be redirected to their proper, divine, subject. But how could a genre associated principally with cynical and trivial mockery be adopted for divine purposes? While the typical focus of a secular epigram might be the grotesque nose of a fool, the religious epigram might seek to treat in limited space Christ's walking on the waters, or the healing effect of Peter's shadow. The reputation for scandalous subject matter dogged all users of the form in the period, and, as noted in earlier chapters, epigrammatists frequently apologize for and dismiss their own works.

In addition to its brevity, the epigram's reputation for scandal and its typical tone of urbane cynicism would also seem to render it unsuitable for a religious subject.[7] Martial's habitual tone is one of detached bemusement at a paradox or ironic situation, as found, for example, in Book 2:80, wherein a man kills himself in the process of fleeing death. The paradox of the situation is queried through a rhetorical question and juxtapostion: 'ne moriare, mori?' [to die to avoid death?].[8] Can such an attitude, such a habitual tone, be successfully translated for use in a sacred epigram, applied to a holy mystery to express committed awe rather than detached bemusement?[9] Henry Vaughan's 'Regeneration' famously ends with a paradoxical couplet on just that concept ('"Lord," then said I, "on me one breath, / And let me die before my death!"'), but that comes at the climax of eighty lines of spiritual searching. The challenge with the religious epigram proper is to achieve the same sense of religious paradox in just a few lines. Abrupt detached whimsy, when applied to divine subjects, can be unsettling, as in Crashaw's epigram on John the Baptist (John 1:23):

Vox *ego sum*, dicis: tu vox es, sancte Ioannes?
   Si *vox* es, genitor cur tibi *mutus* erat?
Ista tui fuerant quam mira silentia patris!
   Vocem non habuit tunc quoque cum genuit.

[*I am the voice*, you say: you are the voice, Saint John?
   If you are *the voice*, why was your father *silent*?
How strange that silence of your father was!
   He did not have a *voice* even then while he fathered [one].] [10]

Ultimately, in religious epigrams like this the ironic detachment of the traditional epigram remained, but shorn of its Martialian cynicism. Hence, they are very different in tone from devotional lyrics, and, even where the first person pronoun is used, there is no scope for development or spiritual struggle as one might find in Donne or Herbert.

The epigram's conventional dynamics of detachment could fit a religious purpose, but in a very different sort of verse than the intense lyric introspection and emotion of other devotional poems. Like the secular epigram the religious variety directs attention first of all to the object or incident under consideration. An epigram on St Peter's shadow maintains that as its subject, rather than becoming a poem about the poet/speaker's own situation. [11] And most sacred epigrams of the period do maintain a focus on a particular object or occasion: the nails of the crucifixion, not salvation in general or the response of the poet to the event. Perhaps, then, the sacred epigram functions primarily by fixing attention upon that which was most worthy. In their triviality epigrams point to that which is not trifling. The reader remembers Peter's shadow, but not the particulars of any of the epigrams written upon that subject. [12] The poets move towards erasure of the self, and there is little scope for hubris in the composition of epigrams, or for the conflicted state of mind found in many of Herbert's poems or Marvell's 'The Coronet'.

The varieties of epigram tones identified by Scaliger (see Chapter 1) were invoked by composers of religious epigrams, who most often associated their tone with saltiness. Abraham Wright in his preface to *Delitiae Delitiarum* suggests the poems are like 'sale theologico' [theological salt] needed for a proper sacrifice, [13] thus bringing together the classical and the biblical. He explicitly evokes the traditional use of salt in sacrifice (Lev. 2:13 and Ezek. 43:24), and finds precedent for salty speech in Colossians 4:6: 'Let your speech always be gracious, seasoned with salt.' Thus, a conventional dimension of the epigram drawn from the classical tradition proved consistent with certain Biblical imagery and acceptable for divine purposes. Francis Quarles, however, embraced a different tone, promising readers that his epigrams provide 'honey' (associated with the naive epigram by Scaliger): 'There are no *Waspes*; there are no *Hornets*'[14] – a seeming allusion to Goddard's satiric epigrams, *A Neste of Waspes*, published in 1615. He also notes, however, that his bees will sting if provoked.

In addition to these theoretical subdivisions of the genre, would-be epigrammatists could also invoke authoritative precedents and models as part of their defence. The *Greek Anthology* included Christian poems by early Church Fathers, which in the Palatine version were placed first, with the following motto: 'Let the pious and godly Christian epigrams take precedence, even if the pagans are displeased.'[15] However, this collection was rediscovered only in 1606 and not published *in toto* until the eighteenth century, so its significance for the epigrams of the period is probably limited to those poets who were part of the more elite scholarly and literary circles who saw manuscript copies of it. Also reflected in the *Greek Anthology* and the *Anthologia Latina* is the tradition of inscribing epigrams on church buildings. These 'tituli' may have developed in imitation of pre-Christian inscriptions on pagan temples.[16]

Eminent Church Fathers are among those whose religious epigrams survive. Prudentius's *Dittochaeon* consists of epigrammatic four-line verses on biblical figures and situations.[17] Paul the Silentiary has approximately a hundred epigrams in the *Anthology*, and those of St Gregory of Nazianzus, although fewer in number, seem to have been most influential. Thomas Drant's 1568 translation of his poetry, *Epigrams and sentences spirituall in vers*, provides some indication of the means by which this example became known: 'Perusing (right honorable) some of the Germaine wryters, and delighting in their pretie & wittie verses, which to the texts and common places of holy scriptures they fitly have applied: I found no sayinges in them of a more quicke and godly sence, then those whiche they bringe oute of *Gregorie Nazanzen*, a Doctour of the Greeke churche very wel learned, and very eloquent' (sig. A2r). The influence of the Greek Christian epigrammatists was thus mediated for Drant through German poets, which is symptomatic of the pan-European literary culture of epigrams. However, Drant is a very early example of this awareness in England.[18] These precedents became most important and influential in the scholarly circles of Cambridge and Oxford in the 1620s and 1630s after such scholars as Isaac Casaubon and Thomas Farnaby had furthered English familiarity with the *Anthology*. James Duport, a Cambridge scholar and poet, in an undatable poem from the mid-seventeenth cen-

tury, praised George Herbert by placing him within this tradition of
Gregory of Nazianzus, thus finding a continuity of devout poetic use of
the epigram form.[19]

In addition to these relatively scholarly and lofty defences, epigram collections frequently offer a more humble justification: that the poet could
be doing something worse with his time. John Heath writes of his 1610
volume of epigrams:

> I mought be better busied; I graunt so:
> Could I be better idle? surely no.
> Then hold your idle chat, for I professe,
> These are the fruits but of my idlenesse. (2:2)

Frequently, this justification was put forth in the terminology of *otium
theologicum* [religious leisure]. Thus, Crashaw asserts in a dedicatory
letter to his manuscript epigrams: 'Neque sane hoc scriptionis genere
... quid esse potuit otio Theologico accommodatius' [Nor clearly could
anything be more suitable for theological repose than this kind of writing]
(630–1). Saltmarsh refers to his epigrams as 'hoc otio nostro' (sig. ¶3v),
and Wright uses the term 'otium Theologium' as part of his defence (sig.
t3v).[20] This concept of *otium theologicum* is a very different idea from that
which lies behind most devotional poetry: it accepts the tendency of fallen
human nature to succumb to indolent leisure, and, given that, finds that a
sacred leisure is preferable. This is not a high and lofty defence of a central
Christian genre, but a humble acceptance of human limitations.

Brian Vickers has established beyond a doubt that the critical commonplace that *otium* was a positive classical and Renaissance term is badly mistaken.[21] In fact, *otium* was more commonly seen as the breeding ground
of a host of vices, and typically any positive use of the term depends upon
qualifying adjectives or nouns, such as Cicero's 'otium cum dignitate
[leisure with dignity]' or 'otium honestum [honest leisure]'.[22] The former
suggested leisure used for the public good; the latter an undesired exclu-
sion from public life (10). Similarly, Seneca – often presented by scholars
as an advocate of retirement – suggested that *otium* might be redeemed
only by using it for study: 'Otium sine litteris mors est [leisure without
books is death]' (34). *Otium* was certainly not something to be embraced in
itself. Likewise, within the Christian tradition *otium* provoked suspicion,
if not hostility. Both the early Church fathers (including St Jerome in the
Vulgate) and the medieval Church use it in largely negative contexts: as
otium could so often lead to vice, it was a sirenic threat.[23] Petrarch's *De*

Otio religioso builds upon Roman writers and Church Fathers to elaborate a heavily qualified *otium* that is only worthwhile if dedicated to virtue.[24] *Otium theologicum* functions in a similar way for Crashaw and Wright: if they are to wantonly spend their time in trifles, the dangers of doing so can at least be mitigated by making it a sacred *otium*. Still, there is something a bit shame-faced about the whole pastime; like the genre itself, there would seem to be some doubt whether *otium* could be Christianized.[25] Nevertheless, Christian epigrams were produced and defended as examples of theological leisure; that is, leisure turned to a worthier end, devotion relaxed from its usual high pitch, and an acceptance that intensity of study and devotion was not always possible. Such an approach might also justify the reading of them. A defence of epigrammatic brevity as more attuned to the limitations of the human attention span was posited in a commendatory poem to Saltmarsh's *Poemata Sacra*: 'Tam pietate doces, quam brevitate places' [You teach with piety, while you please with brevity].[26]

Compositional contexts

While published epigrams were often *defended* as the consolatory fruit of *otium*, it is clear that the original composition of religious epigrams in fact often stemmed from *negotium* (dutiful labour). They were composed as part of some regular, often daily, exercise – either a self-imposed exercise or one that was prescribed as part of educational or religious duties, as described in Chapter 3 in reference to Crashaw's sacred epigrams.

For other surviving English and Latin sacred epigrams, the compositional practice is less clear. W. Hilton Kelliher speculates that the twenty-one epigrams on the elements of the crucifixion in George Herbert's *Passio Discerpta* 'may have been composed as part of his Holy Week devotions' (35), but he offers no external evidence.[27] The largest collection of English religious epigrams, Quarles's *Divine Fancies*, first published in 1632, also provides some limited evidence of compositional practice.[28] The volume is a fairly unstructured compilation of what Quarles describes as 'Epigrammes, Meditations, and Observations', without clear distinction among these forms. At times, a general pattern of movement through the Bible is evident: in the early part of Book II, Quarles seems to be reading (and writing) his way through Judges and I Samuel, while in Book III he draws more heavily from the Gospels. However, these strings are broken by other unrelated poems. I suspect that Quarles composed some on the basis of daily readings, but other, more topical, compositions were added in response to developments in the Church, or in response to other writers. On a few occasions, Quarles works metaphoric variations upon a theme: thus, 'My Sinnes are like the hayres upon my head' (2:67) is followed a few poems later by 'My Sinnes are like the Sands upon the shore' (2:70), and then, again, after two intervening poems, 'My Sinnes are like the Starres, within the skyes' (2:73). While clearly linked, the separation of the three poems in this way mitigates the sense of them as a sequence, or even a three-stanza poem.[29]

Saltmarsh's *Poemata Sacra* (1636), a collection of Latin epigrams followed by English 'Meditations', roughly follows the sequence of the Bible. It begins with the Creation and the Fall and continues methodically through Genesis and Exodus. However, from that point the order breaks down, with poems based on random passages throughout the Old Testament, occasionally pointing forward to New Testament events in a typological fashion. Herrick's sacred epigrams, gathered in his 'Noble Numbers' at the end of *Hesperides* (1648), show some traces of compositional practice. A few epigrams seem to be based on particular biblical passages, but in the latter part of 'Noble Numbers', which consists almost wholly of epigrams, a significant number clearly arose from readings in the Church Fathers, indicated by such parenthetical phrases as 'says Cassiodore' or 'as S. Aug'stine saith'. Some are more general: 'as from the Learn'd I gather' or 'some say'; however, the editors of the recent Oxford edition of Herrick show that many of these were based upon his reading of John Gregory, *Notes and Observations upon Some Passages of Scripture* (1646).[30] Thus, it would seem that Herrick composed some of these epigrams in response to his theological studies, and, of course, many more might be of this nature without the indicating feature of a parenthetical identifier. In these same pages we also find epigrams that refer to Jewish customs and lore; these too may derive from readings in the Fathers, or may have been based on Herrick's own direct reading of Jewish material. The implication is that the epigrams were composed as an extension of his studies and devotional practice. While we can trace some compositional practice in these volumes, they seldom highlight any organization when printed. As discussed in Chapter 6, this disregarding of organization stems from the tradition of the epigram itself.

Religious epigrams: manuscripts and readership

Of the great many epigrams composed as educational or devotional exercises it seems likely that only a small percentage achieved any widespread circulation or publication. Those of Crashaw offer the most evidence in this regard. His epigrams, in fulfilling his scholarship requirements, were publicly displayed; they were to be 'set on ye skreene before dinner'.[31] This was not the end of their public life, however. A significant number of manuscripts of Crashaw's epigrams survive; some are clearly based on the printed edition (and show the popularity and continued influence of them later in the century), but others are probably pre-publication presentation copies. BL MS Add. 33219 'gives the impression of having been designed as a gift to a lady';[32] and the Tanner manuscript, which belonged to Archbishop Sancroft later in the century, is entitled 'Mr. Crashaw's poems transcribed from his own Copie, before they were printed; among which are some not printed'.[33] In some cases, such as Trinity College, Dublin, MS 659 (formerly F.4.28), Crashaw's poems share manuscript space with similar religious ones by other, usually unidentified, writers (39–68). These anonymous epigrams from the Trinity manuscript are like Crashaw's in being tightly focused on a passage from one of the Gospels, and it is plausible that they arose from the same exercises that produced Crashaw's.

In the final poem in his *Divine Fancies*, Quarles contemplates the potential circulation of his epigrams; they were dedicated to the infant Prince Charles, and, like his earlier biblical paraphrases, he hopes that they might eventually reach the court. While gesturing towards the patronage network, Quarles also concedes that the work may take its place in the market:

Perchance, thy Fortune's to be *bought and sold*;
Was not young *Joseph* serv'd the like of old? (4:117)

He hopes, however, that if they are bought and sold, like the Old Testament Joseph, these transactions might prove 'A *steppe to Honour*'. Joseph was sold into slavery but through the favour of the Pharaoh became steward of all Egypt. We do not know if *Divine Fancies* achieved a Joseph-like prominence at court, but it certainly was successful in the marketplace, with eleven subsequent editions in the seventeenth century.[34]

Publication offered epigrammatists another opportunity to organize or contextualize their work, but such organizing was in tension with the longstanding tradition of the epigram. The majority of published volumes of seventeenth-century epigrams follow Martial in offering no overarching structure, and thus those who composed both religious and secular epigrams frequently presented them in a completely mixed fashion. Owen's epigrams provide an excellent example of how religious epigrams might be scattered in a largely secular collection. John R. C. Martyn's chart of Owen's subjects shows that 247 of the total 1492 are broadly 'religious' in subject. Especially in the first two books, many of these 'religious' poems are satiric and mocking, often of the Roman Church. In later books, some epigrams have a more devotional nature: for example, 9:58, 'Sacrificium Mundum', presents the world as the temple of God and Christ as the sacrifice. Book 3 includes by far the most religious epigrams, with some extended series of them (3:15–34 and 3:40–64). However, in most cases the sacred epigrams are arbitrarily, and sometimes joltingly, juxtaposed to typical secular epigrams on sexual matters and personal caricatures.

A minority of those composing both religious and secular epigrams resisted this tradition of mixed presentation, and neatly separated the two in publication. This was the approach of the influential German epigrammatist Andreas Gryphius: Book 1 of his *Oden und Epigramme* (1663) consists of one hundred religious poems, while Books 2 and 3 are secular and satirical.[35] John Pyne's title *Epigrammata religiosa, officiosa, jocosa* (1627) signals the threefold division of his Latin epigrams. Stradling's *Epigrammatum libri quatuor* (1607) includes a series of some thirty-five largely biblical epigrams in Book 3 of what is otherwise a strictly secular collection. Herrick offers his 'Noble Numbers' as an apologetic corrective to the main body of his *Hesperides*:

> For Those my unbaptized Rhimes,
> Writ in my wild unhallowed Times;
> For every sentence, clause and word,
> That's not inlaid with Thee, (my Lord)
> Forgive me God, and blot each Line
> Out of my Book, that is not Thine.
> But if, 'mongst all, thou find'st here one
> Worthy thy Benediction;
> That One of all the rest, shall be
> The Glory of my Work, and Me.[36]

Finally, without comment Bancroft devotes the first book of *Two Bookes of Epigrammes* (1639) to secular epigrams and the second to religious ones. The first half of the religious book uses biblical passages to consider ethical points rather than mystical or devotional ones. For example, an epigram on the deceitful actions of Jacob's uncle Laban uses them to show that there is no truth in the world.[37] Repeatedly, a biblical story or moment serves as a starting point for Bancroft; it functions as an example of more general ethical truths, or that from which an analogy might be drawn. Further on, the epigrams, much more than most written in this period, move toward the devotional realm of Donne and Herbert as he hopes that 'My Muse shall bring / Strong Lines, that binde the passions of a King'.[38]

As noted in Chapter 6, Edward May frontloads his collection with religious epigrams to mask the overwhelmingly secular and satiric nature of the volume with the title *Epigrams Divine and Moral*. The volume begins with a series of Christ-centred epigrams not unlike those of Crashaw; and then from no. 12 onward there is another series that is moral rather than divine. However, a more striking shift takes place at no. 36, where without announcement May turns to wholly secular epigrams typical of the tradition of Martial, Jonson and Owen. There was precedent for this in the manuscript epigram collection by the tenth-century Byzantine scholar Constantine Kephalas, who opened his compilation of largely secular (and frequently sexual) Hellenic epigrams with some Christian ones.[39]

Multi-author collections

Single-author published collections, like those of Crashaw, Quarles, May and Bancroft, were not the only possibility for epigrams, religious or otherwise. A tradition of multi-author anthologies of Latin epigrams had long prevailed across Europe. Wright's *Delitiae Delitiarum* (1637) is a pre-eminent example of this type of volume: it is a collection of religious epigrams by various authors from the sixteenth and seventeenth centuries. The title gestures towards the broader European phenomenon: *Delitiae Poetarum Germanorum*, including 'nearly 250,000 pieces',[40] was published at Frankfurt in 1612, and similar volumes of Italian, French, Dutch and Scottish extraction followed. The title of Wright's volume presents it as the 'delights of the delights'; that is, a compilation of the best material from those books based on nationality already published.[41] Wright's role as collector or editor is to ensure that nothing of the frequently unchaste epigram tradition, nothing of Martial's ribaldry, appears in the work: 'si qui Bilbilici cinaedi occurrebant, illos extinxi, hos castravi; & ex Cleocritis puros redidi Gallos' [If there is anything of wanton Martial, these I have extinguished, I have cut them out [castrated them], and out of Cleocriti I have made pure priests].[42] This language embraces the idea of a 'castrated Martial' that Donne and Jonson had mocked in the expurgated Jesuit editions of the poet (see Chapter 1). Wright also claims that he has produced gardens 'sine Priapo' [without Priapus]. Statues of the phallic fertility god Priapus were common in Roman gardens, and in the Renaissance it was commonly believed that the *Priapeia*, a collection of obscene epigrams related to these statues, had been composed by various poets, posted on a statue of Priapus in the garden of Maecenas, and then anthologized.[43] This allusion connects Wright's anthology with a classical precedent, but also distances his compilation from the ribald associations of the classical epigram.

Uthalmus's *Fasciculus florum: or, A nosegay of flowers* (1636) is another multi-author collection of the period, which differed from Wright's in its attempt to broaden the potential audience for such compilations of Latin poems by providing a translation for every epigram.[44] The volume straddles the divide between anthology and epigram book. All the selections are brief and 'epigram-like', but many are excerpts from longer works rather than free-standing epigrams. Uthalmus's intent, however, is not entirely clear: his pseudonym identifies him as a presenter of silly talk and salty nonsense, and his jesting preface seems inconsistent with the largely ethical epigrams he later provides. Unlike Wright, who, as typical of the 'Delitiae' volumes, organizes by author and provides an index of authors, Uthalmus presents the poems anonymously; in this he follows in the common tradition of English miscellanies, where it is the potential social use, not the origins, that give the individual pieces value.[45]

The polemical epigram

The sub-category of polemical religious epigrams deserves separate attention, as they emerged and circulated in different contexts, and were defended in different ways from the more devotional epigram. While these epigrams on religious topics might be call 'satiric', the term 'polemical' better captures their partisan participation in the aggressive strife within the Christianity of the time. The term also has precedent from the period, in that Prynne called his 1642 volume *A Pleasant Purge* a collection of 'polemicall epigrams'. Such poems were most often provoked by moments of theological and ecclesiastical controversy, or sometimes by the epigrams of others. They figured prominently in the early stages of the continental Reformation, and Sullivan has suggested that German Lutheranism 'was less offended by the earthy and frank language of the epigram, accepting as it did the vagaries of the flesh as against the supposed celibate asceticism of the Catholic Church'.[46] While sixteenth-century examples most often reflect conflicts between Reformers and Roman Catholics, by the seventeenth century many satiric religious epigrams involve quarrels within Protestantism.

The best-known British polemical epigrams were from the mid- to late sixteenth century: John Parkhurst, Bishop of Norwich, published his Latin epigram collection *Ludicra* in 1573. It echoed and responded to a wide range of continental religious epigrams in order to castigate the Roman Catholic Church.[47] Parkhurst even invoked the example of Christ's outspoken criticism of the hypocritical to defend his treatment of 'otiosos, inertes, hostes Evangelii' [indifferent, lazy men, enemies of the Gospel].[48] George Buchanan, tutor to King James VI and a highly regarded scholar, used the genre to satirize the pope and monastic orders. Within Protestantism, the Presbyterian Andrew Melville became known across Europe in the 1590s and early seventeenth century for his scathing epigrams on English liturgy and ceremony.[49] These polemical poems frequently elicited epigrammatic replies, reflecting the *responsa* tradition traced above. George Herbert participated in this sort of exchange in his *Musae Responsoriae*, which defended English church ceremony against the Presbyterian Melville, and in the collection *Lucus*, where he mocked Pope Urban VIII.[50]

Some references from the 1620s connect these sorts of polemical epigrams with the Pasquil of Rome, and they manifest a Protestant admiration of his outspoken criticism of Roman Church figures. An anonymous work of 1623, *The abuses of the Romish church anatomised*, draws on particular sixteenth-century Pasquils against popes, and a similar work from the next year, *The popes pyramides*, credits Pasquil with an exposure of the corruption of the Roman Church. Its preface celebrates the volume, 'As *Pasquill* sent it to our *Britany*'.[51] In this way, the English Protestant satiric attacks on the Church of Rome were connected with Pasquil and the whole tradition of epigrammatic critique from within Rome itself.

Some Neo-Latin polemical epigrams were disseminated through quotation in printed prose works of religious controversy. This happened repeatedly with the well-known epigrams of Buchanan and Melville. However, a lesser known one by Giles Fletcher (the elder) (1546–1611) will serve as an example here. Fletcher was a significant diplomatic figure who wrote an influential account of Russia (*Of the Russe commonwealth*, 1591), and composed Latin verses, many of which manifest a firm Protestant perspective. He is also noteworthy for his family connections: two of his sons, Phineas and Giles the younger, became known as poets in the first decades of the 1600s; his brother Richard was Bishop of London in the 1590s; and through Richard he was uncle to John Fletcher the playwright.

His epigram survives in manuscript (next to a similar anti-papal poem by Melville):[52]

Non ego mirarer Stygiae si forsitan aulae
    Romuleus possit claviger esse Petrus
Innumeris etenim ditavit manibus umbras
    et reserat stygias ingrediturque fores
Sed miror quòd[53] cum spatiis[54] sic distet ut*rumque*
    possit et aetherei claviger esse poli.
Sed neque iam miror: caeli nam claudere forsan
    tecta solet: stygias sed reserare fores.[55]

[I would not marvel if perhaps the Romulean Peter [the Pope] could be the key-bearer of the Stygian courts, and even enriched the shades with innumerable hands, and unlocked the Stygian doors and entered in. But I wonder because with the spaces between the two of them [Heaven and Hell] that he could be the key-bearer of the heavenly city. But now I do not wonder: for, perhaps, he is accustomed to shut the heavenly abodes but open the Stygian doors.]

The poem was somehow obtained by Lionel Sharpe, who used it within his long argument against papal authority in *Novum fidei symbolum* (1612), which was published in English translation a few years later as *A looking-glasse for the Pope* (1616). That which follows is from the lead-up to the quotation of the (translated) poem:

Peters key is altogether the key of heaven, whereby by the preaching of the eternall Gospell hee hath opened heaven to the faithfull and penitent, and shut it to the unfaithfull and impenitent, which the Pope the counterfet successor of Peter doth use otherwise, as somtime an elegant Poet played upon this princely porter.

I should not marvaile much
If that the Popes good grace,
Did happily beare the key
Of that darke stigian place.
For he enriched hath
that place with many an elfe,
And opened wide hell gate,
And entred in himselfe.
But sith that heaven and hell
Are set so far asunder,
That he should beare the key
Of heaven it is a wonder.

> But now tis none at all,
> From heaven he all shuts out,
> And opes the gate of hell,
> And letteth in that rout.

As the falling starre in the prophecie of *John* he hath changed the key of heaven
into the key of the bottomles pit.[56]

Fletcher's original poem is thus given a new home as a witty ornament
within a very long and decidedly unwitty argument on why Peter's keys of
the kingdom are not a justification for papal authority.

Quarles's occasional polemical religious epigrams in *Divine Fancies* provide a typical example of the sub-genre in English. Towards the end of
this large volume Quarles's tone becomes mildly satiric and reminiscent of
the secular epigram.[57] Representative men, identified by Latinate names,
are mocked for their sins, theology and ecclesiology. At times, he is clearly
partaking in the intense debates of the 1630s over liturgy, ceremonial garb
and Church government. These are partisan poems, reflecting Quarles's
commitment to the Church of England as it was; they are consistent with
his religious position throughout his life, despite the posthumous accusations of Papism and later scholarly perceptions of him as a Puritan. The
figure of Rhemus, a Roman Catholic whose name derives from Rheims,
the site of a major Catholic English seminary on the continent, is the
subject of a number of Quarles's epigrams. These offer little sense of the
individual: it is clearly the broader tenets of the Roman Catholic that
Quarles is questioning through this figure. Towards the end of Book 4
Quarles presents a number of epigrams on Zelustus, a name which reflects
the zeal of the person, a quality closely associated with the Puritans or
godly of the time. In 4:91 Zelustus is mocked for his devotion to keeping the first four commandments, which pertain to loving God, while
flagrantly ignoring the final six on the love of neighbour. Two epigrams
(4:103 and 4:105) chastise the same figure's attitude toward clerical garb:
Quarles finds Zelustus guilty of stubbornly and proudly insisting on the
out-of-fashion 'Geneva Ruffe' and 'steeple Hat', as if these were in themselves 'Symptomes of Regeneration' (4:103) or liked of Heaven (4:105).
Thus, the implied resistance to the more formal attire of the high churchmen is presented by Quarles as being itself an affectation and source of
pride. Similarly treated is the character Phares, whose name recalls the
Pharisees, and who adopts the standard Puritan refusal to kneel for communion (4:115).

These epigrams fit more comfortably in the mainstream epigram tradition by simply changing the target of ridicule from general human behaviour to religious life and thought. But Quarles faced a challenge different from the epigrammatist who limited himself to secular subjects: could the epigrammatist who engaged in religious satire escape the cynical voice or pose that was so much a part of Martial's epigrams? Martial, after all, expresses a commitment to nothing; Lessing wrote of him 'I know of no Latin poet from whom fewer morals can be taken'.[58] Such urbane detachment is not ultimately sustainable for a religious epigrammatist who was ridiculing another from a committed position of loyalty to his own Church, beliefs or customs.

Other volumes, both manuscript and print, present much more focused sequences of epigrams of religious controversy, arising from very clear contexts, and in the process discard urbane detachment for committed polemic. A fragment of one such is found in Knatchbull MS U951/Z18 at the Kent History and Library Centre, Maidstone. This manuscript preserves fourteen epigrams on the issues stemming from the Hampton Court Conference of 1604. The author defends the godly who had argued before the King against such ceremonial elements as clerical garments, the sign of the cross in baptism and kneeling at communion. The poems average about twenty lines each, and are epigram-like only in their derisive tone: they mock 'syr Sapience' and the 'Cross-munger' who uphold the traditional ceremonies. The plentiful marginal notes, which recall the practice in printed books of prose polemic, defend the use of such abusive (and even scatological language) by invoking previous examples from the Bible, Chaucer, Calvin and King James himself. They also establish the context of the poems: they were written between 1604 and 1607 and reflect the bitterness of the militant Protestants who felt their concerns had been unfairly rejected at the Conference. The arguments are the common ones found among the godly in the early years of King James's English reign – that these ceremonies may be things indifferent to the King and bishops, but not to those who object to them. They take the advanced Protestant line that that which is not explicitly ordained in scripture is to be rejected. Thus, the tender consciences of the godly should be considered. The specific triggers here are the sign of the cross in baptism and kneeling at communion, but the larger issue is that of conformity and the authority of the King and bishops.

A variety of rhetorical strategies are used in the Knatchbull epigrams. Most frequent is the hyperbolic deriding of the ceremonial elements themselves: if the cross in baptism is so important, why not actually engrave it in the child's skin, one epigram asks:

Were I a cannon-wright, I would perswade
You should imprint it in his skin; or paint
With some deepe dye, which time can never fade.[59]

Frequently, the poet reminds his opponents of how their rituals approach those of the Church of Rome. Some epigrams drop the mocking tone to address King James directly, and remind him of his earlier opposition in Scotland to such ceremonies. What survives is clearly a fragment of a larger sequence, as the poems are numbered 60 to 73. The extensive marginal annotations (added by the author in 1609 or 1610) gives the impression that the volume was being prepared for the press, but, given its subject and vitriolic nature, it is not surprising that it was not printed.

These manuscript epigrams are similar in approach to Laurence Anderton's *Epigrammes* (1630?), written under the pseudonym John Brereley.[60] Like the poet of the Knatchbull manuscript, Anderton uses the genre as an aggressive tool of religious polemic. Generally, his approach is to castigate Protestants on doctrinal grounds, but he adopts a variety of means to do so. At times, he takes the voice of a famous Protestant, at others he uses the youthful amatory epigrams (*Basia*) of the noted Reformer Beza against him. Like Quarles, Brereley invents fictional Latinate names in the course of providing satiric character sketches. In length, these poems stretch the definition of an epigram, running from twenty to forty lines. As with the Knatchbull manuscript, Anderton's *Epigrammes* are marked by heavy marginal annotation: nearly every point of each poem is footnoted with direct reference to a Reformer's own work (both early and late, continental and English), and in most cases the notes are longer than the epigrams themselves. This framing suggests that the work is a learned one, set apart from other epigram collections by its seriousness: these are not mere trifles, but contributions to a longstanding theological and ecclesiastical debate.

Occasional anti-Catholic poems were a standard part of the English epigram tradition in the Elizabethan and early Stuart period, but some poets went further in presenting larger collections of such epigrams. The section devoted to epigrams in Taylor's *Water-workes* begins with a batch addressed 'To the whole kennell of Anti-Christs hounds, Priests, Friers, Monks, and Jesuites, Mastiffes, Mongrels, Islands, Spanniels, Bloudhounds, Bobtale-tike, of Foysting-hounds':[61] these are largely attacks on the Church of Rome; many of them feature marginal notes like those of Brereton/Anderton. Like many other 'epigrams' of religious controversy in these decades, they show little concern for the attributes of brevity and sharpness usually associated with the genre.

Although he calls them 'polemicall epigrams', the poems in Prynne's *Pleasant Purge* (1642) are even less epigram-like in tone. Written in the late 1630s when he was imprisoned for his anti-Laudianism, they are an anti-papist series based upon discussions with Roman Catholic fellow prisoners. He presents the epigrams as allowing him greater latitude:

> On this occasion, to helpe passe the time,
> I some of our *Discourses* turn'd to *Rime*.
> That so I might with *greater Liberty*,
> And *lesse Offense*, their *Errors* lash, descry.[sig. *r]

This explanation combines two disparate justifications: the notion of *otium theologicum* informs the first two lines, but in the latter two he suggests a clear, pragmatic function. The poetic form allows a 'greater Liberty' to correct errors without causing offence.

Prynne's verses are not really much like epigrams, but rather extended arguments (often forty lines or more) set in couplet verse: he is accurate in describing them as '*Discourses* turn'd to Rime'. They generally lack the sharpness or wordplay associated with the form. Anderton and Prynne were clearly using the term 'Epigram' in a very loose sense to denote a spirit of controversial opposition and little else. Anderton admits little concern with stylistic niceties: as long as his poems 'gall' they have served their purpose. He imagines how his volume might be read by an opponent. Unable to find fault with the theological method, the 'carping' minister would turn to literary criticism:

> But finding all exact, he carpes my stile,
> Censures my verse, and with a scornfull smile
> Fy on this Priest (*sayth he*) what rime is this?
> What words are heere, this couplet is amisse;
> That phrase is of his owne invention, new;
> This over-harsh, that England never knew. (6)

In Anderton's view, all this misses the point: his are religious not literary works, and any legacy of Martial, either in style or reputation, seems to have been lost.

Notes

1 The continental sacred epigram has been better served by scholars; see, for example, R. K. Angress, *The Early German Epigram: A Study in Baroque Poetry* (Lexington, KY: University Press of Kentucky, 1971).

2 Published collections include Thomas Bancroft, *Two Bookes of Epigrammes* (1639); John Brereley, pseud. [Laurence Anderton], *Epigrammes* (ca. 1630); Richard Crashaw, *Epigrammatum sacrorum liber* (1634); George Herbert, *Musae Responsoriae* (written ca. 1620); Herbert, *Passio Discerpta* (written ca. 1623); Arthur Johnstone, *Epigrammata* (1632); Edward May, *Epigrams Divine and Moral* (1633); John Pyne, *Epigrammata religiosa, officiosa, jocosa* (1626); Frances Quarles, *Divine Fancies* (1632); Andrew Ramsay, *Poemata Sacra*, (1633); Alexander Ross, *Three Decades of Divine Meditations* (ca. 1630); John Saltmarsh, *Poemata Sacra, Latine et Anglice* (1636); Lerimos Uthalmus, [pseud.], *Fasciculus Florum: Or, A Nosegay of Flowers, Translated out of the gardens of severall Poets, and other Authors* (1636); and Abraham Wright, *Delitiae Delitiarum* (1637), Thomas Bancroft, *Two Bookes of Epigrammes* (1639).

3 *The Complete Poetry of Richard Crashaw*, ed. George Walton Williams (New York: Norton, 1974), p. 642.

4 Ruth C. Wallerstein, *Richard Crashaw: A Study in Style and Poetic Development* (Madison, WI: University of Wisconsin Press, 1959), pp. 59–60.

5 John Saltmarsh, *Poetices libri septem* (1636), sig. A1v.

6 Crashaw, *Complete Poetry*, ed. Williams, p. 642.

7 On the fashion of 'urbanité' in the seventeenth century spurred by Martial, see Sullivan, *Martial*, pp. 2701.

8 Trans. Walter C. A. Ker, from Martial, *Epigrams*, vol. 1, p. 155.

9 Averil Cameron suggests that a similar secular stigma was attached to the epigram in early Byzantine times: 'If there were few Christian epigrams in the *Cycle* it is because of the overwhelmingly conventional and conservative nature of the genre itself, not because they were specifically excluded. Though Gregory Nazianzen had shown that literary epigrams (of a sort) could indeed be written on Christian subjects, Agathias and his friends were writing in an essentially secular form. The question whether or not to compose Christian epigrams for the most part simply did not arise.' *Agathias* (Oxford: Clarendon Press, 1970), p. 17.

10 Crashaw, *Complete Poetry*, ed. and trans. Williams, pp. 302–3.

11 This incident from Acts 5:15 seems to have come in for repeated treatment: George Herbert, *Lucus*, 14, in *The Works of George Herbert*, ed. F. E. Hutchinson (Oxford: Clarendon, 1941), p. 413, and a number in Crashaw, *Complete Poetry*, ed. Williams, pp. 410–11.

12 Fitzgerald, *Martial*, p. 193, notes how Burmeister's parody of Martial takes 'the generic self-deprecation of the epigrammatist into the territory of Christian humility'.

13 'ubi epigrammata, sale Theologico tanquam undis lustralibus conspersa, e sacro-sanctis Musarum prodiisse videbuntur' [where epigrams just as if with theological salt sprinkled among the sacrificial waves, seem to have been brought forth out of holy chambers of the Muses] (sig. ¶4r).

14 Francis Quarles, *Divine Fancies* (1632), sig. A3r.

15 *The Greek Anthology*, vol. 1, p. 3.

16 Kay, *Epigrams from the Anthologia Latina*, p. 70.

17 Kay, *Epigrams from the Anthologia Latina*, p. 77. Prudentius, vol. 2, pp. 347–71.

18 *STC* also notes a 1545 publication that includes St Gregory: *Verse epigrams and prose sentences*, *STC* 12345. John Stockwood, *Progymnasma Scholasticum*, (1597), offered Latin translations of many poems from the *Greek Anthology*. See Jean-Louis Quantin, *The Church of England and Christian Antiquity: The Construction of a Confessional Identity in the 17th Century* (Oxford: Oxford University Press, 2009), on the significance of the Church Fathers for the English Church at this time.

19 See my article, with Antony Prancic, '"Ora pro me, sancte Herberte": James Duport and the Reputation of George Herbert', *The George Herbert Journal*, 24 (2000–01), 35–55.

20 On *otium* in the classical tradition, see J. P. Toner, *Leisure and Ancient Rome* (Cambridge: Polity Press; Malden, MA: Blackwell, 1998).

21 'Leisure and Idleness in the Renaissance: The Ambivalence of Otium', *Renaissance Studies*, 4 (1990): pp. 1–37, 107–54. Vickers also puts to rest the oft-repeated statement that *otium* is 'usually opposed to *negotium*'. The belief in this statement, and its relevance to the epigram tradition, is reflected in Robert Fletcher's title of his translation of Martial, *Ex Otio Negotium, or, Martiall his Epigrams Translated* (London, 1656).

22 Vickers, 'Leisure and Idleness in the Renaissance', pp. 9–12.

23 Vickers, 'Leisure and Idleness in the Renaissance', pp. 107–10. In the Middle Ages there were attempts to develop a sense of redeemed *otium* consistent with the contemplative life, St Hilary, for example, identifying the Sabbath as an 'otium Domini' (Jean LeClercq, *Otia monastica: études sur le vocabulaire de la contemplation au Moyen Age* (Rome: Herder, 1963), p. 37).

24 Vickers, 'Leisure and Idleness in the Renaissance', pp. 112–13. He also notes that 'It may well be that the association of otium with the writing of lyric poetry is a new development in the mid-seventeenth century, a "baroque" phenomenon rather than a Renaissance one', p. 147. He cites the examples of

Constantine Huygens's *Otia* (1625) and Mildmay Fane's *Otia Sacra* (1648).
I suspect that the cultural landscape had shifted for Fane in the 1640s: *otium*
for him and other defeated Royalists might represent the life of cultivated
leisurely retreat into which they had been forced. Richard Lovelace's 'The
Grasshopper' is the best-known poem within this tradition. See Leah Marcus,
*The Politics of Mirth: Jonson, Herrick, Milton, Marvell and the Defense of
Holiday Pastimes* (Chicago: University of Chicago Press, 1986), and Robert
Wilcher, *The Writing of Royalism, 1628–1660* (Cambridge: Cambridge
University Press, 2001), pp. 308–48.

25 This sense of *otium theologicum* is consistent with the broader pattern: 'a general sense of guilt, or at least embarrassment attended many manifestations of *otium* in the Renaissance' (Vickers, 'Leisure and Idleness in the Renaissance', p. 129).

26 Saltmarsh, *Poemata Sacra*, sig. A1r.

27 Cf. the German epigrams of Andreas Gryphius, a century of which focus on the Incarnation, and within which century a series (61–70) is 'openly autobiographical' (Angress, *The Early German Epigram*, pp. 108–9).

28 An allusion to 'one good Friday' in the final poem ('To my Booke', Ep. 4:117) may mean that the epigrams were all composed in less than two years; William Liston suggests that 'Quarles probably did not begin writing until he completed *The Historie of Samson*, published in the previous year, 1631' (Francis Quarles, *Divine Fancies*, ed. William T. Liston (New York: Garland, 1992), p. 236).

29 Quarles also includes a number of poems that compare the world to a more limited human institution ('The world's a Printing-house' (Ep. 4:3), 'The World's a Theater' (Ep. 1:6), 'The World's an Inne' (Ep. 2:61), 'The World's a Booke' (Ep. 4:35)), but these are scattered among the four books.

30 Tom Cain and Ruth Connolly (eds), *The Complete Poetry of Robert Herrick*, 2 vols (Oxford: Oxford University Press, 2013), vol. 1, p. 415.

31 Qtd in Kenneth J., Larsen, 'Richard Crashaw's *Epigrammata Sacra*', in J. W. Binns (ed.), *The Latin Poetry of English Poets* (London: Routledge & Kegan Paul, 1974), pp. 93–120; p. 95).

32 Crashaw, *Poems: English, Latin, and Greek*, ed. Martin, p. lxxiv.

33 Crashaw, *Poems: English, Latin, and Greek*, ed. Martin, p. lviii.

34 Editions appeared in 1633, 1636, 1638, 1641, 1652, 1657, 1660, 1664, 1671, 1675, 1687 and 1722. On these later editions of *Divine Fancies*, see Karl Josef Höltgen, *Francis Quarles* (Tübingen: Niemeyer, 1978), p. 128.

35 Angress, *The Early German Epigram*, p. 108.

36 Herrick, *Poetical Works*, ed. Moorman, p. 339.

37 Thomas Bancroft, *Two Bookes of Epigrams* (1639), Ep. 2:78.

38 Bancroft, Ep. 2:138.

39 Edward N. Luttwak, *TLS*, 13 Feb. 2009, p. 7. Kephalas's collection was a precursor to the Palatine version of the *Greek Anthology*.

40 Hudson, *The Epigram in the English Renaissance*, p. 24.

41 The conclusion of Wright's preface 'Lectori' coyly refuses to explain why he has not included epigrams by English poets. It may have been that a *Delitiae Poetarum Anglorum* was in the works.

42 Kleokritos appears in Aristophanes' *The Birds* and *The Frogs*, in both cases as a ridiculous ostrich figure, unable to fly (*Birds*, ed. Nan Dunbar (Oxford: Oxford University Press, 1993), p. 512, and *Frogs*, ed. Kenneth Dover (Oxford: Oxford University Press, 1995), p. 376). However, this does not explain the obscene nature suggested here.

43 W. H. Parker (trans. and ed.), *Priapea: Poems for a Phallic God* (London and Sydney: Croom Helm, 1988), pp. 32–4. Through the Middle Ages the *Priapea* had been commonly ascribed to Virgil; however, Renaissance scholars felt they were too be obscene to have been that poet's work, and developed the multi-author theory, or the theory that they had all been the work of Martial (Parker, pp. 34–6).

44 *STC* suggests that 'Lerimos Uthalmus' may be an acronym for Thomas Willmers or Thomas Sumervill.

45 Smyth, *Profit & Delight*, p. 52.

46 Sullivan, *Martial*, p. 280.

47 Hudson, *The Epigram in the English Renaissance*, pp. 96–8.

48 John Parkhurst, *Ludrica* (1573), sig. Aiiiv.

49 See my chapter on Melville in *King James I and the Religious Culture of England* (Woodbridge: Brewer, 2000), pp. 57–72.

50 James Doelman, 'The Contexts of George Herbert's *Musae Responsoriae*', *George Herbert Journal*, 2 (1992), pp. 42–54, and 'Herbert's *Lucus* and Pope Urban VIII', *The George Herbert Journal*, 32 (2008–09), pp. 43–53.

51 *The popes pyramides* (1624).

52 University of Texas at Austin, MS HRC 79. The transcription of this (and many other poems) by Farmer, *Poems from a Seventeenth-Century Manuscript*, is error-filled; hence, I have provided the text based on my reading of the facsimile, and compared it with the printed version in Lionel Sharpe discussed below. The poem is not listed in Lloyd E. Berry, 'Giles Fletcher, the Elder: A Bibliography', *Transactions of the Cambridge Bibliographical Society*, 3 (1961), pp. 200–15.

53 Based on copy in Lionel Sharpe, *Novum fidei symbolum* (1612).

54 Sharpe: 'spacio'.

55 Sharpe: 'foret' (but 'fores' really does make sense here).

56 *A looking-glasse for the Pope*, pp. 295–6. A marginal note identifies the author as 'Dr Giles Fletcher'. The manuscript had simply attributed it to 'D Fletcher'.

57 The satiric tendency of the later epigrams is reflected in the final poem, 'To my Booke', where Quarles 'weans' the work, because its 'Teeth grow sharp' (Ep. 4:117). The image of satire as a biting beast was a longstanding tradition; see my '"Born with Teeth": Christopher Brooke's *Ghost of Richard the Third* (1614)', *Seventeenth Century*, 14 (1999), pp. 115–29; Kernan, *The Cankered Muse*; and, on such biting's imagined effect on the body and feelings of its subjects, William Kerwin, 'Epigrammatic Commotions', in Katharine A. Craik and Tanya Pollard (eds), *Shakespearean Sensations: Experiencing Literature in Early Modern England* (Cambridge: Cambridge University Press, 2013), pp. 157–72.

58 Lessing, 'Essay on Epigram', p. 176.

59 Knatchbull MS U951/Z18, fol. 3r.

60 A second edition of this appeared under the title *The Mirror of New Reformation* (1634). Appended to this edition are four poems not in *Epigrammes*.

61 John Taylor, *Water-workes: or the scullers travels, from Tiber to Thames* (1614), sig. B2r.

Coda: Harington's 'Of Moyses'

The polemic poems of Prynne, Anderton and the Knatchbull manuscript with which the last chapter concluded represent a sort of endpoint for the evolving idea of the epigram in the period 1590 to 1640. While *called* epigrams, they were a far cry from the detached, pointed and brief poems, modelled on Martial above all, that represented the mainstream of the genre. As such, they manifest an extreme example of the modulation of genres and drift in terminology which was already present in the first flourishing of the epigram in late 1590s England.

Hence, it is fitting to conclude with a final epigram by Harington, one which embraces religious subject matter but does so in a way consistent with the Martialian tradition. A tension between jesting detachment and religious commitment is manifest in Harington's religious epigrams, which, as Gerard Kilroy has shown, are the 'decades' that provide a structure for his gift manuscript collections. In them, the sub-genre of the religious epigram and the mainstream Martialian tradition come together. However, there are also occasional epigrams on religious topics scattered amongst the other satiric epigrams. Such is the case with 'Of Moyses':

Most worthy Prophet that by inspiration
Didst tell of heav'n and earth and seas creation,
    That first deserv'dst the name of sacred poet,
    Now so prophan'd, that fooles on fooles bestow it.
Thou for thy peopl's libertie and good,
didst scorne the tytle of the Royall blood
    thou that by grace obtayned from thy God
    from rocks derivedst[1] rivers by thy rod,
And in that Rod's true reall alteration,
didst show undoubted transubstantiation.

thou that didst plague all Egipt with their prince
that ten such plagues were ne're before nor since;
Thou that didst by thy makers speciall grace,
Speake with him in the mountayne face to face,
and there receavdst of him ten hy Behests,
in stony bookes, for our more stony brests.
Thou that twise forty dayes, tookst no repast,
and gav'st two samples, of one Lenton fast,
thou that in zeale revenge didst take so sore,
upon that damned crew Dathan and Core
And at another time in rightfull yre,
consumedst some with sword, and some with fyre
Obtayn my pardon, if (untoward Scholler)
I prove in nothing like thee, but in choller.
And now give leave unto my awfull Muse,
to tell one fault of thine in mine excuse,
For though I needes must graunt my foollish wrath,
those lawes to breake sometimes me caused hath.
I breake but one and one, none for the nonce,
thou in thy wrath, didst breake them all at once.[2]

Through the first twenty lines Harington adopts an approach widely found in sacred epigrams: focused reflection upon a biblical moment or figure. Here, he recounts the roles and accomplishments of Moses as he addresses him in praise. However, there are already subtle elements that suggest that this will not be a conventional religious epigram. Along with his other roles, Moses is identified as a 'sacred poet'; this allows Harington a brief barb at his contemporary poets (Tasso, Spenser, du Bartas?) who have been labelled such by their fellow fools. The poem also briefly flirts with religious polemic, but in the subtle playful way that is typical of Harington: he reads Moses' bringing forth of water from the rock as showing 'undoubted transubstantiation', a major issue of dispute between Protestants and Catholics. As often found in Harington's epigrams, there is a playfully provocative espousing of the Catholic position here; however, it is a far cry from the intense partisan polemic in the epigrams discussed above. Such an approach, consistent with the epigram tradition, always allows the poet to claim that it is simply jest.

The major twist, however, comes in the second half, as he turns the poem back on himself and moves toward a final jesting epigrammatic point. He is like Moses only 'in choller', and whereas Moses broke the laws 'all at once' (i.e., the two tablets), 'I breake but one and one, none for the nonce'. The conclusion thus engages in a typically Protestant consideration of a biblical figure as a paradigm for a life in the New Covenant, but here it is the weakness or sinfulness of the figure rather than his devotion or prophetic powers that form the basis of similarity. Moses has, rather oddly, become a subject of jesting treatment in an epigram. However, as is typical of Harington, the poem moves beyond conventional detachment in its treatment of its subject, becoming ultimately about the poet himself.

Such a treatment of the biblical Moses is, at least in part, deliberately provocative (something very frequent in Donne's devotional poems as well) and the poem that follows gives voice to the scandalized reader. 'Against Leda for carping' addresses one who has read his epigram on Moses and responds, 'What; have wee byble storyes ioyn'd with bables,[3] / Oh Sacriledge, unexcusable cryme'.[4] Harington's response is that God knows he has reverence for all the saints, but also knows that on earth they were subject to passions. He then turns the jest on Leda by concluding,

> Thy Husband like to Moyses picture ys,
> For Moyses ever painted ys with hornes.

What had begun as a seeming attempt to write a redeemed epigram has reverted to one of the most conventional uses of the genre: the mockery of cuckoldry. *Vicisti, Bilbilitane.*

Notes

1 Other manuscripts have the more likely 'dividedst' here.
2 Harington, Ep. 3:33 (Kilroy ed.).
3 Some manuscripts have 'fables'.
4 Harington, Ep. 3:34 (Kilroy ed.).

Appendix

The educational experience of major epigrammatists

Name	Elementary	University	Inns of Court
Adamson, Patrick	Perth	St Mary's College at St Andrews	
Anderton, Lawrence	Blackburn	Christ's College, Cambridge; English College, Seville	
Andrews, Richard	Merchant Taylors' School	St John's College, Oxford	
Anton, Robert		Magdalene College, Cambridge	
Ayton, Sir Robert		St Leonard's College at St Andrews	
Bancroft, Thomas		St. Catharine's College, Cambridge	
Bastard, Thomas	Winchester College	New College, Oxford	
Brathwaite, Richard		Oriel College, Oxford, then Cambridge, probably Pembroke College	Gray's Inn
Breton, Nicholas		possibly Oriel College, Oxford	
C[ooke], J[ohn]	unknown		
Campion, Thomas		Peterhouse, Cambridge	Gray's Inn
Chamberlain, Robert		Exeter College, Oxford	
Crashaw, Richard	Charterhouse School	Pembroke College, Cambridge; Peterhouse, Cambridge	

Name	Elementary	University	Inns of Court
Davies, John of Hereford		no higher education, but active at Oxford as a writing master	
Davies, Sir John	Winchester College	Queen's College, Oxford	New Inn; Middle Temple
Donne, John	private	Hart Hall, Oxford	Thavies Inn; Lincoln's Inn
Drummond, William	high school of Edinburgh	College of Edinburgh	studied law in Bourges, France
Dunbar, John	unknown		
Edes, Richard	Westminster School	Christ Church, Oxford	
Farlie, Robert	unknown		
Fitzgeffry, Charles	under Richard Harvey and Henry Wallis in Cornwall	Broadgates Hall, Oxford	
Fitzgeffrey, Henry	Westminster School	Trinity College, Camb.	Lincoln's Inn
Freeman, Thomas		Magdalen College, Oxford	
Gamage, William	unknown	Oxford	
Gill, Alexander	St. Paul's School	Trinity College, Oxford; Wadham College, Oxford	
Goddard, William	unknown		
Guilpin, Edward	Highgate School	Emmanuel College, Cambridge.	Gray's Inn
Gwyn, Walter	unknown		
Harington, John	Eton College	King's College, Cambridge	Lincoln's Inn
Hayman, Robert		Exeter College, Oxford	Lincoln's Inn
Heath, John	Winchester College	New College, Oxford	
Hoskins, John	Winchester College	New College, Oxford	Middle Temple
Hutton, Henry		St John's College, Cambridge; possibly Oxford	Gray's Inn
Johnston, Arthur	Kintore School	University of Aberdeen, likely King's College	
Jonson, Ben	school of St Martin-in-the-Fields, then Westminster School	possibly at St John's, Cambridge, for a short time	

Name	Elementary	University	Inns of Court
Julius, Alexander	unknown		
Latewar, Richard	Merchant Taylors' School	St John's College, Oxford	
Leech, John		University of Aberdeen	studied law in Poitiers
Martin, James		Christ Church, Oxford; Broadgates Hall, Oxford	
Martyn, Joseph	unknown		
May, Edward	unknown		
Melville, Andrew	Montrose	St Mary's College, St Andrew's	studied law in Poitiers
Michelborne, Edward		St Mary's Hall, Oxford; Gloucester Hall, Oxford	
Michelborne, Laurence		Oxford	
Michelborne, Thomas		Broadgates Hall, Oxford	Gray's Inn
Middleton, Richard		Jesus College, Oxford	
Niccols, Richard		Magdalen College, Oxford	
Owen, John	Winchester College	New College, Oxford	
Peacham, Henry	near St Albans	Trinity College, Cambridge	
Percy, William	studied in Paris	Gloucester Hall, Oxford	
Plumptre, Huntingdon		St John's College, Cambridge; Trinity Hall, Cambridge	
Pyne, John	unknown		
Quarles, Francis	'schoole in the countrey', probably in Essex	Christ's College, Cambridge	Lincoln's Inn
R[ichards], Nathaniel	unknown		
Ramsay, Andrew		Marischal College, Aberdeen	continued schooling in France
Reynolds, John	Winchester College	New College, Oxford	
Ross, Alexander	grammar school in Aberdeen	university in Aberdeen[1]	
Russell, John	grammar school in Norwich?	Magdalene College, Cambridge	

Name	Elementary	University	Inns of Court
Saltmarsh, John		Magdalene College, Cambridge	
Storer, Thomas		Christ Church, Oxford	
Stradling, Sir John	educated at Bristol by Edward Green	Brasenose College, Oxford; Magdalen Hall, Oxford	possibly the Middle Temple
Taylor, John	elementary school in Gloucester; then a grammar school, perhaps Crypt School	no higher education	
Thorius, Raphael		Oxford; Leiden	
Thynne, Francis	Tonbridge School, under John Proctor[2]		Lincoln's Inn
Weever, John	by his Uncle (possibly Thomas Langton) Lancashire	Queens' College, Cambridge	
West, Richard		Pembroke College, Cambridge	
Wroth, Sir Thomas		Gloucester Hall, Oxford; Broadgates Hall, Oxford	Inner Temple

Notes

1 Arguments have been made for both King's College and Marischal College.
2 F. J. Furnivall (ed.), *Animadversions* (1875; Rpt London: Oxford University Press, 1965) suggests with evidence the Cathedral School at Rochester.

Select bibliography

Manuscripts

Alnwick Castle MS F392 509
Bodl. Ashmole MS 38
Bodl. Ashmole MS 781
Bodl. Don. MS c.54
Bodl. English History MS c.272
Bodl. Eng. poet. MS e.14
Bodl. Holkham MS 436
Bodl. James MS 35
Bodl. Malone MS 16
Bodl. Malone MS 19
Bodl. Malone MS 23
Bodl. Rawl. poet. MS 26
Bodl. Rawl. poet. MS 62
Bodl. Rawl. poet. MS 147
Bodl. Rawl. poet. MS 246
Bodl. Sancroft MS 48
Bodl. Sancroft MS 53
Bodl. Selden Supra MS 81
Bodl. Tanner MS 465
BL Add. MS 15227
BL Add. MS 27343
BL Add. MS 32464
BL Add. MS 39829
BL Add. MS 73542
BL Egerton MS 2877
BL Egerton MS 2982
BL Harl. MS 1221

BL Harl. MS 3910
BL Sloane MS 1889
Camb. Add. MS 29
Camb. Add. MS 57
Camb. Add. MS 4138
Camb. UL MS Gg.I. 29. Part II
Chetham's Library, Manchester, MS A.3.47
College of Arms, London, MS 218
Folger MS V.a.262
Folger MS V.a.345
Huntington MS 4
Huntington MS 172
Huntington Ellesmere MS 2727
Kent History and Library Centre, Maidstone, Knatchbull MS U951/Z18
PRO SP 14/103/61
Queen's College, Oxford, MS 121
Westminster Abbey MS 41

Printed primary sources

Unless otherwise indicated, London is the place of publication for premodern
   books

An Italians dead bodie Stucke with Englishe Flowers (1600).
Anderton, Laurence. *Epigrammes* (1630).
[Anon.]. *The life and death of Queene Elizabeth* (1639).
—— *Ulysses upon Ajax* (1596).
Armstrong, Archie. *A banquet of jests. Or Change of cheare Being a collection of
   moderne jests. Witty jeeres. Pleasant taunts. Merry tales* (1634).
Aubrey, John. *Brief Lives* (Harmondsworth: Penguin, 1962).
Ayton, Robert. *The English and Latin Poems*, ed. Charles B. Gullans (Edinburgh:
   Blackwood, 1963).
Bancroft, Thomas. *Two bookes of epigrammes* (1639).
Bastard, Thomas. *Chrestoleros: Seven Bookes of Epigrams* (1598).
Beedome, Thomas. *Poems, divine and humane* (1641).
Black, Joseph, ed. *The Martin Marprelate Tracts* (Cambridge: Cambridge
   University Press, 2008).
Brathwaite, Richard. *The Good Wife: or, A rare one amongst women* (1618).
—— *Strappado for the Divell* (1615).
—— *Times curtaine drawne, or the anatomie of vanitie* (1621).

Breton, Nicholas. *The Works in Verse and Prose,* ed. Alexander B. Grosart, 2 vols (1879; Rpt New York: AMS, 1966).

Brinsley, John. *Ludus literarius: or, the grammar schoole* (1612).

Bruch, Richard. *Epigrammatum Hecatontades Duae* (1627).

C., J. *Alcilia: Philoparthens loving folly. To which is added Pigmalions image. With the love of Amos and Laura. And also epigrammes by Sir I.H. and others* (1613).

Camden, William. *Remaines concerning Britaine.* (1637).

Campion, Thomas. *Two bookes of ayres* (1613?).

—— *Works,* ed. Percival Vivian (1909; Rpt Oxford: Clarendon Press, 1966).

Carew, Richard, 'The Excellency of the English Tongue', in *Elizabethan Critical Essays,* ed. G. Gregory Smith, 2 vols (Oxford: Clarendon Press, 1904).

Chamberlain, John. *The Letters of John Chamberlain,* ed. N. E. McClure, 2 vols (Philadelphia, PA: American Philosophical Society, 1939).

Cockburn, David. 'A Critical Edition of the Letters of the Reverend Joseph Mead, 1626–1627, Contained in British Library Harleian MS 390', PhD, University of Cambridge, 1994.

Collins, Arthur (ed.). *Letters and Memorials of State,* 2 vols (1746; Rpt New York: AMS, 1973).

C[ooke], J[ohn]. *Epigrames. Served out in 52. severall Dishes for every man to tast without surfeting* (1604).

Cooper, Thomas. *Thesaurus Linguae* (1565).

Corbet, Richard. *Poems,* ed. J. A. W. Bennett and H. R. Trevor-Roper (Oxford: Clarendon Press, 1955).

Covell, William. *Polimanteia, or, The meanes lawfull and unlawfull, to judge of the fall of a common-wealth, against the frivolous and foolish conjectures of this age* (1595).

Craigie, James (ed.). *The Poems of James VI of Scotland,* 2 vols (Edinburgh: W. Blackwood, 1955–58).

Crashaw, Richard. *The Complete Poetry of Richard Crashaw,* ed. George Walton Williams (New York: Norton, 1974).

—— *Poems: English, Latin, and Greek,* ed. L. C. Martin (Oxford: Clarendon Press, 1957).

Crawford, Robert (ed. and trans.). *Apollos of the North: Selected Poems of George Buchanan and Arthur Johnston* (Edinburgh: Polygon, 2006).

Davies of Hereford, John. *Scourge for paper-persecutors* (1625).

—— *The Scourge of Folly* (1611).

—— *Wits Bedlam* (1617).

Davies, Sir John. *Poems,* ed. Robert Krueger (Oxford: Clarendon Press, 1975).

Davison, Francis. *A poetical rapsody containing, diuerse sonnets, odes, elegies, madrigalls, and other poesies, both in rime, and measured verse* (1602).

Dekker, Thomas. *The Seaven Deadly Sinnes of London* (1606).

A Description of Love with Certain Epigrams (1620).

Denbo, Michael Roy. 'The Holgate Miscellany: The Pierpont Morgan Library, MA 1057', PhD, City University of New York, 1997.

D'Ewes, Simond. *Autobiography*, ed. James Orchard Halliwell, 2 vols (London, 1845).

The Dr. Farmer Chetham Manuscript being a Commonplace Book in the Chetham Library, ed. Alexander B. Grosart, vols 89 and 90 in the Publications of the Chetham Society (Manchester, 1873).

Donne, John. *Letters to Severall Persons of Honour*, ed. John Donne, Jr (1651).

—— *Life and Letters*, ed. Edmund Gosse, 2 vols (Gloucester, MA: Peter Smith, 1959).

Ellis, Henry (ed.). *Original Letters Illustrative of English History*, 3 vols (London, 1824).

Elyot, John. *Of the knowledeg [sic] whiche maketh a wise man* (1533).

Esops eables [sic] translated grammatically (1617).

Farmer, Norman K. *Poems from a Seventeenth-Century Manuscript with the Hand of Robert Herrick*, in *Texas Quarterly*, Supplement to 16:4 (1973).

Farnaby, Thomas. *HE TES ANTHOLOGIAS ANTHOLOGIA: Florilegium epigrammatum Graecorum, eorumque Latino versu à variis redditorum* (1629).

Fennor, William. *Fennors defence: or, I am your first man* (1615).

Fitzgeffry, Charles. *Affaniae* (Oxford, 1601).

Fitzgeffrey, Henry. *Certain Elegies done by sundrie excellent wits With satyrs and epigrams* (1620).

—— *Satyres: and satyricall epigrams* (1617).

Freeman, Thomas. *Rubbe, and a great cast Epigrams* (1614).

Fuller, Thomas. *The history of the worthies of England* (1662).

Gamage, William. *Linsi-woolsie or two centuries of epigrammes* (1613).

Gawdy, Philip. *The Letters of Philip Gawdy, 1579–1616*, ed. I. H. Jeayes (London: J. B. Nichols and Sons, 1906).

Goddard, William. *A Mastif Whelp, with other ruff-Island-lik Currs fetcht from amongst the Antipedes* (1616?).

Gomersall, Robert. *Poems* (1633).

The Greek Anthology, trans. W. R. Paton (Loeb Classical Library), 2 vols (Cambridge, MA: Harvard University Press, 1916).

Greville, Fulke. *Poems and Dramas*, ed. G. Bullough, 2 vols (Edinburgh: Oliver and Boyd, 1939).

Guilpin, Everard. *Skialetheia: or, A shadowe of truth, in certaine epigrams and satyres* (1598), ed. D. Allen Carroll (Chapel Hill, NC: University of North Carolina Press, 1974).

Harington, Sir John. *A briefe view of the state of the Church of England as it stood in Q. Elizabeths and King James his reigne* (1653).

—— *Epigrams for Lady Rogers*, ed. Simon and Ben Cauchi (Wellington: Pharaoh, 1992).

—— *The Epigrams of Sir John Harington*, ed. Gerard Kilroy (Farnham: Ashgate, 2009).

—— *The Letters and Epigrams of Sir John Harington*, ed. Norman Egbert McClure (Philadelphia, PA: University of Pennsylvania Press, 1930).

—— *A New Discourse of a Stale Subject, Called The Metamorphosis of Ajax*, ed. Elizabeth Story Donno (London: Routledge & Kegan Paul, 1962).

—— *Nugae Antiquae*, 2 vols (1804; Rpt New York: AMS, 1966).

—— *A Tract on the Succession to the Crown (A.D. 1602)* (London, 1880).

Harvey, Thomas. *John Owen's Latine epigrams* (1677).

Hayman, Robert. *Quodlibets* (1628).

Heath, John. *Two Centuries of Epigrammes* (1610).

Herbert, George. *Works*, ed. F. E. Hutchinson (Oxford: Oxford University Press, 1941).

Herrick, Robert. *The Complete Poetry of Robert Herrick*, ed. Tom Cain and Ruth Connolly, 2 vols (Oxford: Oxford University Press, 2013).

—— *Poetical Works*, ed. F. W. Moorman (Oxford: Oxford University Press, 1921).

Heywood, Thomas. *The English Traveller* (1633).

Holland, Abraham. *Hollandi post-huma* (1626).

—— *Naumachia* (1622).

Holland, Henry. *Monumenta sepulchraria Sancti Pauli* (1633).

Holles, Sir John [Earl of Clare], *Letters*, ed. Peter Seddon, 3 vols (Nottingham: Thoroton Society, 1975–80).

Hoole, Charles. *A New Discovery of the old Art of Teaching Schoole* (1661).

Jonson, Ben. *Ben Jonson*, ed. C. H. Herford, and Percy Simpson, 10 vols (Oxford: Clarendon Press, 1925–52).

——. *The Cambridge Edition of the Works of Ben Jonson*, ed. David Bevington, Martin Butler, and Ian Donaldson, 7 vols (Cambridge: Cambridge University Press, 2012).

Joyner, Robert. *Itis, or three severall boxes of sporting familiars* (1598).

Kay, N. M. (ed.), *Ausonius: Epigrams* (London: Duckworth, 2001).

—— *Epigrams from the Anthologia Latina: Text, Translation and Commentary* (London: Duckworth, 2006).

Kendall, Timothy. *Flowers of epigrammes, out of sundrie the most singular authours* (1577).

King, Humphrey. *An halfe-penny-worth of wit, in a penny-worth of paper. Or, The hermites tale* (1613).

Lee, Maurice Jr (ed.). *Dudley Carleton to John Chamberlain, 1603–1624: Jacobean Letters* (New Brunswick, NJ: Rutgers University Press, 1972).

Leishman, J. B. (ed.), *The Three Parnassus Plays (1598–1601)* (London: Nicholson & Watson, 1949).

Marcus, Leah S., Janel Mueller and Mary Beth Rose (eds), *Elizabeth I: Collected Works* (Chicago: University of Chicago Press, 2000).

Marston, John. *Poems*, ed. Arnold Davenport (Liverpool: Liverpool University Press, 1961).

May, Edward. *Epigrams Divine and Moral* (1633).

Meres, Francis. *Palladis Tamia* (1598).

Middleton, Richard. *Epigrams and Satyres* (1608).

Nashe, Thomas. *The Returne of the Renowned Cavaliero Pasquil of England* (1589).

Niccols, Richard. *The Furies. With Vertues Encomium. Or, The Immage of Honour. In two Bookes of Epigrammes, Satyricall and Encomiasticke* (1614).

Nixon, Anthony. *Blacke Yeare* (1606).

Osborne, Francis. *The works of Francis Osborne* (1673).

Overbury, Sir Thomas (And Others). *Characters, together with Poems, news, Edicts, and Paradoxes based on the eleventh edition of 'A Wife Now the Widow of Sir Thomas Overbury'*, ed. Donald Beecher (Ottawa: Dovehouse, 2003).

Owen, John. *Ioannia Audoeni Epigrammatum*, ed. John R. C. Martyn. 2 vols (Leiden: Brill, 1976).

Parkhurst, John. *Ludicra sive Epigrammata iuvenilia* (1573).

Parrot, Henry. *Cures for the Itch* (1626).

—— *Epigrams by H.P.* (1608).

—— *Laquei ridiculosi: Or Springes for Woodcocks* (1613).

—— *The Mastive – or Young-Whelpe of the Olde-Dogge* (1615).

—— *The Mous-trap* (1606).

Peacham, Henry. *Compleat Gentleman* (1622).

—— *Thalia's Banquet* (1620).

Penkethman, John. *The epigrams of P. Virgilius Maro* (1624).

Percy, William. *Mahomet and his Heaven*, ed. Matthew Dimmock (Aldershot: Ashgate, 2006).

Pestell, Thomas. *The Poems*, ed. Hannah Buchan (Oxford: Blackwell, 1940).

Pontanus, Jacobus. *Poeticum institutionem*, in Johann Buchler, *Sacrarum profanarumq[ue] phrasium poeticarum thesaurus.* (1632).

Poole-Wilson, Nicholas (ed.), *John Owen's Epigrams for Prince Henry: The Text of the Presentation Manuscript in the Library of Trinity College Cambridge* (London: Bernard Quaritch, 2012).

Prynne, William. *A pleasant purge for a Roman Catholike to evacuate his evill humours consisting of a century of polemicall epigrams* (1642).

Puttenham, George. *The Art of English Poesy: A Critical Edition*, ed. Frank Whigham and Wayne A. Rebhorn (Ithaca, NY: Cornell University Press, 2007).

Quarles, Francis. *Divine Fancies* (1632).

Redding, David C. 'Robert Bishop's Commonplace Book: An Edition of a Seventeenth-Century Miscellany [Rosenbach MS 187]', PhD, University of Pennsylvania, 1960.

Reynolds, John. *Epigrammata* (1611).

Rous, John. *Diary of John Rous*, ed. M. A. Green (London, 1856).

Rowlands, Samuel. *A Fooles Bolt is Soon Shot* (1614), in *The Complete Works of Samuel Rowlands, 1598-1628* (Hunterian Club, 1880; Rpt New York: Johnson Reprint, 1966).

—— *Roome, for a messe of knaues* (1610).

Rudick, Michael (ed.). *The Poems of Sir Walter Ralegh: A Historical Edition* (Tempe, AZ: Renaissance English Text Society, 1999).

Russell, John. *The Spy* (1628).

S., T. *Fragmenta aulica* (1662).

Saltmarsh, John. *Poemata Sacra* (1636).

—— *Poetices libri septem* (1636).

Sanderson, James. 'An Edition of an Early Seventeenth-Century Manuscript Collection of Poems (Rosenbach MS. 186)', PhD, University of Pennsylvania, 1960.

Scaliger, Julius Caesar. *Poetices* (Stuttgart: Frommann-Holzboog, 1987).

Shepherd, Samuel. *Epigrams Theological, Philosophical, and Romantick* (London, 1651).

Stow, John. *A Survey of London: Reprinted from the Text of 1603*, ed. Charles Lethbridge Kingsford, 2 vols (Oxford: Clarendon Press, 1908).

Stradling, John. *Epigrammatum libri quatuor* (1607).

Suckling, John. *Works*, ed. Thomas Clayton (Oxford: Clarendon Press, 1971).

Taylor, John, the Water-Poet. *The Sculler* (1612).

—— *Water-workes: or the scullers travels, from Tiber to Thames* (1614).

Thompson, Howard H. 'An Edition of Two Seventeenth-Century Manuscript Poetical Miscellanies (Rosenbach MSS 188 and 191)', PhD, University of Pennsylvania, 1959.

Thynne, Francis *Animadversions uppon the annotacions and corrections of some imperfections of impressiones of Chaucers workes*, ed. F. J. Furnivall, EETS, old series, 9 (1875; Rpt London: Oxford University Press, 1965).

—— *Emblemes and Epigrames*, EETS old series, 64 (London, 1876).

The Time's Whistle: or, A new daunce of seven satires, and other poems: compiled by R. C., gent., ed. J. M. Cowper (London: EETS, 1871).

Turner, Richard. *Nosce Te* (1607).

Twisse, William. *A Discovery of D. Iackson's vanitie* (1631).

Tyro, T. *Tyros Roring Megge Planted against the walles of Melancholy. One Booke cut into two Decads* (1598).

Ussher, James. *The Whole Works*, 16 vols (Dublin, 1847).

Weever, John. *Ancient Funerall Monuments* (1631).

—— *Epigrams in the Oldest Cut and Newest Fashion* (1599).

—— *The Whipping of the Satyre* (1601).

Wheare, Degory. *Degorei Wheari Prael. Hist. Camdeniani. Pietas erga benefactores* (1628).

Willes, Richard. *Poematum Liber* (1573).

Wits recreations (1640).

Wood, Anthony à. *Athenae Oxoniensis* (1691).

Wotton, Henry. *Life and Letters*, ed. Logan Pearsall Smith, 2 vols (Oxford: Oxford University Press, 1907).

Wroth, Thomas. *The Destruction of Troy* (1620).

Yonge, Walter. *Diary*, ed. G. Roberts (London, 1848).

Secondary sources

Angress, R. K. *The Early German Epigram: A Study in Baroque Poetry* (Lexington, KY: University Press of Kentucky, 1971).

Atherton, Ian. '"The Itch Grown a Disease": Manuscript Transmission of News in the Seventeenth Century', in Joad Raymond (ed.), *News, Newspapers and Society* (London: Frank Cass, 1999), pp. 39–65.

Attwater, Aubrey. *Pembroke College Cambridge: A Short History* (Cambridge: Cambridge University Press, 1936).

Babbage, Stuart Barton. *Puritanism and Richard Bancroft* (London: SPCK, 1962).

Barkan, Leonard. *Unearthing the Past* (New Haven, CT: Yale University Press, 1999).

Bawcutt, N. W. (ed.), *The Control and Censorship of Caroline Drama: The Records of Sir Henry Herbert, Master of the Revels, 1623–1673* (Oxford: Clarendon Press, 1996).

Beal, Peter. *Index of English Literary Manuscripts, Volume 1, Part 2* (London: Mansell, 1980–93).

Bellany, Alastair. 'A Poem on the Archbishop's Hearse: Puritanism, Libel and Sedition after the Hampton Court Conference', *Journal of British Studies*, 34 (1995), pp. 137–64.

—— 'Libels in Action: Ritual, Subversion and the English Literary Underground, 1603–42', in Tim Harris (ed.), *The Politics of the Excluded* (Basingstoke and New York: Palgrave, 2001), pp. 99–124.

—— *The Politics of Court Scandal in Early Modern England: News Culture and the Overbury Affair: 1603–1666* (Cambridge: Cambridge University Press, 2002).

—— 'Railing Rhymes Revisited: Libels, Scandals, and Early Stuart Politics', *History Compass*, 5 (2007), pp. 1136–79.

Birch, Thomas (ed.). *The court and times of Charles the First*, 2 vols (1848).

—— *The court and times of James the First*, 2 vols (1849).

Boehrer, Bruce. 'Martial', *Ben Jonson Journal*, 14 (2007), pp. 259–62.

Bolwell, Robert. *The Life and Works of John Heywood* (New York: AMS, 1966).

Boutcher, Warren. 'Pilgrimage to Parnassus: Local Intellectual Traditions, Humanist Education and the Cultural Geography of Sixteenth-century England', in Niall Livingstone and Yun Lee Too (eds), *Pedagogy and Power: Rhetorics of Classical Learning* (Cambridge: Cambridge University Press, 1998), pp. 110–47.

Bowen, Catherine Drinker. *The Lion and the Throne: The Life and Times of Sir Edward Coke, 1552–1634* (London: Hamish Hamilton, 1957).

Bradner, Leicester. *Musae Anglicanae; A History of Anglo-Latin Poetry, 1500–1925* (London: Oxford University Press, 1940).

Brady, Jennifer. '"Beware the Poet": Authority and Judgment in Jonson's Epigrammes', *SEL*, 23 (1983), pp. 95–112.

Brown, J. Howard. *Elizabethan Schooldays: An Account of the English Grammar Schools in the Second Half of the Sixteenth Century* (Oxford: Blackwell, 1933).

Cameron, Averil. *Agathias* (Oxford: Clarendon Press, 1970).

Capp, Bernard. *The World of John Taylor the Water-Poet, 1578–1653* (Oxford: Clarendon Press, 1994).

Carlson, David. 'The Writings and Manuscript Collections of the Elizabethan Alchemist, Antiquary, and Herald Francis Thynne', *HLQ*, 52 (1989), pp. 203–72.

Cathcart, Charles. 'John Davies of Hereford, Marston, and Hall', *Ben Jonson Journal*, 17 (2010), pp. 242–8.

Cecil, Algernon. *A Life of Robert Cecil, First Earl of Salisbury* (Westport, CT: Greenwood Press, 1915).

Chambers, D. S. *Cardinal Bainbridge in the Court of Rome, 1509 to 1514* (Oxford: Oxford University Press, 1965).

Chynoweth, John. *Tudor Cornwall* (Stroud: Tempus, 2002).

Clegg, Cyndia Susan. *Press Censorship in Elizabethan England* (Cambridge: Cambridge University Press, 1997).

—— *Press Censorship in Caroline England* (Cambridge: Cambridge University Press, 2007).

Cogswell, Thomas. 'Underground Verse and the Transformation of Early Stuart Political Culture', in Susan D. Amussen and Mark A. Kishlansky (eds), *Political Culture and Cultural Politics in Early Modern England: Essays Presented to David Underdown* (Manchester: Manchester University Press, 1995), pp. 277–300.

Coiro, Ann Baynes. *Robert Herrick's Hesperides and the Epigram Book Tradition* (Baltimore, MD: Johns Hopkins University Press, 1988).

Colclough, David. '"The Muses Recreation": John Hoskyns and the Manuscript Culture of the Seventeenth Century', *HLQ*, 61 (1998), pp. 369–400.

—— *Freedom of Speech in Early Stuart England* (Cambridge: Cambridge University Press, 2005).

Cooper, J. P. (ed.). *Wentworth Papers, 1597–1628* (London: Royal Historical Society: 1973).

Cope, Esther S. *The Life of a Public Man: Edward, First Baron Montagu of Boughton, 1562–1644* (Philadelphia, PA: American Philosophical Society, 1981).

Cousins, A. D. 'Feigning the Commonwealth: Jonson's *Epigrams*', in A. D. Cousins (ed.), *Ben Jonson and the Politics of Genre* (Cambridge: Cambridge University Press, 2009), pp. 14–42.

Cressy, David. *England on Edge: Crisis and Revolution, 1640–1642* (Oxford: Oxford University Press, 2006).

Croft, Pauline. 'The Reputation of Robert Cecil: Libels, Political Opinion and Popular Awareness in the Early Seventeenth Century', *Transactions of the Royal Historical Society*, 6th ser., 1 (1991), pp. 43–69.

Dent, C. M. *Protestant Reformers in Elizabethan Oxford* (Oxford: Oxford University Press, 1983).

DiPasquale, Theresa. 'Donne's Epigrams: A Sequential Reading', *Modern Philology*, 104 (2007), pp. 329–78.

Doelman, James. 'The Contexts of George Herbert's *Musae Responsoriae*', *George Herbert Journal*, 2 (1992), pp. 42–54.

—— *King James I and the Religious Culture of England* (Woodbridge: Brewer, 2000).

—— 'The Comet of 1618 and the British Royal Family', *Notes and Queries*, new ser., 54 (2007), pp. 30–5.

—— 'Herbert's *Lucus* and Pope Urban VIII', *The George Herbert Journal*, 32 (2008–9), pp. 43–53.

Doelman, James and Anthony Prancic, '"Ora pro me, sancte Herberte": James Duport and the Reputation of George Herbert', *The George Herbert Journal*, 24 (2000–01), pp. 35–55.

Dubrow, Heather. *The Challenges of Orpheus: Lyric Poetry and Early Modern England* (Baltimore, MD: Johns Hopkins University Press, 2008).

Duffin, Anne. *Faction and Faith: Politics and Religion of the Cornish Gentry before the Civil War* (Exeter: University of Exeter Press, 1996).

Duncan-Jones, Katherine. 'Preserved Dainties: Late Elizabethan Poems by Sir Robert Cecil and the Earl of Clanricarde', *Bodleian Library Journal*, 14 (1992), pp. 136–44.

Dutton, Richard. *Ben Jonson: To the Folio* (Cambridge: Cambridge University Press, 1983).

Eckhardt, Joshua. *Manuscript Verse Collectors and the Politics of Anti-Courtly Love Poetry* (Oxford: Oxford University Press), 2009.

—— 'Verse Miscellanies in Print and Manuscript: A Book Historiography' at *Verse Miscellanies Online* (http://www.academia.edu/3623473/_Verse_Miscellanies_in_Print_and_Manuscript_A_Book_Historiography_).

Enenkel, Karl A. E. 'Introduction: The Neo-Latin Epigram: Humanist Self-Definition in a Learned and Witty Discourse', in Susanna De Beer, Karl A. E. Enenkel and David Rijser (eds), *The Neo-Latin Epigram: A Learned and Witty Genre* (Leuven: Leuven University Press, 2009), pp. 1–24.

Evans, Robert C. *Ben Jonson and the Poetics of Patronage* (Lewisburg, NY: Bucknell University Press, 1989).

Finkelpearl, F. J. *John Marston of the Middle Temple* (Cambridge, MA: Harvard University Press, 1969).

Fitzgerald, William. *Martial: The World of the Epigram* (Chicago: University of Chicago Press, 2007).

Fleming, Juliet. *Graffiti and the Writing Arts* (Philadelphia, PA: University of Pennsylvania Press, 2001).

Forshaw, Cliff. '"Cease Cease to bawle, thou wasp-stung Satyrist": Writers, Printers and the Bishops' Ban of 1599', *EnterText*, 3 (2003), pp. 101–31.

Foster, Joseph. *Alumni Oxonienses: The Members of University of Oxford, 1500–1714* (Oxford: Parker, 1891–92).

Fowler, Alistair. *Kinds of Literature: An Introduction to the Theory of Genres and Modes* (Cambridge, MA: Harvard University Press, 1982).

Fox, Adam. 'Religious Satire in English Towns, 1570–1640', in Patrick Collinson and John Craig (eds), *The Reformation in English Towns* (Basingstoke: Macmillan, 1998), pp. 221–40.

—— *Oral and Literate Culture in England, 1500–1700* (Oxford: Clarendon Press, 2000).

Frank, Tenney. 'Naevius and Free Speech', *American Journal of Philology*, 48 (1927), pp. 105–10.

Gaisser, Julia. *Catullus and His Renaissance Readers* (Oxford: Oxford University Press, 1993).

Ghosh, Ranjan. 'Ben Jonson and His Reader: An Aesthetics of Antagonism',

Comparatist: Journal of the Southern Comparative Literature Association, 37 (2013), pp. 138–55.

Greg, W. W. *Licensers for the Press to 1640* (Oxford: Oxford Bibliographical Society, 1962).

Grendler, Paul F. *Critics of the Italian World (1530–1650); Anton Francesco Doni, Nicolo Franco & Ortensio Lando* (Madison, WI: University of Wisconsin Press, 1969).

Guillen, Claudio. *Literature as System: Essays toward the Theory of Literary History* (Princeton, NJ: Princeton University Press, 1971).

Gutzwiller, Kathryn J. *Poetic Garlands: Hellenistic Epigrams in Context* (Berkeley, CA: University of California Press, 1998).

Hardison, O. B. *The Enduring Monument: A Study of the Idea of Praise in Renaissance Literary Theory and Practice* (Chapel Hill, NC: University of North Carolina Press, 1962).

Harries, Byron. 'John Owen the Epigrammatist: a Literary and Historical Context', *Renaissance Studies*, 18 (2004), pp. 25–9.

Harrison, G. B. *The Life and Death of Robert Devereux Earl of Essex* (1937; Rpt. Folcroft, PA: Folcroft Library, 1973).

Hart, E. F. 'The Answer-Poem of the Early Seventeenth Century', *RES*, 7 (1956), pp. 19–29.

Haskell, Francis and Nicholas Penny. *Taste and the Antique: The Lure of Classical Sculpture, 1500–1900* (New Haven, CT: Yale University Press, 1981).

Healy, Thomas F. 'Crashaw and the Sense of History', in John R. Roberts (ed.), *New Perspectives on the Life and Art of Richard Crashaw* (Columbia, MO: University of Missouri Press, 1990), pp. 49–65.

Helgerson, Richard. *Self-Crowned Laureates: Spenser, Jonson, Milton and the Literary System*. Berkeley, CA: University of California Press, 1983.

Heninger, S. K., Jr. *The Subtext of Form in the English Renaissance: Proportion Poetical* (Philadelphia, PA: Pennsylvania State University Press, 1994).

Hess, Peter. *Epigramm* (Stuttgart: Metzler, 1989).

Hester, M. Thomas. 'The Titles/Headings of Donne's Epigrams', *ANQ*, 3 (1990), pp. 3–11.

Hillenbrand, Harold N. 'William Percy: An Elizabethan Amateur', *HLQ*, 1 (1938), pp. 391–416.

Hobbs, Mary. *Early Seventeenth-Century Verse Miscellany Manuscripts* (Aldershot: Scholar Press, 1992).

Hodgart, Matthew. *Satire* (New York: McGraw-Hill, 1969).

Höltgen, Karl Josef. *Francis Quarles* (Tübingen: Niemeyer, 1978).

Holstun, James. *Ehud's Dagger: Class Struggle in the English Revolution* (London: Verso, 2000).

Honigmann, E. A. J. *John Weever: A Biography of a Literary Associate of Shakespeare and Jonson, Together with a Photographic Facsimile of Weever's Epigrammes (1599)* (Manchester: Manchester University Press, 1987).

Hop, Susanna. '"What Fame Is This?": John Davies's *Epigrammes* in Late Elizabethan London', *Renaissance Journal*, 2 (2005), pp. 29–42.

Hudson, Hoyt Hopewell. *The Epigram in the English Renaissance* (New York: Octagon, 1966).

Humez, Jean. 'The Manners of Epigram: A Study of the Epigram Volumes of Martial, Harington, and Jonson', PhD, Yale University, 1971.

Hutton, James. *The Greek Anthology in Italy* (Ithaca, NY: Cornell University Press, 1935).

—— *The Greek Anthology in France and in the Latin Writers* (New York: Johnson Reprint, 1967).

Ingram, Randall. 'Lego Ego: Reading Seventeenth-Century Books of Epigrams', in Jennifer Anderson and Elizabeth Sauer (eds), *Books and Readers in Early Modern England: Material Studies* (Philadelphia, PA: University of Pennsylvania Press, 2002).

Jones, William R. '"Say They Are Saints Although That Saints They Show Not": John Weever's 1599 Epigrams to Marston, Jonson, and Shakespeare', *HLQ*, 73 (2010), pp. 83–98.

Kamholtz, Jonathan Z. 'Ben Jonson's *Epigrammes* and Poetic Occasions', *SEL*, 23 (1983), pp. 77–94.

Kaplan, M. Lindsay. *The Culture of Slander in Early Modern England* (Cambridge: Cambridge University Press, 1997).

Kernan, Alvin B. *The Cankered Muse: Satire of the English Renaissance* (New Haven, CT: Yale University Press, 1962).

Kerwin, William. 'Epigrammatic Commotions', in Katharine A. Craik and Tanya Pollard (eds), *Shakespearean Sensations: Experiencing Literature in Early Modern England* (Cambridge: Cambridge University Press, 2013), pp. 157–72.

Kilroy, Gerard. *Edmund Campion: Memory and Transcription* (Aldershot: Ashgate, 2005).

Larsen, Kenneth J. 'Richard Crashaw's *Epigrammata Sacra*', in J. W. Binns (ed.), *The Latin Poetry of English Poets* (London: Routledge & Kegan Paul, 1974), pp. 93–120.

Laurenson, Ian. 'A Pasquinade for John Owen', *Notes and Queries*, 26 (1979), pp. 403–5.

Lauxtermann, Marc D. 'Janus Lascaris and the Greek Anthology', in Susanna De Beer, Karl A. E. Enenkel and David Rijser (eds), *The Neo-Latin Epigram: A Learned and Witty Genre* (Leuven: Leuven University Press, 2009), pp. 41–66.

LeClercq, Jean. *Otia monastica: études sur le vocabulaire de la contemplation au Moyen Age* (Rome: Herder, 1963).

Lessing, Gotthold. 'Essay on Epigram', in *Fables and Epigrams*, trans. J. and H. L. Hunt (1825).

Loewenstein, Joseph. *Ben Jonson and Possessive Authorship* (Cambridge: Cambridge University Press, 2002).

—— *The Author's Due: Printing and the Prehistory of Copyright* (Chicago: University of Chicago Press, 2002).

Love, Harold. *Attributing Authorship: An Introduction* (Cambridge: Cambridge University Press, 2001).

—— *Scribal Publication in Seventeenth-Century England* (Oxford: Oxford University Press, 1993).

Macleane, Douglas. *History of Pembroke College, Oxford, Anciently Broadgates Hall* (Oxford: Clarendon Press, 1897).

Manley, Lawrence. 'Proverbs, Epigrams, and Urbanity in Renaissance London', *English Literary Renaissance*, 15 (1985), pp. 247–76.

Marotti, Arthur F. *Manuscript, Print, and the English Renaissance Lyric* (Ithaca, NY: Cornell University Press, 1995).

May, Steven W. 'The Circulation in Manuscript of Poems by King James VI and I', in James Dutcher and Anne Lake Prescott (eds), *Renaissance Historicisms: Essays in Honour of Arthur F. Kinney* (Newark, DE: University of Delaware Press, 2008), pp. 206–24.

May, Steven W. and William A. Ringler, Jr (eds), *Elizabethan Poetry: A Bibliography and First-line Index of English Verse, 1559–1603*, 3 vols (London and New York: Thoemmes Continuum, 2004).

McCabe, Richard. 'Elizabethan Satire and the Bishops' Ban of 1599', *Yearbook of English Studies*, 11 (1981), pp. 188–93.

McConica, James. 'The Rise of the Undergraduate College', in James McConica (ed.), *The History of the University of Oxford, Volume III: The Collegiate University* (Oxford: Clarendon Press, 1986).

McGee, J. Sears 'A "carkass" of "mere dead paper": The Polemical Career of Francis Rous, Puritan MP', *HLQ*, 72 (2009), pp. 347–71.

McRae, Andrew. 'The Literary Culture of Early Stuart Libeling', *Modern Philology*, 97 (2000), pp. 364–92.

—— *Literature, Satire, and the Early Stuart State* (Cambridge: Cambridge University Press, 2004).

Milligan, Burton A. 'Humor and Satire in Heywood's Epigrams', in Don Cameron Allen (ed.), *Studies in Honor of Thomas Whitfield Baldwin* (Urbana, IL: University of Illinois Press, 1958).

Morgan, Victor. 'Cambridge University and "The Country" 1560–1640', in Lawrence Stone (ed.), *The University in Society*, 2 vols (Princeton, NJ: Princeton University Press), vol. 1, pp. 183–245.

Mullaney, Steven. *The Place of the Stage: Licence, Play, and Power in Renaissance England* (Chicago: University of Chicago Press, 1988).

Newstok, Scott. *Quoting Death in Early Modern England: The Poetics of Epitaphs Beyond the Tomb* (Basingstoke: Palgrave Macmillan, 2009).

Nicholls, Mark. 'The Authorship of "Thomas Bastard's Oxford Libel"', *Notes and Queries*, 52 (2005), p. 187.

—— 'The Enigmatic William Percy', *HLQ*, 70 (2007), pp. 469–77.

Nichols, John. *The progresses, processions, and magnificent festivities of King James the First*, 4 vols (1828; Rpt New York: AMS, 1968).

Nisbet, Gideon. *Greek Epigram in the Roman Empire: Martial's Forgotten Rivals* (Oxford: Oxford University Press, 2004).

Norbrook, David. *Writing the English Republic: Poetry, Rhetoric, and Politics, 1627–1660* (Cambridge: Cambridge University Press, 1999).

North, Marcy L. 'Anonymity in Early Modern Manuscript Culture: Finding a Purposeful Convention in a Ubiquitous Condition', in Janet Wright Starner and Barbara Howard Traister (eds), *Anonymity in Early Modern England: 'What's In A Name?'* (Farnham: Ashgate, 2011), pp. 13–42.

Nussdorfer, Laurie. *Civic Politics in the Rome of Urban VIII* (Princeton, NJ: Princeton University Press, 1992).

O'Callaghan, Michelle. *The English Wits: Literature and Sociability in Early Modern England* (Cambridge: Cambridge University Press, 2007).

—— '"Thomas the Scholer" versus "John the Sculler": Defining Popular Culture in the Early Seventeenth Century', in Matthew Dimmock and Andrew Hadfield (eds), *Literature and Popular Culture in Early Modern England* (Farnham: Ashgate, 2009).

Osborn, Louise Brown. *The Life, Letters, and Writings of John Hoskyns, 1566–1638* (New York: Archon, 1973).

Parker, W. H., trans. and ed., *Priapea: Poems for a Phallic God* (London & Sydney: Croom Helm, 1988).

Partner, Peter. *Renaissance Rome, 1500–1559: A Portrait of a Society* (Berkeley, CA: University of California Press, 1976).

Partridge, Eric. 'Jonson's *Epigrammes*: The Named and the Nameless', *Studies in the Literary Imagination*, 6 (1973), pp. 153–98.

Perry, Curtis. '"If Proclamations Will Not Serve": The Late Manuscript Poetry of James I and the Culture of Libel', in Daniel Fischlin and Mark Fortier (eds), *Royal Subjects: Essays on the Writings of James VI and I* (Detroit, MI: Wayne State University Press, 2002), pp. 205–34.

—— *Literature and Favoritism in Early Modern England* (Cambridge: Cambridge University Press, 2006).

Perry, Kathryn. '"I do it onely for the Printers sake": Commercial Imperatives and Epigrams in the Early Seventeenth Century', *EnterText*, 3 (2003), pp. 204–26 (www.brunel.ac.uk/faculty/arts/ EnterText/3_1_pdfs/perry.pdf).

Petti, Anthony G. 'Beasts and Politics in Elizabethan Literature', *Essays and Studies*, 16 (1963), pp. 68–90.

Philips, Ambrose. *The life of John Williams* (1700).

Pitman, Margaret C. 'The Epigrams of Henry Peacham and Henry Parrot', *Modern Language Review*, 29 (1934), pp. 129–36.

Prouty, Charles Tyler. *George Gascoigne: Elizabethan Courtier, Soldier, and Poet* (New York: Columbia University Press, 1942).

Reynolds, Anne (ed. and trans.), *Renaissance Humanism at the Court of Clement VII: Francesco Berni's Dialogue against Poets in Context* (New York and London: Garland, 1997).

Rickard, Jane. *Authorship and Authority: The Writings of James VI and I* (Manchester: Manchester University Press, 2007).

Riddell, James A. 'The Arrangement of Ben Jonson's *Epigrammes*', *SEL*, 27 (1987), pp. 53–70.

Rijser, David. 'The Practical Function of High Renaissance Epigrams: the Case of Raphael's Grave', in Susanna De Beer, Karl A. E. Enenkel and David Rijser (eds), *The Neo-Latin Epigram: A Learned and Witty Genre* (Leuven: Leuven University Press, 2009), pp. 103–36.

Rollins, Hyder E. 'Samuel Pick's Borrowings', *Review of English Studies*, 7 (1931), p. 204.

Roman, Luke. 'The Representation of Literary Materiality in Martial's *Epigrams*', *Journal of Roman Studies*, 91 (2001), pp. 113–45.

Rose, Margaret A. *Parody: Ancient, Modern and Post-Modern* (Cambridge: Cambridge University Press, 1993).

Rowe, George E. 'Ben Jonson's Quarrel with Audience and Its Renaissance Context', *Studies in Philology*, 81 (1984), pp. 438–60.

Sanderson, James L. 'Epigrames p[er] B[enjamin] R[udyerd] and Some More "Stolen Feathers" of Henry Parrot', *Review of English Studies*, 17 (1966), pp. 241–55.

Scodel, Joshua. *The English Poetic Epitaph: Commemoration and Conflict from Jonson to Wordsworth* (Ithaca, NY: Cornell University Press, 1991).

Scott-Warren, Jason. 'Reconstructing Manuscript Networks: The Textual Transactions of Sir Stephen Powle', in Alexandra Shephard and Phil Withington (eds), *Communities in Early Modern England: Networks, Place, Rhetoric* (Manchester: Manchester University Press, 2000).

―― *Sir John Harington and the Book as Gift* (Oxford: Oxford University Press, 2001).

Small, Roscoe Addison. *The Stage-Quarrel between Ben Jonson and the So-Called Poetasters* (1899; Rpt New York: AMS Press, 1966).

Smyth, Adam. *Profit & Delight: Printed Miscellanies in England. 1640–1682* (Detroit, MI: Wayne State University Press, 2004).

Stapleton, Paul J. 'A Priest and a "Queen": Donne's Epigram "Martial"', *John Donne Journal: Studies in the Age of Donne*, 28(2009), pp. 93–118.

Steggle, Matthew. *The Wars of the Theatres: The Poetics of Personation in the Age of Jonson* (Victoria: English Literary Studies, 1998).

Stone, Lawrence. *An Elizabethan: Sir Horatio Palavicino* (Oxford: Clarendon Press, 1956).

Sullivan, J. P. *Martial: The Unexpected Classic: A Literary and Historical Study* (Cambridge: Cambridge University Press, 1991).

Swann, Bruce W. *Martial's Catullus: the Reception of an Epigrammatic Rival* (Hildesheim: Olms, 1994).

Swann, Marjorie. *Curiosities and Texts: The Culture of Collecting in Early Modern England* (Philadelphia, PA: University of Pennsylvania Press, 2001).

Toner, J. P. *Leisure and ancient Rome* (Cambridge: Polity Press; Malden, MA: Blackwell, 1998).

Upton, C. A. 'John Jonston and the Historical Epigram', *Acta Coventus Neo-Latini Bononiensis: Medieval and Renaissance Texts and Studies* (Binghamton, NY: Center for Medieval & Early Renaissance Studies, 1985), pp. 638–44,

Van Dorsten, J. A. *Poets, Patrons, and Professors: Sir Philip Sidney, Daniel Rogers, and the Leiden Humanists* (Leiden: University of Leiden, 1962).

Venn, John. *Alumni Cantabrigienses: A Biographical List of All Known Students, Graduates and Holders of Office at the University of Cambridge, from the Earliest Times to 1900* (Cambridge: Cambridge University Press, 1922–54).

Vickers, Brian. 'Leisure and Idleness in the Renaissance: The Ambivalence of Otium', *Renaissance Studies*, 4 (1990), pp. 1–37, 107–54.

Wallerstein, Ruth C. *Richard Crashaw: A Study in Style and Poetic Development* (Madison, WI: University of Wisconsin Press, 1959).

Warren, Austin. 'Crashaw's *Epigrammata Sacra*', *Journal of English and Germanic Philology*, 33 (1934), pp. 233–9.

Watson, Foster. *The English Grammar Schools to 1660: Their Curriculum and Practice* (Cambridge: Cambridge University Press, 1908).

Whipple, T. K. *Martial and the English Epigram from Sir Thomas Wyatt to Ben Jonson* (New York: Phaeton Press, 1970).

Whitlock, Baird W. *John Hoskyns, Serjeant-at-Law* (Washington, DC: University of America Press, 1982).

Williams, Franklin B. Jr, 'Henry Parrot's Stolen Feathers', *Publications of the Modern Language Association*, 52 (1937), pp. 1019–30.

Wilson, P. N. 'A Best-Seller Abroad: The Continental Editions of John Owen', in Ton Croiset van Uchelen et al. (eds), *Theatrum Orbis Librorum: Liber Amicorum Presented to Nico Israel on the Occasion of His Seventieth Birthday* (Utrecht: HES, 1989).

Wilson-Okamura, David Scott. *Spenser's International Style* (Cambridge: Cambridge University Press, 2013).

Winner, Jack D. 'Ben Jonson's *Epigrammes* and the Conventions of Formal Verse Satire', *SEL*, 23 (1983), pp. 61–76.

Woudhuysen, Henry R. *Sir Philip Sidney and the Circulation of Manuscripts 1558–1640* (Oxford: Clarendon Press, 1996).

Wykes, David. 'Ben Jonson's "Chast Book" – The *Epigrammes*', *Renaissance and Modern Studies*, 13 (1969), pp. 76–87.

Young, R. V. Jr. 'Jonson, Crashaw, and the Development of the English Epigram', *Genre*, 12 (1979), pp. 137–52.

Index

Note: literary works can be found under authors' names